Muslims

The revised, second edition of this authoritative and accessible text combines the previous two separate volumes, providing a survey of Islamic history and thought, from its formative period to the present day. Many aspects of the discussion have been updated and there are two new chapters on intellectual thought and medieval developments. In seeking to redress the lack of critical thought that appears in so many introductory textbooks on Islam, Andrew Rippin examines the elements that come together to form Islam, in particular the Qur'ān and the traditions from Muhammad. He traces the way these sources have interacted through history to create the disciplines of theology and law, as well as provide the basis for the 'alternative visions' of Islam found in Shī'ism and Sufism. The trajectory of Muslim interaction with these sources is followed down through the medieval period to contemporary times, with speculation on what the future might hold for Islam.

With a combination of well-documented source material, recent research in the field and thorough critical analysis, Andrew Rippin provides an introduction to this important and frequently misunderstood religious group in a concise, challenging and refreshing way. Teachers, students and interested lay people will find this an invaluable introduction to the subject.

Andrew Rippin is Professor of History and Dean of Humanities at the University of Victoria, British Columbia, Canada, and is the author of many works on the Qur'ān and its interpretation.

Library of Religious Beliefs and Practices

Series editors:

John Hinnells and Ninian Smart

This series provides pioneering and scholarly introductions to different religions in a readable form. It is concerned with the beliefs and practices of religions in their social, cultural and historical setting. Authors come from a variety of backgrounds and approach the study of religious beliefs and practices from their different points of view. Some focus mainly on questions of history, teachings, customs and ritual practices. Others consider, within the context of a specific region, the interrelationships between religions; the interaction of religion and the arts; religion and social organization; the involvement of religion in political affairs; and, for ancient cultures, the interpretation of archaeological evidence. In this way the series brings out the multi-disciplinary nature of the study of religion. It is intended for students of religion, philosophy, social sciences and history, and for the interested lay person.

Other titles in the series include:

Hindus
Their Religious Beliefs and Practices
Julius Lipner

Mahayana Buddhism
The Doctrinal Foundations
Paul Williams

Religions of Oceania
Tony Swain and Garry Trompf

Theravada Buddhism
A Social History from Ancient Benares to Modern Colombo
Richard Gombrich

Zoroastrians
Their Religious Beliefs and Practices
Mary Boyce

Muslims

Their Religious Beliefs and Practices

Second edition

Andrew Rippin

London and New York

First published 2001
by Routledge
11 New Fetter Lane, London EC4P 4EE

Simultaneously published in the USA and Canada
by Routledge
29 West 35th Street, New York, NY 10001

Routledge is an imprint of the Taylor & Francis Group

© 2001 Andrew Rippin

Typeset in Times by Florence Production Ltd
Stoodleigh, Devon

Printed and bound in Great Britain by
Clays Ltd, St Ives plc

British Library Cataloguing in Publication Data
A catalogue record for this book is available from the
British Library

Library of Congress Cataloging in Publication Data
has been applied for

ISBN 0–415–21781–4 (hbk)
ISBN 0–415–21782–2 (pbk)

For my children: Courtney, Casey and Lucas

Contents

Preface

The present book is a revised edition of *Muslims: Their Religious Beliefs and Practices* which was published in two volumes, Volume 1 on the "formative period" (1990) and Volume 2 on the "contemporary period" (1993). In preparing this edition, I have benefited from a number of the reviews which were published on the first edition, from the publisher's reader reports for this proposed new edition, and from conversations with colleagues who have shared some of their opinions on my previous efforts. I would especially like to thank Christopher Buck and Gordon Nickel for their input and help. The debt to numerous colleagues and students which I incurred in writing the first edition of this book still remains, of course, but one of those people especially must be mentioned once again. In undertaking this revised edition, I deeply missed the advice and inspiration of my friend and colleague Norman Calder, whose help in both volumes of the first edition was so crucial and in whose person and writing I found, and continue to find, such inspiration. I know that Norman, had he been writing this book, would have approached many of the topics differently and he would have crafted the English language in ways in which I am totally incapable. Our field lost a very special voice with his untimely death, and many of us lost a man whom we were honoured to consider our friend.

Transliteration and other technical considerations

The transliteration system followed in this book accords with that popularly used in many scholarly works; common place names, anglicized Arabic words and the word "Islam" itself are all spelled as if they were English words, however. Note should be made of the fact that the transliteration system employed in the major reference tool in the field, the *Encyclopaedia of Islam* (Leiden, E.J. Brill, first edition 1913–36, reprinted 1987; new edition in preparation, up to the letter "t" so far, 1960–, now available on CD-ROM [version 1, 1999]; the *Shorter Encyclopaedia of Islam*, 1953, gathers together articles on religion from the first edition with some updated material) is slightly different. The main differences[1] are to be seen in the letters "j" (*jīm*) and "q" (*qāf*). For "j" the *Encyclopaedia of Islam* uses "dj," so, for example, an entry for *ḥajj* ("pilgrimage") will be found under *ḥadjdj*, or *jihād*, "holy war," under *djihād*. For "q," the *Encyclopaedia of Islam* uses "k" with a subscript dot, thus intertwining the entries with "k" representing the letter *kāf*. The reader must remember that where "q" is found in a word in this book, the *Encyclopaedia* entry will have a "k." Examples are *qāḍī*/*ḳāḍī* ("judge"), *ṭarīqa*/*ṭarīḳa* ("Ṣūfī brotherhood") and *Qurʾān*/*Ḳurʾān*.

In common with the practice in religious studies, all dates are cited according to the "Common Era" (CE), numerically equivalent to Christian AD.

I have provided my own rendering of the Qurʾān in this book, generally working on the basis of translations previously crafted by A. J. Arberry, *The Koran Interpreted* (London, Allen and Unwin, 1955) and T. B. Irving (al-Hajj Taʾlim ʿAli), *The Qurʾan: The First American Version* (Brattleboro, VT, Amana Books, 1985). In citing the Qurʾān, the verse numbering of the Arabic text known as the Cairo edition (as used in Irving's translation) is employed. Readers using some other translations of the text (especially older European ones, including that of Arberry) will find a slight variation in the numbering scheme. In citing the Qur'ān, the form "chapter (*sūra*) number"/"verse number" is generally employed.

Because this book is designed as a textbook, I have resisted the temptation to document everything, including contrary views, in the endnotes. Instead, in most cases, the endnotes are limited either to providing the source of a quotation or to giving a source for further reading in which more details of the topic, including arguments pro and con, will be found. The further reading section supplements the endnotes with a list of standard works in the field of Islamic studies with which all students should be acquainted.

Introduction

In the ten years since the first edition of this book appeared, writing in the field of Islamic studies has proceeded at a rapid pace. In every aspect of the discipline – original research, new syntheses of knowledge, and general introductions to Islam – there has been a proliferation of books and articles. Yet, when it comes to basic textbooks on Islam, the situation as I described it ten years ago has not changed substantially. In teaching undergraduate students, I continue to encounter individuals who come to the study of Islam with a background in the historical study of the Hebrew Bible or early Christianity, who express surprise at the lack of critical thought that appears in introductory textbooks on Islam. In dealing with the formation of the religion, the idea that "Islam was born in the clear light of history" still seems to be assumed by a great many writers of such texts. While the need to reconcile varying historical traditions is generally recognized, usually this seems to pose no greater problem for the authors than having to determine "what makes sense" in a given situation. To students acquainted with approaches such as source criticism, oral formulaic composition, literary analysis and structuralism, all quite commonly employed in the study of Judaism and Christianity, such naive historical study seems to suggest that Islam is being approached with less than academic candour. The situation is little better in dealing with the medieval or modern periods of Islam. While topics of interest are often broached, there seems to be little concern for a critical analysis of the approaches to the sources which modern Muslim writers are employing, continuing the general lack of critical reflection upon the Muslim historical sources in general.

In recent years, however, some scholarly analyses of Islam have started to broaden their methodological perspective. There has especially been a trend away from historical positivism (a notion already disposed of in a great many fields) and a move towards an approach which attempts to take into account the literary character of the so-called historical sources. This new effort has resulted in a recognition of the ideological aspects of the literary texts involved. Central has been the critical appreciation of the attempts made in the texts to define and legitimize an understanding of Islam in which the religion functions as a normative system which acts, in a convenient and stabilizing manner, to justify the right to rule of a certain group of people. Islam is, of course, a "religion" in the common meaning of the word; the character that the system has adopted in its tenets and practices, however, can be seen in many instances to reflect an ideological significance for its society. This insight is as true of the formative period as it is of the modern period.

The historical picture of Islam which results from this mode of research leaves a great deal of ambiguity concerning precisely what can be known of the very early times, however. What must be recognized is the nature of the source material in which one sees a theological/ideological backreading of history. As a result, what one can know, and what is explored and emphasized in this book, is how Muslims from the early ninth century (when the documentation of Islam becomes fully available) up to the present day viewed the history of their own religion and how they have developed that understanding into the various manifestations of "orthodox" Islam. Given the scope and length of this book, in most instances it has only been possible to sketch out the issues rather than actually argue the proof for them as fully as may be desirable. Some Islamicists may well feel that this book has glossed over too many details which are crucial in the debate over sources and their implications. Yet it seems to me that the attempt to write a very general textbook such as this, one which paints its picture in very large brush strokes and suggests – in some places at least – a modified view of the accepted version of the emergence, development and future directions of Islam, is worthwhile and potentially fruitful for students. Certainly there seems to be no good reason to withhold the basic approach from this audience, especially since the methodological assumptions underlying it are so commonplace in the study of other religions. I should also add that, while the new tendencies in scholarship have produced a good deal of debate within scholarly circles over the last 10 years, I have not seen any reason to change my basic ideas about the formation, development and enunciation of Islam from those which I attempted to articulate in the first edition.

It should be kept in mind that this book does not attempt to provide an entire "history of Islam." Likewise, this book does not endeavour to take into its purview the expansion of Islam into the many different regions of the world. The intellectual struggles, which played a vital part in the emergence of Islam as the religion we have come to know, appear to have taken place in the Islamic "heartland" of the Arabo-Persian empire; it is to that region, then, that the major attention must be paid in the first parts of the book. In dealing with the modern period, the Middle East region of the world is of central interest as well, although reference is also made to people and ideas emanating from the Indian subcontinent, Malaysia, North America and Europe. Islam in the contemporary world does not mean the Arab world alone, although the sense in which modern Islamic nations look to the Arab world for leadership in intellectual, political and economic spheres must be acknowledged. Furthermore, the role of the Arabic language as the lingua franca of discussions of Islam and as the vehicle for the enunciation of the classical Islamic vision (to which some contemporary spokespeople make frequent reference, in both positive and negative ways) certainly argues for an emphasis on the Arab world in coming to an understanding of the intellectual vision of Islam in today's world.

The emphasis in this book, from the formative period down to today, is that there exists a religious group of people, which, like all peoples, has moved through and been influenced by (as well as being an influence upon) history (even if recapturing that history in words may well be almost impossible). This study, then, is not of a single entity but rather something which has changed over time, has moved with the historical circumstances and has varied for reasons which sometimes are very obscure. As a religion, Islam is also a phenomenon in which people believe and which has created its own sense of historical development. But this Muslim sense of the past has varied over time according to the needs of the situation. To try, therefore, to understand this picture is, once again, the task of this book. Furthermore, central to the presentation of the emergence and history of Islam is the idea of "identity": that is, how a religion functions on both a personal and social level to provide that "stable niche in a predictable environment."[1] The role Islam has played, and continues to play, in creating and developing an understanding of the world and of the relationship between individuals is vital; yet this too is not an unchanging mechanism but one which has gradually and subtly changed in response to the realities and pressures of the world. To try to understand this role of the sense of

Islamic identity and the ways in which this role has responded to the needs of the situation and continues to respond is also the task of this study. Looking into the future, this study also speculates, in Part VI, about possible faces of Islam which may emerge.

Writing about modern Islam poses special problems, and the current turmoil in various parts of the world – many of them Muslim – certainly does not make it any easier. The attempt to come to terms with what is going on in a very fluid situation has often made me long for the relative stability of the study of past history while writing about modern debates. Even then, however, the value placed upon the past by various contemporary religious positions makes the security of the anonymity of history illusory. To understand the reasons why the contemporary religious sensibility sees itself as having something at stake in the study of history, then, brings this book together in yet another way. The reflection upon manifestations of Islam in the past may be complemented by reflections upon the present.

While the material which must be dealt with in this book is fairly complex, the basic notions underlying it are straightforward. Islam, as the religion of the people known as Muslims, was revealed by God, the same God who revealed himself to the Jews and the Christians; he is known in Arabic as Allāh. He revealed his religion to a native of the Ḥijāz on the Western side of the Arabian peninsula, by the name of Muḥammad ibn 'Abd Allāh, in the beginning of the seventh century. Over a period of 22 years, a scripture which is called the Qur'ān (also spelled "Koran") was revealed to Muḥammad by God. A work roughly the same length as the New Testament, the book calls on polytheists along with the Jews and the Christians to declare and put into action their commitment to God's final revealed religion. Heaven awaits those who heed the call, a fiery damnation in hell for those who ignore it. Clearly this is a message which fits within the overall Judeo-Christian tradition and, at the same time, is one which sees the whole world as eventually having to respond one way or the other to its call. As the person to whom this religion was revealed, Muḥammad is considered to have had a perfect understanding of the meaning of the message. Thus, everything which he did in his life is worthy of emulation by his followers, being the perfect expression of the will of God for humanity. Those who follow (or "submit to," as the word *muslim* suggests in its root meaning) this path of Islam form the *umma*, the community of Muslims whose common bond in religion symbolically reflects the central Islamic concept of the unity of the Divine.

Part I

Formative elements of classical Islam

Significant dates

570	traditional birth date of MUḤAMMAD
622	MUḤAMMAD's move to Medina – the *hijra*
632	death of MUḤAMMAD
634	death of ABŪ BAKR, first caliph
644	death of ʿUMAR, second caliph
656	death of ʿUTHMĀN, third caliph
661	death of ʿALĪ, fourth caliph and figurehead of the Shīʿa
661–750	UMAYYAD dynasty
750	ABBISID dynasty begins
767	death of biographer IBN ISḤĀQ
819	death of historian IBN AL-KALBĪ
823	death of historian AL-WĀQIDĪ
824	death of exegete/literary scholar ABŪ ʿUBAYDA
830	Christian polemicist AL-KINDĪ active
833	death of historian/editor IBN HISHĀM
845	death of historian IBN SAʿD
870	death of *ḥadīth* collector AL-BUKHĀRĪ
875	death of *ḥadīth* collector MUSLIM IBN AL-ḤAJJĀJ
887	death of *ḥadīth* collector IBN MĀJA
889	death of *ḥadīth* collector ABŪ DĀWŪD
892	death of *ḥadīth* collector AL-TIRMIDHĪ
915	death of *ḥadīth* collector AL-NASĀʾĪ
923	death of exegete/historian AL-ṬABARĪ
996	death of grammarian/theologian AL-RUMMĀNĪ
1111	death of theologian-mystic AL-GHAZZĀLĪ

1   Prehistory

Arising when Rabbinic Judaism and Christianity were still in the process of firmly establishing themselves institutionally, Islam traces its origins to Arabia of the seventh century. Revolving around a prophet named Muḥammad with a scripture named the Qur'ān, Islam became the ideology which served to unite the Arab empire which asserted itself first in the area of the Fertile Crescent and Egypt, and then across North Africa and Persia. In doing so, it displaced to a large extent the older religions, including that of ancient Persia, Zoroastrianism.

The foundations of Islam

Common wisdom would suggest that in order to understand the foundation of Islam we must have some knowledge of the historical, social, political and economic context from which the religion emerged. As a generalization, of course, this has a degree of validity. However, it is quite possible to question the value of this approach to Islam's historical contextualization because it is highly dependent upon a notion of the religion of Islam existing as a conceptually defined entity from the very beginning of its proclamation. A more stimulating model of the foundation of Islam pictures the religion as emerging gradually, coming to a fixed sense of identity (and all that entails in terms of sources of authority) over a period of some two centuries. Certainly the gradual intertwining of developing Islamic ideology and the immediate environment presents a complex and confused picture, and thus a sketch of the political and religious situation in the Near East in the sixth through the eighth centuries can definitely help to put some of the matter in focus. The provision of such information should not be taken, however, in the sense of looking for "influences upon Muḥammad" from this pre-Islamic period (as so many studies of Islam seem to suggest), but, rather, as an attempt to sketch the context in which Islam did eventually emerge and to see the combination of factors in the society that made the religion successful and made it into the religion that it is today. While the point may seem surprising at first, the relevance of the geographical region of Central Arabia to that emergent definition of what we have come to know as the religion of Islam is highly questionable; Islam (in its clearly defined and developed form) had its formative developing period outside the Arabian context and, while the initial impetus for the religion is clearly tied to the Ḥijāz in Arabia, the character the religion adopted was moulded by more widespread Near Eastern precedents than would appear historically possible within the narrow isolation of Arabia.

The Near East before Islam

There are three foci of interest in the centuries preceding the wave of Arab conquests of the Near East region in the seventh century. The Christian Byzantines had some influence over the Red Sea, extending at times to an alliance with the Monophysite Christians of Abyssinia; the Zoroastrian Persians, with their capital in Ctesiphon in Mesopotamia, had influence which reached at times the eastern side of Arabia and along the south coast to the Yemen; and the South Arabian kingdoms whose fluctuating fortunes, last manifested in the Himyar dynasty of the sixth century, had lost virtually all semblance of vitality by the time of the rise of the Arabs. The Arabian peninsula, although having had settled centres for several millennia, did not contain a power to be reckoned with in the world at the time. The only partial qualification to this resided in the various tribal areas which had become pawns in the hands of external kingdoms, perhaps thereby creating the human forces which would eventually expand out of the peninsula and subjugate the earlier rulers.

In the year 527 Justinian I came to the throne of the Byzantine empire at Constantinople. He was determined to restore unity with the remnants of the decaying Roman empire, the western parts of which had been lost to the Germanic tribes, especially the Vandals and the Goths. He was successful in directing the re-conquest of Italy, North Africa and part of Spain but, by his death in 565, much of this accomplishment was being nullified as the result of continual local uprisings. The Persians took advantage of the subsequent unstable situation and undertook military initiatives on their western border with Byzantium. Heavy taxes, however, provoked instability on the edges of this newly expanded area. Heraclius, the Byzantine leader who died in 641, managed to gain supremacy in Constantinople in 610, only to witness the Persians take Antioch in 613 and Jerusalem in 614, and then march into Egypt in 619. An attempt to move on Constantinople itself in the year 626 left the Persians disorganized and overstretched. Before this final move by the Persians, Heraclius had begun a counterattack and had successfully invaded Persian territory as far as Ctesiphon in 628, recapturing Jerusalem in 629, forcing a retreat on the part of the Persian empire, and eventually causing the murder of Shah Khusro II. The overconfident Byzantines relaxed and fell victim to the Arab conquest, which started most significantly with the initial capture of Damascus in 635.[1]

The situation in the Arabian peninsula

From the point of view of Arabia, this political situation was further confused and made more unstable by two additional factors: the interaction of the Arabs with the two major world powers and the religious rivalry between Jews, the various sects of Christians and, to a lesser extent, Zoroastrians.

Through a system of states functioning as tributaries to the Byzantines and Persians, the nomads of Arabia were kept within the confines of the desert area, and thus did not pose any great danger to the frontier area. As well, these tributary states, Hira (whose people are also known as the Lakhmids) under the Persians in the northeast of Arabia, and Ghassan under the Byzantines in the northwest, provided troops to their respective overlords. By the sixth century, these areas were populated by settled bedouin tribes, and Christianity especially was making its presence felt.[2] The Arabs of this area were, however, of little practical consequence to the world powers of the time, although towards the end of the sixth century, independence was seized by the Ghassanids, while the Lakhmids were forced into an even more subservient relationship with the Persians than had previously been the case. Overall, the tributary system, while it had been in operation for a number of centuries by the time of the Arab conquests, was becoming increasingly unstable at this time.

In the south of Arabia, inter-tribal warfare was bringing an end to the Himyar kingdom, the last in a long line of impressive states in the Yemen area. One of the reasons for the gradual decline in this region was the diminishing importance of the incense trade in the fourth century, in the wake of the Christian takeover of the pagan world and the weakening of the Roman economy.[3] South Arabia, the major source of incense for the world from antiquity (at least since the seventh century BCE), had based a great deal of its economy on the production and trade in this material which was used in Greco-Roman religious festivals and in medicinal preparations. With the shift in the world situation, this economy suffered greatly. Some scholars have also suggested that, around the year 300, the whole area of Arabia suffered a drought, bringing about a collapse of the traditional agricultural basis of the local economy, although the evidence for this is not overwhelming.

Religion in the Arabian peninsula

The sedentary lifestyle of south Arabia had produced a society deeply involved in the various religious systems of the ancient Near East. Evidence, coming from inscriptions found in the area, reflects a developed stage of this religious growth and we have no information on how this religious system actually came into being. Clearly, the region was closely linked to the Mediterranean and Mesopotamian worlds. Until the fourth century, all of the evidence points to the existence of a polytheistic religion with a northern Semitic character. The worship of 'Athtar, a male god who was the most prominent of the pantheon (he is always mentioned first in lists of gods), is often said to have been related to the Ishtar cult of the north, whose female god manifested herself in the Venus star. 'Athtar was believed to be the bestower of blessings who could ensure good crops, many children and success in war. There were a number of other prominent deities whose identity varied with the locality and the historical era. Keeping these different deities clear and distinct is extremely difficult, given the complexities of dealing with the inscriptional source material, but a few observations can be made. The moon god was variously known as Almaqah, 'Amm, Sīn and Wadd (the name of the latter is also known from Qur'ān 71/23), and the sun goddess was known as Shams.[4] These gods and several others were held to be tribal patrons. As well, deities of the clan and the family also existed and these were often described simply as "the god [*'Ih*] of so-and-so." Each level of deity was seen to govern a different sphere, each in a power relationship to the next level: personal to village to tribal land to world. According to the evidence of archaeological remains from various temples, sacrifices were a prominent part of religious worship. Incense offerings on stone altars and blood offerings were likely to have played a role in acquiring benefits for the person doing the sacrifice. All these activities took place within temples which were apparently attended by both men and women, with the purpose of the rituals being seen as the acquisition of the benefits which these various gods could bestow. Other features attested by inscriptions include pilgrimage activities, ritual meals and a code of personal purity.

Starting in the fourth or fifth century, south Arabian inscriptions speak of a monotheistic cult of Raḥmanan, "the Merciful," frequently qualified as "Lord of heaven and earth."[5] Very little evidence is found in the inscriptions for a continuation of the earlier polytheistic cult (although since inscriptions necessarily reflect an élite and official segment of society, whether the general populace so quickly gave up its polytheistic belief is open to question). Apparently the rise of the kingdom of Himyar in about the year 380 marks this change, coming about probably as a result of, or in order to accomplish, a unification of the various South Arabian tribes. The monotheistic impetus is often seen to be a result of Jewish influence in the society, although some scholars wish to see this as a natural, independent development (based on an evolutionary picture of religion in general). Some scholars also wish to connect this development to the Quranic notion of a *ḥanīf*, the quality of being a monotheist in the face of paganism; whether this is really a reference to a historical reality in terms of a movement among people or whether it refers to moral qualities of certain people is open to question. There is no independent evidence that incontrovertibly supports the existence of a native Arabian pre-Islamic monotheism.[6] The Biblical echoes found in some of the monotheistic inscriptions, such as the phrase "the Merciful [*raḥmanan*], who is in heaven" and the use of the grammatical plural in reference to God (as in the Hebrew *elōhīm*) found in the inscriptional statement "the God(s) to whom belong the heaven and earth" suggest that Judaism is the most likely influence on the formation of this cult. Little is known of the religious character of this monotheistic trend, so additional information is not available to settle the matter definitively. It is likely that Judaism was supported by the Persians as a tool against Byzantine influence in the south of Arabia.

Certainly Judaism was present within this period of the monotheistic cult and perhaps even predated it slightly. There is clear and explicit evidence of a Jewish presence in South Arabia, attested towards the end of the fourth century. References are found to the "community of Israel" as well as "Lord of Jewry." The presence of

Jews in the Yemen continued until the mid-twentieth century when most were removed to the newly formed State of Israel.

Christianity, meanwhile, was not in evidence in south Arabia before the sixth century, at which time it appears to have been present in a community centred in the town of Najrān. It is thought to have spread there from Abyssinia. Accounts are found of persecution of the Christians early in the sixth century by the Jewish ruler Yūsuf Asʿar, probably as a result of fears of Byzantine influence over the Christian community. Sixth-century retaliations by Abyssinian troops seem to mark the demise of Judaism as a power, with inscriptions thereafter speaking of belief in "God and His Messiah and the Holy Spirit" on the part of the rulers. There is no doubt that the Christianity which spread from Abyssinia was supported by the Byzantines against Persian influence in the area, even though it was, from the Byzantine perspective, of the heretical Monophysite persuasion. By the end of the sixth century, the Persians started to encourage Nestorian Christianity, another strain of that faith which was abhorrent to both the Byzantines and the Abyssinians, and aided the Yemenites in their removal of the Abyssinian overlords. The country was so fractured and destroyed by being subject to the manipulation of the various foreign powers that little remained by the time of the rise of the Arabs to be of any particular significance to either major empire.

The significance of Central Arabia

The area of central Arabia remains a vast unknown territory during this historical period, of little significance to anyone in the ancient world except as a natural barrier of desert. Despite the extensive work done by scholars studying early Muslim literary texts concerned with the subject (archaeological digs have not been permitted in crucial religious areas), the evidence for the role of the region as a focal point for a rich and economically explosive trade between south Arabia and the fertile crescent, as was once suggested, is virtually non-existent.[7] Any solid evidence of the religious character of the region reveals a polytheistic system having basic features in common with Semitic religion in general; this includes worship of gods associated with the astral cults and beliefs in spirits inhabiting rocks, trees and the like.[8] The role of Mecca as a sanctuary is fairly evident, although the character of this sacred area becomes rather muddled as a result of the manipulations of the data by later historians who have overlaid what would appear to be native Arabian sanctuary traditions with Jewish ones.[9]

Overall, given this situation, a number of things become clear in historical retrospect. Politically, the area of the Near East was unsettled at the time of the Arab conquests and was certainly in a condition which would allow for the emergence of a new configuration in political power. The interactions which did occur between the Arabs and the world at large saw the tribes being manipulated by the foreign policy of the empires, with no particular significance being given to the people themselves; this was true both in the north and in the south. The connection between the ancient empires and their religions was close, meaning that a new religious dispensation, separate from the notions connected with the old regimes, may well have found itself in a favourable position.

Prehistory in Muslim identity

There is, however, far more significance to the pre-Islamic period than the preceding interpretation of the historical data would seem to suggest. In terms of Muslim identity, the pre-Islamic period serves most emphatically as a historical, ideological and ethical counterpoint to the Islamic ethos. It is, therefore, an era in which Muslim writers have tended to be very interested and they have provided an abundant amount of material purporting to portray the period. Therefore from the standpoint of attempting to comprehend the foundation of the Islamic religion, the Muslim understanding of the period takes on a crucial and considerable role. The appreciation of this Muslim view, however, must be distinguished from reconstructing the history of the era itself; what is at issue here is the role of understanding the past and the kinds of pressures and interpretations to which such understanding becomes subject. This process, embodied within Muslim writings about the past, is one which is common to humanity: the re-creation of the past embodied in the idea of "tradition," selectively formed and reshaped into a new and relevant context.[10]

The notion of *jāhiliyya*

The pre-Islamic period is an era contrasted to the time and ethos of Islam, a contrast which is embodied in the term *jāhiliyya*. This term is found in the Qur'ān four times in reference to the idea itself and ten times in reference to people, and is also used in verbal derivations related to the word with the same sense. The word would appear to be used in the text of scripture as the opposite of "Islam," in that those who are connected to the *jāhiliyya* are those who are "ignorant of God" – at least this is the way most Muslim commentators on the Qur'ān have taken the word. For example, Qur'ān 48/26 states:

> When those who disbelieved set in their hearts fierceness, the fierceness of ignorance [*jāhiliyya*], God sent down His Shechina upon His messenger and the believers, and obliged them to the word of godfearing to which they have a better right and of which they are worthy.

The religious accomplishment of Islam, encompassed in the word "godfearing" (*taqwā*) contained in this passage, can only be judged by comparing it to what came before it. Even more significantly, the impulse to demonstrate this accomplishment of Islam appears to rest ultimately upon the desire to prove the divine status of the religious dispensation itself. What Islam has accomplished in transforming society from one of *jāhiliyya* to a "godfearing" one is, in fact, proof of the divine nature of the religion.

A consequence of this apparent impulse to illustrate the separation between *jāhiliyya* and Islam is that a large amount of material emerged which was designed to prove and provide the appropriate pre-Islamic contrast. The starting point of all this material was, of course, the Islamic position – that is, only what was needed in order to provide this counterpoint to Islamic values is presented in the texts. In no sense do the Islamic sources attempt to provide a dispassionate presentation of pre-Islamic society, politics and religion (although many recent scholars of Islam have certainly attempted to take the material and recreate that era, despite the selectivity and biases of the material itself).

Discontinuity of Islam with the past

How this approach to portraying the past works can most easily be illustrated through an example dealing with a point of law. In legal issues the impulse to demonstrate the benefits of Islam are quite pronounced, for this often reflects very tangible elements within everyday Muslim life. Qur'ān 2/168 reads: "O people, eat anything lawful and good that exists on earth, and do not follow the steps of

Satan; he is a manifest enemy of you." Common to a number of
sources which deal with interpretation of the Qur'ān and which
provide anecdotes about the "context" of the revelation of a verse[11]
is the following: "This verse was revealed about [the Arab tribes of]
Thaqīf, Khuzā'a and 'Āmir ibn Ṣa'ṣa'a who prohibited to themselves
cultivated produce and grazing livestock. They also forbade the
baḥīra, sā'iba, waṣīla and *ḥāmī* camels."[12]

The picture that is painted is one of various people before the
revelation of the Qur'ān doing things, in this case prohibiting to
themselves various foods, which were to be permitted under the
Islamic dispensation. Of course, it is not possible to prove that this
was not actually so, that this event did not "really happen," but that
is not the point. What is of interest here is how the anecdote works
within the Islamic context, for the function of such stories would
seem to be the prime reason Muslim writers transmitted such
accounts. The purpose of the anecdote is to provide a measure of
the accomplishment of Islam and to differentiate Islam clearly from
what existed previously.

In fact, it is quite possible to demonstrate in individual cases that
later Muslims did not know the "facts" of the pre-Islamic period
but, rather, that the anecdotes emerged for the purpose of anchoring
Islam to history more firmly; other writers have provided many lucid
examples of this phenomenon[13] and further instances are easy to
locate. Concerning Qur'ān 2/158, "Ṣafā and Marwa are among the
waymarks of God. Whoever goes on the pilgrimage to the house or
performs the visitation ['*umra*], there is no fault on him if he circum-
ambulates them," anecdotes are repeated which speak of the
pre-Islamic practices concerning the hills of Ṣafā and Marwa but they
are unclear as to whether the pre-Islamic Arabs did or did not run
between them. One anecdote reads as follows:

> On Ṣafā was the image of a man called Isāf, while on Marwa
> was the image of a woman called Nā'ila. The people of the book
> [i.e. the Jews and Christians] claimed that these two had
> committed adultery in the Ka'ba [in Mecca], so God converted
> them into stone and placed them on Ṣafā and Marwa in order
> to act as a warning to others.... The people of the *jāhiliyya*
> stroked the idols when they circumambulated them [during their
> pilgrimage rituals]. When Islam came and the idols were broken,
> Muslims detested the circumambulation between the hills
> because of [their association with] the idols. So God revealed
> this verse.[14]

Another explanation of the verse is found in this report:

'Urwa ibn al-Zubayr said to 'Ā'isha: "I see no fault in someone who does not run between Ṣafā and Marwa, nor would it concern me if I did not run between them." 'Ā'isha answered: "You are wrong, O son of my sister! Muḥammad ran between them and so did the Muslims. Rather it was [the pagans] who sacrificed to Manāt, the idol on the mountain of Mushallal, who did not run between them. Then God sent down this verse. If it were as you say, the verse would read, 'there is no blame on whoever does not run between them'."[15]

Illustrated in these anecdotes is the ambivalence of the information. Either the pre-Islamic Arabs did or did not run between the two hills. Both reports certainly provide a justification for the Muslims running between them (which, after all, is the central question for later Muslim jurists) and, at the same time, both reports provide a contrast with the pre-Islamic period. This contrast, note, can be positive or negative – either things are different from the past or they are the same. A similar phenomenon can be seen in many legal discussions, for example, regarding foods being prohibited to Muslims "by virtue of not being eaten by pre-Islamic Arabs,"[16] where the evaluation as compared to the past is positive once again.

The role of the Abrahamic myth

In general, it can be said that this pre-Islamic material was recorded not with "historical" reasons in mind, if by that we mean modern principles of historical research. Rather, the accounts were transmitted and written down in order to provide the necessary information for understanding the Qur'ān within a context of Arabia, and for evaluating Islam as a whole. An extremely popular work was written by Hishām ibn al-Kalbī, who died in 819, which was entitled *The Book of Idols*. The text gathers together poetical references to various "pre-Islamic" deities, especially those cited in the Qur'ān. Once again, however, it must be noted that the origins of this poetry is by no means obviously from the historical period before Muḥammad; it is non-Islamic religiously (but not necessarily pre-Islamic historically), and that suggests the possibility at least that, in the period after Muḥammad, vestiges of earlier religious sentiments still remained.

Of special interest is the very beginning of Ibn al-Kalbī's book which provides a clear theological understanding of Islamic prehistory; the example illustrates well the approach of works such as these. History is presented (indeed, as one should expect) through Islamic eyes and told according to Islamic principles and includes in its retelling an implicit condemnation of the corruption and immorality of the pagan era which preceded Islam.[17]

> When Ishmael, son of Abraham, may God bless them both, settled in Mecca, many children were born to him such that the number of people became so numerous that they were crowded there. They displaced the original inhabitants, the Amalekites. Later on, Mecca become so overcrowded that rivalries and strife arose among them, causing them to fight one another and as a result they spread out throughout the land seeking a livelihood. ... No one left Mecca without carrying a stone from the sanctuary as a sign of veneration of it and of love for Mecca. Wherever they settled they would erect the stone and circumambulate it as they had done at the Ka'ba, thereby seeking blessing and affirming their attachment to the Ka'ba. They continued their veneration of the Ka'ba and Mecca despite this practice and still journeyed there on the pilgrimage and the visitation ['umra] according to the tradition inherited from Abraham and Ishmael, may God bless them both. In time, this led them to worship whatever they liked. They forgot their ancient beliefs and changed the religion of Abraham and Ishmael for another. They worshipped idols and returned to the practices of the nations before them. After discovering the images which the people of Noah (on him be peace!) worshipped, they adopted the worship of those which were remembered. Among the practices were some which came down from the time of Abraham and Ishmael, including the veneration and circumambulation of the temple (in Mecca), the pilgrimage, the visitation ['umra], the standing on 'Arafāt, the rituals of Muzdalifa, offering sacrifices, and uttering the ritual formulae during the pilgrimage and the visitation.[18]

The problem that such a passage is trying to solve for its readers is the following. Muslims know that the rituals connected to the Meccan pilgrimage were continuations of pre-Islamic rites; such rites had pagan connotations. How could God legitimize such activities? The answer is found in Abraham and Ishmael who, having lived in Mecca and performed the pilgrimage rites there (implicitly the same ones which Muslims perform until the present time), left the heritage of the activities but the meaning (although not the actions themselves) of them was forgotten among the pagan inhabitants of the area.[19] While this Abrahamic background is not appealed to in every case of a positive connection between the *jāhiliyya* and Islam, it certainly is sufficiently frequent to be seen as a generalized tool for the Muslim understanding of the past. Abraham remains the "first Muslim," putting into practice the activities which would have to be revived by Muḥammad; the people in the intervening centuries are the ones who distorted the true religion which God had made available to His creation through Abraham.

The significance of prehistory

Thus we can see that the "prehistory" of Islam is a significant conceptual notion both for historians concerned with understanding the emergence of Islam and for the Muslim community itself in the understanding of its relationship to its religio-cultural heritage. For the latter, the evaluation of the accomplishment of Islam in separating its faith from the past is understood in two ways, as a radical split from the past or as a continuation of the valuable (i.e. divinely sanctioned) elements. For the former, the reliance on material preserved within the framework of the evaluation of the Muslim faith means that the assessment of the rise of Islam is fraught with difficulties. In the absence of assuredly contemporaneous sources, literary or epigraphic, our knowledge of "prehistory" will remain filtered through the theologically inspired picture of the past provided by the later Muslim sources.

2 The Qur'ān

Islam as a religion focuses on its scripture, the Qur'ān. Written in Arabic, the Qur'ān is a short book which holds a special appeal for its listeners and readers. It is relatively easy to give a brief description of the Qur'ān in terms of the book as we have it before us today. Even the Qur'ān's contents are readily summarized, as long as one does not attempt to perceive a necessarily systematic theological position within it. But accounting for how, why and when the Qur'ān came into being as a text and why it looks and sounds the way it does, is far more difficult. It will be beneficial to start with the easy tasks and then attempt the more difficult ones afterwards.

The Qur'ān as a book

The Qur'ān consists of 114 chapters, called *sūra*s, arranged roughly in order of length from the longest (some 22 pages of Arabic text for *sūra* 2) through the shortest (only a single line for *sūra* 108). The major exception to this principle of ordering is the first chapter, called "The Opening," *al-fātiḥa*, which is essentially a prayer and is used as such in Muslim ritual. Each chapter is divided into verses, *āya*s, the total number amounting to somewhere between 6204 and 6236, differing according to various schemes of counting. These verse divisions do not always correspond to the sense of the text but are generally related to the rhyme structure of the individual *sūra*s. Twenty-nine chapters are preceded by disconnected letters of the Arabic alphabet, some single letters (Q – *qāf*, *sūra* 50; N – *nūn*, *sūra* 68) or up to five letters together. The significance of these so-called mysterious letters has eluded traditional Muslim and modern scholarship alike. Also prefacing each chapter, with the exception of *sūra* 9, is the *basmala* – the statement "In the name of God, the Merciful, the Compassionate" (a statement which also occurs at the beginning of a letter which is cited in Qur'ān 27/30). The text as it is generally found today indicates both the Arabic consonants and the vowels according to a standard system of notation, along with a variety of other marks connected to recitation practices and verse divisions. Early manuscripts of the Qur'ān dating from the eighth and ninth centuries provide only the consonantal form of the Arabic, however.

Reading the Qur'ān discloses a thematic preoccupation with three major topics: law, the previous prophets and the final judgement. The three combine to create what has been termed by some "a curious amalgam" of an assumption of Biblical knowledge on the part of the reader with another element, which would appear to be some sort of native Arabian tradition.[1]

God as the central theme

Ruling over all of the Qur'ān, and the reference point for all the developments of the themes, is the figure of God, *Allāh* in Arabic. The all mighty, all powerful and all merciful God has brought the world into being for the benefit of His creatures, has sent messages to His creatures in the past to guide them in the way of living most befitting to them and to Him, has given them the law by which they should live – and which has reached its perfection and completion in Islam – and will bring about the end of the world at a time known only to Him when all shall be judged strictly according to their deeds. The basic message is a familiar one in the Judeo-Christian tradition.

The Qur'ān declares in *sūra* 20, verses 7–8, "Be loud in your speech, yet surely He knows the secrets and what is even more hidden. God, there is no god except Him! His are the most beautiful names." This emphasis on the uniqueness of God, that He is the only god who exists, is presented both in opposition to the Jewish–Christian tradition and in opposition to the polytheist idolaters.

> The Jews say, "Ezra is God's son;" the Christians say, "Christ is God's son." That is what they say with their mouths, conforming with the unbelievers before them. May God fight them off! How they are perverted! They have taken their rabbis and monks as lords apart from God, and the Messiah, the son of Mary – and they were ordered to serve God alone; there is no god except Him. Glory be to Him, above what they may associate [with Him]!
>
> (Qur'ān 9/30–1)

While the precise reference of the charge that Ezra is the son of God according to the Jews has never been made clear, the overall emphasis of the passage on the association of simple mortals alongside God is obvious enough. As far as Jesus is concerned, there is a clear denunciation of his divine sonship throughout the Qur'ān, and, while he is called al-Masīḥ, the Messiah ("the anointed one"), this is presented as his name only and not as an indication of his function or status.

> They have set up *jinn* as associates with God, even though He created them! They have imputed sons and daughters to Him without any knowledge. Glory be to Him! Exalted is He over whatever they describe! The creator of heaven and earth – how can He have a son while He has no consort, and He created everything and He has knowledge of everything? That then is God, your Lord; there is no god except Him, the Creator of everything. So serve Him for He is trustee over everything.
>
> (Qur'ān 6/100–2)

The reference to the *jinn*, or the "genies" of the Arabian Nights, is mentioned here in such a way as to object to their being considered as divine powers of any sort (as apparently the polytheists thought), but their existence is quite obviously accepted. Along with the angels and humanity, the *jinn* are seen as part of creation but existing in a different dimension. The creation of humanity from clay (Qur'ān 15/26, 55/14) is paralleled by the creation of the *jinn* from fire (Qur'ān 15/27, 55/15). The belief that the angels were created from light is a strong tradition in Islam but it is not actually mentioned in the Qur'ān.[2] Overall, each part of creation has its own sphere and its own specific duties in its relationship to God.

The prophets of the past

The figure of God in the Qur'ān is clearly the same God who communicated to the prophets of the past. Qur'ān 20/9–14 states:

> Has Moses' story ever reached you? When he saw a fire, and told his family, "Wait here; I have glimpsed a fire. Perhaps I can bring you a brand from it, or I shall find some guidance at the fire." When he came to it, [a voice] called out: "Moses, I am your Lord! Take off your sandals; you are in the sacred valley, Tuwa. I Myself have chosen you, so listen to this revelation.

Indeed I am God! There is no god except Me; therefore serve
Me and perform the prayer of My remembrance."

This passage illustrates nicely the Quranic approach to previous
revelation. The story itself is familiar from the Hebrew Bible (Exodus
3) but is presented here shorn of the extensive narrative element
which seems so essential to the Judeo-Christian way of understanding
scripture. In contrast, the Qur'ān simply presents a summary of the
story and gets directly to the religio-moral point, each aspect of
which is, in fact, central to the Islamic message. In this case, clearly,
the emphasis is upon the oneness of God, but it is also on the institution of prayer and the instruction of obedience to God as the
essential element of faith. To understand such passages fully in terms
of a coherent overall narrative it is frequently necessary to place the
Quranic accounts into the framework of the Biblical tradition. This
fact emphasizes the need to consider an area far broader than Central
Arabia when thinking of the original context of the message of Islam.

Twenty-eight figures other than Muḥammad are named in the
Qur'ān as having been commissioned or selected by God to spread
the message of the true way of obedience to Him. Only a limited
number of these figures were given scriptures of some sort to share
with the community. Abraham, Moses, David and Jesus are specifically cited in this regard. Not all of the messengers are familiar from
the Biblical tradition (or, at least, their identification with person-
ages of the past is less than clear): Hūd, Ṣāliḥ, Shuʿayb and Luqmān
are generally treated as prophets of the specifically Arabian context
prior to Muḥammad. Dhū'l-Qarnayn is identified as Alexander the
Great according to the legends which have gathered around the
name. Dhū'l-Kifl, the "lord of the portion" (mentioned in Qur'ān
21/85 and 38/48), is variously and very uncertainly identified as
Obadiah of I Kings, Ezekiel or Elijah, but is often left as "unknown"
from the perspective of history.

The stories of these prophets are recounted frequently in stereo-
typed passages, reflecting the general Islamic message. The prophet
is commissioned by God, the prophet confronts his people, the people
reject him and the people are, as a result, destroyed, and the prophet
and any persons faithful to his message are saved by the mercy of
God. A *sūra* such as the eleventh, entitled "Hūd," is typical in its
presentation of these stories. Here we find, joined together in narratives always similar in structure and even in wording in some
instances, accounts of Noah, Hūd, Ṣāliḥ, Abraham, Lot, Shuʿayb and
Moses. The moral is always the same. God will triumph over the

unbelievers and His message will always remain in the world in one form or another. A few other prophets have their stories told in more expansive form. The story of Joseph, recounted in *sūra* 12 and one of the most cohesive narratives found in the Qur'ān, is presented in a form quite full and in parts even more elaborate than the Biblical account. This elaboration indicates that the Qur'ān is not simply a retelling of the Biblical stories but a reflection of the popular form of the prophet stories in the Near Eastern milieu of the seventh century. Elements in the Quranic versions of these stories are sometimes found in works such as the Jewish Talmud or Midrash, for example. Thus, the context within which the Qur'ān must be read is far more than the framework provided by the text of the Bible alone; rather, the living tradition of Judaism and Christianity, and all the other faiths and folklore of the area are reflected in the Qur'ān and provide the necessary background for its comprehension.

The famous story from Genesis 22 concerning the sacrifice of the son of Abraham is also retold in the Qur'ān, but the son is not identified by name and his identity became, for a time, subject to great debate in Islam.[3] The context of the Quranic passage would seem to suggest that Ishmael was the one who was sacrificed, since after the discussion of the sacrifice in the Qur'ān (*sūra* 37, verses 102–9) the passage goes on in verse 112 to say, "then We gave him the good tidings of Isaac, a prophet, one of the righteous," suggesting that this was a totally separate character. The reading of Ishmael as the intended victim gained further standing through the later ideology of the Muslim community which argued that the Jews had changed the Biblical account to reflect well on their own heritage traced through Isaac; the Jews had done this rather than enhance the status of the Arabs and their descent through Ishmael (as related in the Bible, although that genealogy is nowhere echoed in the Qur'ān). Regardless, the story provides another illustration of the approach of the Qur'ān to Biblical narratives. Qur'ān 37/102–9 states:

> and when [the son] had reached the age of running with him, he said, "My son, I saw in a dream that I will sacrifice you. Consider, what do you think?" He said, "My father, do as you are ordered; you will find me, God willing, one of the steadfast." When they had surrendered and he flung him down on his brow, We called out to him, "Abraham, you have confirmed the vision! Thus We reward the good-doers. This is a manifest trial." We ransomed him by means of a mighty sacrifice and left for him among the later people, "Peace be upon Abraham!"

Compacted here into a few lines is a chapter of the Bible which has often been cited as one that was well crafted for dramatic impact and for its use of narrative tension in having the young Isaac travelling to the sacrifice not knowing the fate in store for him. The Qur'ān, however, removes the drama but saves the message, the supreme faith of both Abraham and his son. This faithful attitude on the part of Isaac is also emphasized in the development of the tradition in Jewish and subsequently Christian circles, in which Abraham's son becomes the prefigurement of Jesus in his willing self-sacrifice. Also significant in the Quranic story is the emphasis on the fact that Abraham and his son "surrendered," in Arabic *aslama*, essentially "became Muslims"; even here then (or, perhaps, especially here), the story is told with Muslim understanding and insights.

Jesus

Similar observations may be made concerning the story of Jesus which, while it is found scattered throughout the Qur'ān rather than in one cohesive narrative, presents a picture that has often been seen to reflect varying tendencies within Christianity – Gnostic, Monophysite and Nestorian.[4] Born of the Virgin Mary (Qur'ān 19/16–34), Jesus spoke his first miracle from the cradle. His task on earth was to provide the "clear proofs" or "explanations" (Qur'ān 2/253 and elsewhere) and his mission was punctuated by miracles as in Qur'ān 3/49: healing, knowing secrets and fashioning birds out of clay into which he breathed life, the latter being a story known from Christian apocryphal Gospel of Thomas. The crucifixion of Jesus, spoken of in Qur'ān 4/157–8, has created the greatest amount of interest, with a view to its possible reflection of sectarian Christian disputes: "[The Jews] neither killed nor crucified him, only a likeness of that was shown to them. . . . God lifted him up to Himself." The notion that Jesus did not "really" die on the cross has been seen as a continuation of Christian discussions over the nature of Jesus – divine and/or human. Once again, however, the Qur'ān would seem to reflect a strange amalgam, on the one hand supporting the argument for the truly divine nature of Jesus and thus denying the reality of his death, while on the other hand denying that Jesus was anything other than a human being.

The message of the judgement day

All these prophets, and many additional figures who are not mentioned by name in the Qur'ān but who are said to have been sent (as Qur'ān 10/47 states: "Every nation has its messenger"), brought the same message of the coming judgement for those who do not repent and follow the law of God. Qur'ān 19/59–61 states:

> There followed after them ["the prophets"] a succession who neglected prayer and followed passions. So they shall meet error except for anyone who repents and believes and acts righteously; those – they will enter paradise and they will not be wronged in any way; the gardens of Eden which the Mercy-giving has promised His servants in the unseen.

The message is a simple one. All people shall die at their appointed time and then, at a point known only to God, the resurrection shall take place, at which each person shall be judged according to the deeds they have performed on earth. "The agony of death will come in truth; that is what you have been trying to escape! The trumpet shall be blown: that is the day of the threat!" states Qur'ān 50/19–20, making reference to the eschatological trumpet, one of many Quranic elements familiar also from the visions of John recorded in the Book of Revelation. The scene of the judgement is painted in graphic style. For each person, a book of deeds shall be brought forth, bearing witness to his or her good or evil state (Qur'ān 83); the image of the balance and the weighing of deeds is also employed (Qur'ān 21/47). The judgement shall determine the ultimate fate of the individual, be that either the bliss of paradise in the gardens or the burning torment of hell. Both of these places are depicted in vivid terms quite frequently in the Qur'ān, as for example in *sūra* 55 where the "flare of sparks and fire" and the "seething bath" of hell are contrasted to the "two gardens" of paradise which have "every kind of fruit, flowing springs" and exotic rewards for the righteous.

The fate of the individual is described as being in the hands of God but also as up to the individual. God as the all-powerful creator can control His world fully but humanity must accept responsibility for its own actions. The tension which such statements create proved to be a major topic for theological speculation in Islam. Be that as it may, the Qur'ān is clear that each individual is expected to follow the law which God has set down in His scripture, if there is to be any hope of entry into paradise in the hereafter. People are capable of sin, that being defined as an "error" in parting from the ways of God. The figure of Satan is introduced to explain the presence of this potential for evil in the world.

The path to paradise

Qur'ān 4/136 proclaims, "O you who believe, believe in God and His messenger, and the book which He has sent down on His messenger as well as the book which He sent down previously. Anyone who disbelieves in God and His angels, His books, His messengers and the last day has surely gone astray." Here is a veritable creedal statement, bringing together all the elements considered essential for reaping the final reward in paradise. One must believe in the truth and the contents of the scripture; and what is the evidence of belief in it, if it is not putting the words into action? The previously quoted Qur'ān 19/60 emphasizes the reward "for anyone who repents and believes and acts righteously." Fulfilling the law of God – "acting righteously" – is a prerequisite for an individual to achieve salvation. The law, as proclaimed in the Qur'ān, is reminiscent of the Jewish law in matters such as its continuation of the prohibition of pork and the institution of ritual slaughter (e.g. Qur'ān 2/173, 5/1–3), some purity regulations (especially as regards women, Qur'ān 2/222, and within a ritual situation, Qur'ān 4/43, 5/6) and the emphasis on the regulation of marriage (e.g. Qur'ān 4/23), divorce (e.g. Qur'ān 4/19–22) and inheritance (e.g. Qur'ān 4/6–12). Clearly Islam sides with Judaism against Christianity in its position on the role of the law as the appropriate implementation of faith, a law given by God as a gift to humanity to provide guidance in living the proper, fully human life. As well, various emblems of Islam are mentioned in the Qur'ān, but often only in an unelaborated form. The pilgrimage (e.g. Qur'ān 2/196–200), the month of fasting (e.g. Qur'ān 2/183–7), the institution of prayer (e.g. Qur'ān 2/142–52, 2/238–9) and the idea of charity (e.g. Qur'ān 9/53–60) are all dealt with to varying degrees; regardless of the somewhat vague nature of some of the descriptions of these activities within the Qur'ān (as compared to their elaborate formulation in other Muslim sources, a topic dealt with in more detail in Chapter 7 below), it is clear that they are conceived as a compulsory part of Muslim life.

Some parallel has been seen between the biblical "ten commandments" and *sūra* 17, verses 22–39. Certainly the moral aim of many of the statements is similar: belief in only one God, showing respect to parents, not committing adultery and so forth. In terms of its narrative structure, however, the law is quite clearly not presented in the same way in the Qur'ān as it is in the Bible. In no sense is this passage a pivotal or focal point of the text; nor is it portrayed in Muslim tradition as central within the context of Muḥammad's career. Thus, the passage does not stand parallel to the traditional understanding of the "ten commandments" in relationship to Moses and the Bible. Rather, the law in the Qur'ān is an integral part of the text with nothing to mark it off from the rest of the word of God. This presentation of the law does not preclude it being stipulated in great detail in numerous places, however, just as in the Bible:

> Forbidden to you [in marriage] are your mothers, your daughters, your sisters, your aunts on your father's side and on your mother's side, your brother's and your sister's daughters, your foster mothers and your foster sisters, your mothers-in-law and step-daughters who are under your guardianship being born of your wives with whom you have consummated marriage (however, if you have not consummated it with them, there is no fault on you) and the wives of your sons who are your own flesh-and-blood; nor may you take two sisters together unless this is a thing of the past. God is Forgiving, Merciful.
>
> (Qur'ān 4/23)

The Qur'ān speaks also of the law as it was revealed to the previous communities. Both the Torah of Moses and the Gospel of Jesus are specifically cited as previous revelations.[5] The Qur'ān is seen as confirming both scriptures and as acting as a resolver of disputes between them: "We sent down to you the Remembrance [i.e., the Qur'ān] so you may make clear to people what was sent down to them, so perhaps they may reflect" (Qur'ān 16/44). But the Qur'ān also serves a correcting function, according to Muslim understanding, because humans have misinterpreted and tampered with the earlier revelations, infusing the word of God with human perversions (see Qur'ān 5/48). The Qur'ān provides a clear and perfect version of the will of God, the correct rendition of revelation.

The character of the Qur'ān

A summary of the contents of the Qur'ān, such as that just provided, while necessarily incomplete, glosses over an important point about the composition of the book itself – its apparent random character and seeming arbitrary sense of organization.[6] This unique composition is illustrated by examining the contents of any of the longer *sūra*s which are clearly a composite of many different themes and strata of thought. *Sūra* 2, for example, the longest in the Qur'ān, presents a startling picture when looked at in outline:

Verses	Topic
1–29	Faith and disbelief
30–9	Creation, Adam, Satan
40–86	Biblical history – Moses
87–103	Biblical history – Jews, Jesus, Moses
104–21	Polemic – Muslim, Jewish, Christian
122–41	Biblical history – Abraham
142–67	Islamic identity (direction of prayer, prayer itself, pilgrimage)
168–203	Juridical problems (food, wills, fast, pilgrimage, etc.)
204–14	Salvation history
215–42	Juridical problems (holy war, marriage, divorce, etc.)
243–53	Salvation history
254–60	(mixed)
261–83	Juridical problems (charity, usury)
284–86	Faith

Such a brief outline does not do justice to the complexity of the thematic structure of the *sūra* by any means,[7] but, even so, it does provide some material for provoking thought. How did the Qur'ān come to look the way it does, with the subject matter within individual chapters jumping from one topic to the next, with duplications and apparent inconsistencies in grammar, law and theology abounding? To the source critic, the work displays all the tendencies of rushed editing with only the most superficial concern for the content, the editors/compilers apparently engaged only in establishing a fixed text of scripture. Within this perspective, a logical historical point for the emergence of this fixed text is provided by the rise of the Qur'ān to a status of absolute authority in matters of law and theology (as opposed to the authority of tradition, of the caliph or of reason). Creating a stable text of scripture, canonizing the various elements into a whole, may be seen as going hand-in-hand with the text being confirmed as the major source of legal and theological authority for the Muslim community.

Muslim accounts of the collection of the text

The Muslim community itself has, of course, an explanation for why the Qur'ān looks the way it does, but the contradictory nature of the accounts within the multiplicity of versions of the story has raised grave doubts on the part of many scholars as to their motivation. Generally, Muḥammad himself is excluded from any role in the collection of the text, although it is possible to find some accounts which talk of him going over the whole text with 'Alī, his cousin, son-in-law and figurehead of the later Shī'a. Zayd ibn Thābit, a companion of Muḥammad, is generally credited with an early collection of the scripture and the pages of the text are said to have been entrusted to Ḥafṣa, one of Muḥammad's wives. Under the instructions of 'Uthmān, the third ruler of the empire after the death of Muḥammad, the major collection of the text "as we now have it" (as the Muslim claims have it) is said to have taken place. Working on the basis of pieces of text written "on palm leaves or flat stones or in the hearts of men," the complete text (deemed to have survived in full) was written out in full and distributed to the major centres of the early empire. Thus, within 30 years of the death of Muḥammad, it is understood that the Qur'ān existed in its fixed, if skeletal form; theologically, it is held that the form that the text was in at this point was an image of the "heavenly tablet," suggesting that its structure and content were precisely that which God desired for it.[8] From this skeleton text, which indicated only the consonants of the Arabic script in a rudimentary form, the final text of the Qur'ān was developed over the next two centuries, such that all the subtleties of the language and the script were indicated. Most important from the Muslim perspective, it is held that an oral tradition preserved the full text from the time of its revelation, the written form serving only as a mnemonic device for memorization of the text. There are, in a sense, two ways of dealing with the Qur'ān within Muslim tradition: the oral, the tradition about which stems from Muḥammad, and the written, the tradition stemming from the caliph 'Uthmān.

The evidence of the manuscripts

In 1972, a treasure trove of ancient manuscripts of the Qur'ān was discovered in the Great Mosque of Sana'a during renovations. In 1979, a German team of scholars started working through some 12,000 fragments of parchment and paper, some of which (twenty-two groups of fragments) have been dated to the eighth century primarily on the basis of their use of the early Arabic script known as the *Ḥijāzī* style.[9] This discovery has excited a good deal of scholarly and popular interest. The existence of early copies of the text of the Qur'ān might well be thought to help answer some of the riddles about its composition. So far, however, that has not been the case and only very tentative conclusions have been put forth.

Certainly, the existence of manuscripts of the Qur'ān indicates that the text (or, at the very least, substantial parts of it) existed in some sort of collected form by the eighth century. That, of course, does not tell us anything about the status of the text itself within a community of believers. Some discrepancies in the order to the *sūra*s as they are found in a few manuscripts may indicate some variability in the overall form of the text. More interesting, though, is the fact that the text contains variant readings of a minor nature that suggest to some scholars that the idea of an oral tradition running parallel to the written one cannot be given historical credence. What we may have evidence of is the interpretative nature of the detailed annotations that were added to the text later: that is, that the current text is the product of reflection upon a primitive written text and not upon the parallel transmission of an oral text as the Muslim tradition has suggested.

Examples can be provided, on the evidence of the early manuscripts, of instances in which words, because of the way they were written in the primitive script of the time, were likely mispronounced as a result of a misunderstanding of the script and in the absence of a firm oral tradition. Examples include the name Ibrāhīm, more easily and better understood in a version closer to the Hebrew, Abrāhām, and Shayṭān, once again closer to the Hebrew if read Sāṭān. Both of these developed readings depend upon the misunderstanding of the early writing of the long "a" sound in the middle of the word.[10]

Another different type of example may help to indicate what is at stake here. The very last verse (112) of *sūra* 21 starts "He said [*qāla*], 'My Lord, judge according to the truth. Our Lord is the All-Merciful.'" The reference to "My Lord" and "Our Lord" in the text indicates that the subject of "He said" cannot be God but is the reciter of the Qur'ān, in the first place understood to be Muḥammad. Such a passage, in fact, falls into a common form of Quranic speech found in passages normally prefaced by the imperative "Say!" (*qul*). The significant point here is that in the text of the Qur'ān, the word here translated as "He said" is, in fact, more easily read as "Say!" due to the absence of the long "a" marker (something which commonly happens in the Qur'ān, to be sure, but the word *qāla* is spelled this way only twice – the other occasion being in Qur'ān 21/4 and that only occurs in some of the traditions of the writing of the text). In the early Sana'a manuscripts, the absence of the long "a" in the word *qāla* is a marker of an entire set of early texts. But why should it be that this particular passage should be read in the way that it is? It really should read "Say!" to be parallel to the rest of the text. This opens the possibility that there was a time when the Qur'ān was understood not as the word of God (as with "Say!") but the word of Muḥammad as the speaking prophet. It would appear that in the process of editing the text, most passages were transformed from "He said" to "Say!" in both interpretation and writing with the exception of these two passages in *sūra* 21 which were not changed. This could have occurred only because somebody was working on the basis of the written text in the absence of a parallel oral tradition.

It is fair to say, then, that the manuscript tradition may have a significant impact upon our understanding of the early history of the text of the Qur'ān. The study of these manuscripts is still in its infancy, however, and the impact of these texts has yet really to be felt.

The authority of the Qur'ān

The value and the point of the stories about the collection of the Qur'ān are still under debate among scholars but, whatever the case, one thing remains quite clear. The Qur'ān is, and has been from the beginning of the emergence of Islam as a firmly established religion, the primary point to which reference must always be made in order to define something as "Islamic." The Qur'ān is the defining point of Islamic identity. The emergence of the Muslim community is intimately connected with the emergence of the Qur'ān as an authoritative text in making decisions on matters of law and theology. What research has revealed is that scripture's status and authority were debated in early times, especially between the various religious communities of the Near East and also within the newly emerging Islamic community itself. Elements of the process by which the Qur'ān emerged as the authoritative source, side-by-side with the emergence of the community of Islam itself, can be traced in the writing of various texts of Quranic interpretation in the early centuries of Islam,[11] in early works of law, and in several documents of interreligious polemic. The ultimate enshrinement of the text of the Qur'ān as we now know it, understood to be literally the word of God, miraculous, inimitable, linked to an illiterate prophet, and thereby having its authority within the community, was the result of two to three centuries of vigorous debate as reflected in these texts.

Supporting the status of the authority of the Qur'ān are a number of theological dogmas connected directly to the book by which institutionalized Islam was able to argue for the Qur'ān as the prime source in law and theology. These dogmas have as their end result the skirting of issues connected to the construction of the text. They do this by seeing the very shape of the book as evidence of the divine hand at work. But it is on this point that early polemical texts reveal a great deal of discussion, and early Islamic exegetical texts dealing with the Qur'ān indicate that the argument concerning the form of the text as evidence of divine authorship took at least three centuries to reach its fully developed formulation.

The Qur'ān as the proof of Islam

It would appear that, early on, Muslims had to defend their nascent religion against Christian theological attack in the area of the Fertile Crescent, especially Iraq. The following argument was constructed: miracles prove the status of prophethood and the Qur'ān is Muhammad's miracle; therefore, Muhammad was truly a prophet and Islam is a true, revealed religion. All participants in the debate appear to have agreed on the first premise. What Muslims had to prove, and Christians disprove, was the validity of the second, for the conclusion, the truth of Islam, stood or fell on its credibility. Over time, the argument became one concerned to prove the "inimitability" of the Qur'ān, an argument which, its proponents were quick to point out, had a basis in the Qur'ān itself, although whether that was clear before the demands of the argument were put upon those verses is not entirely obvious. Known as the "challenge verses," the production of a text "like" the Qur'ān is encouraged but known to be impossible: "Produce a *sūra* like it [i.e. the Qur'ān], and call on whom you can, besides God, if you speak truthfully (Qur'ān 10/38); Well then bring ten chapters the like of it, forged!" (Qur'ān 11/13). God has given the Qur'ān to Muhammad and because of its divine origin, no text "like" it can, in fact, be produced. The inimitability of the text proves its divine authorship and thus its status as a miracle, confirming Muhammad's role and the veracity of Islam.

Polemical texts from some 150–200 years after Muhammad indicate the sorts of discussions that were going on; the existence of the arguments indicates that there were no clearly formulated Muslim answers to these concerns at the time. That suggests that the Qur'ān as a fixed text of scripture was still in the process of finding support for its authority within the community; indeed, it took at least 100 more years before the full enunciation of the doctrine of inimitability could respond cohesively to such challenges. The Christian al-Kindī, who wrote a text around the year 830, starts off by demanding the following: "Show me any proof or sign of a wonderful work done by your master Muḥammad, to certify his mission, and to prove what he did in slaughter and rapine was, like the other, by Divine command." The isolation of one of the central elements of Christian polemic against Islam – that Muḥammad's religion was spread by the sword – is combined here with the demand for proof of a miracle. Anticipating the Muslim response that the Qur'ān was that evidence, al-Kindī continues:

> The result of all of this [process by which the Qur'ān came into being] is patent to you who have read the scriptures and see how, in your book, histories are all jumbled together and inter-mingled; an evidence that many different hands have been at work therein, and caused discrepancies, adding or cutting out whatever they liked or disliked. Are such, now, the conditions of a revelation sent down from heaven?[12]

The literary state of the Qur'ān is used against the Muslims by al-Kindī as proof of its non-divine origin.

The doctrine of inimitability

The Muslim response to these charges did not reach its full defensive literary expression until towards the end of the tenth century in the hands of the theologian-grammarian al-Rummānī (d. 996) who argued for the *i'jāz*, "inimitability," of the Qur'ān on the basis primarily of its literary qualities, especially its easily quantifiable merits such as its concision.[13] At one point in his argument, al-Rummānī cites a popular Arab saying, suggests that its meaning is close to a Quranic statement but then points out that the Qur'ān expresses the same sentiment (and even more, he claims) in a fewer number of letters. Furthermore, what to polemical writers of earlier centuries were faults within the Qur'ān – evidence of its human production and thus non-miraculous status – become for al-Rummānī positive elements within the book. Ellipses within the text, for example, were considered positive rhetorical devices rather than evidence of rushed or careless writing. Much of this sort of argumentation became tied to an understanding of the nature of the Arabic language, a language full of rhetorical potential of which, naturally, the Qur'ān must take full advantage. The Qur'ān, according to its own statements (Qur'ān 12/2, 26/192–5) was revealed by God "in a clear Arabic tongue" and, the argument is made, it must partake in all the features of that language. This sort of argument is difficult, if not impossible, to evaluate, due to the lack of contemporaneous profane literature by which the rhetorical accomplishment of the Qur'ān can actually be assessed. The argument remains a dogmatic one, essential to the proof of the status of the text, but one which operates (like many other religious arguments) within the presuppositions of Islam alone.

Interpretation of the Qur'ān

In fact, Muslims, in the two centuries for which there is some literary evidence before al-Rummānī, appear to have had slightly different feelings about their scripture. They appear to have been more concerned with cataloguing the peculiarities of the text itself and facing the practical job of understanding the text, rather than worrying about defending its intricacies. Therefore, the more general problem of interpretation and, hand-in-hand with that, the consolidation of its authority through clear enunciation of its meaning, were of far greater concern.

The text of the Qur'ān presents many ambiguities, difficult words whose precise readings are unsure, problems of textual division, and apparently incompatible statements. With the text's rise to the status of authority, or perhaps parallel to it and stimulating that very rise to authority, there emerged the discipline of interpretation, known as *tafsīr* or, in a more general sense, the Quranic sciences called *'ulūm al-Qur'ān*.

Fundamentally, a work of *tafsīr* provides an interpretation of the Arabic text of scripture and is defined by a number of formal characteristics: it will follow the text of the Qur'ān from beginning to end and will provide an interpretation of the text segmented either into words, phrases or verses. While exceptions are found to these characteristics in some works which would be accepted as *tafsīr*s, the vast majority of works fit into this pattern. Early works tend to focus on certain tendencies in interpretation, Some pursue the narrative ("haggadic") aspects of the Qur'ān, developing the text into an entertaining and edifying whole, paying attention to the needs of the reader who will approach the text of scripture with a curious and speculative mind. Thus, providing the historical background to the various pieces of revelation (in a format which later becomes known as *asbāb al-nuzūl*, the "occasions of revelation") and identifying people, places and things which are only alluded to (known later as *ta'yīn al-mubham*) become important aspects.

Other works pursue the legal ("halakhic") aspects of the text, focusing on the early community's need to support legal practice by reference to the text of scripture, sometimes facilitated by organizing the Qur'ān into topics rather than follow the text *ad seriatim*. Yet other works examine textual matters, including lexicographical and more narrowly "masoretic" issues. Another tendency is seen in the work of Abū 'Ubayda (who died in 824) called *Majāz al-Qur'ān*, which focuses on literary figures and expressions. It presents a listing of types of "problematic" verses in the Qur'ān and their explanation; items such as ellipses due to omission, grammatical numerical discord (e.g. plural verbs with singular subjects), and variation in the treatment of the gender of nouns are all recorded. This cataloguing of difficulties in the Qur'ān is also found in other works treating the vocabulary of the text itself as well as the text's stylistic features and variant readings. With the emergence of the doctrine of inimitability, the attitude towards these sorts of elements changed, as has already been suggested.

More major works of interpretation of the Qur'ān emerged in the ninth century, and they aimed to clarify the text in light of contemporary understandings and conditions. Not only was this the result of the maturation of the Muslim community and a consolidation of opinion about the scripture but it was also the result of practical pressures. As the Islamic community expanded, it incorporated a large number of people who did not know Arabic and who were not fully acquainted with the Biblical tradition, which, as was pointed out earlier, seems to be an assumed basis for understanding the Quranic text. The first landmark of what became a vast library of books providing comprehensive interpretations of the Qur'ān, was written by Abū Ja'far al-Ṭabarī who died in 923.[14] A verse-by-verse analysis provides a detailed discussion of every major interpretational trend (except sectarian tendencies, for example, Shī'ī); every idea is documented by the transmission of the opinions said to derive from Muḥammad or his closest companions, who are pictured as having the best information regarding the understanding of the text. It also becomes clear that grammar along with theological perspective become the main guiding tools for constructing a mature exegesis of the Qur'ān. Grammar served to assert the scholar's status and authority within the whole discipline of *tafsīr*, such that the ability to pursue the minutia of Arabic constructions became a focal point of argumentation over how a meaning of the text could be derived. Theology tended to play a lesser role, usually subsumed under grammatical or legal wrangling.

While a brief quotation cannot do justice to the complexities of al-Ṭabarī's text, the following short section gives some indication of his own bases for reasoning, although we do not here see his constant reference to reports from Muḥammad and his companions which provide the material basis to many discussions and variations in interpretations. In dealing with Qur'ān 3/7, "It is He who sent down upon you the book in which there are clear verses – they are the mother of the book – and others are ambiguous," al-Ṭabarī makes the following statement:

> Then God described these *clear verses* by saying that they are the *mother of the book*, meaning that they are the source of the book which contains within it all the duties of the religion, including the responsibilities and the penalties and everything else which creation needs in the law of its religion. Also included are the responsibilities which are assigned in this world and the hereafter. These are called *the mother of the book* because they are the major portion of the book and they are a place of refuge for the people of the Qur'ān when they are in need of such. That is the practice of the Arabs in calling the gathering of a major portion of something its "mother." So they named the banner of the people under which they gathered in their fighting groups their "mother;" also the leader who handled the majority of the matters of the village or district was called its "mother." ... *Mother of the book* is in the singular; it is not made plural as in "They are the mothers of the Book." *They* is used, however, because all of the *clear verses* are intended by *the mother of the book*, but not each verse of them is the *mother of the book*. If the meaning was such that each of the *clear verses* was the *mother of the book*, there would be no doubt in the matter, because then it would have been said: "They are the mothers of the book." The analogous statement of God to *They are the mother of the book* as we have interpreted it in the singular sense of *mother* being the grammatical complement of *they* is in Qur'ān 23/50, *We made the son of Mary and his mother a sign.* He did not say: "two signs" because the meaning is "We made the two

of them together a sign." The meaning is singular because they gave a single warning to humanity. If the intention had been that each one of them independently gave a warning to humanity, then it would have been stated, "We made the son of Mary and his mother two signs," because then in each one of them there would have been a warning. The signs are that Mary had a child not by a man and that her son spoke from the cradle as a baby. So, in each of those events there is a sign for the people.[15]

The historicization of the text of the Qur'ān was another important element in the production of many works of exegesis. The integration of the text with the stories of the prophets of the past (primarily Biblical) in the material known as the *qiṣaṣ al-anbiyā'*, "stories of the prophets," and with the story of the life of Muḥammad as embedded in books of *Sīra* ("life story") such as that of Ibn Isḥāq (d. 767), was designed both to prove the theological fact of the reality of revelation and to provide a context for interpretation for an otherwise historically opaque text. The result was a text which was grounded in day-to-day human existence with an emphasis on the period of the formative Muslim community.

The Qur'ān as an object of faith

For the Muslim community, the Qur'ān is the word of God as revealed to Muḥammad, the focal point of the Islamic faith. As a symbol of that faith, the book has naturally garnered far more importance for the individual believer than the polemical discussions sketched above would suggest. After all, for Muslims there is no doubt about the status of their scripture; at every moment, their faith confirms for them the veracity of the book. There arose a great number of beliefs about the text of the book itself, separate from its contents, which reflect the honour and significance which is accorded to the scripture as a book. Within at most two hundred years of the death of Muḥammad, traditions arose speaking of the significance of individual sections of the Qur'ān. The first chapter, *sūrat al-fātiḥa*, is not only argued to be an essential element of the ritual of prayer,[16] but also the "greatest" of all the *sūra*s, the recitation of which is recorded as curing the bite of a scorpion, for example; likewise, *sūra*s 113 and 114 are seen as effective in curing illnesses. Reciting specific individual portions of the Qur'ān, the last two verses of *sūra* 2 especially, are spoken of as giving protection from Satan for the night. Recitation of *sūra* 18, *sūra* 48 or *sūra* 112 brings merit and benefits.[17] The result of these practices has been the emergence of a complex group of medical and spiritual beliefs all connected to the book, known as *khawāṣṣ al-Qur'ān*. The history of these practices, like most popular beliefs, is not well known but it is likely that modern practices,[18] such as wearing a tiny copy of the Qur'ān or the name Allāh as an amulet, in the manner in which Christians wear a crucifix or Jews, a star of David, have a heritage which extends well back into the early Islamic period. The Qur'ān has been the central symbol of Islam as well as its vital source and, as is true of Jesus in Christianity, its power to move and motivate individuals has never been underestimated by Muslims.

3 Muḥammad

Muḥammad is the central figure in Islam. Chosen by God to receive the revelation of the Qurʾān, he has been taken by all Muslims to be the ideal man, the perfect embodiment of what it means to be a Muslim. Having lived a fairly normal existence in sixth century east central Arabia, at the age of 40 Muḥammad revolutionized his society in ways which were both unexpected and long lasting.

Contemporary scholarship on Islam has generally not seen fit to postulate that Muḥammad did not exist. That someone named Muḥammad embodied the rallying point for the Arab conquests and provided the tag for a religious doctrine in the name of which the conquered lands were united, there really is little doubt; at the very least, no profit is to be gained from denying those facts in terms of providing a cohesive historical picture.[1] Sources external to the nascent Islamic society itself provide evidence, albeit somewhat at variance with the "accepted" portrait of the Arabian prophet, that confirms the role of the figure himself. These sources are limited in number, extremely hard to date (raising questions of Muslim influence upon the writers, if the source is, in fact, much later than claimed) and questionable in their supposed "disinterested" or "objective" presentation of history.[2]

Despite the existence of these external sources and the proliferation of documentation from within the community, the fact of the matter remains that it is very difficult to talk about Muḥammad, in either his political or religious guise, free from the perspective which later Muslim tradition has imposed upon him. The biography of Muḥammad has served a number of important functions in Islam, each of which has coloured it in crucial ways. There are two major aspects which must be confronted here. One, Muḥammad's biography must be understood as a framework for the revelation of the Qurʾān and two, it must be understood as a source for the normative example, *sunna*, of Muḥammad.

Muslim sources for the life of Muḥammad

Material on the life of Muḥammad is available in ample if, in fact, not excessive quantities. The earliest complete extant text stems from a version of the biography (*Sīra*) of Muḥammad by Ibn Isḥāq (d. 767) edited by Ibn Hishām (d. 833). This may be supplemented by other fairly early texts such as those by al-Wāqidī (d. 823) and Ibn Saʿd (d. 845). Also useful are the later *ḥadīth* collections which gather together anecdotes about Muḥammad and his life, generally organized according to legal topics and communicated by Muḥammad's closest followers, his so-called "companions." In broad outline, all these sources present the same story but matters of chronology and detail are always problematic.

The account of the events during Muḥammad's life is fairly standardized, despite the multiplicity of sources available and the numerous disagreements among scholars of Islam as to how to interpret the material in a meaningful way. Most accounts go back to the text of Ibn Isḥāq, supplemented by the various other sources. Despite valiant attempts by some scholars to elicit information, the Qurʾān has proven very opaque when it comes to Muḥammad: the name is mentioned four times – Qurʾān 3/144, 33/40, 47/2, 48/29 – but without prior knowledge of the *Sīra* accounts of Ibn Isḥāq, the material provides no data beyond asserting Muḥammad's existence and a conception of his prophetic role. Furthermore, since in many places the *Sīra* may well be attempting to explain, make sense of, or clarify the elliptical and allusive text of the Qurʾān, there is the danger of going around in interpretative circles. The absence of biographical material is but one example of a general tendency in the Qurʾān not to provide any overall context. The Qurʾān simply does not provide the necessary clarifying keys by which it would be possible to extract data concerning the contemporary Arabian context, beyond the citation of a few names.[3] It is in this vein, then, that one of the roles of the biography of Muḥammad in Islam is to be understood as providing the contextual framework for the revelation of the Qurʾān. While the details of this framework are frequently vague and contradictory, the basic theological point stands, underpinning the entire biographical corpus: God has revealed the Qurʾān to Muḥammad, an ordinary man living among the Arab tribes, over a 22-year period.[4] As a result, the entire biographical account has been coloured by these efforts to situate and interpret the Qurʾān.

The life of Muḥammad in the sources

Muḥammad is said to have been born around 570; this is a date fixed by a tradition which records that the "Expedition of the Elephant," the expedition by a ruler of south Arabia named Abraha, into the homeland of Muḥammad, the Ḥijāz, was in the same year. The evidence for the date of the expedition being 570 is undermined by inscriptional material found in south Arabia, which makes it more likely to have been at the end of the 540s. The significance of the date in the Muslim context is that it serves to establish Muḥammad's age as 40 when he started to receive revelations, the number forty being one of general spiritual significance in the Near East region.[5]

Muḥammad was born into the family of Banū Hāshim in the tribe of Quraysh; his family was a prominent but not dominant group in the society at the time. He was orphaned at an early age, and lived a meagre existence until he married Khadīja, an older woman with financial involvement with the camel-caravan trade. Muḥammad is thought to have been involved in the trade himself. At the age of 40 he is said to have gone on a solitary retreat in the hills near Mecca, following a religious practice of the time, at which point the angel Gabriel came to him to inform him of his commission as a prophet of the one God, Allāh. To this event is traditionally connected the Quranic passage contained in *sūra* 96: "Recite in the name of your Lord who created, created humanity from a blood clot! Recite, for your Lord is most Generous, who taught by the pen, taught humanity what it knew not." Stories of self-doubt are connected with this call to prophethood, but eventually Muḥammad followed his orders and preached the message of the Qur'ān. He had little success to begin with, perhaps converting some of the lower-class members of his society, along with his wife Khadīja and his cousin 'Alī, his future son-in-law, fourth Caliph and figurehead of the Shī'ī movement in Islam. As Muḥammad hardened his attack on the polytheistic society of Mecca, its inequalities and hypocrisies, the inhabitants became more resentful of his presence. It has been speculated that the cause of some of this resentment was his attack upon the institutions of the Meccan society, especially the town's connection to the religious shrine, the Ka'ba, which gave it a degree of prominence in Arabia at the time. Persecution of the members of this new religion is said to have increased substantially, and traditions tell of a group of believers who emigrated to Abyssinia, perhaps going there to find asylum among the Christians or to attempt to make more converts among an audience who may have been thought to be sympathetic to the message of the movement. Meanwhile, Muḥammad made efforts to find a new place to live in Arabia, trying the neighbouring town of al-Ṭā'if, before being invited to Yathrib (later to be called Medina, or fully, Madīnat al-nabī, the "City of the prophet") some 350 kilometres northeast of Mecca. Communities of Jews were living in Yathrib and these people are suggested to have been part of the attraction of the location, for a sympathetic audience for the message of Muḥammad was anticipated among these "people of the book."

The move to Yathrib is referred to as the *hijra* ("emigration" or "flight") and the year in which it happened (622) serves as the focal point of the Muslim calendar. An event to which the Qur'ān provides only ambiguous reference, it is regardless seen as the time at which the Muslim community came into being and thus the appropriate starting point for calendar dating (the notion of "community," *umma*, being a defining point of the Islamic sense of identity). There do not appear to be any instances of the mention of the idea of a *hijrī* calendar in coins or documents from the seventh century; rather, an undefined era is employed or reference is made to an era (apparently starting in 622, however) as the "rule of the Arabs."[6] Defining the calendar in terms of the *hijra* appears to be linked with the rise of Islam as a state religion, a notion to be explored further in Chapter 4.

It was in Yathrib/Medina that Muḥammad emerged as a forceful religious and political leader, leading the Medinan community under the terms of a type of treaty, the so-called "Constitution of Medina," within which his authority was said ultimately to derive from God: the ideal religio-political aspects of Muslim community life are embodied here. Controlled in this "constitution" were the political and civil relations of the various tribes within the Medinan federation, with all disputes to be brought before Muḥammad for arbitration. The "constitution" explicitly states: "Whenever a dispute or controversy likely to cause trouble arises among the people of this document, it shall be referred to God and to Muḥammad, the apostle of God. God is the guarantor of the pious observance of what is in this document."[7]

The actual conversion of the inhabitants of Medina to Islam was not immediate and the Jewish communities were accused of treachery and, eventually, all were either removed or attacked.

Muḥammad's strategy in Medina, especially after his realization that the Jews were not the ready audience for his message which he had anticipated, was to return to Mecca. This aim was pursued through an attempt to curtail the trade of Mecca by random attacks on the camel caravans, producing unstable conditions for reliable conduct of business as well as bringing the profits of such raids into Medinan hands, thus producing power and prestige for the community in the eyes of the Arabian tribes.[8] The most important of these raids was known as the battle of Badr; taking place in 624, it started as an attack on a Meccan caravan and then became a battle with the Meccan Quraysh tribe. It provided a great victory for Muḥammad and his followers, a victory which was interpreted as a sign of divine pleasure with the strategy. In the year 625 an attack by Quraysh tribesmen in the Battle of Uḥud, resulted in a defeat for Muḥammad's followers, while in 627, a Meccan army laid siege to Medina in the Battle of the Ditch. The Medinans were able to withstand the onslaught, however, and the Meccans were forced to withdraw after 40 days. This success was followed by an attack directly on Mecca led by Muḥammad, which ended not with a battle but with the Treaty of Ḥudaybiyya, the terms of which allowed the Medinans to enter Mecca the next year in order to perform the pilgrimage; that treaty was honoured. By that time, the power of the Medinan community had grown significantly in Arabia and, by the next year, 630, Muḥammad was able to attack and take over Mecca, meeting little resistance to his efforts. The final 2 years of Muḥammad's life were spent in Medina, with him attempting to consolidate his position in Arabia with alliances, and at least nominal conversion to Islam, of the nomadic Bedouin of Arabia.

Difficulties with the biography

This is the basic account of the life of Muḥammad as it is presented in the narrative sources available to us. Many aspects of it are debatable, especially in matters of precise dating and, on that basis alone, the summary of the "life of Muḥammad" as presented here is fraught with difficulties and insoluble problems. Evidence of such things as the sources' tendency to "improve" over time – such that later sources are able to provide specific data when earlier ones are vague – and the overt intention of much of the material to interpret unclear passages of the Qur'ān as mentioned above, suggests that texts such as Ibn Isḥāq's *Sīra* are far more complex in literary terms than a historical biography might popularly be conceived today. Essentially, these texts were involved in a creative story-telling in which the raconteur's ability to elaborate, entertain and enhance were highly praised merits. Underlying the whole structure, however, is the attempt to provide a context for the revelation of the Qur'ān, such that ambiguous references may be made clear through the process of interpretation.

The mythic dimension of Muḥammad's biography

One other related factor acts to restrict the amount of confidence that may be placed in these accounts of Muḥammad's life, even disregarding disputes over small details. The religious importance of Muḥammad is such that it is not really feasible (nor necessarily desirable) to distinguish later religiously-inspired fiction from what might be called historical "fact." The entire structure of a work such as that of Ibn Isḥāq suggests that many elements are constructed from what have been termed by one scholar "mythic *topoi*," or basic religious narrative and thematic conventions. Such *topoi* were employed throughout the Near Eastern area in the construction of literary lives of religious figures. In addition, the *Sīra* text is composed of lists, documents, genealogies, chronologies, poetry and formal prose.[9] The overall effect is to create a picture of both Muḥammad and the Muslim community in its "pristine" form. This means that the picture which emerges, as well as the impulse behind its composition, is a normative one: this is a picture of how the Muslim community should be, projected back into the times of its founder who has been described in mythic terms. Its intention is to portray the religion of Islam as conceptually identifiable from the time of Muḥammad.

A part of the reason for having produced such a picture of Muḥammad was to create an expression of Islam which separated it clearly from Judaism and Christianity. The role of the figurehead of a religion in producing identity for the religious community is evident in all three of the monotheistic traditions and Muḥammad's place in this interreligious rivalry was established both through the Qur'ān (as the book given specifically to him, as the Oral and Written Torahs were revealed to Moses) and through the biographical material. The major concern displayed through a work such as Ibn Isḥāq's *Sīra* is the acceptance or rejection by various groups of the credentials in the hands of the messenger, that is the scripture. At stake, then, is the authority of the person of Muḥammad, not in terms of law but as a prophet. The connection of Muḥammad to the revelation of the Qur'ān then becomes central.[10]

The significance of the figure of Muḥammad

Another reason for the emergence of this elaborated, detailed picture of Muḥammad is far more complex and vital to the enterprise of Islam itself. In fact, regardless of how interesting the events of Muḥammad's life may be, the significance for Muslims of the person himself and the actual "facts" of the narrative (as opposed to its overall theological point) does not lie particularly in the historical narrative at all. Rather, it is the anecdotes about his life, the *ḥadīth*, and the more generalized aspects of what that behaviour represents, that concern the community most of all. This is the *sunna*, the "example" provided by the life of Muḥammad which every Muslim attempts to emulate. Of course, the two aspects – the historical and the anecdotal – are intertwined and, for the historian, indistinguishable; this is, as a consequence, what has created some of the problems in trying to reconstruct the "historical Muḥammad."

The information which is found in works such as that of Ibn Isḥāq (at least in germ form) and which has been gathered together into the works of *ḥadīth* especially, is believed by Muslims to have been transmitted from the earliest generations of community members down to the collectors of these books. Such transmissions are documented by what is known as the *isnād*, the "chain" of transmitters of a report (listed backwards chronologically), while the actual text is known as the *matn*. An example is the following:

> Isḥāq told me that 'Ubayd Allāh told him on the authority of Shaybān on the authority of Yaḥyā on the authority of Muḥammad ibn 'Abd al-Raḥmān, client of Banū Zuhra, on the authority of Abū Salama on the authority of 'Abd Allāh ibn 'Umar that he said, "The messenger of God (may the prayers and peace of God be upon him) said to me, 'Recite all of the Qur'ān in one month.' I said, 'But I am able to do more than that!' So (Muḥammad) said, 'Then recite it in seven days, but do not do it in less than that'."[11]

Reports such as these comprise the text of a series of books devoted to the gathering together of the material, which may be arranged either according to the transmitter of the report or according to the legal topic. This latter method of organization proved the most successful, it being the principle employed in the six works which are accepted as being of major importance by the majority of Muslims. These books collect together what were considered genuine *ḥadīth* reports (and, as such, the reports serve as the theoretical basis for Islamic law). The books were each compiled by al-Bukhārī (d. 870), Muslim ibn al-Ḥajjāj (d. 875), Ibn Māja (d. 887), Abū Dāwūd (d. 889), al-Tirmidhī (d. 892) and al-Nasā'ī (d. 915).

All the reports in these books deal with what Muḥammad said and did, and of what he approved or disapproved implicitly (as indicated by his general behaviour). They are classified into subjects which would appear to follow the legal discussion taking place at the time of their compilation. Al-Bukhārī, for example, has a total of 93 chapters with sub-headings but in some chapters there are in fact no *ḥadīth* reports to be found under some of the sub-headings; it is clear, therefore, that he was working with a prearranged structure and was attempting to document the issues under discussion. The structure of the book reflects the concerns of Muslim life, ones which go beyond any narrow definition of "law" and encompass many different aspects. To take al-Bukhārī as an example again, his work starts with what might be considered "theological" topics: revelation, faith and knowledge. He then deals with various aspects of prayer (Chapters 4 through 23), followed by charity, pilgrimage and fasting (Chapters 24 to 32). Covered there are what have become the central symbols of Islam, enshrined in the concept of the "five pillars" (see Chapter 7 below). After that, the book covers, in Chapters 33–53, general interactions between people (with special emphasis on commerce) and then turns to certain religious concepts such as the merit of the prophets and the Qur'ān. Marriage and divorce follow, then a wide variety of topics, ranging from medicine and good manners to apostasy and dreams. The work finishes with "The Unity of God," thus bringing the sequence to closure. Muḥammad, therefore, is conceived to have had some bearing on all aspects of Muslim life, both the personal and the interpersonal, as reflected in this categorization of the *ḥadīth* material.

The problem of *ḥadīth* reports

For an individual report itself, the *isnād*, or chain of transmitters, is considered to act as a guarantor of the genuineness of the text of the report. However, the *isnād* mechanism was, according to Muslims, subject to a great deal of fraud in the early period. Muslims therefore created several methods of evaluating these *isnād*s, using criteria which dealt in particular with the life and character of the individual transmitters found in the sequence of names. The desire was to document *isnād*s which were complete in their testimony to the transmission of the text of the report from generation to generation. The citation of people of high moral integrity who conceivably could have met in their lifetimes so that the reports could have been passed on physically was the important factor in the assessment of the chains of transmitters. Not surprisingly, perhaps, such methods could really only sort out the inept *isnād* fabrications from the less inept.

The tendency to fabricate *ḥadīth* reports extended so far as to include reports which could justify the employment of *ḥadīth* reports themselves in trying to settle legal issues and others which warn against false transmission of reports. One of the most famous of all such reports is the following:

> Abū Bakr ibn abī Shayba told us that Ghundar told him on the authority of Shuʿba, and also that Muḥammad ibn al-Muthannā and Ibn Bashshār both told him that Muḥammad ibn Jaʿfar told him that Shuʿba also told him, on the authority of Manṣūr on the authority of Ribʿī ibn Ḥirāsh who heard ʿAlī, may God be pleased with him, giving a sermon in which he said that the messenger of God, may the prayers and peace of God be upon him, said, "Do not spread lies about me! Whoever spreads lies regarding me will enter the fires of hell."[12]

The forces which tried to stem the tide of extensive spreading of unreliable *ḥadīth* reports appear to have used the very practice it was trying to condemn in order to stop the practice.

We also find in the collections of *ḥadīth* reports instances which clearly are concerned with matters of interest to the community in generations after Muḥammad but which have been framed as predictions made by him. An example is the following which raises the divisive issue of free will versus predestination as discussed by theologians several centuries into the Islamic era:

> Bundār told us that ʿAbd al-Raḥmān ibn Mahdī told him that Shuʿba told him on the authority of ʿĀṣim ibn ʿUbayd Allāh who said that he heard Sālim ibn ʿAbd Allāh reporting on the authority of his father who said that ʿUmar said: "O messenger of God, what do you think? Are the works which we do of our own creation or are they settled in advance by God?" (Muḥammad) said: "They are indeed settled in advance, O Ibn al-Khaṭṭāb, and everything has been made easy [see Qurʾān 80/20]. Whoever is of the people of happiness will do that which

leads to happiness, and whoever is of the people of misery will do that which leads to misery."[13]

Here Muḥammad is employed as a spokesperson for the theological party which supported the doctrine of predestination; in that way, those people tried to assert the rightness of their position by citing Muḥammad as their proof. *Ḥadīth* reports may also be found which also support the opposite position.

It has also been discovered by modern researchers that *isnād*s had a tendency to "grow backwards." In certain early texts a statement will be found attributed to a caliph of the Umayyad dynasty, for example, or will even be unattributed, as in the case of certain legal maxims; elsewhere, the same statements will be found in the form of *ḥadīth* reports with fully documented *isnād*s going back to Muḥammad or one of his companions. There are instances where it would have been appropriate on the basis of the arguments being conducted in texts to cite the given report from Muḥammad, had such reports been available; but, in fact, unattributed statements are found. The conclusion to be drawn from this is that at a certain point in time the *isnād* had not yet been fully developed and was not yet considered by some authors necessary to establish a report's authority. Only when the significance of a given statement was fully established did the *isnād* "grow backwards" to include Muḥammad and thus invest an opinion with the authority of the prophet of Islam.[14]

The authority of Muḥammad

This fabrication of *ḥadīth* reports arose because of the importance which Muslims attributed to Muḥammad in the elaboration of Islam. Muḥammad's example became the legal basis for substantiation of individual items of Muslim behaviour. As we shall see in Chapter 6 on the development of law, Muḥammad's practice or *sunna* became a source of law in Islam (second only to the Qur'ān) as a result of the desire to introduce both some uniformity and a sense of defined authority into the Muslim community. Because of this, the name and the authority of Muḥammad were used to substantiate legal positions; what a given group of Muslims felt was the correct or appropriate legal practice would, at the same time, sincerely be felt to be the practice of Muḥammad.

The crucial question, which is much debated in modern scholarship, is when did Muḥammad emerge as being the source of authority for the community, which is clearly the position attributed to him by the ninth century? Certainly the status of the authority of Muḥammad in the early Muslim community is not clear. Coins which refer to him as *rasūl Allāh*, the "messenger of God," start appearing only in the 60s and 70s of the *hijrī* calendar and even then such citations need not be taken as necessarily invoking his authority; rather, his symbolic value as an emblem of Islam – a part of an emerging self-definition – would appear to be the point of such references, since the caliph was at the same time proclaiming himself the authority in the living community as the *khalīfat Allāh* (a matter discussed in Chapter 4 below). This same question also arises in the context of the discussion of the law as to when the notion of the "local tradition" as being the basis of legal practice was supplanted by the *sunna* or guided practice of Muḥammad specifically as second only to the Qur'ān.

Clearly, then, the status of Muḥammad as the legal grounding for the community's actions and beliefs had an impact on the biographical material which is available to us today. Much of the material tells us more about the developments within the later Muslim community – the issues which were being elaborated, the debates which were going on – than it does about Muḥammad as a person. All the material is of great value to the historian, therefore, but it must be treated with a discerning, critical eye, always alert to the ideological value contained within any reminiscence or anecdote.

The significance of Muḥammad

In sum, then, the life of Muḥammad may be recounted on the basis of various sources and its details may be debated. The value of it as a grounding for the Qur'ān may be examined. The development of Muḥammad's role as an authority in the community can be analyzed and evidence cited. All such discussions, however, miss the essence of Muslim feelings about the significance of Muḥammad.

It has often been commented that while Muslims may think those who deny the existence of God or who utter blasphemies about Him are misguided, such discussions will not offend in the same manner in which discussions over Muḥammad will. Those who insinuate evil of Muḥammad or who cast aspersions on him are considered to be insulting Islam. This, upon consideration, is not surprising. The charges laid by Christians against Islam in medieval times always focused on Muḥammad and his use of "holy war," *jihād*, the permission of polygamy and the number of marriages consummated by

Muḥammad himself. "Insulting" Muḥammad in any way, therefore, always recreates the image of those times and raises the suspicion that such charges are being laid once again, even if they are in different words. But further thought reveals that "attacking" Muḥammad is, of course, attacking the way of life of individual Muslims, for their way of life is understood to rest on the example of the founder of their religion. If something is felt by Muslims to be a denigration of one aspect of the life of Muḥammad, then by implication such may be seen as an attack on the whole way of life of each and every Muslim, at least in its idealized conception.

Muḥammad, as is implied in the basis of the entire concept of the *sunna*, is the "perfect man." He is the most liberal, the best, the bravest. Most of all, Muḥammad is considered to have lived his life in a state of sinlessness (*'iṣma*). With such a doctrine, everything Muḥammad did is considered to be the perfect embodiment of the will of God – nothing at any point of his life would have been in contravention of that will. This is a doctrine which took a number of centuries to become firmly established in Islam, as evidenced by some early, divergent material which presents Muḥammad as capable of making mistakes, even on very basic religious issues.[15] It is quite likely that the significance of the doctrine should be viewed in tandem with that of the *i'jāz*, "inimitability," of the Qur'ān; Muḥammad's sinlessness not only protects the concept of the *sunna* but also the contents of the Qur'ān from any lack of perfection.

The picture of Muḥammad has, as a result of the notion of sinlessness, been subject to all sorts of "fantastic" elaborations, creating a mythic image of the prophet of Islam. A portrait of the "perfect man" emerges, providing details even of his physical description:

> [Muḥammad's hair was] neither lank nor short and woolly. It touched his shoulders. Muḥammad used to make four plaits with each ear exposed between two plaits. The number of white hairs did not exceed seventeen. His eyes were very wide and black. His nose was hooked. He had a broad chest. Between his navel and upper chest there was a single hair. He had three belly folds.[16]

Descriptions such as these are not abundant in Muslim texts but they do display at least one aspect of the devotion to Muḥammad who, although he is only ever said to have been an ordinary mortal with no supernatural attributes, inevitably became the focus for much popular speculation and devotion to his person.

The night journey of Muḥammad

More prominent in this elaboration of the picture of Muḥammad is the story of his night journey (*isrāʾ*) to Jerusalem and his ascension into heaven (*miʿrāj*). Not only is the narrative a favourite in and by itself, but the stories have been the subject of numerous artistic endeavours.[17] The story also provides at least some of the sanction for the significance of Jerusalem in Muslim piety (this is the place from which Muḥammad ascended into heaven). As well, the account of the ascension stands as a model of Muslim spiritual devotion when interpreted on a metaphorical level as the inner journey leading to the vision of God. Issues dealing with the nature of heaven and hell, their existence and the conditions for entrance often find themselves attached to this story. Finally, the stipulation of five prayers a day as the requirement for Muslims also finds its support in the narrative. The story functions on many different levels, therefore, and is not only a vehicle for flights of popular imagination.

Traditionally pegged[18] to Qurʾān 17/1, "Glory be to Him, who carried His servant by night from the holy mosque to the further mosque whose surroundings We have blessed, so that We might show him some of Our signs. He is the All-hearing, the All-seeing," the story tells of Muḥammad travelling to Jerusalem on the back of the winged horse Burāq, and from there ascending through the seven levels of heaven, meeting the great prophets of the past as he progresses: Adam, John, Jesus, Joseph, Enoch, Aaron, Moses and Abraham. He is given a view of various aspects of hell as well. Finally he is allowed a vision of God and is given the command of fifty prayers a day for his followers. In a narrative reminiscent of the Sodom and Gomorrah account in Genesis 18, Muḥammad, at Moses's insistence, returns to God to bargain for a lower requirement; the final result is the five daily prayers.[19] Muḥammad returns to Mecca and tells of his adventure and is able to prove the veracity of his story by knowing of the imminent arrival of a caravan in his home town which he saw when returning on Burāq. The proof of the mission provides a rousing climax to the account. When asked what proof he had for his journey to Jerusalem, Muḥammad replied that,

> he had passed a certain caravan in a certain valley and the animal which he was riding on scared them and a camel ran away. [He said], "I showed them where it was while on my way to al-Shams. I carried on until I reached Ḍajanān where I passed by another caravan. The people were sleeping; they had a jar of water which

was covered with something. I uncovered it, drank some water and replaced the cover as I had found it. The evidence of this is that their caravan is now approaching from al-Baydā' at the pass of al-Tanʿīm; it is led by a dark-coloured camel with two sacks on it, one black, the other multi-coloured." The people hurried to the pass and it was as Muhammad had described.[20]

The basic substance of the entire story of the night journey and ascension is found in Ibn Ishāq's *Sīra* and it has continued to be elaborated up until today.[21] Such miraculous stories are not abundant in the popular life accounts of Muhammad (as compared to Jesus's for example) but they do tend to play an important role both in providing a guarantee of Muhammad's status and in supplying a focal point for popular belief. Other instances of popular stories are frequently connected to Muhammad's birth and youth. Very popular is the account of angels visiting him to cleanse his heart. The story exists in many renditions. One version speaks of two men in white clothes seizing the infant Muhammad, opening his chest and removing his heart. They then proceed to wash his heart in a golden basin with purifying water from the well of Zamzam which was located next to the Kaʿba in Mecca. This type of story and many others like it reveal a colourful adaptation of Jewish and Christian legends regarding prophetic qualifications and initiation; the stories frequently combine this thematic borrowing with anecdotes spun around statements from the Qur'ān, as in the instance of the account of the heavenly journey.[22]

Muhammad as intercessor

Another aspect of the popular Muhammad which is of great significance is that of his role as intercessor on behalf of the members of his community on the day of judgement. While not finding any explicit support within the Qur'ān (which emphasizes individual responsibility on this point), it is commonly held that Muhammad will act as an advocate before God on behalf of his people. While this sort of idea has not developed into a notion of redemption through the prophet by his suffering on other's behalf, as in Christianity, nor into an idea of Muhammad having a store of merit which he can share, his role is clearly enunciated in the texts of classical Islam which concentrate on the events on the day of judgement. A text ascribed to the famous Sūfī-theologian al-Ghazālī (d. 1111) pictures Muhammad saying in the afterlife scene, "I am the right one! I am the right one [to intercede] insofar as God allows it for whomever He wills and chooses." God then says to him, "O Muḥammad, lift your head and speak, for you will be heard; seek intercession and it will be granted."[23] Once again, the popular portrait of Muḥammad constructs him as an extremely important element in the salvation of his community, someone far more significant than simply the recipient of the revelation of the Qur'ān. Islam very much revolves around its twin sources of authority, the Qur'ān and Muḥammad, with both of those entities being firmly situated in the prehistory of the community in Arabia.

Part II

Emergence of Islamic identity

Significant dates

632	death of Muḥammad
634	death of ABŪ BAKR, first caliph
644	death of 'UMAR, second caliph
656	death of 'UTHMĀN, third caliph
661	death of 'ALĪ, fourth caliph and figurehead of the Shī'a
661	MU'ĀWIYA becomes caliph
661–750	UMAYYAD dynasty
680	death of ḤUSAYN, son of 'Alī
	death of caliph MU'ĀWIYA
685–705	rule of caliph 'ABD AL-MALIK
691	DOME OF THE ROCK built
728	death of writer AL-ḤASAN AL-BAṢRĪ
750	ABBASID dynasty begins
767	death of jurist ABŪ ḤANĪFA
	death of historian IBN ISḤĀQ
795	death of jurist MĀLIK IBN ANAS
798	death of jurist ABŪ YŪSUF
805	death of jurist AL-SHAYBĀNĪ
813–833	rule of caliph AL-MA'MŪN
820	death of jurist AL-SHĀFI'Ī
838	death of theologian/exegete ABŪ 'UBAYD
855	death of jurist AḤMAD IBN ḤANBAL
870	death of ḥadīth collector AL-BUKHĀRĪ
875	death of ḥadīth collector MUSLIM IBN AL-ḤAJJĀJ
884	death of jurist DĀWŪD IBN KHALAF, founder of Ẓāhirī school
912	death of Mu'tazilī theologian AL-KHAYYĀṬ
935	death of theologian AL-ASH'ARĪ

944	death of theologian AL-MĀTURĪDĪ
945	BUWAYHIDS take over Baghdad
1025	death of Muʿtazilī theologian ʿABD AL-JABBĀR
1037	death of jurist/theologian AL-BAGHDĀDĪ
1055	rise of the SELJUKS
1065	death of Ẓāhirī jurist/theologian IBN ḤAZM
1096	death of jurist AL-SARAKHSĪ
1142	death of theologian AL-NASAFĪ
1197	death of jurist AL-MARGHANĀNĪ
1258	Mongol takeover of Baghdad
1453	Turkish takeover of Constantinople/Istanbul

4   Political action and theory

Muslim sources, frequently confirmed by the unintentional witness of contemporaneous Greek and Syriac writers, make it clear that the Arabs came surging out of the Arabian peninsula in the seventh century, with the initial attack on Damascus in 635 (the city being taken finally in 637), Ctesiphon in 637 and Jerusalem in 638. The area had been made ready for such an invasion by the political situation of the Near East as sketched above in Chapter 1. A critical matter of dispute among historians is the extent to which religion was a motivating factor in these wars of expansion. The simple explanation that religion, in the common sense of the word, provides the underpinning of the whole phenomenon is not necessarily supported by the archaeological data available; nor is it substantiated by the historical texts, at least not when they are critically assessed in light of an understanding of the theological back-reading of history which took place well after Islam was fully established. What appears fairly plain is that, in the first century of Arab rule in the Near East, a religious ideology was being employed both by those in power and by those struggling for power; it was by means of this ideology that authority was established in the community. Once again, then, one must be careful in speaking of the religion in the earliest period. To call it "Islam" leads easily to the glossing of the difference between what was conceived then and what the religion became by the beginning of the third Muslim century when a fixed religious system had certainly emerged (although its orthodox form was still at least a century off even at that point). Some scholars have suggested that we should refer to this early religion of the Arabs as "Hagarism," a word derived from the name used in some Greek and Syriac sources when talking about the "Muslims."[1] Others have suggested a term such as "Muhammadanism" or even "Arab monotheism."[2] Be that as it may, in general some of the most important evidence for making some distinction between the earlier and later roles and forms of the religion in the area comes from the political actions of the early rulers of the conquered territory, especially as the rulers affected the religious ideology and symbolism through their employment of it.

History of the Arab conquests and empire

Abū Bakr took over rule of the community in the position of "caliph" (*khalīfa*), upon the death of Muḥammad in the year 632; he was selected by a group of elders, according to traditional reports, as being the person most qualified to rule. At that time the Arabs controlled no territory outside Arabia, as far as the contemporary sources let us know. It was under Abū Bakr's leadership in the year 633 that early victories in Iraq (the city of Hira) took place. The year 634 saw the beginnings of the conquest of Syria as well as the accession of ʿUmar ibn al-Khaṭṭāb, the second caliph. Syria gradually fell into Arab hands with the battle of Yarmuk in 636 inflicting a crushing defeat on the Byzantine army. Damascus, Antioch, Jerusalem and finally the whole Syrian area came under Arab control by 638. Meanwhile, Iraq was falling also, with the conquest of Ctesiphon (Madāʾin) and the defeat of the Sasanian army in 637, followed by the founding of the garrison towns of Basra and Kufa in 638. By 641, the Sasanian empire was coming close to its final end, with virtually all of Persia open to the Arabs after the battle of Nihavand. The conquest of Egypt was begun in 639 and completed by 642. With ʿUmar's death in 644, ʿUthmān ibn ʿAffān, the third caliph, took over; in his time, the armies made westward gains, coming near the Roman outreach of Carthage by 647, but the area proved much harder to subdue than the former Sasanian or Byzantine territories. Some of the islands of the Mediterranean came under Arab domination at this time, with Cyprus being taken in 649 and Rhodes and Crete occupied shortly thereafter; these conquests came as a result of the emergence of Arab sea power, which provided a means of defence for the armies against the initially superior Byzantine naval forces.

ʿUthmān was assassinated in 656, reputedly by a group of disaffected tribesmen from Egypt, and his rule was followed by that of ʿAlī ibn abī Ṭālib, cousin and son-in-law of Muḥammad. ʿAlī's position was challenged, however, by a group consisting of ʿĀʾisha, one of the widows of Muḥammad, Ṭalha and al-Zubayr, members of the group of close followers of Muḥammad. The "Battle of the Camel" was the result of this uprising, leading to the death of Ṭalha and al-Zubayr, and the removal from a position of influence of 'Ā'isha. 'Alī was effectively in charge until a kinsman of 'Uthmān, Mu'āwiya, revolted. Power and authority were clearly the issues at stake in this civil war once again, although rivalries between groups of Arabs, both on matters of tribal loyalties and political/practical problems, have also been seen to be partially responsible.

'Alī and Mu'āwiya met in what is known as the Battle of Ṣiffīn which was, in the end, submitted to arbitration because of the indecisive outcome of the clash. The fact of submitting the matter to this sort of resolution led to a clear erosion of 'Alī's power, for it acted to legitimize the challenge to his position as ruler. Probably by the year 660, Mu'āwiya had full control of his home province of Syria. In 661, 'Alī was murdered by a rebel, creating a situation in which Mu'āwiya was able to take over Kufa in Iraq, the power base of 'Alī, and emerge as the clear leader; thus was formed what became the Umayyad dynasty which lasted until 750. Certainly not all the people rallied behind Mu'āwiya; some supporters of 'Alī, who gained the name the Shī'a, or "party," of 'Alī, remained outside the control of the new leader. Others who are thought to have felt that the whole process was somehow illegitimate, declared themselves opposed to both sides and became known as the Khawārij, those who had "gone out" from the community. The stance of such people plays a major role in the debates over theological issues, as will be discussed in the next chapter. It is tempting to see people such as the Khawārij as the earliest bearers of the religious impulse which became Islam; thus their rejection of the political powers of the day might be seen in religious as well as political terms. Such a reading of history remains fairly speculative at this time, however.[3]

Meanwhile, the expansionist wars were continuing. By 661, the armies had already arrived in Afghanistan, making their way to India, as far as the Indus river and the province of Sind. Under a succession of Umayyad rulers, the armies went into central Asia, with Bukhara being raided in 674 and Samarkand in 676, although it took until 711 for the area to be fully settled. Sporadically from 670 onward, Constantinople was besieged, although it was never actually captured until 1453 under the Ottomans. Eastern sections of Anatolia, and Armenia, fell towards the end of the seventh century. Likewise, the conquests in the west continued, with Kairouan in present-day Tunisia being founded in 670, and Carthage finally falling into Arab hands in 693. From there, the armies went to the Atlantic and crossed into Spain in 710, taking over Toledo in 712. Southern

France was invaded in 725 but the overstretched army was stopped from further incursions into Europe by the Battle of Tours in 732. Muʿāwiya ruled from 661 until 680 when he died and, by previous arrangement, the leadership of the empire went to his son Yazīd. This transfer of power did not go uncontested. Almost immediately upon assuming power, Yazīd faced a rebellion by one of ʿAlī's sons, Ḥusayn, whose efforts appear to have been pitiful, although his actions had an enormous mythic power among the later Shīʿa. A more serious and lasting challenge came from ʿAbd Allāh ibn al-Zubayr who was a member of the Quraysh tribe to which Muḥammad had belonged and a resident of Medina. Amassing power in his home base, Ibn al-Zubayr was attacked by Yazīd's Medinan governor in 680 but he was able to flee to Mecca, where he gained power especially when Yazīd died in 683. His rebellion continued, even reaching such an extent that he was the most significant leader within the Arab empire for a certain period of time, until a strong power re-emerged within the Umayyad family, that of ʿAbd al-Malik (685–705), and he was defeated. It was also under the rule of ʿAbd al-Malik and his son al-Walīd (705–15) that the final surge of conquests in the east and the west were accomplished.

By 744 the power of the Umayyads was being challenged again and, despite a strong ruler, Marwān II (744–750), an apparently Shīʿī-inspired rebellion fomented in the eastern province of Khurasan. This eventually led to civil war and the rise of the Abbasid dynasty in 750. The Shīʿa were quickly disavowed by the new rulers, but the change in ruling families did have far-reaching consequences beyond the actual political structure of the state. A socio-economic restructuring of the empire took place, with the partial removal of the "old guard" who were entrenched in positions of power within the social system and the eventual emergence of a new and powerful class of bourgeoisie and religiously devoted scholars. The capital of the empire was moved from Syria to Baghdad and this action provided the pretext for the splintering of various areas of the new empire. For the western reaches of the empire, this eastward shift of the caliphal seat of power was cited as an example of the lack of interest exhibited by the central administration for the more far-flung portions of the empire. A descendant of the Umayyads, ʿAbd al-Raḥmān, became the independent ruler of Spain in 756. Similar independence movements affected North Africa during the late eighth and ninth centuries. Likewise, separate dynasties emerged in the East, especially in the provinces of Khurasan and Transoxiana, in the ninth century, leading eventually to the Buwayhid family taking over Baghdad itself in 945 and reducing the caliph to a person of little influence who acted only as a puppet of the real military rulers. The Mongol takeover in 1258 spelled the end of even this remnant of Abbasid caliphal prestige.

Such were the political events of the early centuries. There is little reason to harbour substantial doubts concerning the overall chronological ordering of these conquests. What is significant, however, is that, during this period, the gradual emergence of the classical form of Islam may be seen. But just what was the role of Islam in all of this political activity? What was the role of politics in enunciating the classical form of Islam? What was the position of the caliph as the leader of the community and how did he use the idea of Islam in his ruling of the community?

The Dome of the Rock and its significance

During the rule of the Umayyad caliph 'Abd al-Malik an event of major significance took place; the Dome of the Rock in Jerusalem was built. This is the oldest extant building of Islamic architecture and one which can be dated with significant precision due to the presence of an important inscription which is found on both sides of the outer arched octagonal colonnade within the building. The inscription was tampered with by al-Ma'mūn, the Abbasid caliph (ruled 813–33). He had ordered some repairs done to the Dome in about the year 831, and he appears to have followed a general policy of attempting to obliterate signs of the accomplishments of the earlier Umayyads. Significant original information still remains in the inscription, however, apparently due to an "oversight" on the part of those who changed it. The end of the inscription, at the east end of the south face on the outer band of the colonnade reads, "The servant of God 'Abd Allāh the *imām* al-Ma'mūn, commander of the believers, has built this Dome in the year 72 [i.e. 691], may God accept him. . . ."[4] Not only is the shade of the mosaic in which the inscription has been written different when the name of the caliph is stated, but also the name is written in crowded characters. Most telling, however, is the fact that the date which is given (and is written in mosaics of the same shade as the rest of the inscription) is that of 'Abd al-Malik who, as all the other sources tell us, had the Dome built and who ruled from 685 to 705. A similar tampering is also witnessed on the copper inscriptions over the north and east doors which are also held to have been written in the time of 'Abd al-Malik, according to the evidence of the shape of the script itself.[5]

Why was the Dome of the Rock built?

Later Muslim historians provide several reasons for ʿAbd al-Malik having built the Dome. As stated earlier, during the revolt of Ibn al-Zubayr, control of Mecca fell to the rebel leader. In order to assert his authority and independence, ʿAbd al-Malik, according to this tradition, had the Dome of the Rock built as a place of pilgrimage. This explanation attempts to account for the unique (within Islam) architectural style of the Dome, for it is not a mosque nor is it an imitation of the Kaʿba. It is, however, clearly a place where pilgrimage type activities – especially circumambulation – were designed to take place within the colonnaded passageways. Modern historians have objected to this interpretation, suggesting that it is unlikely that any caliph would attempt to displace Mecca as a point of pilgrimage for this would be likely to entail, as a result, the total rejection of that person's legitimacy to be ruler of an "Islamic" state. Such an objection, however, is based upon a supposition that the pilgrimage to Mecca was already a central symbol of nascent Islam. It would seem just as possible to conceive that, in the era of ʿAbd al-Malik, the activity of pilgrimage was being used as a political symbol and that two pilgrimages, one in Mecca under Ibn al-Zubayr and another in Jerusalem under ʿAbd al-Malik, emerged at roughly the same time in competition with one another.

Another suggestion classically put forth to explain the existence of the Dome of the Rock is that it was a sanctuary built to commemorate the "ascension" (*miʿrāj*) of Muḥammad as related above in Chapter 3; the rock from which Muḥammad ascended into heaven is covered by the commemorative Dome. Such an interpretation is clearly late, however, for no part of the colonnade inscription of ʿAbd al-Malik found in the building makes any reference to this journey; nor do any elements of the texts which are found in the inscription and which are also found in the Qurʾān even contain an allusion to this myth. It is also worthy of note that early Muslim interpretation of Qurʾān 17/1, the key text cited as related to the *miʿrāj*, is ambiguous about the identification of *al-masjid al-aqṣā* which is mentioned in this verse. One interpretation is that this term refers to a town near Mecca on the boundary of the sacred *ḥaram* (and, in parallel, *al-masjid al-ḥaram* refers not to a specific building but to the town of Mecca itself). Another idea is that *al-masjid al-aqṣā* is in a celestial location. Third, the term is taken as a reference to the Temple Mount in Jerusalem as a whole, or even to Jerusalem as a whole. The association of the Muslim buildings with this term is quite late, with the so-called Mosque of ʿUmar, located on the southern end of the sanctuary platform, being identified as *al-masjid al-aqṣā* (as it is now commonly called) for the first time only in the eleventh century.

Finally, texts from various Muslim historians suggest that the Dome was built to rival the beauty of the Christian Holy Sepulchre in Jerusalem.[6] This is an account which has echoes throughout Islamic history, for example in the accounts of Sultan Ahmet I and his commissioning the architect Mehmet Aga early in the seventeenth century to build the Blue Mosque (Sultan Ahmet Camii) in Istanbul directly opposite the Christian church of Justinian, Haghia Sophia, dedicated in 537, in order to rival its magnificence.

The interpretation of the Dome of the Rock

This latter explanation may, in fact, contain an element which is meaningful historically when the building is interpreted as a whole in its architectural form and in light of the contents of the inscriptions. It would appear that the desire of the builder was not only to rival but to outshine all other buildings and, most importantly, to symbolize the triumph of the conquerors over the land and over the rival religions. The Dome of the Rock embodies the arrival of nascent Islam and underlines the religion's rising presence. It is a piece of work representing the ultimate propaganda of the Arab rulers over their subjects through the use of religion. That is why the building is so important to any understanding of the rise of Islam. Still, though, why the Dome should have been built over this specific rock in Jerusalem remains unclear; a suggestion that, in fact, the Muslims were completing a Christian project from an earlier time is possible but, once again, there does not seem to be an overwhelming amount of evidence for such a notion.[7]

The evidence of the inscription on the colonnade (which people circumambulating the rock would see and perhaps be able to read, especially the one on the inner surface) also suggests significant aspects of the Arab propaganda effort. The outer face of the colonnade contains a series of passages, found today in the Qurʾān, which comprise five groups of short phrases, each emphasizing the unity and absolute unrivalled power of God, that He has had no offspring, and that Muḥammad is His messenger. The text on the inner face declares the unity of God and Muḥammad's status, and continues with verses addressed to the "people of the book," admonishing that no mistakes be made in religion, declaring the Trinity to be false, and telling of the correct view of Jesus, the spirit from God. "Do not speak of three (gods)," one of the passages warns. The polemical aspect of the inner text especially is clear. The testimony to the development of Muslim doctrine is significant also. Here we have evidence of the status of key beliefs in Islam – the non-messianic and non-divine status of Jesus, the acceptance of a multiplicity of prophets, Muḥammad's receipt of revelation and the designation of the religion itself by the name of Islam.

The stylized architecture of the building is also significant in understanding the rise of Islam. The Dome itself is clearly modelled after Syrian Christian churches – it may be seen as the final achievement of the Byzantine architectural style[8] – although it has also been suggested that it contains in its decorations many Sasanian traits. Certainly, the only true Arab element in the building is the inscriptional calligraphy. A close connection has been noted between the Dome and various earlier buildings of the Byzantines, including the Church of the Holy Sepulchre and the cathedral in Bosra (southern Syria) built in 512.[9] The resemblance extends most importantly to the geometrical structure of the buildings themselves. By employing a clear tradition in Byzantine architecture, the Dome was able to provide evidence to the conquered people of the power of the new rulers. It should be noted that circumambulation appears to have been practised by Christians who went around the tomb of Jesus in the rotunda of the Holy Sepulchre; thus, the entire rite connected to the building in early times is likely to have been one which would have reinforced this assertion of authority.

It has also been suggested that the inscription of 'Abd al-Malik inside the Dome aimed to provide spiritual guidance to the believers and to show the fundamental difference between Christianity and Islam. That is, the Dome was built as a symbol of, and a vehicle for, the emergence of the self-definition of Islam over against Christianity. This was done through the means of a splendid building, undoubtedly built to surpass the beauty of Christian churches, but yet done in the model of a Christian edifice. It was situated in Jerusalem as a political symbol of triumph – symbolized in the very fact of its being built. Its construction served to indicate the gradual emergence of Islamic identity in a form expressive and meaningful for all to behold.

Indeed, one of the statements in the inscription refers to Islam as "the religion with God" (compare Qur'ān 3/19); from this point on, therefore, those in power are clearly arguing for their religion "Islam." The copper inscription over the north door also refers to

Muslims as those who believe in God, and what He revealed to Muḥammad, and that there are no differences among the prophets, all of whom God sent (compare Qur'ān 2/136 or 3/84). Additionally, the inscription also indicates the direction of early theological self-definition in the sense that the emphasis on Christianity can be seen to suggest Islam's supersession of the Christian faith, especially in light of its doctrine of Jesus. The connection of the rock over which the Dome was built to King David and the Jewish Temple may well be intended to suggest both the fulfilment of the promise of Judaism, as well as the abrogation of that dispensation – Islam has taken over the Davidic heritage in both religious and political ways.

The caliph and his authority

The Dome of the Rock represents, therefore, a conscious attempt on the part of 'Abd al-Malik to assert the authority of the new rule and to champion the new religion of Islam. That this was very much a personal matter, one which established his own authority not only among the new subjects of the empire but also among the members of the Arab community, appears to be evidenced by the self-conception of the caliph in this early period. Thus, while the Dome of the Rock provided the symbol of the caliph's authority, the actual conception of the position provided the source of his authority.

Classical Islam displays the phenomenon of religious authority residing with a scholarly élite and ultimately, it would be claimed, with the entire community. Some evidence has been interpreted to suggest, however, that this situation was not always so. Early on, the caliph, referred to by the title *khalīfat Allāh*, the "representative (or deputy) of God," appears to have combined religious and political power, only to have the religious dimension of the power removed in the third Muslim century (as reflected in the later theory of the caliphate), in recognition of the *de facto* change in the power structure by that time. This revamping of power appears to have occurred at the hands of the scholars after a struggle involving an explicit attempt by the caliphs to impose a specific religious system of thought which upheld their position and asserted their authority; this was put forth in opposition to the efforts and interests of scholars who stood for their own independent authority.

Evidence for this position of the early caliph comes from the use of the title *khalīfat Allāh* as testified most significantly on coins from the reign of 'Abd al-Malik, the builder of the Dome of the Rock. This title is used in the place of the later *khalīfat rasūl Allāh* ("deputy of the messenger of God"), which was employed by the Abbasids alongside the earlier formulation, a fact which has often (mis-)led historians to believe that the two titles were directly equivalent.

Some recent scholarship[10] has suggested that the early caliph saw himself in a mode very similar to the Shī'ī Imām. Obedience to the caliph was deemed to be necessary for salvation because the caliph's authority came straight from God. For the individual in the early period, therefore, the choice of to whom to give one's allegiance was a religious one, since salvation was connected to it; at least, that was the argument that those in power appear to have been suggesting.

Concomitant with his stress on divine authority, the caliph acted as judge, creating the sacred law and acting as the reference point for decisions on difficult items of law. The argument was made that his rulings were based on the Qur'ān, the practice (*sunna*) – not that of a fixed practice of the past embodied in the person of Muḥammad but the practice as found in the territory concerned – and his own (superhuman) insight.

The "inquisition" and the emergence of the scholarly élite

The early ninth century institution of the *miḥna*, or "inquisition," unintentionally put an end to this type of conception. The final result of the attempt to assert caliphal control over religious dogma embodied in this "inquisition" was the emergence of an independent scholarly group of people (symbolized in the figure of Aḥmad ibn Ḥanbal, d. 855) in whom religious authority, to the extent which that was conceived to exist, was vested. Under the Abbasid caliph al-Ma'mūn (ruled 813–33), various attempts were made to assert the power of the caliph in the community in a variety of areas concerned with religion.[11] Significantly, beginning in 829, al-Ma'mūn declared that all government officials and religious leaders must believe in the doctrine of the "created Qur'ān"; in 833 an "inquisition," *miḥna*, was initiated, such that only those who agreed with the caliph's dogma would be allowed to hold official positions. Those who refused, including Aḥmad ibn Ḥanbal, were removed from their positions and imprisoned. This practice continued in the following reigns of al-Mu'taṣim (ruled 833–42) and al-Wāthiq (ruled 842–47). Al-Mutawakkil (ruled 847–61) put an end to the enterprise in 849 but by then it was too late.

The significance of the actual doctrine which al-Ma'mūn and his successors tried to enforce is not as important as the actual act of their trying to impose it. Until this point, the authority of the caliph to enunciate and represent Islam, while not totally unchallenged, appears to have been accepted. That is, for the Umayyad and early Abbasid rulers, Islam was to a significant extent an ideological tool in the hands of the ruling powers. Al-Ma'mūn's actions in attempting to enforce a version of Islamic orthodoxy backfired and led to the increasing prominence of those who rejected the caliphal authority in favour of the authority of a scholarly élite; their authority was said to lie in their transmission and interpretation of the Qur'ān and the *sunna* of Muḥammad. It is at this point that classical Islam as we know it today began to come into existence, as is reflected in the literary sources, virtually all of which stem from a time after this period and reflect those scholarly concerns, perceptions and interpretations of Islam.[12]

The final implication of this change in power structure is that religion and politics in Islam became disentangled. This is reflected in the later theories of the caliphate which recognized the fact that the two spheres were in practice separate, although mutually supportive. The caliphate was defined as a "form of government which safeguards the ordinances of the Sharia [Muslim law] and sees that they are put into practice."[13] Beyond that, the relationship between the person of the caliph and the actual mechanism of rule in both military and religious spheres was left open, such that practical realities of the Islamic empire could be accommodated to the theory and thus legitimized.

5 Theological exposition

Chapter 4 examined the role of the caliph and the learned classes in defining what Islam was to stand for, both theologically and politically. That discussion focused on the role of authority; both within and behind the debates which went on in the early centuries, however, lie the actual doctrines which were to emerge as the central elements of Islamic self-definition in theological terms. Certainly, no other element in the understanding of the formation of Islam has consumed such a great deal of intellectual effort among modern scholars as has the development of theology. Ironically, the resulting picture is one of considerable confusion, perhaps a consequence, once again, of the abundance of late source material, the variety of ways of interpreting the data provided, and the absence of a substantial quantity of texts traceable to the early period itself. Some relatively early works do exist, but the picture they combine to create remains disjointed.

Theological writing is the end result of an attempt at religious self-definition; it attempts to enunciate what is believed within a certain group of people in terms of certain tenets. Within the Near Eastern milieu, various elements emerged among the religions of Judaism, Christianity, and Islam which defined what they held in common and where they differed. The process of defining where Islam was to differ from the other religions and where it was to agree was what the early theological tracts attempted to accomplish. The texts do not do this in an explicit way. They do not set up interreligious comparisons. Rather, the efforts were conducted under topics which were, to a great extent, already predefined within the general religious milieu and were then enunciated from within each religious perspective.

The emergence of Islamic theological identity

The basic elements of Islamic theology find their expression within the Qur'ān and the *sunna*, and are elaborated to some extent in works such as the *Sīra* of Ibn Isḥāq (d. 767). In these contexts, the statements are not theology, of course, but rather simple creedal formulae which have been isolated as being summaries of what Islam stands for. It took several centuries of scholarly reflection to mould this raw material into the mature formulations of Islamic faith. Belief in the oneness of God, in angels, in all the prophets and their scriptures, in the final judgment day, and in God's decree for humanity are often seen to be the core elements of faith for all Muslims; such simple summations arose, however, only after extensive reflection and debate concerning some very basic theological issues in the formative centuries of Islam.

The definition of a Muslim

From the available sources, one prime question emerges which seems to have been of major concern and may well have provided the stimulus toward developed theological writing. This was the issue of determining who was and who was not a Muslim. The later Muslim sources, which provide us with additional data on the origins of this dispute, picture it as first arising within the context of the history of the early Muslim community, in common with the general trend in the sources to put the origins of Islam as back as far as possible. Disputes over succession within the Arab ruling groups appear to have been read and understood by later generations of Muslims in theological terms as well as political ones. At stake was whether 'Alī, the fourth leader of the Arabs after Muḥammad, had the responsibility for avenging the death of his assassinated predecessor 'Uthmān; the clan of 'Uthmān, led by Mu'āwiya, championed the claims of its kinsman, suggesting that 'Alī had lost rightful claim to rule because of his failure to follow up on this obligation. Civil war erupted and Mu'āwiya and the Umayyad dynasty eventually took over. From today's perspective, there seems to be little reason to dispute the basic historico-political events. Muslim theological sources, however, see far more in these events and view them as paradigms for the discussion of issues of religious self-definition; they use these earlier events for discussion of the theological disputes which were, in fact, taking place at least a century after the fact. From a historical perspective, it is worth noting that the use of military force in trying to decide the issues concerning 'Uthmān and 'Alī indicates immediately that there certainly was a great deal at stake at this time, and the issue really was far more involved than the question concerning the death of 'Uthmān. In the later reading of these historical events, the notions of piety and the "rightful" (i.e. moral) assassination of an "unjust" ruler become the operative elements.

What emerges from the sources is a picture of a variety of groups, each going under a name which is often provided with a connection back to the times of 'Alī and 'Uthmān, each taking its own position on what constitutes the definition of membership within the emergent Muslim community. The reasons for being concerned with this question were likely to have been of both a practical and a legal nature, over and above being the result of polemical discourse with Jews and Christians in the Near Eastern milieu.

The Khawārij

The Khawārij held a strict, activist position: all those who fall short of the total adherence to the Islamic precepts are unbelievers. Any of those who might happen to slip are thus rendered targets for the Islamic *jihād* against all non-believers; membership in the community, at the very least, provided protection from such attacks. In origin the group may well have been involved in even more basic discussions over the sources of authority in the community. Their slogan is said to have been *lā ḥukm* illā li-llāhi*, "there is no judgment except that of God," which would suggest that they held that only God, through His expression in the Qur'ān, has made binding laws for humanity. At least in part, therefore, the Khawārij may be pictured as the scripturalist party who rejected those who attempted to supplement the single source of authority in the community with a notion of the *sunna*. For the Khawārij, this *sunna* was not a part of the divine revelation and therefore had no particular status in the framework of Islamic law. It may well be, then, that they are to be identified as a pietistic group in the context of emergent Islam, facing off against the asserted power and authority of the caliph and his *sunna*.[1] Later, however, a part of the ammunition of the Khawārij against other groups was sought in *ḥadīth* reports (that is, the *sunna* of Muḥammad), which they saw as equating certain actions, for example, adultery, as taking one out of the category of "believer."[2]

The Murji'a

The Murji'a adopted a conservative position, preserving the status quo. They argued that those who appeared not to be following the outward precepts of Islam must still be accepted as Muslims; only God truly knows their religious state. A profession of faith along with an inward assent to Islam was all that was required to confirm community membership; faith (*īmān*) is "of the heart and of the tongue." The position starts with the emblem of theological identity implied by the questions concerning 'Alī and 'Uthmān. Were these two men guilty of sin? Were their assassinations justified? The Murji'a are pictured in the sources as holding that the decisions on these questions must be left to God. As a theological position, this stance holds that "works" are not a part of faith; that is, as long as a person professes belief in Islam (through the single "act" of confession of faith), then that person is a Muslim. The actual performance of the ritual acts of Islam is not a criterion for membership in the community. This position was supported in the view of the Murji'a by the notion that in the Qur'ān God called those who had confessed their faith (and that alone) "believers." According to Abū Ḥanīfa (d. 767), good works will be rewarded primarily in the hereafter:

> Whoever obeys God in all the laws, according to us, is of the people of paradise. Whoever leaves both faith and works is an infidel, of the people of the fire. However, whoever believes but is guilty of some breach of the law is a believing sinner, and God will do as He wishes with that person: punish the person if He wills, or forgive the person if He wills.[3]

In the here and now, it was frequently argued that any increase in faith as manifested in pious works was really only an increase in conviction on the part of the individual. The whole doctrine thus had a practical result in terms of the ease of conversion to Islam, as may be seen especially in the case of the spread among the Turks in Central Asia in the eleventh century of the later theological school of al-Māturīdī which followed Abū Ḥanīfa's legal teachings.[4]

Abū Ḥanīfa is generally pictured as the major early enunciator of the Murji'a position; certainly his name has become associated with documents which are seen as coming from the Murji'a in their details. One such document is *al-Fiqh al-Akbar*,[5] another the *Risāla* ("letter") to 'Uthmān al-Battī.[6] These documents, and others from the same school of thought, seem to have the preservation of the unity of the

Muslim community as their central concern, as is suggested by the tolerant nature of the definition of faith according to the Murji'a.

The Traditionalists

A group generally termed the Traditionalists (often calling themselves, as do other groups, *ahl al-sunna*, "the people of the *sunna*"; the name "traditionalist" refers to the use of *ḥadīth* materials in preference to the independent powers of reason) are generally connected to the figure of Aḥmad ibn Ḥanbal (d. 855) in the early period. Their stance represents yet another position on this question of faith, essentially arguing that there are degrees of "being Muslim." Works do count towards one's status in the community although one can still be a believer and commit sin – there are, therefore, what may be termed "degrees of faith." This position is enunciated in works ascribed to Ibn Ḥanbal and to Abū 'Ubayd (d. 838), and is also found embodied in the books of *ḥadīth*; it becomes the position of the later theological school of al-Ash'arī and thus of the majority form of Islam. Ibn Ḥanbal is said to have summarized his position as "faith consists in verbal assent, deeds and intention and adherence to the *sunna*. Faith increases and decreases."[7]

Abū 'Ubayd was a scholar with broad intellectual interests who "contributed pioneer studies of major significance, and in all of them he displayed a degree of erudition and reached a level of achievement which won the acclaim of contemporary scholars."[8] Theologically, he argued that faith is submission to God through intention, statement of belief, and works all combined. Such faith varies by degrees, beginning with the basic confession of faith and then building from there; whoever makes the first step is entitled to be called a Muslim (and thus, in practical terms, the doctrine has the same consequences as that of the Murji'a) but perfection of faith is something to be reached through works. One can be termed a believer on the basis of the statement of faith but there are ranks among the believers in accordance with the extent to which such people conform to the requirements of the religious system of Islam. The Muslim who commits a grave sin, therefore, is still to be termed a believer but is not as good a believer as someone who has not committed a sin; such a person is not a believer in the full definition of that term.

The Qadariyya

A fourth position in the overall debate became associated with some people from within a group known as the Qadariyya (for example, al-Ḥasan al-Baṣrī, d. 728); here, as with the Murji'a, a person who professes faith in Islam is considered a member of the community, but those who can be observed not following the requirements of Islam are to be considered neither believers nor unbelievers, but somewhere in between – they are hypocrites. The end result in practical terms is, once again, the same as with the Murji'a, but the claim is being made that it is, in fact, possible to have an opinion about the status of a believer's adherence to Islam. The position does not distinguish, however, between levels of faith as does that of the Traditionalists.

The problem of free will and predestination

The Qadariyya were centrally involved in another theological dispute, one which is generally understood to have provided them with their name. The Qadariyya are those who discussed the issue of *qadar*, the preordination of events in the world by God. This group held to the position of the free will of humanity and was opposed in this matter by those often said to be more closely aligned to the political powers of the day. That is, the Qadariyya were on the more revolutionary wing of the theological groupings; their espousal of free will was frequently connected to those agitating for a new political order which was opposed to the ruling Umayyad caliphs who had appropriated both political and theological authority under the guise of having been appointed by God (and thus destined to fulfill this function).[9] If individuals were accountable for their actions, then so were governments, according to the argument of the Qadariyya. The Murji'a are frequently pictured as those most supportive of the ruling powers, for their doctrine of faith as a personal concern did not facilitate judgements being made on people as to their status in the faith (beyond the actual statement of faith), whether that person be a peasant or the ruler.

The *Risāla* (often translated "Treatise" in this instance) of al-Ḥasan al-Baṣrī is generally seen as one of the earliest documents concerned with the argument for free will, although both the ascription of an early date to the text and its status as one of the earliest texts have been questioned.[10] Al-Ḥasan argues in the treatise for the position of the individual's free will on the basis of the Qur'ān; any suggestion made in the Qur'ān that predestination is to be supported (as his opponents suggested) is to be countered by an interpretation of the passage in light of other statements. Most obvious in this regard, statements such as Qur'ān 13/27, "God sends anyone He wishes astray" (implying that the individual's fate is in the hands of God alone and there is nothing that can be done about it) are to be interpreted in the light of other statements such as Qur'ān 14/27, "God sends wrongdoers astray," where, it is asserted, the people are *already* astray (they are already "wrongdoers," by the act of their own free will) before God confirms them in their "fate." This became the standard interpretative tool of all those who argued for the free will position in Islam. From a more positive angle, the argument also ran that God says in Qur'ān 51/56, "I have only created *jinn* and people so they may worship Me," meaning that all people must be free to worship God, for God would not command them to do something and then prevent them from doing it.

The Mu'tazila and the role of reason

Out of this political protest party of the Qadariyya there appears to have developed a group known as the Mu'tazila. Clearly, this party adopted the theological stance of the Qadariyya. Most importantly, though, the Mu'tazila are generally credited with the perfection of the art of theological speculation in Islam in the form of *kalām* – the dialectical style of discussion where objections are put forth and then the response, in the form "If they say ... , it is said to them. ..." While this style of discussion originated neither with the Mu'tazila nor even within Islam itself,[11] it was through this means that this group argued their position, one which was based around the dual principle of the justice and unity of God. Working from this starting point, all the implications were systematically laid out on the basis of the use of reason in the argumentation. While the Qur'ān had its place in the discussions, it was not so much a source when used by the Mu'tazila as a testimony to the veracity of the claims which they were making. The basic assumptions of the Greek philosophical system (as understood and transmitted through Christian scholars) formed the fundamental element underlying the whole position; it was argued that reason, and not only traditional sources, could be used as a source of reliable knowledge for human beings. The Mu'tazila were the first to introduce the Greek mode of reasoning and argumentation into the Islamic religious discussions, changing the face of Muslim theology for all time as a result.

Greek philosophical learning remained a discipline in and by itself among Muslims (as will be explored in Chapter 10 below), being developed by people such as al-Kindī (d. *c.* 870), al-Farābī (d. 950) and Ibn Sīnā (d. 1037). The subject (known in Arabic as *falsafa*) was one which aroused the ire of many traditionalists and remained, for the most part, a rival to theology as a discipline, except in the hands of the Muʿtazila who used its tools to their advantage.

The justice of God

The notion of the justice of God, something demanded of the divinity by Greek logic, led to extensive discussions concerning the nature of the divinity and His relationship to humanity. "Justice" for the Muʿtazila was equated with "good," such that it was not possible to conceive that God would be unjust or evil. The basic Muslim principle that God will reward the true believers after death and punish the unbelieving wrong-doers is then connected to this. God must be just in assessing this punishment or reward, and therefore humanity must have a fair chance to perform on the side of good or evil. Any sense of predestination must be removed from the Qurʾān, therefore, by reinterpretation. Al-Khayyāṭ (d. *c.* 912), the earliest author of the Muʿtazila from whom we have a complete text directly, speaks, for example, of the Quranic notion of God "sealing hearts":

> [the idea of "sealing"] is not that He prevents people from doing what He orders them to do – He is above that! – rather, it refers to the name, the judgment and the testimony [concerning an act]. Do you not notice that He said [in Qurʾān 4/155] "because of . . . their disbelief"? Thus He sealed their hearts because of what was in them of disbelief.[12]

The power to act given by God to humanity carries with it the power to decide which action to undertake; individuals must therefore be fully responsible for their own fate. Evil deeds must originate in individual actions and have nothing to do with God, a problem which the doctrine of predestination seems to create. However, unjust acts do seem to occur in nature – death of young infants, death through natural disasters and so forth. This theological problem was faced in a variety of ways by members of the Muʿtazila. Some said, for example, that while God could have created a perfect world where such things did not happen, He chose not to. All this is, for the Muʿtazila, a necessary consequence of the doctrine of the justice of God.

The created Qur'ān

The Mu'tazila had their moment of political support under the 'Abbāsid caliph al-Ma'mūn (ruled 813–33) with the institution of the *miḥna* serving as an inquest body investigating the creedal stance of leading figures at the time, as discussed in the previous chapter. Here the figure of Aḥmad ibn Ḥanbal looms large for his role in resisting the creed of the Mu'tazila. A crucial issue at this time, started with the notion that the Qur'ān was the word of God, therefore the resultant discussion was concerned whether the "scripture" was created "in time" or uncreated and thus existent from eternity. The argument, it is worth noting, was not a new one within the Judeo-Christian world, as may be witnessed by ideas of the "pre-existent Torah" and Jesus as the Logos who "was with God at the beginning."[13] The Mu'tazila championed the notion of the created Qur'ān as a part of their understanding of the inherent free will of humanity, often pointing to Abū Lahab and his being condemned to hell in *sūra* 111. The Qur'ān must have been created at the time of its revelation, they argued, for otherwise the fate of Abū Lahab would have been established beforehand, thus removing his freedom to determine his own fate. This issue was also related to the reality of God's speech. Some took God's speaking to mean that He spoke as humans speak, with the organs of speech, a point which was then rejected as impinging upon God's "otherness." For a Traditionalist such as Ibn Ḥanbal, the reality of God's actually speaking must be so, because such is stated in the Qur'ān.[14] In the beginning, it was this element which seems to have been crucial in the development of the argument and only later did the argument turn to one of the emergence of the Qur'ān "in time," as was the issue in the *miḥna*.

The unity of God

The debate over the created Qur'ān relates to the other important element of Mu'tazilī thought, the concept of the unity of God, *tawḥīd*. Polemic with Christianity and Manicheism appears to have been part of the reason for the emphasis within Mu'tazilī thought on this doctrine, and the use of the Greek mode of reasoning by protagonists from these other two religions may well account for the introduction of rationalism into Islam as well, occurring initially within this polemical framework. Al-Khayyāṭ's work paints the portrait of a real threat posed by the radical dualism of the Manicheans, although it is likely that the Christian Trinity was a far more important topic of discussion. The position adopted by most of the Mu'tazila was that God can only be described in negatives. Any attempt to ascribe positive attributes to God was seen as impinging upon His unity, for such would suggest that He could be divided into a series of eternal aspects. The closest that one may come to saying something positive about God would be to say that God is "knowing," but this "knowing" occurs not by an attribute of God, but rather by and through God Himself in His essence. Once again, the parallels in these arguments to Christian discussions over the nature of Jesus in his relationship to the Father cannot be overlooked.[15]

An implication of this position on the unity of God was the emphasis on de-anthropomorphization of the divinity especially as He is described in the Qur'ān. Any suggestion that God might have a "face" (Qur'ān 2/272, 6/52, etc.) or be "sitting upon a throne" (Qur'ān 2/255, etc.) in reality was to be rejected and taken as a metaphorical statement; no reference to the human form could be applied to God in its usual meaning. God's "face" was to be understood as His "essence," according to al-Khayyāṭ, for example. Thus, the discussion conducted during the *miḥna* over the status of the Qur'ān was not limited only to the matter of free will. For the Mu'tazila at least, both major aspects of their doctrine, unity and justice, were encapsulated in the idea of a created Qur'ān; an eternal Qur'ān would suggest an attribute of God (speech) which existed separately (in the concept of the "heavenly tablet") alongside God, impinging thereby on His unity, as well as suggesting predestination of events.

The fall of the Mu'tazila

The role of reason for the Mu'tazila was such that the main principles of the conduct of life – the principles of good and evil – were seen to be discoverable by any rational human. Revelation is necessary only in order to supplement what reason can discover, especially in such matters as the ritual law of Islam. For example, 'Abd al-Jabbār (d. 1025), one of the last major medieval Mu'tazilī thinkers, suggests that the eating of meat would not be allowed in Islam if it were not for the fact that scripture supports the practice; reason, therefore, cannot be seen to provide necessarily the full delineation of the law and scripture must provide the additional pointers needed.[16] Revelation also serves to motivate people with its emphasis on the promise and the threat of the afterlife; the Mu'tazila recognized that humanity was in need of guidance and that, in its "natural state," it would not follow the dictates of reason.

This view of the role of reason is significant in terms of the ultimate fate of the Muʿtazila, for it implied that the legal scholars of Islam had, in fact, no particular claim to sole possession of the right interpretation of all Muslim dogma. For the Muʿtazila, all humans are, in theory, capable of making the correct decision on issues of faith and law because of their God-given intellect. There is, therefore, implicit in this stance an anti-jurist bias that may well have proven to be a part of the cause of their ultimate downfall. Agitation by the scholarly élite whose job it was to provide the interpretation of the law is likely to have brought about the eventual political action, by the caliph al-Qādir in the years 1017 and 1041, of demanding a profession of faith which rejected the Muʿtazilī stance. This finally put a stop to the movement (at least until more recent times when it re-emerged in the guise of modernism).[17]

In the eleventh century, however, the Buwayhids, the rulers in Baghdad, were backing politically the remnants of the supporters of the fourth caliph, ʿAlī, known as the Shīʿa; the desire of the majority of the Muslims at the time (known as the Sunnīs) to present a united front against this pressure was probably part of the reason for this final move against the Muʿtazila (whose theology had already influenced the Shīʿa by this time and was probably perceived as a threat by the Sunnīs for that reason also.)[18] So, the eventual downfall of the Muʿtazila was undoubtedly a result of political circumstances of the time as much as their doctrine.

Al-Ashʿarī

Abūʾl-Ḥasan al-Ashʿarī (d. 935) emerged out of the context of the Muʿtazila in the tenth century to enunciate a theological position which may be characterized as midway between the scripturalism of the Traditionalists and the audacious rationalism of the Muʿtazila; this was a position which was to last as the most significant statement of Islamic theology. In his book *al-Ibāna*, for example, he uses *kalām*-style argumentation, setting up questions to be posed to his opponents who are stipulated to be especially the members of the Muʿtazila who "interpret the Qurʾān according to their opinions with an interpretation for which God has neither revealed authority nor shown proof."[19] To the questions which he poses in his arguments, he responds: "If they say 'yes', then it follows that . . . or if they say 'no', then it follows that . . . ," with the arguments being pursued to the point of logical contradiction or contradiction with the twin sources of authority in Islam, the Qurʾān and the *ḥadīth*.

Al-Ash'arī's method was based upon extensive use of the Qur'ān and the *ḥadīth* in order to formulate his rational arguments. He fully supported the position of predestination, God being pictured in the Qur'ān clearly as all-powerful and all-knowing; that God should not know and not be in control of what people were doing is clearly a problem if the free will position is embraced. For al-Ash'arī, God creates the power for people to act at the moment of action (God being the only one who actually has the power to create), yet the individual is responsible for all he or she does. This responsibility is referred to as *kasb*, "acquisition" – that is, that people "acquire" the ramifications of their actions, perhaps to be thought of as similar to the workings of the "conscience" in modern terminology. Says al-Ash'arī, "No human act can occur without His willing it, because that would imply that it occurred out of carelessness and neglect or out of weakness and inadequacy on His part to effect what He wills."[20]

God's attributes are real for al-Ash'arī because the Qur'ān clearly states them and so it must be meaningful to speak of God's hand and God's face; de-anthropomorphization was one of the central elements of Mu'tazilī thought which al-Ash'arī denounced, for he saw it as a symbol of rationalist excesses and wilful ignorance of the sense of the Quranic text. Still, he did not wish to deny that reason indicates that speaking of these attributes of God would seem problematic when put in conjunction with an infinite God. His solution was to speak of the reality of the attributes but that these are not attributes in the same way that humans have such. God does have a hand, but we just "do not know how" this is to be conceived. The phrase *bilā kayf*, "without knowing how," became a key term in Ash'arī theology, to be used whenever reason and the Qur'ān or *ḥadīth* met head-on in conflict.

Al-Ash'arī saw the Qur'ān as the eternal and uncreated word of God, precisely because it was the word of God and, therefore, must partake in the character of His attributes. Those attributes (most importantly knowing, powerful, living, hearing, seeing, speech, and will)[21] are all strongly affirmed by al-Ash'arī who argued that if God does not have these attributes in reality, then He is somehow deficient and that, of course, cannot be the case. For example, al-Ash'arī states:

> one who is living, if he be not knowing, is qualified by some contrary of knowledge such as ignorance, doubt or other defects. ... But if He had been ever qualified by some contrary of knowledge, it would have been impossible for Him ever to know. For

if the contrary of knowledge had been eternal, it would have been impossible for it to cease to be; and if it had been impossible for it to cease to be, it would have been impossible for Him to have made works of wisdom. Hence, since God has made such works, and since they prove that He is knowing, it is true and certain that God has always been knowing, since it is clearly impossible for Him to have been ever qualified by some contrary of knowledge.[22]

Al-Māturīdī

Abū Manṣūr al-Māturīdī (d. 944) was another of the tenth-century theologians whose influence at the time seems to have been significant in the emergence of Sunnī Islam. Living in Transoxiana, he attacked the doctrines of the Muʿtazila and set down the foundations of his theological system. Like al-Ashʿarī, al-Māturīdī followed a middle path between traditionalism and rationalism, forging an Islam which saw the written sources of the faith dominate but which found a place for the activities of the human mind.

Only a few texts have come down to us from al-Māturīdī and his school, but one of the most important, his *Kitāb al-Tawḥīd*, is available in Arabic.[23] The work commences by declaring that unconditional following of the teaching of another person is not valid. God has given humanity intelligence so that all may think and that gift must be used. This, of course, is a doctrine held in common with the Muʿtazila. Reason leads to knowledge, as do the senses and transmissions from the past, either from authoritative sources or from prophets. Reason must be used to judge the information provided by the other sources of knowledge. Reason also allowed knowledge of God before prophets were sent, a position contrary to al-Ashʿarī who held that prophets were necessary and thus belief not incumbent upon those who had not been reached by God's messengers. Following this in al-Māturīdī's work come arguments concerning the temporality of the world, the necessary and eternal existence of God, and that God is the creator of the world. This is all demonstrated using rational proofs. Likewise, the oneness of God is proven and the matter of His attributes dealt with such that what the text of the Qurʾān says about God must be believed, although we cannot know "how" God is to be conceived of as "sitting" on His throne, for example; this suggests a greater tendency towards interpretation of such matters than in al-Ashʿarī. Al-Māturīdī supports the idea of the free will of humanity, although God is, in fact, the only creator and

He creates the actions of His creation; using the same notion as al-Ash'arī of individuals "acquiring" their actions, al-Māturīdī suggests that this acquisition is connected to the choice or intention which precedes an act. This is to be distinguished from al-Ash'arī's sense of acquisition being the contemporaneous coming into the possession of the capacity to act at the time of the action. Evil deeds, while predetermined by God, are the actions of the individual as a consequence of the choice and intention to do such acts.

Al-Māturīdī was the inheritor and perpetuator of the position of the Murji'a on the question of faith. Only two states exist: having faith or not having faith. The essence of faith is in the belief in one's heart but there must be some practical consequence of this within Islam.

For a century after the death of al-Māturīdī, his teaching does not seem to have been of much importance, for some 150 years not drawing the attention of even Ash'arī opponents. The reason for this neglect undoubtedly lies in the fact of al-Māturīdī's residency in Samarqand, and thus his being well away from the centre of Islamic intellectual activity; his doctrines appear to have remained of local concern to the community in that region, with little external note taken of the development. The position of al-Māturīdī is generally presented as being a outgrowth of Abū Ḥanīfa's stance which had already spread to Samarqand by al-Māturīdī's time. Abū Ḥanīfa's position as eponym of the Ḥanafī legal school allowed al-Māturīdī's later followers to argue for the acceptance of their theological stance in areas outside Samarqand which were already dominated by the Ḥanafī legal school; they argued this on the basis of the previous relationship between the two sets of beliefs.

The spread and the eventual success of the school were a result of the conversion of Turks in central Asia to Islam of this Ḥanafī-Māturīdī persuasion. The liberal theological implications of Ḥanafī juridical requirements – such that faith is present in the individual even if all religious duties are ignored – is thought to have allowed for the gradual conversion of these nomadic peoples. With the expansion of the Turks, starting in the Seljuk period, adherence to the ideas of the Māturīdī school came to the attention of other groups in the Islamic community. The theological position of later Māturīdī school is represented for example in the *'aqīda* or creed of al-Nasafī (d. 1142) which has proven popular throughout the Muslim world, attracting many commentaries and elaborations even from the followers of al-Ash'arī.[24] In form, the creed presents what had become the classical sequence of argumentation, starting with the enumeration of the sources of knowledge and moving through discussion of God and His attributes and His nature, belief, and the communication from God via messengers, to be concluded by a discussion of life in the world. The whole theological position is thereby argued to be one cohesive whole, leading its reader from simple observations on how we know things to the compelling implication that, therefore, the Muslim way of life is the true and divinely desired one.

The role of theological writing

Theological writing became an art in Islam, although, as will become clear in the next chapter, it never had the place of honour in the community which legal discussions held. To some extent certainly, this is because the theological enterprise was dedicated more to the theoretical than the practical aspects of Muslim life. Islam is, to a great extent, predicated upon the idea of responding to the call from God through action; thus, the most crucial and relevant discipline to the vast majority of Muslims has been the one which guides human behaviour – Islamic law – rather than theology, with its dedication to the realm of human thought. Theology did provide some of the intellectual basis for the enunciation of the distinction between Islam on the one side, and Judaism, Christianity, and a multitude of other "lesser" religions on the other; it was, therefore, a crucial element in the formation of Islam as an independent and individual mode of existence within which a religious way of life could be led.

6 Legal developments

Sunnī Islam (as compared to the Shī'a, to be dealt with in Chapter 8) is defined not by theological allegiance but by practice. Following one of the four schools of law authenticated by the agreement of the community as being true implementation of the *sunna* or practice of Muḥammad makes one a member of Sunnī Islam. It is the individual believer's perspective on the law which becomes the central element of self-definition as a Muslim and which has thus evolved as the controlling element of the community's identification as a whole. Law in this sense, however, is a far broader concept than that generally perceived in the English word. Included in it are not only the details of conduct in the narrow legal sense, but also minute matters of behaviour, what might even be termed "manners," as well as issues related to worship and ritual. Furthermore, the entire body of law is traditionally viewed as the "revealed will of God," subject neither to history nor to change.

The role of law in defining Islamic allegiance is emphasized by the fact that the theological schools of Islam, discussed in the previous chapter, gained their fullest support in the guise of appendages to groups of legal scholars; this support occurred in correlation to the attitudes manifested by those theological groups towards the roles of speculative reason and tradition in human life.[1] Theology, therefore, is not only subordinate in importance to law as a discipline but also incorporated within the whole legal framework. Since all law comes from God, law is, in fact, theology as such, for both topics deal with the contemplation of human action in relationship to the divine; because of the practical aspects of Islamic life, law requires study in a way that theology does not.

The idea of *sunna*

The focal point of the law in Sunnī Islam is the *sunna*, the concept of the practice of Muḥammad, as embodied in the *ḥadīth* and transmitted faithfully by Muḥammad's followers through the succeeding generations down to the present. The *sunna* presents, for the individual Muslim, the picture of the perfect way of life, in imitation of the precedent of Muḥammad who was the perfect embodiment of the will of God. The *ḥadīth* reports are the raw material of the *sunna*, and must be sifted through by jurists in order to enunciate the details of rightful practice; the *sharīʿa* is the "way of life" for the Muslim which has been developed by the Muslim jurists on the basis of certain jurisprudential principles, the *uṣūl al-fiqh*.[2]

The history of Islamic law indicates that the idea of the *sunna* was not always perceived in this fashion, nor indeed was the *sunna* always considered to be the authoritative body of law for members of the community. Such a position took time and much argument before it emerged. It is to Muḥammad ibn Idrīs al-Shāfiʿī (d. 820) that most of the credit must go in developing this aspect of the overall legal theory of Islam.

In contemplating that transformation, however, it must be remembered that the concept of the law of Islam was a part of the emerging ideology and symbol system which provided a sense of identity to the Muslim community. Much of Islamic law, in substantive terms, can be seen to reflect a Jewish background and concerns common to Judaism. At the same time, portions of the law appear to have developed in a pragmatic way, with the adoption of laws and practices as they were found in the lands which were conquered; this is especially evident in elements of Roman law which were adopted in the Muslim environment.[3] These two trends – Jewish and Roman – often merged, and they were reshaped as the distinct Muslim law emerged. This process was aided by many of the legal elements being recast by Muslims such that they were seen as emerging from the context of the *jāhiliyya*, as was suggested above in Chapter 1.

In the early community, law was employed as a tool by which unity was imposed from above and for which an authority was needed to justify the requirements of that law. In the earliest period after the conquests, it would appear that the caliphs themselves were pictured as the authorities within the community on legal matters,[4] and it took some time before a unifying concept of the authority of Muḥammad as enunciated in the notion of the prophetic *sunna* actually emerged.

When the word *sunna* is used in texts from the early period it refers not to the *sunna* of Muḥammad but to the *sunna* of the caliphs and/or the *sunna* of a particular area, often combined with a sense of an ideal behaviour which is normative.[5] That is, as the Arab territories expanded and Islam became the emblem of that region, the law developed in a non-uniform manner under the general umbrella of "Islam." Each local area developed, in a pragmatic style, a law based upon the practice of its own region. This appears to have been supplemented to some degree by the centralized efforts of the caliph to unify his domain.

The emergence of schools of law

From the early stages of developing the law in a pragmatic and authoritative way, various "schools," *madhāhib* (*madhhab* in the singular), emerged in which people sharing common positions derived from their own personal legal deductions gathered together. The schools formed around the name of a single person, a teacher who had instructed students in the law, although it is doubtful that any of the individuals actually intended to start a "school" as such.[6] The schools themselves did not (and do not now) demand adherence or conformity, nor did the term *madhhab* imply any particular teaching activity. What a school shared was a common interest in a specific body of legal material which, in one way or another, was connected to the eponymous founder of the school and his followers.

There can be little doubt that these schools emerged through the pious motivation and efforts of those involved in the study of law, combined with the emergence of a class of scholarly élite whose desire it was to wrest authority from the hands of the caliph. For Muslims to be sure that they were fulfilling the will of God as completely as possible, it was necessary that every detail of the law be expounded; this required that every aspect be discovered. As new situations arose, never before encountered within Muslim society, it was the jurists' responsibility to discover "the will of God" in such instances. The rules of jurisprudential theory (*uṣūl al-fiqh*) were eventually established in order to allow individual jurists to make these sorts of decisions in an orderly and "Muslim" way.

The schools of law first emerged as local centres, reflecting the geographical diversity in the law from the beginning. Basra, Kufa, Medina, and Damascus are to be distinguished as the major regions, developing their own traditions and influencing others. In Basra, the only lasting school of importance was that which became the Ibāḍī *madhhab*, a surviving relation of the theological school of the

Khawārij. In Kufa, there emerged the Ḥanafiyya, under the eponym of Abū Ḥanīfa (d. 767) but developed by Abū Yūsuf (d. 798) and al-Shaybānī (d. 805) in Baghdad, as well as various Shīʿī groups, including the Imāmīs, the Zaydīs and the Ismāʿīlīs. Al-Awzāʾī (d. 774) was associated with a school in Syria although it did not last very long. Medina produced Mālik ibn Anas (d. 795) and provided the impetus, at the very least, for al-Shāfiʿī (d. 822). A later group, known as the Ḥanbalī school (the Ḥanābila), developed from Ibn Ḥanbal (d. 855) with a substantial debt to Medinan practices.[7]

The differences between these groups should not be exaggerated; the main contrast between the groups tends to be schematized best as a difference between the early groups in Iraq (who seem to have had close contact with Jewish law) and those in Medina (who had a more "liberal" attitude than their Iraqi counterparts), with the later schools following the Medinan position.[8] The issues at stake were generally matters dealing with customary practice and local conditions rather than disputes primarily over principles or methods. This sort of differentiation between the schools actually increased over time, as the schools developed what had been the early core of the law according to their own practices. Each school developed its own practice, its own *sunna*, which as time went on and authority was sought for individual practices, was traced back, first to prominent jurists in the past, then to companions of Muḥammad, and finally to Muḥammad himself. This "backwards growth" in authority is a tendency which has already been mentioned in Chapter 3 in terms of the growth of *isnād*s; this is the same phenomenon but on a larger, more theoretical scale. The final result was the emergence of the *sunna* of Muḥammad. The ultimate motivation behind this development was to create a structure of law which was Islamic through and through, by denying all foreign elements and justifying all the law in terms of the twin sources of Muslim life, the Qurʾān and the *sunna*.

The role of al-Shāfiʿī

It took al-Shāfiʿī to make the *sunna* of Muḥammad the authoritative source of law for all Muslims. Stimulating his efforts were claims made by Traditionalists to the effect that it was not sufficient for a jurist to simply assert that such and such an item was the *sunna* of Muḥammad, using what the Traditionalists felt was simply independent reasoning; there was, for these people, a need to prove each and every one of these statements. This is where the role of the *ḥadīth* with its *isnād* came in. The tendency to demand proof did not arise without a great deal of opposition, as evidenced most obviously within the Muʿtazilī movement which championed the use of reason in all matters of religion. For the most part, the schools of law, to the extent to which they had emerged by this point, only accepted the arguments and the demands of the Traditionalists in so far as the latter's points would support the former's legal traditions. Where traditions from Muḥammad could be seen to agree with a legal practice, all fine and good; there was not, at this point, any sense of changing the law in order to agree with the *ḥadīth*.

Al-Shāfiʿī systematized what appears to have been chaos by developing a procedure for legal reasoning. While other jurists prior to him and contemporary with him, people such as Abū Ḥanīfa, Abū Yūsuf and al-Shaybānī, were involved in this process also, modern scholarly research (especially that of Joseph Schacht) has shown al-Shāfiʿī to be the pivotal person in the emergence of the legal system of Islam as we know it.[9] Al-Shāfiʿī demanded the use of systematic reasoning without arbitrary or personal deduction in formulating the law and thus he created a system that was far more cohesive on a theoretical level than had previously been the case. He argued for the authoritative *sunna* being that of Muḥammad, a *sunna* which was to be found only in traditions transmitted from Muḥammad himself; the acceptance of traditions from the companions was not to be considered sufficient. As al-Shāfiʿī states, "the enactments of the Prophet are accepted as coming from Allāh in the same way as the explicit orders of the [Qurʾān], because Allāh has made obedience to the Prophet obligatory."[10] Furthermore, the Qurʾān could not contradict the *sunna*; the *sunna* could only explain the Qurʾān – such had to be the hierarchy of the sources of the law. A controlled notion of *naskh*, "abrogation," was implemented in order to handle cases of apparent contradiction between and within the sources. The community of Muslims could be said never to be in contradiction of the *sunna* if they agreed on a certain practice:

We accept the decision of the public because we follow their authority, knowing that, wherever there are *sunna*s of the Prophet, their whole body cannot be ignorant of them, although it is possible that some are, and knowing that their whole body cannot agree on something contrary to the *sunna* of the Prophet and on an error, I trust.[11]

This, in fact, must be the case in order to guarantee the transmission of *ḥadīth* reports from Muḥammad. It is not surprising, then, to note that the books of *ḥadīth* were all compiled after the time of al-Shāfiʿī when the need for these sources was crucial.

The development of the schools of law

The major schools of law which have survived down until today have their development in the time of al-Shāfiʿī and after. The process was not one of transforming the local practice into a school as such, but of championing the doctrine of a teacher and the tradition which that teaching represented. In Kufa the Ḥanafī school including the star pupils al-Shaybānī (who attributed his writings to Abū Ḥanīfa and thus created the literary tradition which is the school of law, *per se*) and Abū Yūsuf, became paramount and drew into their system the city of Basra. Similarly, in Medina and followed by Egypt and Mecca, Mālik ibn Anas, the person associated with the book called *al-Muwaṭṭaʾ*, one of the first written compendiums of legal traditions, became central as the Mālikī school, destined to find its major development in North Africa. The book ascribed to Mālik was an attempt to provide a very limited number of traditions concerning a given topic, and then to interpret them in light of the prevailing legal system of Medina. This latter element is the controlling factor in the whole book, rather than the traditions themselves.[12]

Al-Shāfiʿī's school was more personally based, he considered himself a member of the school of Medina, but he ended up not following the tradition of that area. His efforts were directed towards combining the pragmatic approach and position of Medina with the demands of the Traditionalists for adherence to the *sunna* of Muḥammad. Cairo proved to be the focal point of the development of his school, an area where al-Shāfiʿī spent the last part of his life. The school emerged by the ninth century as one of the three major groupings which continued their efforts in developing the *sharīʿa*, or law, of Islam and out of which eventually came the *uṣūl al-fiqh*, the principles of jurisprudence.

Principles of jurisprudence

The emergence of a fully enunciated theory of jurisprudence was not an instantaneous development of the law schools. The works of the earliest representatives of the law schools display a measure of disorder in their treatments of the law and rarely put forth the full basis of the reasoning in individual cases. It was not until the eleventh century that matters became more precise, so that definition of terms and reformulation of earlier decisions took place in works such as that of al-Sarakhsī (d. 1096) in the Ḥanafī school. This was not a simple reiteration of, or commentary upon, the earlier works, but a creative reworking of the entire structure of the *fiqh* process. The underlying drive behind the literature was a theological one. The desire was to demonstrate the completeness of Islamic law. Since it must be possible to answer every legal question on the basis of the sources of law, these works are dedicated to demonstrating that this is so. In order to do that, cases with the most remote possibility of occurring in human interaction are dealt with, precisely to show that the law (or the skill of the jurist) was such as to cover every potentiality.[13]

According to the developed jurisprudential theory in Sunnī Islam which has its ultimate basis in the work of al-Shāfiʿī, there are four sources from which law can be derived: the Qur'ān, the *sunna* of Muḥammad, consensus (*ijmāʿ*) of the community and/or the scholars, and analogy (*qiyās*). The first two provide the material basis upon which *qiyās* must operate. The vast majority of laws have, in fact, been fashioned by *qiyās* because the Qur'ān and the *sunna* provide a fairly limited selection of detailed legal provisions.

In general terms, an individual jurist first had to scour the works of previous jurists to find another case under consideration that was the same, or a case with similar facts. Should he not find one, he was faced with an unprecedented instance for which he would then use *qiyās*, using as his starting point legal information found in the Qur'ān, *sunna* or rendered absolute law by *ijmāʿ*. *Qiyās* works on the basis of finding the *ʿilla*, the common basis between a documented case and a new situation; this process depends upon the powers of deduction of the jurist and the results of his work will depend upon *ijmāʿ*, the consensus of opinion, in whether or not it supports his judgement. Should the decision find general support, it becomes an irrevocable law and thus may serve as the basis for further deductions by means of *qiyās*.

The operation of *ijmāʿ*, consensus, was a major issue in the development of the principles of jurisprudence, one which jurists took pains to prove was in fact a legitimate process substantiated by the Qur'ān and the *sunna*; only in this way, it was argued, was it possible to distinguish between jurists who delegated to themselves the right to make laws (perhaps an accusation resulting from polemical discussions with Jews and Christians) and those who worked legitimately within the Muslim framework. *Ijmāʿ* functions to confirm rulings. While, in theory, this could take place at the time of a given ruling, in practice it occurred in retrospect. If no dissenting voices were heard by the time of the following generation, then it could be taken that *ijmāʿ* had confirmed a ruling. *Ijmāʿ* is often seen to be the most crucial element of the whole legal structure, for it is through its action that all elements are confirmed, especially individual *ḥadīth* reports and even, one might say, the Qur'ān itself, which is only authoritative because all Muslims agree that it is so. This is emphasized by the fact that there is no centralized authority (in Sunnī Islam) by which such a matter can be established. Muslim theorists, however, did not view the process in this manner, since they still needed to confirm the validity of *ijmāʿ* as a concept by means of *ḥadīth* and Qur'ān. For them, the twin scriptural sources were authenticated by customary usage and their miraculous nature, rather than by consensus itself; thus no circular reasoning was involved.[14]

Relations between the schools of law

The Traditionalist school, which had demanded a complete rejection of personal reasoning, was not totally satisfied by al-Shāfiʿī's compromise in working out the relationship between the sources of law. Ibn Ḥanbal (d. 855), who was the eponym of the Ḥanbalī school, structured his thought on the principle of adherence to *ḥadīth* in preference to personal reasoning. He manifested this attitude in his compendium of traditions, the *Musnad*. The anecdote is related that Ibn Ḥanbal never ate a watermelon because he could not find a tradition which suggested that Muḥammad had done so or that he had approved of such.[15] Over the centuries, however, even this school, by the time it was accepted within the structures of Islamic juristic orthodoxy, came to the position of accepting the *uṣūl al-fiqh* as enunciated by the other schools, and thus embraced reasoning and consensus; watermelons were deemed acceptable.[16]

Another school emerged in the ninth century, known as the Ẓāhirī group, founded by Dāwūd ibn Khalaf (d. 884). Claiming allegiance to the *ẓāhir* or "literal" sense of both the Qur'ān and prophetic *ḥadīth*, the school rejected all aspects of systematic reasoning employed in the application of *qiyās*. This led to peculiar combinations of stances on the part of the school in contrast to the others, appearing liberal in some instances – because it followed the letter of the law and did not extend it into the many other areas deemed analogous by other schools – and being far more strict in others. Ibn Ḥazm (d. 1065) remains the intellectual high point of this school which, in fact, lost much of its influence after his time.

By the end of the tenth century, the four schools – Ḥanafiyya, Mālikiyya, Shāfiʿiyya and Ḥanābila – had solidified their position to the extent that no further schools of law emerged from that point on. This did not mean that no further legal judgements were to be made, but, rather, that the principles for which the schools stood and the legal stances which they had developed were to be the points within which all further discussions were to be conducted.[17]

The extent to which the schools disagree on points of law is of little concern to Muslims, for there is a tradition ascribed to Muhammad (although it is not found in the canonical collections of *hadīth*) which addresses itself precisely to the situation: "Difference of opinion in the community is a token of divine mercy."[18] An attitude of mutual recognition among the schools has prevailed, such that orthodoxy in matters of law is defined only by acceptance of the roots of the law; this means that the Zāhirī school was excluded due to its rejection of *qiyās*. Where a difference of opinion exists between the schools, it is to be taken that each opinion is an equally probable expression of God's will. On a matter seemingly as basic as the food laws, differences may be noted in whether certain animals are declared to be permissible or disapproved:

> The followers of al-Shāfi'ī disagree concerning aquatic animals. Some claim that fish are permissible but that frogs are forbidden. Others say that if the animal is in the form of a fish or of an animal ritually slaughtered in good faith, then it is permissible to eat it if it comes from the sea without being ritually slaughtered; however, if it is in the form of something which is not permitted to be eaten in good faith, then one is forbidden to eat it. This is the judgement of Abū Thawr. Others say that everything from the sea is to be judged by the law of fish, except the frog which is forbidden because the prophet forbade killing it. This is the judgement of 'Alī ibn Khayrān.
>
> Mālik and Rabī'a declare all aquatic animals allowable, even the tortoise and the like. This is suggested by a report from Abū Bakr who said, "There is nothing in the sea besides animals which God would slaughter for you."
>
> Abū Hanīfa forbids everything which does not have the form of a fish among the aquatic animals.[19]

Thus, the Hanafī school allows aquatic animals to be eaten only if they have the form of a fish, while the Mālikī school considers all aquatic animals permissible. Both positions are considered equally valid and equally "orthodox" for all Muslims.

Law and morality

After considering a given legal case, a jurist is able to declare whether
the resultant action itself is to be classified as being obligatory
(*wājib*), recommended (*mandūb*), permissible (*mubāḥ*), disapproved
(*makrūh*), or forbidden (*ḥarām*). Speaking in very broad terms,
performance of obligatory actions will bring reward in the hereafter
for the person concerned, while omission of the actions will bring
punishment. Recommended actions bring reward but no punishment
for their omission. Forbidden actions will bring punishment for being
committed, but reward for being avoided, while disapproved actions
bring reward for being avoided, but no punishment should they be
performed. The vast majority of actions fall into the "permissible"
category, the ramifications of which will not be felt in the hereafter.
There are many subtleties in the application of these categories, but,
in principle, they apply whether the concern is ritual, moral or legal;
all activities are considered in the same way and all are under the
rule of Islam. It is in the nature of this law, however, that even an
act which is declared to be disapproved can still bring about a binding
result. Marriages, for example, can be dissolved in a number of ways.
According to the Ḥanafī jurist al-Marghinānī (d. 1197), the most
laudable way of divorce is for "the husband to repudiate his wife
within a single sentence during the time she is not menstruating",
and then leave her alone for the next three months. This is best
because such a divorce is revocable until the end of the three-month
waiting period, since it has only been pronounced once. Repeating
the repudiation regularly each month over a period of three months
is simply "laudable." However, "an irregular divorce is where the
husband repudiates his wife with three divorces in a single statement
or three (arbitrary) times during a three month period"; this is
declared to be "disapproved" but, most significantly the marriage is
still considered to have been terminated in fact.[20] There is, thus, a
separation between what might be considered law and morality,
although it is all a part of one whole in the Muslim system, for all
law ultimately has as its purpose gaining entry for the individual into
paradise in the hereafter. At the same time, it is a sign of the realistic nature of Islamic law that the five moral categories of actions
were adopted rather than a bipolar system of good versus bad (a
position championed by the Muʿtazila at one point in history). The
law recognizes that not all Muslims are going to be saints in every
aspect of their behaviour and that they will need the urging forth
towards perfection that the law can provide.

Underlying this system are certain assumptions about the ethical nature of the law. In general Muslim understanding, the law has been determined by God in a manner that determines what is good and what is evil according to God's will. Reason cannot determine morality because God and His will cannot be constrained in any way. At the same time, God's will is not arbitrary: it is deemed to be purposeful. Because of this, the law is not limited to the literal statements of the Qur'ān and *sunna* as they apply to specific situations. Rather, it is reasonable for humans to extrapolate on the basis of one situation to a similar one because God's will is understood to be purposeful and thus somewhat predictable. Furthermore, because the laws found in the sources which set the dimensions of ethical action are specific, they are not stated as ethical principles from which further guidance may be deduced. However, the Muslim jurists did determine three general principles which were deemed to be within the framework of Islamic law: necessity (*ḍarūra*), public welfare (*maṣlaḥa*) and equity (*istiḥsān*). These three "are invoked to promote a good that would appear to be threatened by absolute adherence to the revealed command of God or to prevent an evil that is likely to result from such adherence,"[21] although all three principles were applied very cautiously in classical juristic thinking in order to avoid permitting the law from departing from the plain meaning of scripture in too many situations.

The role of the judge

The administration of the law in the Muslim community developed institutionally first under the Umayyads, but it came into its more lasting form under the Abbasids. A judge, known as a *qāḍī*, was appointed by the government to administer the *sharīʿa*. A central chief judge was also appointed by the government, to whom all other judges as well as the ruler himself would refer on all legal issues. He became the person who recommended to the caliph the appointment of all the judges and became the major legal counsellor of the ruler. The fact that all the judges (including the chief judge) were appointed by the government often led to conflicts; although in theory once a judge was appointed he was to be independent of the government, in practice such things as implementing decisions against high government officials was extremely difficult.

One of the qualifications for being a judge was, obviously, full knowledge of the Islamic law; other requirements included having sound sight and hearing, and being free (that is, not a slave), honest and a Muslim.[22] Such scholars were often the most strenuous upholders of Islam and they frequently saw the activities of the government as not being as fully "Islamic" as would be desirable. Their ability to criticize those who gave them their jobs, however, was tenuous. This led to a great deal of discussion over legitimacy of rule and explains why there was such a lot of debate in Islam[23] concerning the need to follow an unjust ruler and the right of rebellion. The position of the judge and the legitimacy of the appointment to that post were never held to be affected by the nature of the ruling powers who appointed him (or her, for a woman, according to some lines of thought, could be a judge, although she certainly did not have the right to rule in the imposition of the *ḥadd* penalties – those penalties specifically prescribed in the Qur'ān for crimes such as adultery, stealing, armed robbery, drinking wine, false accusation of unchastity, and apostasy). However, many of the leading jurists found it impossible to accept a position as a *qāḍī* and made much of their refusal to do so; their principles always dictated that since, in their opinion, the ruler of the time was not fulfilling his responsibility to Islam, accepting a judicial appointment from such a person would be morally reprehensible.

The administration of justice

The judges depended upon the power of the government to put their decisions into action. This was crucial in issues of criminal justice, for example. Although the law had been structured by the jurists such that essentially there were no crimes against the state – a crime is against another person or against God – the imposition of the prescribed penalties, especially the *ḥadd* penalties found the Qur'ān, had to be enforced by some means. Eventually a police force was devised to deal with such cases. Judges were further hampered by the terms of Islamic law which only allowed them to receive evidence that was submitted to them, rather than being able to search it out or conduct interrogations; the law was founded on the notion that blameless witnesses would always tell the truth and that oaths of innocence would always be forthcoming from all honest persons. The jurists saw themselves "in the role of spiritual advisors to the conscience of Islam rather than authoritarian directors of its practical affairs."[24] The result of this was the inevitable situation of the political powers having to assume some of the responsibility for direct administration of justice; several additional institutions emerged to deal with a variety of situations as a consequence. Among the legal officials in the community was the "investigator of complaints" (*naẓar fī'l-maẓālim*). This was an office originally designed to hear charges concerning the miscarriage of justice, and was thus to act as a check on judges; additional issues such as matters dealing with unjust taxes and enforcing the decisions of the *qāḍī*s were also within its purview. Later, the office emerged as a parallel system of justice, especially in matters of lawsuits; this was the result of the *maẓālim* courts having powers which the *qāḍī*s did not enjoy: the right to double-check and investigate evidence, to restrain acts of violence, and to refer people to binding arbitration.

An "inspector of the market" (*muḥtasib*, holding the office of the *ḥisba*) was also appointed, who was responsible for encouraging Islamic morality in general and thus provided the possibility of prosecutions in the general public interest. Specific duties of this office included matters relating to defective weights in the marketplace and commercial transactions where fraud or unpaid debts were suspected. Once again, the role of the judge was to a certain extent duplicated.[25]

The nature of Islamic law

Overall, Muslim law is recognized to be an "ideal" system, one which will be corrupted and will suffer at the hand of corruption in the world. This is even more so because the law is, in the first instance at least, a theoretical development and an enunciation of jurists, rather than a body of law emerging from precedents, although this position is tempered to some extent by practical considerations. The theoretical nature of the law may be best described as existing in tension with its practical aspects. Islamic law is, to a degree, of a purely religious character, carrying with it only the threat of punishment by God; failure to follow the law of Islam concerning the prayer, for example, will not involve any juridical penalty in this world. An exception would be the case of a person who went so far as to deny the obligatory character of the prayer, which would then be evidence of the rejection of Islam itself. The law is flexible also to the extent that any law may be broken under duress or necessity; in such conditions, a given act previously considered forbidden becomes valid, including such things as eating pork when no other food is available or drinking wine in the absence of all other liquids.

One final implication of the character of Islamic law is to be noted in the treatment of Jewish and Christian communities living within territories controlled by Muslims. These groups were not subject to the specific provisions of Islamic law, precisely because it was for those who were Muslims alone. Rather, these communities were allowed to be self-governing, following their own legal codes and principles, although they were considered citizens at a lower level than their Muslim neighbours, with certain restrictions on their public rights and a requirement of paying of a special poll tax. Security of life, property and religion was guaranteed by the payment of this tax, but no new religious buildings were to be erected nor was the public display of religion to be allowed.[26] In practice, the tolerance shown for these communities fluctuated in the Muslim world according to the political and social pressures of the time, but the theory, at the very least, echoed the character of Islamic law and its integrative religious nature.

7   Ritual practice

To a person standing on the outside observing the presence of a religion, ritual is the most obvious sign of the character and existence of believers in that faith. Ritual activities and their attendant buildings, clothes, and assorted paraphernalia provide the emblems of a religion and become, for the members of the religion themselves, modes for the expressions of their identity. Such ritual symbols also fulfill an obvious political function for the ruler, as a way of declaring his own dedication to the values embodied in the symbols and as a way of unifying his people behind him in one common symbolic expression.

For classical Islam, the notion of the "five pillars" represents the epitome of the revealed law as enacted through ritual activity. The five actions – the witness to faith (*shahāda*), prayer (*ṣalāt*), charity (*zakāt*), fasting (*ṣawm*), and pilgrimage (*ḥajj*) – are duties for which each individual is responsible, separate from general ethics and rules for interpersonal relationships. They are an integral part of the belief system of Islam, being a part of the explication of theological statements of belief from at least the tenth century onwards, as illustrated by the work of al-Baghdādī (d. 1037), whose *Kitāb Uṣūl al-Dīn* includes an intertwining of theological matters with more formal legal structures.[1]

The concept that "five pillars" were the ritual centre of Islam emerged almost certainly within the second Muslim century; both the *ḥadīth* collections of al-Bukhārī (d. 870) and Muslim ibn al-Ḥajjāj (d. 875) contain early on in their books a report which states that Muhammad said, "Islam is based upon five (principles)," followed by an enumeration of the five. While the term "pillar" is not used in these reports (that term would appear to be a tenth-century coinage), the isolation of these specific ritual activities is clear. Even earlier than the *ḥadīth* collections, al-Shāfiʿī (d. 822), in his *Risāla*,[2] isolated prayer, charity, fasting and pilgrimage as among the central elements of the faith; it would appear that, for him, these elements had not become the actual defining factor of Islam, but the recognition of their prominence is present. A similar observation may be made for the *Muwaṭṭa'* ascribed to Mālik ibn Anas (d. 795), whose work is organized such as to give prominence to the four rituals; that presentation, however, may well be the work of later editors, reflecting a more developed strain of thought than that of Mālik himself. It is equally clear that none of the individual elements of the "five pillars" was simply imposed upon new believers in Islam from the very beginning. Each ritual has its own history and its own significance, both aspects often being very difficult to reconstruct. None of the rituals have their requirements fully expressed in the Qur'ān.

The evidence of archaeological remains from the earliest stages of the Arab conquests, for example in the area of the Negev desert, does not provide us with any clear indication of cultic or ritual emblems in this period either. Inscriptions found in these places reveal the rise of a religious ideology by their use of various religious invocations and also exhibit the emergence of places of worship. No clues are left, however, as to the character of this worship other than the observation that it took place alongside various pagan and Christian (and probably Jewish) worship practices.[3]

Testifying Muslim faith

The witness to faith (*shahāda*) consists of repeating the two phrases, "There is no god but God," *lā ilāh* *illā 'llāh*, and "Muḥammad is the messenger of God," *Muḥammad*ᵘⁿ *rasūl Allāh*. These phrases are recited in order to witness conversion to Islam. Such utterances have practical implications for the political order, therefore, entitling one to the privileges of membership in the Muslim community. The phrases must be recited in Arabic and prefaced by an honest statement of intention. Thus al-Baghdādī states that the person who utters the *shahāda* must know "the truth of the statement" and must repeat it "out of understanding and with heartfelt sincerity."[4] The *shahāda* is repeated as a part of the Muslim prayer, *ṣalāt*, and thus gains more of a sense of being an oft-repeated ritual than simply a once-in-a-lifetime statement.

The two basic statements of the *shahāda* are found in the Qur'ān, but they are not put together as a single statement, nor are they suggested in that book to be some sort of defining notion of what a Muslim is, as is implied within the concept of their ritual use. The refrain "There is no god but God" and variations upon it are frequent in the scripture, found for example in Qur'ān 47/19; "Muḥammad is the messenger of God" and statements to that effect are also found, for example in Qur'ān 48/29, but the sense is never one of a refrain, but rather as a part of an argument.

The emergence of the statement as a key part of Muslim identity is witnessed on coins from the first Muslim century and in the Dome of the Rock inscriptions, as well as in the *ḥadīth* literature. Coins from the eighth decade of the *hijrī* calendar contain phrases such as "There is no god but God alone," a statement reminiscent of Qur'ān 5/73 and similar passages, but obviously it is differentiated by the addition of the word *wāḥid*, "alone," from the first half of the *shahāda*. "Muḥammad is the messenger of God" also appears starting, it would seem, with coins from the years 77 and 78. The that statement is added, "whom He sent with guidance and the religion of truth, that He might make it victorious over all religions."[5] Such invocations continue on many coins from this point on and thus become the standard numismatic phraseology. It would appear to be an accident of history that coins continue to use a formula which does not precisely follow the *shahāda* as might have been expected; this likely occurred because coinage was introduced before the *shahāda* reached its mature formulation. So, while the phrases of the *shahāda* themselves became stock items of the religious vocabulary, it is apparent that, by the time of the issuance of these early coins, the phrases had not yet emerged as the ritual statement which was to identify all Muslims. However, it would appear to be a short step, both historically and phraseologically, before just that occurred.

The same comments hold for the Dome of the Rock inscriptions of ʿAbd al-Malik as they do for the coins. Both phrases in reference to God and Muḥammad are found in the inscriptions, but they are found neither joined together nor distinguished as isolated elements within the texts. For example, there is the statement on the outside of the colonnade on the south side, "There is no god but God alone; He has no partner with Him," followed by "Muḥammad is the messenger of God." Over the north door, the inscription reads "Muḥammad is the servant of God and His messenger whom He sent with the guidance and the religion of truth . . . ," the same as coins from Umayyad times after ʿAbd al-Malik; the lack of emphasis on the formula expressions of later Islam is once again notable and significant for what it reveals of the gradual development of this element of Muslim identity.

As was mentioned earlier, the idea of the "five pillars" is found listed in the *ḥadīth* collection of Muslim ibn al-Ḥajjāj for example, but several of these reports indicate an instability in the matter of the *shahāda*. While all the reports confirm that testifying to faith in one way or another was the first part of the "five" elements stipulated by Muḥammad, it is expressed in a number of ways. For example, this testifying is called "declaring the oneness of God" in one instance.[6] Furthermore, the actual form of the *shahāda* witnessed in the collection of Muslim ibn al-Ḥajjāj is specifically a testimony to faith; that is, it is prefaced by the statement *shahāda an*, "the witness to faith is that. . . ." That statement is, in fact, a part of the ritual prayer (and so the traditions themselves also come within the chapter concerned with the "testimony to faith within prayer"). The fact that the material as presented by Muslim ibn al-Ḥajjāj provides a non-cohesive picture suggests two things: that the isolation of the *shahāda* as an individual part of a concept of the "five pillars" took place at least two centuries after Muḥammad, and that it was a formulation which received its final shape fairly late also.

Islamic prayer

Prayer, *ṣalāt*, is spoken of numerous times in the Qur'ān; the notion of regular times of prayer is stipulated on some occasions, but the text itself can only be made to support the classical Islamic practice of five prayers a day by a tenuous interpretation. Various elements of the ritual connected with the *ṣalāt* are also stipulated in the Qur'ān, including standing, bowing, prostrating, facing in a set direction known as the *qibla* (the word itself is used in the Qur'ān seven times, mainly in Qur'ān 2/142–5), and performing ablutions before prayer (Qur'ān 5/6). The Friday (noon) prayer as one for the whole community is also designated in Qur'ān 62/9. The recitation of the Qur'ān within the prayer is also sometimes seen to be supported by the text itself (Qur'ān 17/78, where reference is made to "reading at daybreak"). None of these elements, however, is presented in a systematic or detailed manner such that one could actually reconstruct a ritual on the basis of these texts alone. Rather, most are presented in a very general manner (for example, Qur'ān 25/63–4: "and the servants of the All-merciful are those . . . who spend the night bowing down to their Lord and standing") and only later did Muslims peg upon these verses the elaborate ritual which had developed in its own way and according to many different impulses.

By the time the collections of *ḥadīth* material emerged, the ritual of the prayer had become quite explicit, although still not with total unanimity in detail. Such differences are to be found manifested in the traditions of the various schools of law, as with all the rituals in Islam, and therefore it is not possible to present a single picture of "prayer" within Islam. Basic elements are common to all schools, however, and may be summarized.

The five times of prayer (*miqāt*) are defined as daybreak (*ṣalāt al-ṣubḥ* or *fajr*), noon (*ṣalāt al-ẓuhr*), mid-afternoon (*ṣalāt al-ʿaṣr*), sunset (*ṣalāt al-maghrib*) and evening (*ṣalāt al-ʿishāʾ* or *ʿatama*), but the precise way in which these times are determined varies. Clearly, it also depends upon where in the world the individual is at a given moment, so Muslims are, in theory, praying all over the world all the time. The call to prayer (*adhān*) is given by the muezzin (*muʾadhdhin*) at each mosque (*masjid*, literally "the place of prostration" but in the Qurʾān meaning "sanctuary") but it is not necessary to go there in order to pray, except for the Friday noon prayer, for anyone may pray in any clean spot alone or in the company of others. Following the ablution, either minor (*wuḍūʾ*) or major (*ghusl*) depending on the state of ritual purity of the individual prior to the ablution, a series of recitations and body movements are undertaken in stages, many of which are liable to be supplemented by other traditional elements which vary according to the school of law. The prayer is done facing the direction of the Kaʿba in Mecca and entails recitation of sections of the Qurʾān, with a special emphasis falling on *sūra* 1. The worshipper moves from a standing position to one of bowing, half-sitting, and full prostration. The whole sequence of the ritual is repeated twice in the morning, three times at sunset, and four times in the noon, afternoon and evening prayers.[7]

The stipulation of these five prayer times is, according to Muslim tradition, a result of instructions given to Muḥammad while on his heavenly journey. Clearly, even on the basis of the text of the Qurʾān alone, the idea of there being five prayers took some time to emerge, but the evidence which is available to us just does not allow any insight into when the number five was decided upon or why. The suggestion that "five" is the median number between the three daily prayers of Judaism and the seven stages of the day of the Syrian Christian monastic orders fits within much of the elaboration of Muslim ritual as a conscious attempt to produce a self-definition which was mid-way between and yet clearly distinct from Judaism and Christianity.[8] The number "five" is often used in Middle Eastern literature as symbolic of half a group – that is, half of "ten" – and the usage of the number itself in the Qur'ān is limited to expressions of large numbers (5000 swooping angels in Qur'ān 3/125; one day is 50,000 years in 70/4), and simply appears to convey a significantly large quantity. The attachment of "five" to ritual matters (not only in the "five" daily prayers, but also the "five" ritual pillars, and the five "pillars" of the creed) is clearly a later development not dependent upon any symbolic or literal sense present in the Qur'ān.

Friday noon prayer

While the daily prayer may be said anywhere and may be said alone (although saying it with others is considered more meritorious), the Friday noon prayer is held in a large *jāmi'* or "congregational" mosque.[9] These buildings are generally supported by government funds, as opposed to the smaller mosques found throughout the Muslim world which have been built with private funds and are typically used by a defined group of people for the prayer at all other times. The Friday noon prayer will always be led by an *imām*, the prayer leader (such a person may be present any time a group of Muslims prays together, however, simply to keep the group in unison), and a sermon will be given by the *khaṭīb* (who may be the same person as the *imām*). Attendance at the Friday noon prayer was declared obligatory for all Muslims who were legally capable, with the exception of "women, slaves, the sick, travellers, those tending the sick and those fleeing oppression," according to al-Baghdādī.[10]

Function of prayer

Additional prayers of a non-compulsory nature, but still of the ritualized *ṣalāt*-type, are also stipulated in Islam. Special prominence is given to the *witr* prayer, performed at night and to which an extra section, *rak'a*, may be added. Additional sections may also be added to the five daily prayers. Also, there is the *wird*, the ritualized private prayer which concentrates on the recitation of the Qur'ān. Another prayer is the *du'ā'*, a non-ritualized individual address to God. Prayer is not therefore restricted to the daily five prayers alone but may be performed on other occasions as the need and desire arise within the individual Muslim. Thus prayer as a phenomenon in Islam does not function simply to bring the community together at regular times of the day and the week; neither is it just a matter of providing structured time periods within the day to Muslim society, nor a way of simply providing a constant reminder of the presence of Islam in the world. Certainly it is all those things, but it also does seem to be conceived as a personal communication with God, providing the opportunity for expressions of thankfulness and worship in the full sense of those words.

The mosque

Even though it is not actually necessary for the ritual of prayer, the mosque has become the central element manifesting the physical presence of Muslims in a given place in the world, a source of identity for the individual believers and a symbol and centre of purity for the Muslim community. The central elements of this physical manifestation of Muslim identity as connected to the mosque may be isolated and, as such, may well provide a statement about the symbols which Muslims consider are essential to their self-definition and self-understanding as Muslims. The phenomenon of churches turned into mosques provides an interesting illustration of such elements.[11] The most obvious examples which allow an insight into this conversion are those found in Istanbul which, while their transformation dates from a late period (the Turkish conquest of Constantinople was in 1453 and thus all such examples are necessarily after that date), include features which are fully representative of classical Muslim self-understanding.

Although overgrown and derelict in the 1980s and suffering from the effects of a partially completed restoration in 1964–5, the church identified as the Myrelaion and known as the Bodrum Camii or the Mesih Ali Paşa mosque in Istanbul, provides a splendid example. Built in about 922, the building is fascinating in its own right for its architectural design and the presence of a crypt underneath the building. In the late fifteenth or early sixteenth century, the church was converted into a mosque. The most obvious evidence of the conversion is the presence of the minaret, built into the southwest corner. The history of the minaret as a form of Muslim architecture is intriguing and, while its practical function of providing a place for the call to prayer is well known and often suggested to be the origin of the edifice, it seems more likely that the form was taken over from earlier buildings. The earliest examples of minarets are those found on the Mosque of al-Walīd in Damascus constructed between 706 and 715; this mosque was built on the base of a Roman temple and incorporated the three original corner towers as minarets. (The absence of a minaret on the Dome of the Rock should be noted.) The generalized symbolism of the minaret in the early period is not hard to comprehend: towering over the inhabitants is the pillar of the conquerors. It is clear, however, that regardless of its early function, in classical Islam a minaret became the central symbol of both the Muslim faith and the place of worship as illustrated in the conversion process of churches into mosques. (It should be noted, however, that it is quite possible for a building to be a mosque without having a minaret.) In the Myrelaion, no other major architectural modifications were required to make the church functional as a mosque. A small window appears to have been installed on the ground level to allow sufficient light for Qur'ān reading. The other changes are all internal and to do with furnishings. A *miḥrāb*, or niche, indicating the direction of prayer, was provided. This indicator would appear to be a necessary feature of converted buildings but a purpose-built mosque would, of course, be properly aligned anyway and thus it appears redundant in such instances. Yet the niche is found in all mosques. It may be that the feature was copied from the design of ancient religious buildings, being the place designated for the presence of the honoured image in Roman temples, for example.[12] A *minbar*, or pulpit, was required for the sermon (*khuṭba*) of the preacher (*khaṭīb*). A women's gallery had to be installed to keep the sexes separate. All these items had to be aligned in the correct Muslim direction, facing Mecca, within the former church structure. Ancillary chambers appear to have been constructed for the *imām* and the muezzin, and a vestibule created for latecomers. No evidence of a place for ablutions appears to exist, although the presence of a cistern within the original building complex may have provided a source for the necessary flowing water.

This pattern of conversion may be witnessed many times in Istanbul and in other parts of the Islamic world. Istanbul provides a further vivid example in the church of Saints Sergius and Bacchus built in 527 CE for Justinian and thus older than Haghia Sophia, which, of course, with its four minarets provides another instance of a conversion. Some churches proved more problematic, as in what is believed to be the Church of St Andrew in Krisei, now known as the Koca Mustafa Paşa Camii, which required a complete reorientation for its successful use as a mosque.

Muslim charity

Alms tax, *zakāt* (the term *ṣadaqa* is often synonymous but can also mean "freewill offerings"), like prayer with which it is often mentioned in tandem, is demanded in the Qur'ān in statements which provide exhortations to believers to give ("You will never attain piety until you spend something of what you love," says Qur'ān 3/92), but few details are actually provided as to what to give and when. The Qur'ān responds to a demand to know how much to give in *sūra* 2, verse 219, with the statement, "As much as you can spare!" An explicit statement is made about the recipients of the alms, with the result that Qur'ān 9/60 has served as the peg for all legal discussions on the issue: "Charity is for the poor, the needy, those working at collecting it, those whose hearts are being reconciled [to yours], for freeing of captives and debtors, and in striving along God's way, and for the wayfarer, as a duty imposed by God." A general emphasis throughout the Qur'ān is made on helping the poor, orphans and widows, and it also suggests that all such payments should be made discreetly, without drawing attention to the one who is giving. The alms tax given should come out of the money or produce which one possesses.

It was up to the jurists of the later centuries to develop a precise system of donation and payment. This development can be seen in the books of *ḥadīth*, and the institution of charity provided endless opportunity for the jurists to work out subtle details and theoretical considerations.

Early *ḥadīth* reports appear to be ignorant of precisely how much should be given as *zakāt* and from precisely what sorts of things it should be paid; such reports simply say that possessing "wealth" is forbidden and thus everything which is in excess should be given away. Within the developed schools of law, however, full rules emerged which, while they vary in their precise detail from school to school, can be summarized fairly accurately. Crops of the field, grapes and dates are liable to *zakāt* on each crop, as an amount stipulated as 10 per cent of the crop, paid at harvest time. Camels, oxen and other small domestic animals which are freely grazing are also liable, the amount paid being a portion of the excess over certain stipulated amounts. Of gold, silver and merchandise, 2½ per cent of the amount held each year is also payable. The amount is payable directly to the recipient, but it is preferred that the tax be paid to the authorities in charge of its distribution (a notion seen to be supported by the fact that the Qur'ān refers to those involved in collecting *zakāt* as one of the groups eligible to receive it). In practice, *zakāt* became difficult to collect, especially in times of high taxation. At various times during Muslim history, however, governments inspired by pious scholars attempted to return to a system of collecting *zakāt* as the only legitimate form of taxation. But the amount collected often proved insufficient and eventually there occurred a reversion to other forms of tax on items more profitable to the government which were not covered in the traditional working out of the *zakāt* laws (for example, by the imposition of import duties).

Zakāt has shown great flexibility over time in adapting to and being adapted by social and political realities. For example, variation in whether the tax was a voluntary one or a required contribution to the state frequently reflected the conditions at the time in terms of the state's prosperity. Also, the imposition of *zakāt* was seen, starting in about the eleventh century, as the central symbol of the revival of Islamic rule; the "proper" (that is, the juridical) implementation of the tax was urged by reformers and initiated by rulers at various points in history in order to bolster Islamic ideological claims. For example, al-Malik al-Kāmil (d. 1238), a ruler during the Ayyubid dynasty centred in Egypt, invoked the Islamic ideal of voluntary payment of taxes under the term *zakāt*, but the programme quickly crumbled under the impact of the revenue lost by the central government.[13]

The Muslim fast

During the ninth month of the *hijrī* calendar, Ramaḍān, a fast called *ṣawm* or *ṣiyām* is enjoined upon Muslims. From sunrise to just after sunset for the thirty days of this month of the lunar calendar, adults are ordered to abstain from all food and drink (the regulation being not to allow any material substance to enter the body in so far as that is possible), from deliberate vomiting, and from having sexual intercourse or emission of semen if that is a result of conscious desire. Menstruation, bleeding after child birth, an unsound mind, and intoxication produce an invalid fast. Numerous legal qualifications surround the fast, including what to do if the fast is violated and what sorts of behaviour in general are permissible during the month; the various schools of law see different implications arising from many of the situations. Because the lunar calendar is followed, the fast moves through the seasons, occurring some eleven days earlier each solar year.

It is considered especially meritorious to read the whole of the Qur'ān during the month of Ramaḍān. To facilitate this, the text has been divided into thirty equal sections, one for each day of the month. When the fasting month is over, the *'īd al-fiṭr* celebration is held; this is the major festival of the Muslim year. The day itself sees a special public prayer for the whole community and, following that, a vast feast is put on, with celebration, visiting, and giving of gifts (called the *zakāt al-fiṭr*) being special features. The Qur'ān contains several fairly detailed explanations of the fast of Ramaḍān, indicating that it was a practice which came into existence early in Islam, being recognized as a symbol of the religion or at least indicating Islam's comparability to Judaism and Christianity. The Qur'ān itself declares in *sūra* 2, verse 183, "O you who believe, fasting has been prescribed for you just as it was prescribed for those before you, so that you will be godfearing." The sense is, therefore, that Islam has a practice equivalent to that of Judaism and Christianity, although it is distinct in its calendar situation and length: "The month of Ramaḍān in which the Qur'ān was sent down as a guidance to the people, and as clear signs of the guidance and the salvation – so let any of you who are present during the month, fast in it" (Qur'ān 2/185). Here we have a case of a ritual which is adopted and adapted from the earlier religions but which is given a distinctly Islamic flavour and mythological significance with the month's connection to the revelation of the Qur'ān.[14]

Stories abound in the *ḥadīth* material concerning an "earlier" fast which Muḥammad instituted on the Jewish Day of Atonement. Suggested to have been a one-day, twenty-four hour fast, the reports are often seen to be an explanation of the Quranic phrase suggesting that there was an earlier fast (that is, Qur'ān 2/183, quoted above); as such, the historical value of the reports is certainly questionable. Most notable, however, is the understanding that these reports provide for the significance of Ramaḍān; the month-long fast is to be understood as the truly Islamic version of the institution of fasting.

Fasting at times other than Ramaḍān

Fasting in Islam is undertaken more often than simply during Ramaḍān. The notion of *kaffāra*, atonement for sin or for duties which have been omitted, is stipulated in the Qur'ān on a number of occasions. In *sūra* 2, verse 196, fasting is to replace the pilgrimage for those unable to go to Mecca under certain conditions; in Qur'ān 4/92, fasting is an atonement for killing a believer by mistake; in

Qur'ān 5/89, fasting is prescribed for breaking an oath; in Qur'ān 5/95, fasting is the penalty for killing an animal while on the *ḥajj*; and in Qur'ān 58/4, one may fast in order to retract a divorce. In each of these situations, fasting is seen as a replacement or another possibility in the suggested ways of making amends for one's moral or ritual errors. All these indicate that fasting as an activity in general is seen to have a certain redemptive effect within Islam; this redemption is sometimes thought to be applicable to the fasting which takes place in the month of Ramaḍān as well, at least in a limited way.

The Muslim pilgrimage

The *ḥajj* to Mecca and its surrounding area is an annual ritual lasting up to seven days which contains within it a fully detailed sequence of events enjoined upon all those who are physically able to come to the city. Performed during the first half of the last month of the year, Dhū'l-Ḥijja, the *ḥajj* requires a state of ritual sanctity for the activities. Prior to the *ḥajj* itself, ritual purification is undertaken, and the Ka'ba is circumambulated and a run is performed between al-Ṣafā and al-Marwa, two hillocks near the Ka'ba (now joined to the central Meccan mosque by a covered arcade); both activities are performed seven times, interspersed with prayers and invocations. On the seventh of Dhū'l-Ḥijja, the pilgrims participate in a prayer service at the mosque around the Ka'ba. On the following morning, the pilgrimage itself starts and, over the next three days, the following activities take place. The pilgrims assemble in Minā, just outside Mecca, and stay there for the night. The next morning, they depart for the plain of 'Arafāt, 15 kilometres east, and assemble on and around the Mount of Mercy where a prayer ritual is performed and a ceremony entitled the "standing" is undertaken, lasting from the time the sun passes the meridian until sunset. That evening, the pilgrims return to Muzdalifa, about half-way back to Minā, where the night is spent. The next day, a journey to Minā brings them to the stone pillar (*jamrat al-'aqaba*) at which seven pebbles are thrown; the column is said to represent Satan. This is followed by a ritual slaughter of sheep, goats and camels, and a meal, the *'īd al-aḍḥā*, "the festival of the sacrifice" (performed by all Muslims whether in Mecca or not and seen as the second major festival of Islam). Returning to Mecca, the Ka'ba is circumambulated and the running between al-Ṣafā and al-Marwa (unless completed prior to the *ḥajj* itself) is performed. The state of ritual purity is also abandoned on this day, symbolized by men having their heads shaved and women having a lock of hair cut off. Three days of celebration at Minā generally follow for most pilgrims, with more stones thrown at the three pillars of Satan, all followed by another circumambulation of the Ka'ba. A visit to Medina will also often be included before the pilgrims return to their own homes.[15]

The Qur'ān's major testimony to this ritual is found in *sūra* 2, verses 196–200 and *sūra* 5, verses 95–7. Various parts of the ritual are detailed, as are some of the legal regulations which bear on the participants, however, no full and cohesive explanation is given. An element which does receive mention on a number of occasions is the relationship of some elements of the pilgrimage to the activities of Abraham and Ishmael. The Qur'ān states in *sūra* 2, verse 127 that "Abraham and Ishmael laid the foundations for the House" [understood to be the Ka'ba] and that they did a number of activities which the later pilgrims also do: performed the circumambulation, ran between al-Ṣafā and al-Marwa, sacrificed a sheep, and stoned Satan.

Historically, the pilgrimage has given tremendous prominence to Mecca but, as has already been mentioned in Chapter 4 above, there was a time when Jerusalem may well have been an alternative pilgrimage destination, although clearly the Dome of the Rock was not constructed with a view to facilitating the vast number of pilgrims which are received at Mecca each year. Notably the inscriptions in the Dome do not exhort people to perform a pilgrimage; the inscriptions are perhaps there, however, to be read while performing a circumambulatory ritual within the domed area.

Other ritual activities

The extent to which Muslim identity is expressed through ritual is not limited to the "five pillars," although the prominence of that grouping is obviously high. The *mawlid* festival, celebrating the birth of Muḥammad (not fully established in Islam until about the thirteenth century) and the informal *du'ā'* prayers are two additional ritual-type activities which are considered by Muslims to be significant in terms of the expression of their faith. Visits to tombs of holy men and women are also a popular activity, especially in areas which have been deeply affected by the mystical side of Islam. Such visits are generally used as occasions either to ask for favours of the deceased saint or to ask for forgiveness. The power of the saint is believed to reside in his or her ability to intercede on behalf of the individual believer with God.

The interpretation of Muslim ritual

Most noticeable when contemplating the sum of Muslim ritual is the emphasis upon the ritualism of the activities; all events are fully planned and formalized. But beyond that, one may observe a general lack of mythological sense in any of the rituals. The only meaning which can be seen in these rituals, according to many classical Muslim thinkers and modern scholars of Islam alike, is its sense of being an expression of an individual's piety and obedience to God's command and as an indication of the person's membership within the Islamic community. There is a very real sense of what has been termed "anti-sacramentalism" and also of the rituals being "commemorative" but at the same time "amythical".[16] That is, many of the actions in these rituals are done with a remembrance of past actions of Muḥammad or Abraham, but without those actions becoming mythological such that the believer becomes, in any sense, the person of the past. Likewise, the animal sacrifice in the *ḥajj* and the performance of the fast of Ramaḍān for the most part do not take on the character of sacraments, conceived to have specific effects for the believer, but, rather, remain acts which individuals do within their sense of obedience. Overall, ritual is the full manifestation of the special character of Islam, separate from other religions by its conscious decision to be unique in its ritual constituents; that process of creating a separate definition appears to have been done, in the case of the development of the ritual practices, in a reasonably arbitrary fashion with no overall consistent pattern imposed in creating that "uniqueness" of Islam within the Judeo-Christian milieu. Islam, in its construction of its rituals, is different from Judaism and Christianity and has rejected, or at least greatly modified, the central ritual activities of its two predecessors. In this way, it has created its "uniqueness" through difference, but that does remain a "uniqueness" which cannot be systematized into a cohesive perspective, at least not within the framework of ritual.

Part III

Alternative visions of Islamic identity

Significant dates

1240	death of mystic IBN 'ARABĪ
1328	death of Sunnī theologian/jurist IBN TAYMIYYA
1501	SAFAVIDS ruling in Iran

8 The Shīʿa

Islam remained, for the most part, remarkably unified in its religious manifestations during the classical period. It is only the split between the legal and theological schools already discussed and what is known as the Shīʿa of ʿAlī that has produced any degree of cleavage and only the latter which has produced a true sense of an "alternative vision" of Islam.

A number of treatises were written by various Muslim authors which detailed a tendency toward sectarianism within the faith which would seem to contradict the preceding statement. Famous works by al-Baghdādī (d. 1037) and al-Shahrastānī (d. 1153) provide lists of the seventy-three "groups" into which the Islamic community fractured. These works, however, reflect less what would normally be considered true variation in expression of Islamic identity, and more a documentation of variations on specific points of Muslim theology. The books are a part of a tendency towards classification of all sorts of sundry matters which was common in classical Islamic times. They also reflect an interpretation and justification of a tradition ascribed to Muḥammad which speaks of his community dividing into seventy-three (or seventy-one or seventy-two) parts. The important concluding statement of this tradition provides its significance: only one of these groups will actually be saved in the hereafter. It was the job of the authors of these texts, then, to enumerate the multiplicity of groups, while, at the same time, providing a clear definition of the group which would be saved: that group, of course, being identical with the author's own allegiances. In some instances, one suspects that, in these books, political rebels have been made into theologically-based heretics, thus once again reinforcing the traditional picture of a well-defined "Islam" as existing from the very earliest times.[1]

One of the groups detailed by these "heresiographers," a group divided into numerous sub-divisions according to their classificatory schemes, was the Shī'a of 'Alī. Once again, how many of these groups really existed as clearly identified units is questionable and certainly few of them actually survived for any substantial period of time. Several main groupings did become prominent, however.

The Shī'ī understanding of its origins

As was mentioned in the discussion of the rise of theology, the Shī'a pictures its roots back in the days of 'Alī ibn Abī Ṭālib and the early caliphs. The Shī'a, or "party," of 'Alī consisted of those who defended his right to rule the early community in the civil war with Mu'āwiya. They claimed, on the basis of statements of Muḥammad and by virtue of 'Alī's relationship to Muḥammad (being his cousin and son-in-law), that he had a legitimate claim to rule. Much is made of traditions from Muḥammad, accepted by both the Sunnīs and the Shī'a, in which 'Alī is designated as having a special relationship to Muḥammad. Al-Tirmidhī (author of one of the canonical Sunnī books of *ḥadīth*) reports, "The prophet said in reply to someone who had complained about 'Alī: 'What do you think of one who loves God and his prophet and who in turn is loved by God and his prophet?'" Also transmitted is, "The most loved of women to the prophet of God is Fāṭima ['Alī's wife, Muḥammad's daughter] and the most loved of men is 'Alī."[2] Such traditions, however, tend to fall into a general category of discussion of the "merits of the companions" found in all *ḥadīth* literature, in which each of the early followers of Islam is honoured. In this way, their authority as "founding fathers," and subsequently as transmitters of *ḥadīth*, was enhanced, and it seems likely that this was the function of such reports in the beginning. It was only when 'Alī as an individual had his persona enhanced by the Shī'a that such reports acquired a greater significance. It would appear, however, that this must have taken place to a great extent after traditions enhancing 'Alī's position were already in circulation in the early community; 'Alī's position within the family of Muḥammad is probably sufficient to explain why early sources would consider him an especially prominent person.

From the Shī'ī perspective, there was more at stake in the whole debate, however, for example concerning the nature of the rule of the early community. Was the leader to be one who combined religious with political authority? Or, with the death of Muḥammad, had religious authority passed to each individual believing Muslim? It remains a matter of debate among scholars as to whether 'Alī received his earliest support because of a nascent belief in his religious significance (which thus suggested that he had authority in religious matters, an element which becomes fully developed among the later Shī'a as we shall see), or whether this was a purely political manoeuvre which later became coloured with religious significance.

However, as was the case for theology, these debates among scholars essentially accept the Muslim accounts at their face value and argue over the various aspects of them, rather than appreciating the ideological viewpoint from which such material was compiled. These debates still work from the standpoint of acceptance of the data provided about the early period and that data's impulse to demonstrate a legitimating and detailed view of Islamic origins.

The Shī'a and the Qur'ān

Most significant in the stance of the Shī'a, *vis-à-vis* their origins, is their general acceptance of the text of the Qur'ān virtually intact, in line with the Sunnīs. While there certainly have been tendencies within the Shī'ī community to debate the accuracy of the text as they have it and even a tendency to suggest modifications to the text – citing additions, omissions, changes and alterations to the version promulgated by 'Uthmān – this sort of activity has been relatively restrained.[3] Much of the contemplated modification to the Quranic text is of such a nature as to take place within the legitimated (from the Sunnī perspective) range of "variant readings." An example of this is found in Qur'ān 3/110, "You are the best community which has been produced for humanity," such that rather than being read *umma*, "community," the Shī'a have read the word as *a'imma* and taken it as referring to the leaders of the Shī'ī community, the Imāms. What all this may be taken to suggest is that the differentiation between the Sunnīs and the Shī'a arose only after the promulgation of an established text of the Qur'ān.

This view of the historical development of the Sunnīs and the Shī'a fits in with the account of the rise of Islam and the caliph's authority given earlier in this book. A fully variant text of the Qur'ān in the hands of the Shī'a would have indicated an earlier establishment of the Shī'a than the evidence concerning the rise of Islam as a whole might otherwise suggest. It might also have suggested a "fixed" text of the Qur'ān being established early on, to which the Shī'a responded with their own version. However, since the Shī'a do *not* have their own Qur'ān, both the late establishment of the Shī'a and the Sunnī community as two interpretations of Islam, and the establishment of a fully fixed text of the Qur'ān prior to that division, are historically possible.

The Shīʿa and *ḥadith*

The other significant element in understanding the rise of the Shīʿa is the observation that the Shīʿa have a distinct body of *ḥadīth* material, much of it traced back to or through the early leaders of the Shīʿī community or, at the very least, containing variants compared to the Sunnī community's versions.[4] In its written form, this material started to emerge during the ninth century. Given the function of the *ḥadīth* in Islam in general, the existence of a separate body of material indicates that the central matter of dispute causing the separation of the Sunnī community and the Shīʿa was one of ultimate authority in the community as a whole and within each group separately. In the early unified community, the caliph appears to have had complete authority, as was discussed earlier in Chapter 4. With the rise of the learned classes in the eighth century, the disputes over authority became more pronounced. The Sunnī community with its trust placed in fixed written sources of authority emerged, leaving what became the Shīʿī group continuing to hold to authority vested in an individual.

The authority of the Shīʿī Imām

This understanding of the development of authority makes sense of what is the most prominent and distinct element in the Shīʿa, and that is the person of the Imām. Designated by Muhammad, ʿAlī was the first Imām for the Shīʿa; this was seen as the designation of a spiritual position, not one of temporal power, and thus the inability of the Imāms in later times to seize power within the community was of no particular concern to their followers. The function of the Imām was to guide his followers by explaining and clarifying the divine law, as well as to direct those believers in the inner spiritual path of Islam. This he was able to do because of his close connection to God, facilitated by *ilhām*, "inspiration," (as distinct from *waḥy*, "revelation," which is the mode through which scripture is produced) and the knowledge passed on to him by the one who designated him. God's mercy and justice indicate that there can never be a time when the world is without an Imām, for, if that were so, people would have no guidance and there would be no proof available of God's beneficence towards His creation. The Imām is thus

termed the *ḥujja*, "proof," and *hādī*, "guide." The people who were
to be Imāms were designated by God from the beginning of creation,
and were even viewed as pre-existent in the form of primordial light
according to some mystically flavoured interpretations. They are, as
a consequence of these ideas, seen as sinless and the best of all
creation. The actual existence of an Imām is to be taken as part of
God's beneficence towards humanity, for he facilitates the salvation
of God's creation by providing a sure guide in the world and a certain
answer to issues of dispute.

The most prominent branch of the Shī'a, known as the "Twelvers"
(in Arabic *Ithnā 'ashariyya*) or more generically as the Imāmīs, iden-
tifies a chain of twelve men through whom the line of authority
passed in the formative centuries of Islam. These people were designated by their predecessors and their birth was generally pictured
as accompanied by various miraculous signs, confirming this designation. That the clear delineation of this line was, up to a certain
point, *ex post facto* would appear likely and is even evidenced by
mid-tenth-century Shī'ī sources who speak of people in their community being unsure of the identity of the Imām. It will only have been
when the need for authority emerged within the community that the
tracing back of a chain of authority (as in the *isnād* of a *ḥadīth*)
would have actually been necessary. The established line of the
twelve Imāms is as follows:

'Alī ibn abī Ṭālib, d. 661
Ḥasan, his son, d. 669
Ḥusayn, 'Alī's second son, d. 680
Zayn al-'Ābidīn, his son, d. 712 or 713
Muḥammad al-Bāqir, his son, d. 735 (?)
Ja'far al-Ṣādiq, his son, d. 765
Mūsā al-Kāẓim, his son, d. 799
'Alī al-Riḍā, his son, d. 818
Muḥammad al-Taqī al-Jawād, his son, d. 835
'Alī al-Hādī, his son, d. 868
Ḥasan al-'Askarī, his son, d. 873 or 874
Muḥammad al-Mahdī, his son, born 868

The formation of the Shī'a

Ja'far al-Ṣādiq appears to have been the pivotal figure through whom
the Shī'a actually came into existence as a religious movement. Up
to that point, the best that one may suppose is that rival groups,

whose primary focus was in the political arena, existed in the community; some of these groups saw their right to rule traced back to ʿAlī. As with the emergence of the whole system of Islam itself, the particular elements manifested in the Shīʿa took time to evolve, even though the sources themselves wish to project the origins back to the earliest period. The rise of the Abbasid caliphate, making its appeal to persons in sympathy with the rights of ʿAlī, would coincide with the dates of Jaʿfar al-Ṣādiq. It is with the sixth Imām and his designated successor, Mūsā al-Kāzim, that the incipient notions of the Imamate would appear to have originated, based on the information provided by various heresiographical works and Shīʿī tradition itself, which sees Jaʿfar as the formative spokesman. One crucial element here is the establishment of a procedure for the designation of the Imām, rather than that person being determined by a process of battle; the Shīʿī platform can then defend a quiescent attitude despite a lineage which would suggest a need to usurp rule in the world; this also had the effect of cutting off a tendency towards proliferation of rival claimants to the position of Imām. Another crucial element was the Imām's receipt of esoteric knowledge passed on from the previous Imām. Regardless of these early elements, it is only in the time of the twelfth Imām that we actually have any Shīʿī sources which provide us with detailed information on the Shiʿa and their beliefs, and it is clear that it is in the post-twelfth Imām period that the Shīʿa as we know it today actually came into being.[5]

The occultation of the last Imām

The twelfth Imām is said to have disappeared and to have entered into his "lesser occultation," being hidden from the view of the world. He designated a series of four persons (in parallel to the first four caliphs perhaps) to whom he communicated his commands; this situation lasted from 874 until 941. He then entered into his "greater occultation" in which condition he no longer communicates with the world. This notion of occultation is a necessary consequence of the line of Imāms ending at a particular point in history. If humanity cannot be without an Imām and the line of Imāms has ended, then the last Imām cannot be dead but must be alive; otherwise, a substitute for him must exist. Known as the *ghayba*, the occultation will last until God determines its end. The return of the twelfth Imām in the role of the messianic Mahdī is awaited; this will occur shortly before the day of judgement. At that time, he will be manifested on earth and will lead the righteous into battle against the forces of evil. Finally, good will triumph over evil, and the Imām will subsequently rule over the world in a period of peace.[6]

The notion that there should be twelve Imāms and that the twelfth should permanently "disappear" took some time to solidify within the Shī'a. Certainly authors writing at the time of the twelfth Imām appear to have expected the line to continue beyond him. Although they admitted that at the time he was "hiding," he was clearly expected to show himself once again. Indeed, the presence of the Imām as a "proof" and a "guidance" was deemed essential and was the major element in polemic against the Sunnī schools whom the Shī'a felt were adrift with no guidance. It would appear to be the case, however, that other Shī'ī groups had already developed the notions of a limited chain of Imāms and of the last one "disappearing." All that was really happening, then, was that the Imāmī group was employing already circulating ideas as an explanation of events taking place in their "twelver-Shī'ī" line. By the time of the Shī'ī writer al-Kulaynī (d. *c.* 941), the idea of there being a line of twelve Imāms was established, although, for the rest of the century, authors still found it necessary to compose works which would explain and defend this notion of an occulted Imām. Arguments in favour of there being a line of only twelve Imāms were found in Quranic references to the number twelve (e.g. twelve months in the year, Qur'ān 9/36) and in Shī'ī and Sunnī traditions which talk of Muḥammad naming twelve successors, which in Sunnī sources are found in texts written in a period before the occultation of the twelfth Imām and perhaps reflect notions regarding "twelve" as a number symbolic of restoration, fulfilment and authority as in the twelve tribes of Israel and the twelve disciples of Jesus.[7]

There seem to be political reasons lying behind the idea of the "disappearance" of the twelfth Imām which account for it becoming a successful doctrine in Shī'ī circles. As long as the Imām was physically present in the world, he represented a threat, albeit ineffectual, to the ruling powers. The Shī'a found themselves virtually always persecuted under the rule of the Abbasids. Removing the worldly reality of the Imām, after enduring some one hundred years of Abbasid rule, was a way of securing a continued existence for the group, but also may be linked to a growing sense of material prosperity among certain groups of Shī'īs which they were unwilling to forego.[8] Cooperation with the ruling powers was far easier without the Imām present, but believing in his "occultation" meant that one's loyalty to him did not have to diminish; cooperation with the rulers brought power as well as a more comfortable existence, something which took place under the pro-Shī'ī Buwayhids and clearly separated political and religious dimensions of existence. The Shī'ī doctrine of *taqiyya* ("religious dissimulation"), by which it was considered acceptable to conceal one's true allegiance in the face of adversity, fitted in with this situation and attitude. It is likely also that, as with Sunnī Islam, a rise in the status and power of the *'ulamā'*, the scholarly classes, put pressure on the Imām whose actual presence proved inconvenient for the learned classes and their expectations and aspirations. As well, for all practical purposes, by the time of the twelfth Imām, the *'ulamā'* had taken over positions of effective authority anyway, the Imām himself generally being kept out of contact with the vast majority of his followers; it was dangerous for the Imām to be in public view, due to his political pretensions. The authority of the learned classes after the *ghayba* resided in the basis of their knowledge of the traditions transmitted by the Imāms. Thus the emergence of the books of *ḥadīth* at approximately the time of the lesser occultation is to be expected.

Shī'ī theology

Much of developed Shī'ī theology follows that of the Mu'tazila, discussed in Chapter 5 above, with a few crucial differences. It is significant to note that, in a sense, the Shī'a represents a re-emergence of Mu'tazilī thought which appears to have lost much of its popular appeal in the Sunnī world in the preceding century or so. The significance and meaning of the Imamate were the major factors which separated the Mu'tazila and the Shī'a. Further significant differences are really a consequence of this stance. One of the Imām's functions is to intercede on behalf of his followers in the hereafter; this function runs counter to the Mu'tazilī insistence on "the punishment and the threat" as applying to all persons, consistent with their perception of the justice of God. Likewise, for the Shī'a, there can be no "intermediate position," that of the hypocrite, applicable to those who appear to sin in their actions but declare their belief; those who declare their allegiance to the Imām are quite clearly members of the community and must be accepted as such. Other than these elements, the theological doctrines are familiar: belief in divine unity and justice, in the role of prophethood and the bringing of the law by sinless prophets, and in the resurrection at the end of time.

The Shī'a did not always hold this theological position, however; the debates in the post-*ghayba* period clearly show an evolution from a tradition-based system to a more fully rationalistic one. Prior to that, however, in the very early period, the information regarding the situation is even less clear and provides at least some evidence of an even greater measure of shift in theological doctrine. However, the fact of the matter remains that there are no sources which can be trusted to be fully reliable, to give us information on the doctrinal stance of the Shīʿa prior to the tenth century. Some scholars have made the suggestion that any sources internal to the group itself suffered destruction at the hands of the later Shīʿa who found the early doctrines unacceptable. The degree to which these early doctrines were contrary to later ones is suggested, perhaps, by Sunnī sources, specifically al-Khayyāṭ (writing around 882) and al-Ashʿarī (writing around 912). The doctrines of these early groups, dubbed the *ghulāt*, "the exaggerators," included notions of transmigration of souls, an anthropomorphic conception of God, God's willing of the evil deeds of humanity, and the possibility of alteration in God's will. At one point, it is also held that some believed in the absolute divine nature of the Imām, although the later Sunnī sources perhaps reflect the lessening of this doctrine for they no longer make that accusation. The trouble here is that the Sunnī sources are clearly polemical in tone and approach, and the items of doctrine with which the *ghulāt* are associated are precisely those items which bring about the greatest reprobation from the Sunnī schools; to represent these doctrines as being held by the largest Shīʿī school at the time may well be a case of attempting to mislead deliberately.

Ibn Babawayh

By the tenth century, when the Buwayhid dynasty took over in Baghdad and made the Abbasid caliph simply a tributary to the ruler, the Shīʿa had become a political force and a clearer picture of its theological stance starts to emerge. Ibn Babawayh (d. 991) appears to have been one of the leading figures in this movement. He wrote against the notion of anthropomorphism – which certainly suggests that some Shīʿīs still held to such doctrines – and, by the end of his life, also seemed convinced that humanity has a degree of free will under God's law:

> "Our belief concerning human actions is that they are created ..., in the sense that Allah possesses foreknowledge ..., and not in the sense that Allah compels mankind to act in a particular manner by creating a certain disposition. ... And the meaning of this is that Allah has never ceased to be aware of the potentialities ... of human beings."[9]

At an earlier stage of his life, however, Ibn Babawayh held to a firmer predestinarian position. What marks all of his works is a reliance on tradition rather than reason and a total rejection of the stance of *kalām* ("The partisans of the *kalām* will perish and the Muslims will be saved");[10] this is similar to the stance of al-Ashʿarī in the Sunnī world who was reacting to the full force of Muʿtazilī doctrine. Ibn Babawayh, on the other hand, came before the major impact of Muʿtazilī thought among the Shīʿa, although some tendency in the direction of rationalism is to be noted in writers from earlier in the tenth century.

Later theologians

Muʿtazilī theology proper came into the Shīʿa through the work of al-Shaykh al-Mufīd (d. 1022), al-Sharīf al-Murtaḍā (d. 1044) and al-Ṭūsī (d. 1067). While the basis for the particulars of the Muʿtazilī position was already firmly established in the Shīʿa (and, some would say, was there since the time of Jaʿfar al-Ṣādiq), it is these authors who emphasized the use of reason in support of the doctrine, seeing the need to defend the religion on that basis. Al-Shaykh al-Mufīd argues for a less radical type of Muʿtazilī stance than some of the later authors; he avoids saying that people are the actual "creators" of their own acts and that the Qurʾān is created. Rather, he says that the Qurʾān "originated in time" and acts are "produced" or "made." God's actions in the world are always in the best interests of humanity (this being provided as an explanation of evil in the world). Overall, al-Shaykh al-Mufīd attempted to avoid going beyond what he sees as the limits of Quranic phraseology in enunciating his theology.[11]

With the later authors, the position became more radical, with reason becoming the basis of all doctrine rather than being the tool by which authoritative doctrine could be defended and enhanced, as it was for al-Shaykh al-Mufīd. Al-Murtaḍā may best be thought of as the Shīʿī al-Ashʿarī in the sense that his writings became the basis for all later Shīʿī exposition of theology, being the virtually unquestioned source.

Why the Shīʿa adopted this rationalist position in theology would appear to be connected to the need for authority. While the Imām was in the world, the source of authority for the Shīʿī community was clear: it was the Imām; being an authoritative source was the very purpose of his presence in the world. The Sunnīs were, in the Shīʿī view, reduced to mere conjecture on all elements of their religion. With the *ghayba* of the twelfth Imām, authority first came through the series of four representatives who were able to put questions to the Imām and bring back answers. With the greater occultation, however, this could no longer happen, although the appearance of the Imām to a worthy individual, either in reality or in a dream, was at least held to be possible. In the absence of the Imām, then, authority was in the hands of the learned classes. But this was no better than the Sunnī position, which the Shī'a had criticized for having no sound basis. Mu'tazilī theology provided a way around this problem, by suggesting that reason alone could provide the certitude which is required. Deduction based on reason, therefore, rather than tradition as used by the Sunnīs, was the ideal replacement for the Imām, whose rulings would only conform to the laws of reason anyway. As the line of Shī'ī thought developed, al-Murtaḍā argued that reason could prove the necessity of the existence of the Imām in the first place, providing the proof for the key element of Shī'ī thought that the Mu'tazila lacked. He argued that the office of the Imām was necessary and that "[t]he way to prove its necessity is reason, contrary to the doctrine of the Mu'tazilites and their like. It is necessary only for bringing those who are under moral obligation close to what is for their interests and for keeping them far from what is harmful."[12]

Shī'ī legal thought and practice

In the legal field, a late development is quite clear also, as in theology. The tenth-century work by al-Kulaynī, *al-Kāfī fī 'Ilm al-Dīn* ("The Sufficient in the Knowledge of Religion"), marks a pivotal point in the emergence of defined Shī'ī law. This work gathers together traditions, either from the Imāms or from Muḥammad and transmitted through the Imāms, which serve as the basis for all discussions (both legal and theological) in this period. The writing of the book is significant and contains, by its very composition, a polemical element. The book clearly wants to argue that the Imām in the world is no more. No longer can that source of authority be utilized, and the Shī'a, like the Sunnīs, must turn to written sources to substantiate their position. The writing of a work such as al-Kulaynī's marks a stage in the emergence of the Shī'a in which the learned classes, who had control of the sources, were starting to assert their authority; in such a way, it was ensured that any potential claimants to the position of the Imām were effectively silenced. Al-Kulaynī's book is one of four, the others written by Ibn Babawayh and al-Ṭūsī (the latter having two to his credit), which are considered the counter-parts to the six authoritative collections of *ḥadīth* in the Sunnī world. Without the Imām, or his representatives, in the world, the specific duties assigned to him were said to be lapsed. These included leading the holy war (*jihād*), division of booty of war, leading the Friday prayer, putting juridical decisions into effect, imposing legal penalties, and receiving the religious taxes.[13] The absence of the Imām left the community leaderless, and it fell to al-Tūsī in the eleventh century to enunciate a theory of juridical authority being in the hands of those knowledgeable in jurisprudence, the *fuqahā'*. Even then, the role of the jurists was limited and it took several centuries and a number of other theorists to develop a more encompassing theory; it was only in the sixteenth century that the *fuqahā'* took over all the duties of the occulted Imām, with the exception of offensive *jihād* which, it was determined, could only be undertaken by the Imām himself.[14]

The absoluteness of this delegation of the authority of the Imām was tempered by the theological speculation over the return of the twelfth Imām. This expected return, though, was of little practical concern to the jurists whose role was to create a legal system with no reference to a living Imām, only to one who existed theologically.[15]

The actual theoretical development of the principles of Shī'ī jurisprudence was, for the most part, late in being written (fourteenth to sixteenth centuries), at least in comparison with the much earlier Sunnī development. To some extent, therefore, the Shī'a depended upon the principles already enunciated within Sunnī thought in order to develop the legal basis of their society; the differences between the two are, as a result, quite slight. The Shī'a, in this view, are little more than another legal school, parallel to the four major Sunnī schools. Minor differences occur in the prayer ritual and the fast of Ramaḍān, but these are precisely of a nature which would be seen as a variation between schools of law. Friday noon prayer is not as important to the Shī'a because of the absence of the Imām who is supposed to lead that prayer, although this became a problem of some seriousness in juridical discussions. Various practices are enjoined such as visiting the tombs of the Imāms, and these visits are conducted with extensive rituals on a par with those of the *ḥajj*.

There are, of course, some significant differences between Sunnī and Shī'ī practices. The phenomenon of "temporary marriage," *mut'a*, considered to be referred to in Qur'ān 4/24, is specifically forbidden in the Sunnī world, where any limit put on the length of a marriage makes a marriage contract null and void.[16] Divorce and inheritance laws also vary. Most striking is a different form of the *shahāda* employed at some points in Shīʿī history. The phrase, "I testify that ʿAlī is the *walī* ['friend'] of God" is added to the two-part Sunnī witness to faith; this is, however, a fairly late addition, mention of it not being made in the earliest texts of Shīʿī law other than that of Ibn Babawayh, who condemns its usage. The sixteenth century saw arguments in favour of its employment, urged probably by the political aims of the rulers at that time, the Safavids, who instituted the Shīʿī position as the state religion of Iran in 1501. The argument for the basis of the statement as opposed to its ritual employment, however, is to be found quite early in Shīʿī thought, for example in al-Kulaynī who argues that the belief in the *wilāya* of ʿAlī is a fundamental tenet of the Shīʿa, and that the belief simply in "There is no god but God and Muḥammad is the messenger of God" is not sufficient to ensure salvation; clearly, the third element of the testimony is needed in the belief of the individual, even if in this early period it was not actually part of the ritual repetition of the *shahāda*.[17]

Additionally, Ibn Babawayh reports the following tradition about Fāṭima bint Asad, the mother of ʿAlī. Muḥammad is quoted as saying that immediately after her death, "She was asked about her Lord, and she said, 'My Lord is Allāh'. And she was asked about her Prophet and she replied, 'Muḥammad'. And she was asked about her Imām and *walī* and she faltered and paused. And I said to her, 'Thy son, thy son'. So she said, 'My Imām is my son'. Thereupon they [the two questioning angels who appear to everyone after death] departed from her and said, 'We have no power over you . . .'."[18] Undoubtedly, it was the pressure of Sunnī condemnation which did not allow this statement to enter the Shīʿī *shahāda* from the very beginning and it was only after many centuries that it was actually approved under more propitious political circumstances.

A prominent celebration which is not found in the Sunnī world revolves around the commemoration of the death of Ḥusayn, the son of ʿAlī. Culminating on the tenth day of the first month of the year, Muḥarram, the day of 'Ashurā', it observes the day of the death of Ḥusayn and his followers which took place at the hands of the forces of the Umayyad ruler Yazīd. This occurred in the year 680. Martyrdom to the cause of the party of ʿAlī became the operative motif in understanding Ḥusayn's death and the celebration of this became the central event of the Shīʿī religious calendar. Visitation of sacred places, especially the tomb of Ḥusayn in Karbala, play an important role in the celebrations on this day.[19] Generally, these ritual differences between the Shīʿa and the Sunnīs have gained symbolic value for the Shīʿa in terms of providing a distinct (and, implicitly, correct) religious identity, especially in times of political antagonism with the Sunnī world.[20]

Variants of the Shīʿa

Given that a fundamental notion among the Shīʿa was the necessity of the identification of an Imām in each generation, it is hardly surprising that rival claimants appeared at various points in history. We thus see the emergence of several branches within the Shīʿa, each of which differed over the line of descent of authority at a certain historical moment. The Ismāʿīlīs, Zaydīs and Druze (Durūz in Arabic) are three such prominent groups. Some of these splits account for their origins in terms of differences over political strategy. The Zaydīs, for example, picture their origins in armed revolt against the Umayyad rulers. They were formed as a group in support of Zayd ibn ʿAlī, a grandson of Ḥusayn ibn ʿAlī, who was defeated and killed in 740. While in certain situations these small offshoots of the Shīʿa have proven politically volatile, throughout a good portion of the history they have been politically quiescent, looking forward to the end of time and the return of the Mahdī. This simply goes along with the doctrine of the occultation of the Imām when faced with the political realities of the historical situation.

9   Ṣūfī devotion

The question of the origins of Sufism (*taṣawwuf*), the mystical aspect within Islam, and its devotees, the Ṣūfīs, seems to have attracted its own particular type of dispute within the academic study of Islam. The reason for this dispute would appear to go back once again to a memory of medieval (and later) polemic between Christians and Muslims. Christians have often pictured Islam as a very sensually-based religion: Muḥammad's multiple marriages, the Qur'ān's very physical and sensual portrayal of heaven and its rewards, and Islam's permitting of polygamy and enjoining holy war (*jihād*) have all been featured in these kinds of characterizations. At the same time, however, Christians have been very well aware of a profound ascetic-mystical trend in Islam. Abū Ḥamīd al-Ghazālī (d. 1111), for example, one of the most famous of all Ṣūfīs, became well known in the medieval West especially in his philosophic guise; this was true of a variety of other mystically-inspired writers also. In trying to reconcile the two natures perceived within Islam, the implicit suggestion given by some early writers on the subject was that the mystical trend could not be inherent in Islam but must have come from Christianity, a far more elevated religion in their view.

It is the case, then, that raising the question of the origins of Sufism today is no less controversial than the question of the origins of the entire religion of Islam, because behind the questions lies the aura, if not the attitude, of medieval polemic. To suggest that Islamic mysticism is, in fact, a borrowing from outside raises the spectre of the denial of the intrinsically spiritual nature of Islam and thence of the spiritual nature of Muslims themselves.

The question of origins here is two-fold. The basic point, much argued by Ṣūfīs themselves in their search for legitimization of their spiritual quest, is whether Islam as a religion contained within itself a spiritual-ascetic tendency from the very beginning; that is, does

Islam inherently see that the mystical way (defined, for the time being, as the quest for some intimacy with God as induced through certain practices of a meditative, repetitive or self-denying nature) is the ideal life that should be aimed for? From the Islamic perspective, is that lifestyle inherently pleasing to God?

The second issue is one concerning the origins of Sufism itself. Regardless of where the original spiritual-ascetic impulse came from, were the practices, aspirations and the mode of expression used by the Ṣūfīs elements developed within Islam or were they the result of influences from another source (be that Christian, Indian, Iranian or whatever) and adapted to an Islamic style?

The source of Sufism in Islam

The problem with answering the first question is, of course, one of interpretation. How do we judge an issue such as "inherent asceticism"? Some would say that a basic world-denying attitude is a part of Judaism, Christianity, and Islam, especially because the overall tradition has been influenced by the radical dualism of Manichaeism with its distrust of the material world. This attitude is difficult to reconcile, however, with the picture of Islam and Judaism especially as "nomocratic," where a very practical attitude towards life in the here and now, as manifested in the law, is a prime characteristic of the religion. The other aspect of the problem is the common one found in all elements of the origins of Islam and that is the lack of contemporary sources. There simply are no ascertainably early sources which give us a glimpse of a spiritual-ascetic lifestyle from before the ninth century, in common with the lack of documentary evidence for the beginnings of Islam in general.

Muslim arguments on the subject revolve around the citation of the Qur'ān and elements of the *ḥadīth* and the *Sīra*, the life story of Muḥammad, which indicate the possibility of, if not the positive encouragement and enactment of, the ascetic ideal. This approach fully answers the question from the internal Muslim perspective. The Qur'ān and Muḥammad, as Ṣūfīs have always said, support the mystical quest. Statements concerning God are popularly cited, for example, Qur'ān 2/186, "Whenever My servants ask you about Me, I am near to answer the call of the caller," and Qur'ān 50/16, "We [God] are closer to him [humanity] than his jugular vein!" Looking inward, therefore, becomes the goal and the quest, although Qur'ān 2/115, "wherever you may turn, there is the face of God," adds another dimension to the quest. The wandering way of life of the early ascetic is supported in Qur'ān 29/20, "Travel in the land and see how He began creation." Qur'ān 9/123 asserts, "God is with the godfearing" whose way of life is echoed in the Quranic refrain to remember God always (for example Qur'ān 33/41, "You who believe, remember God often"). The "light verse," Qur'ān 24/35, is the most famous of all verses for Ṣūfī speculation and its very presence in the Qur'ān is often claimed to be proof of the need for the mystic way:

God is the light of the heavens and the earth. The likeness of His light is as a niche in which there is a lamp; the lamp is in a glass; the glass is just as if it were a glittering star kindled from a blessed tree, an olive neither Eastern nor Western, whose oil will almost glow though the fire has never touched it. Light upon light, God guides His light to anyone He wishes.

As for Muḥammad, his whole experience of revelation and his preparation towards receiving it are seen as models for the ascetic life and its product. This is also true of other Quranic figures, especially Moses and al-Khiḍr whose stories, as told in *sūra* 18, have been elaborated into accounts of the mystic quest. Many of the traditions about Muḥammad most favoured by the Ṣūfīs are not to be found in the major *ḥadīth* collections, generally having been rejected by the collectors as unsound, but the Ṣūfīs kept their traditions going among their own circles. Many aphorisms are found on Muḥammad's lips which are applicable to the Ṣūfī quest, and Muḥammad is also portrayed as following an ascetic way of life. The latter traditions found their way into works such as the *Kitāb al-Zuhd* ("The Book of Ascetic Practices") of Ibn Ḥanbal (d. 855), the eponym of the legal school, who is often seen as a supporter of the early ascetic movement. Poverty especially became an ideal espoused by Muḥammad. For example, Ibn Ḥanbal cites the tradition from ʿĀ'isha who "was asked what the Messenger of God did in his house. She replied, 'He patched clothes, fixed sandals, and did similar things'." ʿĀ'isha also reported that when Muḥammad died, "he did not leave a dinar or a dirham, nor any sheep or cattle, nor did he bequeath anything."[1]

Even more productive for the Ṣūfīs has been the story of the *miʿrāj*, Muḥammad's night journey (based around Qur'ān 17/1), which is seen as a tale of the supreme mystical experience to which every mystic aspires. While the basic account is found in all orthodox sources about Muḥammad, starting in germ form in Muḥammad's early biographer Ibn Isḥāq, the Ṣūfī understanding and interpretation of the account are, of course, unique.[2] The emphasis frequently falls on the role of the journey as a prophetic initiation, leading the way for all mystics after Muḥammad to journey to their own union with the divine presence, not as prophets but as saints or "friends of God."

Interestingly, there is a marked anti-ascetic tendency within the Sunnī books of *ḥadīth*, especially focusing on the rejection of Christian monasticism. For example, these reports are often used in Islam to support the notion that even Ṣūfīs should marry. Other such elements include a rejection of forty-day food restrictions and pleas against poverty (even to the point of denying excessive charity).[3] Most of this material can be seen as anti-Christian in tendency and as reflecting the tension Muslims felt over the status of ascetic tendencies in early Islam.

However, all of this attention to the Qur'ān, *sīra* and *ḥadīth* on the part of the Ṣūfīs simply indicates that they have, like all other Muslims, always gone back to the prime sources of Islam for inspiration as well as justification of their position; in that way they are no different from the jurists in the quest to define the law as closely as possible, for example. For modern historians to take "objective" facts from this type of material and attempt to reconstruct a picture of mystical trends in early Islam is to commit the error of anachronistic reading of texts; one is clearly looking at the texts through the eyes of later people and we learn nothing from them of the earliest meaning given to these sources. The most that may be concluded from this part of the discussion, therefore, is simply to say that Muslims have found the life story of Muḥammad and the Qur'ān itself to be vital sources in their mystical quest. One would not want to discount the possibility that even the early versions of the biography (*sīra*) of Muḥammad have been affected by early mystics and thus reflect some of their concerns and desires, as is reflected also in the *ḥadīth* literature with its books devoted to *zuhd*, asceticism, as practiced by Muḥammad. That the Qur'ān might, in fact, contain such ascetic elements is a possibility that needs to be entertained; however, whether the pieces of the Qur'ān which suggest this background were always understood that way by Muslims, and where those pieces of the Qur'ān actually originated, are vexing questions which still must be faced by scholarship.

Sources of Ṣūfī practice

The solution to this first aspect of the problem of the origins of Sufism, then, would seem to be to put aside the questions about the inherent spiritual asceticism of Islam and perhaps simply admit that the understanding of the nature of God as contained within the Judeo–Christian–Muslim tradition is one which is potentially amenable to the mystical way of life. There only remains, then, the second question of the development of what we may truly call Sufism in Islam, the influences upon it and its role in the emergence of Islam. For the early period there is the major problem of definition, of how to determine for example, whether Ibn Ḥanbal should be considered a Ṣūfī or simply an ascetic Muslim, given his encouragement of that way of life. That he should have combined this role with one of the upholding of traditionalism is significant, of course; one of his works which displays ascetic tendencies is the above-mentioned *Kitāb al-Zuhd*, a collection of traditions about the life of Muḥammad. Indeed, for the earliest period, this emphasis on asceticism is the primary element that one can isolate with certainty as the forerunner of the later mystical way. The evidence suggests that it was in the early to mid-ninth century that these sorts of tendencies found their expression in written form; it was only later in that century that this became combined with speculative thought, producing as a result a true system of mysticism which may accurately and meaningfully be called Sufism. The dating of this era for the emergence of Sufism is confirmed within juridical works, where the disdain for the ascetic way of life is displayed and a resultant attempt on the part of the jurists to restrict its scope can clearly be seen; the end of the eighth and early ninth centuries appears to be the era for the greatest disputes on this matter.[4]

Certainly the influence of Christianity on the foundation of asceticism in Islam is clear in some of the earliest writings. Al-Muḥāsibī (d. 857), for example, has been shown[5] to have borrowed heavily from the New Testament for various sayings and commendations of the Ṣūfī way of life. As well, the practice of wearing woollen garments called *ṣūf*, by means of which it is popularly believed that the term "Ṣūfī" (meaning "those who wear rough woollen garments") was coined, is said to have been done in imitation of Christian hermits; this was done in order to serve as an indication of poverty as well as being an ascetic practice in and by itself.

The development of a mystical litany was also a part of the early enunciation of the movement. Termed *dhikr*, the practice was connected by the Ṣūfīs to the Quranic injunction to "mention God often" as in Qur'ān 33/21. The developed form of this litany consists of the constant repetition of various phrases, often *lā ilāh^a illā 'llāh*, "There is no god but God." This practice serves as the focal point of devotions for virtually every Ṣūfī group.[6] Christian modes of worship once again may have provided some of the impetus for this particular element.

Doctrinally, the early mystics are held to have been devoted to the notion of *tawakkul*, "total trust" in God. The characteristics are complete indifference to the world and its affairs and a full dependence upon God supplying the needs of the individual; this attitude was said to demonstrate one's total trust in the power and mercy of God who will supply those needs. A total lack of possessions and deprivation of any bodily comforts were the mark of such a person. This trend is often seen to have been influenced by Christianity also, that being a tendency of monasticism in the church.

Given the geographical contexts in which Islamic asceticism is generally seen to have emerged – Baghdad, in the environment of the Christian heritage, and Khurasan, a former Buddhist centre – it is not surprising that elements of various religions, especially Christianity as the above examples show, should be present; little would seem to be gained by denying it. However, it has frequently been pointed out that the ascetic lifestyle in Islam developed with a certain overt political motivation. Once again in Islam, a religious position appears to have been used as a rallying point for rebellion against the ruling powers. The whole early ascetic inclination is frequently pictured as a renunciation and rejection of the political strife in the formative Islamic period. The early mystics were the true Muslims who held onto the Islamic spirit in face of the manipulation of the religion by the ruling powers for their own purposes. The emphasis on *tawakkul* would be pictured in marked contrast to the efforts of all other Muslims to secure their places on earth rather than in heaven, at least from the perspective of the mystics. Al-Ḥasan al-Baṣrī (d. 728), famous for his role in the theological debates discussed in Chapter 5, emerges in the literature as one of the central figures of this type of spirituality, going to the extent of denying the value of existence in this world and speaking of the hereafter as the realm free of the contamination of political self-interest. Revolutionary involvement in the political arena was not sanctioned by al-Ḥasan al-Baṣrī, even if that could have meant replacing an unjust ruler by a pious one; the slow persuasion of rulers was about the best that could be hoped for in the effort to improve the lot of all Muslims in the community.

Overall, then, the argument certainly can be made for "foreign influences" on the development of Sufism but, without a doubt, modern scholarship sees the internal tensions of the Muslim community as crucial in the emergence of early ascetic tendencies.

Development of Sufism

The ninth century was marked by a rapid progression of mystics, each famous for adding a certain element to the emergent mystical viewpoint and creating the central tenets of Sufism. Under the influence of neo-Platonism, at least according to some writers, mystical doctrines of the love of God, the beatific vision of the mystical experience, gnosis as the goal of the experience, the image of the mystical ascension, the absorption into God and the theory of the mystical states are all seen to emerge.

Al-Junayd (d. 910), a pupil of al-Muḥāsibī, is often given the credit for establishing a true system of mystical speculation, bringing together the insights of his predecessors and creating a lasting system for all subsequent generations. He is credited with the elaboration of the doctrine of *fanā'*, the goal of the mystic in "dying in one's self," "passing away" or "absorption" into God, supported by the Quranic, "All that is on the earth will disappear while your Lord's face abides, majestic, splendid" (Qur'ān 55/26–7). The mystic quest is based on the need to return to God, the state in which humanity was before creation. *Baqā'*, the "continuance," is the existence of the mystic after *fanā'*, when he or she lives in God. Al-Junayd combined this goal with an ethical theory which demanded of the mystic who has reached the state of "absorption" a return to society; this was so that the individual would make clear "the evidence of [God's] grace to him, so that the lights of His gifts in the return of his individual characteristics scintillate and attract the community to him who appreciate him."[7] This meant, for al-Junayd, that the Ṣūfī had the responsibility to return to his community life and fulfil all the obligations of Muslim existence; the knowledge of the individual's absorption into the divine remains a "secret treasure" which shines through the person in everything done in the world.

Al-Ḥallāj

Contemporary with al-Junayd was al-Ḥallāj (d. 922) who, likewise, was convinced of the necessity of the mystic quest, but who was condemned to death for the blasphemy of considering that individuals could recognize their God-nature through mystical experience. Stories relate that al-Ḥallāj proclaimed, "I am the Truth," which was taken to mean that he felt himself actually to be God incarnate in the world. Such Ṣūfīs (another early example is al-Bisṭāmī, d. 875) have come to be termed "intoxicated" as compared to the "sober" mysticism of al-Junayd, for they had become so overcome by the mystical experience that existence, as such, had no meaning to them; their utterances became the focal point of their understanding of their experiences and vice versa.[8] The ethical aspect of al-Junayd's doctrine became submerged within their experiences.

Later developments

These authors were only starting to develop a truly systematic picture of Sufism; it fell to authors such as Abū Naṣr al-Sarrāj (d. 988) in the following century to construct general accounts of Sufism, its history, and its meaning in the Islamic context. Al-Sarrāj wrote in his *Kitāb al-Lumaʿ* of the legitimacy of Ṣūfī practice, based upon the precedent of Muḥammad and his companions. With this, he combined a great deal of definitional material in an attempt to distil the essence of the mystical path as it existed in his time. He states, for example,

> The meaning of "passing away" and "continuance" ... is the passing away of ignorance into the abiding condition of knowledge and the passing away of disobedience into the abiding state of obedience, and the passing away of indifference into the state of continual worship, and the passing away of the consideration of the actions of the servant, which are temporary, into the vision of the Divine Grace, which is the eternal.[9]

The eleventh century brought greater systematization to the theoretical basis of Sufism in the writings of al-Qushayrī (d. 1072). Writing in 1046, al-Qushayrī was concerned with demonstrating that Sufism was not in conflict with Sunnī Islam. Part of this proof was provided by the biography of many prominent Ṣūfīs. He also presented a picture of the theory of the stations through which a Ṣūfī passes on his or her mystic quest and the states which God may grace the mystic with during that quest. Such had already been detailed by al-Sarrāj before him, but al-Qushayrī added further detail to the schema. Forty-five terms are used to describe the quest, starting with *tawba*, "repentance," which is seen as the manifestation of the conscious desire to follow the mystic way, through "patience," "constant awareness of God," and "satisfaction with God," culminating in "gnosis," "love," and "yearning to be with God."[10]

Abu Ḥamīd al-Ghazālī used the basis established by earlier Ṣūfī theorists for promoting the assimilation of Sufism into orthodoxy in developing his own arguments; his magnum opus, *Iḥyāʾ ʿUlūm al-Dīn*, the "Revivification of the Religious Sciences," written between 1099 and 1102, tried to accomplish just what its title suggests: bring life back into the orthodox "religious sciences" through the inspiration of Sufism. In the process, Sufism itself would be seen to gain total legitimacy as being an essential part of the Islamic way of life. His work is divided into four sections. The first, worship, concentrates on the "inner meaning" of the rituals of Islam. The second, personal behaviour, sees the progression from religious law to mystical training as intimately linked. The third, deadly sins, details the discipline needed for the mystic quest. Finally, the fourth, the way to salvation, concentrates on the interpretation of spiritual experience. This progress in the life of the individual reflects al-Ghazālī's overall view of life and the mystic quest:

> If, then, you ask, What is the Beginning of Guidance in order that I may test my soul thereby? know that the beginning of guidance is outward piety and the end of guidance is inward piety. Only through piety is anything really achieved; only the pious are guided. Piety designates carrying out the commands of God most high and turning aside from what He prohibits . . .[11]

The Ṣūfī orders

The tendency towards increased intellectual support and systematization of Sufism was developed even further in the Ṣūfī orders which are based on the principle of the relationship between the master and the pupil. The authority of the master who has ascended through the stages of the mystic must be accepted wholly by the pupil, for only with guidance will the union with God be possible. The foundation of the *ṭarīqa*, the "way" or "path," and later coming to mean the "order" or "brotherhood," emerged as a way of providing a practical and structured way for the initiate to be guided through the stages of mystical experience. Beginning as an informal group, companionship with an acknowledged master was the focal point of the *ṭarīqa*. Groups emerged early on, centred in dwellings known as *ribāṭ*s, *khānqāh*s, *khalwa*s or *zāwiya*s, all meaning "Ṣūfī retreats" in one part or another of the Muslim world. Such retreats were not organized in any particular way, however; the participants simply wandered from one such place to another. In the eleventh century the institutionalized *ṭarīqa* movement received a boost with the Seljuq reorganization of the *madrasa*, the Islamic school, and the provision of support and supervision of Ṣūfī dwellings at the same time. This trend was encouraged even further by the success of al-Ghazālī's work in bringing Sufism into the fold of orthodoxy. The process culminated in the thirteenth century with the emergence of special centres of Ṣūfī training; focused on the activities and way of a single man, a centre would perpetuate the name, teaching, exercises and rule of life of that person. The *ṭarīqa* was handed down through the *isnād* or *silsila* of the *shaykh*, the leader of the order, passing on to the spiritual heirs of that person. The initiate swore allegiance to the *shaykh*, and thereby became linked to the spiritual chain. Often incorporated into these *silsila*s were famous Ṣūfīs of the past, such as al-Junayd and al-Bisṭāmī; the initial stage of the chain is frequently Muḥammad and from him ʿAlī, although this does not necessarily indicate any Shīʿī leanings on the part of the groups.

All such *ṭarīqa*s, formally at the very least, accept the law and ritual of orthodox Islam as binding. In this way, they provide a supplement to the Islamic way of life, rather than a true "alternative vision," although, obviously, their view of the true nature of Islam and its purpose is different from those who remain outside the *ṭarīqa*. The point remained, however, that in order for the *ṭarīqa*s to ensure their acceptance by orthodoxy (i.e. the jurists), the attention to the externals of Islamic life continued to be necessary.

The major *ṭarīqa*s in classical Islam were the Suhrawardiyya, the Qādiriyya, the Rifāʿiyya, the Yasawiyya, the Kubrāwiyya, the Čishtiyya, the Shādhiliyya, the Badawiyya, the Mawlawiyya and the Naqshbandiyya.[12] These groups trace their foundations to various persons who lived in the twelfth and thirteenth centuries.

The practices of the Ṣūfī orders

Taking the Qādiriyya as an example of the *ṭarīqa* phenomenon, one may see the role these institutions played in the fostering of the Ṣūfī attitude. ʿAbd al-Qādir al-Jīlānī, the *shaykh* of the movement, was born in Jilan in Persia in 1077 and went to Baghdad at the age of eighteen; there he became a popular preacher within the Ḥanbalī tradition at the age of about 50, and he died in 1166. There is no evidence that he ever consciously set out to form a Ṣūfī school, although the legends told in great profusion about his life certainly want to picture him as a Ṣūfī miracle worker. The following story is reported by a disciple of al-Jīlānī:

> Once, while I was still a young man, I entered the presence of Shaykh ʿAbd al-Qādir (may Allah be well pleased with him),

together with a large group. I had with me a book that dealt with questions of abstract philosophy and the speculative sciences of spirituality. As soon as we entered his presence, the Shaykh spoke to me – to me personally, not to the group as a whole – and before he had examined the book, or asked me about its contents, he said, "That book of yours is a bad companion. You had better go and give it a thorough wash!" I reacted to this by deciding to leave his presence, drop the book into some receptacle or other, and then refrain from carrying it with me after that, for fear of offending the Shaykh. My lower self could not accept the idea of giving it a wash, because I had developed quite a fondness for it, and some of its theories and principles had stimulated my intellectual curiosity. I was about to get up and leave, intending to carry out this plan of action, but the Shaykh gave me such a stare, like someone regarding me with incredulous amazement, that I simply could not get up. I felt trapped in a state of paralysis, but then he said to me, "Hand me that book of yours!" So I opened it, and lo and behold, there was nothing inside it but blank paper, with not a single letter written on it! I gave it to the Shaykh, and he thumbed through its pages, then he said, "This is 'The Book of the Excellent Merits of the Qur'ān' by Muḥamad Ibn al-Durays." When he handed it back to me, I saw that it was indeed that book, written in a most handsome calligraphic script! The Shaykh then said to me, "Are you ready to turn in repentance from saying with your tongue what is not in your heart?" I said, "Yes, O my master." So he told me to stand up. I obediently rose to my feet, and I had forgotten all about philosophy and the principles of spirituality! They had been totally erased from my inner being, as if they had never captured my interest.[13]

It was to the two sons of ʿAbd al-Qādir that the formation of the school actually fell and, by the year 1300, centres existed in Iraq and Syria, with the major expansion coming in the fifteenth century. ʿAbd al-Qādir himself is famed as a saint and the belief in his power of intercession is what has made the *ṭarīqa* a significant presence throughout the Islamic world.

The Qādiriyya's practices reflect the beliefs of the group itself but also the general Ṣūfī stance on the role of the master and the efficacy of various mystical practices. The initiation procedure contains the promise to "recite the *dhikr* in obedience to the dictates of the *shaykh*" and the *shaykh* accepts the initiate "as a son." The *dhikr* itself is recited by the group seated in front of the *shaykh* and repeated hundreds of times. The novice members repeat *lā ilāhᵃ illā 'llāh*, "there is no god but God," 165 times, while the more advanced members repeat a series of statements praising God and 'Abd al-Qādir 121 times, followed by 100 repetitions of *sūra* 36, forty-one repetitions of *sūra* 72, 121 repetitions of *sūra* 110, eight repetitions of *sūra* 1 and topped off by one recitation of *sūra* 112.[14] All this is done under the control of the *shaykh* at a pace which increases as it goes on, until individual members, potentially, have a mystic experience appropriate to the level of their spiritual advancement.

Ibn 'Arabī

Muḥyī'l-Dīn ibn 'Arabī represents the culmination of another strand within Islamic Sufism. Born in Spain in 1165, he travelled throughout North Africa and the Middle East, becoming initiated into Sufism in 1194, and eventually dying in Damascus in 1240. He was a prolific author and wrote *al-Futuḥāt al-Makkiyya*, "The Meccan Revelations," a Ṣūfī encyclopaedia, and *Fuṣūṣ al-Ḥikam*, "The Bezels of Wisdom," his most famous work which summarizes his vision. A difficult writer to comprehend, without a doubt, he was fully educated in the Islamic sciences and brought to his work a vast quantity of learning.

His thought represents a true theosophy, believing in the essential unity between humanity and God. Having brought speculative Sufism to its apogee through his emphasis on gnosis (*ma'rifa*) as the way to the experience of truth, Ibn 'Arabī has been accused of monism, of denying the reality of the separation between God and His creation. The doctrine of God's transcendence is often held to be essential to Muslim orthodox theology, denying as it does any possibility of the incarnation of God in the world, a consequence of its ancient polemic with Christianity. In theory, the theosophical Ṣūfīs got around the problem with the notion of "the reality of Muḥammad" in control of the universe, that being the power to which the Ṣūfīs could aspire in their mystical quest. Ibn 'Arabī argued for the doctrine of *waḥdat al-wujūd*, the "unity of being," where certain implications seem hard to avoid: being and existence are all one and are combined in God; being which is apart from God exists only by virtue of His will, but was, prior to its being made separate, one with God; the "perfect human" (*al-insān al-kāmil*) is the one who knows of oneness with God, who loves God, and who is loved by God.

The role of Sufism

The influence of Ibn ʿArabī, despite the complexity of his thought, has been enormous, not only on all Sufism from that point on, but also in the modern scholarly world which is still trying to come to grips with his ideas.[15] But Sufism was not only of this elevated intellectual type, for the role of the brotherhoods in bringing Sufism closer to the popular level cannot be underestimated. It was the efforts of the brotherhoods which spread Islam into many far-flung corners of the contemporary Muslim world, often facilitated by means of mystical poetry and aided by a tolerant attitude towards local religious practices as long as they were accompanied by the basic spiritual impulse of Islam in its Ṣūfī guise. As well, Sufism has served throughout its history as a source of religious revival for Muslims, breathing life into institutions when they tended to reach the point of self-suffocation. While many of the orthodox have remained deeply suspicious of many Ṣūfī practices and, at certain points in history (most notably with Ibn Taymiyya, d. 1328), renewal of Islam has been sought by means of a purge of non-mainstream Ṣūfī influences, Sufism has remained alive and well, catering to those who picture life in terms of the "mystic quest."

Part IV

Consolidation of Islamic identity

Significant dates

632	death of Muḥammad
661–750	UMAYYAD dynasty
750	ABBASID dynasty begins
813–33	rule of the caliph AL-MA'MŪN
889	death of exegete/writer IBN QUTAYBA
925	death of philosopher AL-RĀZĪ
945	BUWAYHIDS take over Baghdad
1037	death of philosopher IBN SĪNĀ
1111	death of theologian/mystic AL-GHAZZĀLĪ
1144	death of exegete AL-ZAMAKHSHARĪ
1209	death of exegete FAKHR AL-DĪN AL-RĀZĪ
1272	death of exegete AL-QURṬUBĪ
1315	death of exegete AL-BAYḌĀWĪ
1328	death of theologian/jurist IBN TAYMIYYA
1350	death of traditionist IBN QAYYIM AL-JAWZIYYA
1373	death of exegete IBN KATHĪR
1382	death of historian/sociologist IBN KHALDŪN
1392	death of exegete AL-ZARKASHĪ
1459	death of exegete AL-MAḤALLĪ
1501	SAFAVIDS ruling in Iran
1505	death of exegete/polymath AL-SUYŪṬĪ
1641	death of mystical philosopher MULLĀ ṢADRA
1762	death of reformer SHĀH WALĪ ALLĀH
1787	death of reformer IBN ʿABD AL-WAHHĀB

10 Intellectual culture

It is possible to see the development of tradition as a dynamic matching of the literary tradition with the needs and capacities of later readers.[1]

In order to study the formative period of Islam, the main evidence we have before us is found embodied in the Muslim literary tradition. This is a tradition which has been creatively formed and read by Muslims throughout their history. This reading and re-reading is not a process which came to an end at a certain point; indeed, the vitality of Islam – of religion in general – may be seen in the way in which it brings forward the past and reforms it – re-reads it – in ways appropriate to its contemporary situation.

In the emergence of Islam as a religion, there are two major factors displayed in the sources which we have isolated and examined in the preceding chapters. One relates to the formation of Islam as a distinct entity alongside Judaism and Christianity. The other relates to social issues and the emergence of structures of authority in the community. The solidification of the identity of Islam appears to have been a dynamic process, working on several levels all at the same time.

At the base of all the discussions over identity or authority are the Qur'ān and the *sunna*, linked to God and the person of Muḥammad. These are the texts which have gained central symbolic authority within the Muslim community by being connected to both divine revelation and divine protection. In that respect, these sources are following the tradition of the past of which they are re-readings, the tradition of the earlier religious dispensations of the Near East. The basis for the establishment of a new tradition called Islam was created thereby for those who wished to embrace that identity, understanding of authority, and relationship to God. This accomplished, it was possible for a true culture and civilization that had Islam at its base to emerge.

The culture of Islam

The formation of Islam and its emergence as an identity in the world were accompanied by a flowering of an integrated culture. It is a mark of a mature religion, perhaps, that it becomes the motivator, supporter and basis for many aspects of the social structure beyond those obviously involved in the religio-legal paradigm itself. Examples may be seen in the developments that took place within medicine and science in the Islamic context. One could also point to the development of the material arts as an additional example. Furthermore, such a mature structure becomes able to tolerate challenges to it and to find ways of integrating those challenges which it deems to be a product of its own culture rather than result of external pressures. Such was the case with philosophy in the Islamic context.

Medicine, science and philosophy share a common rigorous, rational foundation and their presence at the time of the flowering of Islamic culture reflects both internal and external developments. The polemical encounters with Christians and the remnants of the Manichean tradition were paralleled by the internal Muslim development of the Mu'tazila. Greek texts of philosophy, medicine and science were translated into Arabic not only as a result of Arabic becoming the lingua franca of the Christian community in whose possession these texts were, but also because of their appeal to Muslims for their support in developing rational proofs for religious tenets on the basis of empirical data. In doing so, the basis was found for the firm establishment of an Islamic civilization in every aspect.

The influence of Greek philosophy on Islamic theology has already been mentioned in Chapter 5. The need for a systematic presentation and defence of the Islamic faith was apparent as Muslims interacted with Christians in the area of Syria and Iraq. But this apologetic tendency acted in consort with the basic appeal of Greek philosophical thinking to produce a desire and a need to study and Islamicize the Greek works. Initially, through the process of translation, these works were incorporated into the Muslim world.

In the same manner, to achieve such ends within the field of medicine required not only the study of the ancient Greco-Roman texts and intelligent people, but also a process of Islamicization of pre-existing ideas. This can be seen in the emergence of a medical tradition which can be called Islamic. Two elements combine to form this tradition: Greek medical texts and popular Near Eastern medical beliefs and practices.[2]

Medicine

The popular medical beliefs from the time of the formation of Islam which became incorporated into the religion were not unique to the Arabs. Folklore and superstition provided the basis for a common approach to sickness. Such practices were transmitted and supported through custom, and they were referred to by the word which became the common term used for medicine of the developed Islamic system, *ṭibb*. Remedies included the use of plants and herbs as medicines, and incorporated various physical approaches such as cupping and cautery. These fundamentals were intermixed with, and sometimes based upon, beliefs in the power of spirits, *jinn*, and related malevolent tendencies such as the evil eye. Thus, magical remedies and precautions were an integral part of this tradition. Incantations, charms and amulets were important defences. Evidence for these sorts of practices have frequently been discovered in items such as magic bowls with inscriptions and talismanic squares of letters combinations.

At the same time, there existed a learned Greco-Roman tradition of medicine based upon formal investigation and isolation of causes which was continued within the eastern Christian monasteries and which was then encountered and incorporated into the Islamic context. The study of the Greek texts (and their Christian Syriac translations) within the Islamic world likely started in the eighth century, but it did not become systematic until the ninth century. This, of course, coincides with the emergence of an educated élite in Islamic culture and the solidification and flourishing of that culture itself. The interaction between Muslims and Christians, as was so crucial in the development of Islamic theology, exposed Muslims not only to Greek philosophy in a limited sense but also to the medical tradition from which it cannot really be separated. There was even specific support for theological argumentation to be seen in medical texts: "Galen in particular offered powerful evidence for the ancient and much-used argument from design – if the parts of the body worked together for the benefit of the whole, for example, and accord to some principle of harmony and order, then this necessarily implied the giver of harmony and order, i.e. God."[3]

The translation of Greek texts into Arabic entered an enthusiastic phase with the caliph al-Ma'mūn (ruled 813–33) whose support for the rationalist Muʿtazila encouraged pursuit of the Greek tradition for its value in providing a rigorous foundation to discussion and argumentation. One manifestation of this support was the foundation of the *Bayt al-ḥikma* ("House of wisdom" meaning a library) in Baghdad in 832 in which this translation movement set to work. Hundreds of texts were rendered into Arabic, especially works by Galen, before the demise of the school came about in the wake of the loss of caliphal support for the Muʿtazila towards the end of the ninth century. This did not spell the end to the translation of Greek works by any means, for such efforts continued through the tenth century as well, although, as time went by, original Muslim research became more highly valued and relevant than the remaining untranslated Greek classics.

The work of Galen thus established the principle element of the agenda for Islamic medicine, just as the terminology used in the translations set the vocabulary for later generations. The translation movement was also conscious of the need to incorporate the material upon which it was working within the Islamic framework. References to pagan deities were eliminated and specific works were ignored in the translation efforts.

The final manifestation of this is in the Arabic literary tradition, which emerges from the tenth century on, of writing about medicine on the basis of original work. Here, persons often associated famously with philosophy are also seen to have written about medical topics, for example Rhazes (d. *ca.* 925) and Avicenna (d. 1037). The end result is the emergence of vast compendia of medical information following a variety of organizational patterns.

Islamic basis of medicine

The Qur'ān says little about medical matters. Statements about the "lame, blind and sick" tend to fall into moralistic, symbolic exhortations common to the monotheist tradition. One statement about the curative power of honey (Q. 16/69: "Then there comes out of [the bees'] bellies a drink of diverse shades in which is a healing [*shifā'*] for people") is the only substantive statement. The fact that the Qur'ān does mention the *jinn*, however, and makes reference to the purveyors of spells and the like, was also an element in the emergence of the Islamic medical tradition. Some of these elements created controversy. The use of the Qur'ān as a talisman was likely one of the earliest ways of bringing together Islamic elements and popular practices. Such procedures included the Qur'ān's use in amulets, on magic bowls, and in potions (by the washing off of the ink of the written text). More significant than the support of the Qur'ān, however, was the tendency in this popular approach to medicine to use the example of Muḥammad to support various activities. The emergence of *ḥadīth* reports dedicated to the "Medicine of the Prophet," gathered together in medieval works by people such as Ibn Qayyim al-Jawziyya (d. 1350) and al-Suyūṭī (d. 1505), indicate the attempts to suppress those elements considered inappropriate to the Islamic framework and to support those popular practices that were deeply imbedded in society. Accounts of early Muslims have also been retold in order to bridge the gap between ancient medical traditions and the ideas of Islam. Anecdotes are told of al-Ḥārith ibn Kalada who was an "Arab doctor" who used popular remedies in his cures but who is spoken of at the same time as acquiring knowledge of medicine from Persia. Muḥammad used to send people to him for help in their illnesses. The treatments spoken of were "uncomplicated, common sensical, and self-sufficient," reflecting folk tendencies, while the knowledge which al-Ḥārith tapped was foreign and ancient. The combination was legitimized through the person of Muḥammad.[4]

The plague

Perhaps the most significant way in which disputes about medicine versus religion emerged are to be seen in the attitudes towards epidemics, a concern which has been the focus of scholarly study.[5] The plague was a recurring and severe problem at several points during medieval history. Following earlier Greek thought, its cause was generally thought to be spread through bad quality air (miasma) which upset the balance of the four elements (fire, air, water and earth) within the human body. Ibn Khaldūn (d. 1382), a historian and philosopher who is also often spoken of as an early sociologist who studied the rise and fall of societies, reports:

> In the later [years] of dynasties, famines and pestilences become numerous. . . . The large number of pestilences has its reason in the large number of famines just mentioned. Or, it has its reason in the many disturbances that result from the disintegration of the dynasty. There is much unrest and bloodshed, and plagues occur. The principal reason for the latter is the corruption of

the air [climate] through [too] large a civilization [population].
It results from the putrefaction and the many evil moistures with
which [the air] has contact [in a dense civilization]. Now, air
nourishes the animal spirit and is constantly with it. When it is
corrupted, corruption affects the temper of [the spirit]. If the
corruption is strong, the lung is afflicted with disease. This results
in epidemics, with affect the lungs in particular.[6]

Astrological factors and evil spirits were also thought to play their
role in the spread of epidemics. However, ideas of contagion as a
cause were certainly present but frequently downplayed. The recognition that corpses could be the source of the plague, for example,
was certainly known and experimentally confirmed. But the idea of
corrupt air was always firmly held to be the vehicle for such transmission. Fleeing to an area of pure air was generally seen to be the
best preventative step along with fumigation of one's place of
dwelling. Blood-letting was the main method of treatment.

These ideas about the plague were constrained and directed by
religious factors in many instances. Three factors have been isolated:

1   A Muslim should not enter or flee from a plague-stricken land.
2   The plague is a martyrdom and a mercy from God for a Muslim
    and a punishment for an infidel.
3   There is no infection (contagion).[7]

The first and second factors go together, although the first does
suggest a certain medical attitude and understanding of the nature
of epidemics. However, one cannot, and should not, flee from one's
God-given fate, for such is an expression of disbelief. Epidemics
before Islam and those which befell non-Muslim populations were
God's means of rendering justice in the world; when the Muslim
population was afflicted, the incident had to be understood as an
opportunity to reach paradise, just as in dying in battle (*jihād*) for
Islam. Such notions were supported by *hadīth* reports from
Muḥammad. That religious thought did not accept the notion of
contagion finds its basis in the notion that God is the cause of all
things and is supported once again by appeal to *hadīth* reports. Such
attitudes were widespread regarding medicine in general and some
people argued that it was an attempt to "contravene the omniscience
and omnipotence of God."[8]

Philosophy

As in medicine, so too has it be observed that in other scientific endeavours an uneasy relationship existed between those who continued within the "folk" traditions and those who pursued the rational basis. Procedures regarding how to determine the start of a lunar month (especially crucial for Ramaḍān) and how to align a mosque in the direction of Mecca were established by rigorous approaches to astronomy yet they were rarely incorporated into Muslim religious practice. Rather, the time-tried methods of observation and approximation were continued despite significant advances in mathematical reckoning.[9] Underlying the conflicts in these and many other fields of thought on the part of those Muslims who had certainly been influenced by the rational basis of medicine, science and philosophy but who felt the need to protect Islamic theological dogma, was a distrust for those who wished to support the philosophical project wholeheartedly. Those who pursued in-depth study of philosophy (and, frequently, medicine at the same time) were often seen (sometimes justifiably so) to pose a challenge to Islam in their thought. Famous in this regard is Abū Bakr al-Rāzī (d. *ca*. 925), known in the West as Rhazes. As a philosopher, much of al-Rāzī's written legacy has been lost (he states that he wrote about 200 works on medicine, logic, philosophy, theology, natural sciences, alchemy, astronomy, and mathematics), but it is clear that he was a Platonist and a "free thinker" whose challenge to Islam was fully informed by Greek philosophy. He argued for the eternal existence of five principles – the creator, the soul, matter, space and time. Through the study of philosophy, the soul can be released from the cycle of birth and rebirth. Humanity has no need of a belief in prophets and revelation as reason is sufficient as a guide. Material existence poses a constant challenge to pure intellectual existence, the soul always being tempted by the pleasures of nature.

As a doctor, al-Rāzī headed up hospitals in Rayy and Baghdad. Among his significant extant works are a tract on smallpox and measles and two compendia on diet, hygiene, anatomy, physiology, and pathology, along with general descriptions of diagnosis, therapy and surgery. In his work *Fī'l Ḥaṣba wa'l-Judarī*, al-Rāzī distinguished smallpox from measles, a considerable achievement for the time. The details provided are based upon observation rather than dogmatic assumptions:

> The eruption of the smallpox is preceded by a continued fever, pain in the back, itching in the nose and terrors in the sleep.

These are the more peculiar symptoms of its approach, especially a pain in the back with fever; then also a pricking which the patient feels all over his body; a fullness of the face, which at times comes and goes; an inflamed colour, and vehement redness in both cheeks; a redness of both the eyes, heaviness of the whole body; great uneasiness, the symptoms of which are stretching and yawning; a pain in the throat and chest, with slight difficulty in breathing and cough; a dryness of the breath, thick spittle and hoarseness of the voice; pain and heaviness of the head; inquietude, nausea and anxiety; (with this difference that the inquietude, nausea and anxiety are more frequent in measles than in smallpox; while on the other hand, the pain in the back is more peculiar to the smallpox than to the measles;) heat of the whole body; an inflamed colon, and shining redness, especially an intense redness of the gums.[10]

One feature of al-Rāzī's medical system which often gets noted is the emphasis on cures through diet, combined with an acknowledgement of the influence of psychological factors on health. He used animals for the testing of remedies and introduce the use of alcohol for medical purposes. This latter element and related matters created some of the adverse attitude and suspicion of the Islamic religious leaders towards medicine in general. The use of substances banned by the *sharī'a* could not but draw their attention.

Ibn Sīnā

Ibn Sīnā, known in the West as Avicenna (d. 1037) is another example of the physician-philosopher. He is credited with having written 250 works, the most famous of which in the medical field is his *al-Qānūn fī'l-Ṭibb*, "The Canon of Medicine," a rigorously organized treatise based on Aristotelian principles concerned to see medicine within the context of the whole of the natural sciences. The "rational sciences" for Ibn Sīnā were divided into two groupings. One was the "speculative" which searched for truth through physics (which included medicine, astrology, and physiognomy), mathematics, and metaphysics. The other was the "practical", including personal morality, domestic morality, and politics.[11] Philosophy thus covered every item of value to humans.

Neoplatonism was the foundation of Ibn Sīnā's philosophy but he combined that with a mystical aspect and spoke of "the intellectual urge of the soul to achieve contact or conjunction (*ittiṣāl*) with the Active Intellect, or conversely the divine Nous of Plotinus, rather than union (*ittiḥād*) with, or even vision (*kashf, mushahadah*) of, God, who both for Plotinus and Muslim Neoplatonists continues to be unattainable."[12]

The soul aims to exist in conjunction with God (or the "Active Intellect") which will thereby allow the beauty and goodness of the world to be perceived; in that lies true happiness and the meaning of human existence. Such an end can only be reached by the philosopher or the prophet, whereas most people must rely upon the message of the prophets for guidance and, at best, would be able to experience only a shadow of the true happiness after their death.

Attitude to philosophy

Certainly, philosophical thought challenged Islam in this period. This did not mean, however, that it did not flourish, or that the associated ideas of the medical tradition did not have a tremendous impact. Rather, for most Muslims during this period of intellectual development and consolidation, the role of reason as conveyed within the philosophical tradition was accepted as God-given and a useful tool in the development of human existence. Even those more closely associated with traditional approaches to learning in the early period saw the benefits. Ibn Qutayba (d. 889) wrote:

> Knowledge is the stray camel of the believer; it benefits him regardless from where he takes it: it shall not disparage truth should you hear it from the polytheists, nor advice should it be derived from those who harbor hatred; shabby clothes do no injustice to a beautiful woman, nor shells to their pearls, nor its origin from dust to pure gold. Whoever disregards taking the good from its place misses an opportunity, and opportunities are as transient as the clouds. . . . Ibn-'Abbās . . . said: "Take wisdom from whomever you hear it, for the non-wise may utter a wise saying and a bull's eye may be hit by a non-sharpshooter."[13]

That such attitudes did not continue throughout Islamic history is also true and philosophy as such was perceived by many to be a danger to true Islamic belief. The ramifications of that attitude are still being felt today, as will become clear towards the end of this book. That this attitude did not necessarily extend to all aspects of

Greek learning is important to keep in mind, although the tendency to "reclaim" the knowledge by ascribing it to Arab or Biblical predecessors of the Greeks was known in medieval times (just as it is today).

11 Medieval visions of Islam

Despite the emergence and definition of Islamic identity in the earlier centuries, Muslim thinkers did not cease in their efforts to enunciate the substance of their faith, each responding to the needs and conditions of his (and virtually every name which is known to history is male) time. The period from the thirteenth century through the eighteenth century saw a continuance of the distillation of Islam in textual form. The structures employed for this varied, however, often in mutually opposing ways. Super-commentaries emerged, encouraging reflection upon and preservation of some of the great intellectual achievements of the past. Distillations become more popular, in response to general educative aims. Expansions of previous work, ever accumulating the knowledge of the past in celebration of the endless potential of tradition, were popular. Reformulations, often involving a contraction of tradition in response to a perceived need to avoid certain excesses, also abounded. The writings in a discipline such as Quranic exegesis, *tafsīr*, illustrate this, while emphasizing at the same time the continuing perception of the relevance of Islam but also the need to keep the faith ever adaptable, albeit in different ways.

Tendencies in medieval exegesis

Abū'l-Qāsim Maḥmūd ibn 'Umar al-Zamakhsharī (d. 1144) was a philologist, theologian and Qur'ān commentator. For most of his life al-Zamakhsharī lived in the region of his birth, Khwarizm in Central Asia, although he did spend some time studying in Bukhara and Baghdad, and twice he visited Mecca. Motivated by a great appreciation of Arabic (although he was a native Persian speaker) and influenced by rationalist Mu'tazilī theology, al-Zamakhsharī wrote one of the most widely read commentaries on the Qur'ān called *al-Kashshāf*

Muscle

Muslims

'an *Ḥaqā'iq Ghawāmid al-Tanzīl*, "The Unveiler of the Realities of the Secrets of the Revelation." Despite what came to be regarded as a heretical theological slant, the work has been an essential part of the curriculum of religious education throughout the Muslim world for centuries. It attracted many super-commentaries which attempted to explain its terse style and intricacies, as well as refutations (e.g. by Fakhr al-Dīn al-Rāzī [d. 1209]) and bowdlerized versions (e.g. by al-Bayḍāwī [d. probably 1315–16]). Al-Zamakhsharī commented on each phrase of the Qur'ān in sequence, providing philosophical, lexicographical and philological glosses, while displaying a concern for the rhetorical qualities of the text. His text is also imbued with his theological vision which is characterized by a thorough-going de-anthropomorphization and support for the doctrines of human free will and the "created Qur'ān." Al-Zamakhsharī also wrote a number of other works, including works on Arabic grammar, rhetoric, and lexicography, and a collection of proverbs.

The significance of al-Zamakhsharī's work was recognized quickly, with the emergence of explicit commentaries on it written by Ibn al-Munayyir (d. 1284) and Sharaf al-Dīn al-Ṭībī (d. 1343) for example. Super-commentaries such as these are not very common within the *tafsīr* tradition, but the form itself certainly emerged earlier in other disciplines such as grammar. Their existence indicates the nature of learning and of the consolidation of Muslim identity in society in general at the time.

Al-Bayḍāwī's work, *Anwār al-Tanzīl wa Asrār al-Ta'wīl*, "The Lights of Revelation and the Secrets of Interpretation", plus a commentary on it by al-Khāṭib al-Kārūnī (d. 1553), has continued to be an important element in the course of studies at the Muslim religious university al-Azhar in Cairo. Al-Bayḍāwī's text, short, succinct, yet exhaustive, presents the essence of Sunnī doctrine and has attracted a large number of other commentaries as well. While clearly dependent upon al-Zamakhsharī, although avoiding those points of Mu'tazilī doctrine which he deemed unacceptable, al-Bayḍāwī was also indebted to a good deal of the general tradition of exegesis which preceded him.

The commentary on the Qur'ān by Muḥammad Aḥmad al-Qurṭubī (d. 1272), *al-Jāmi' li-Aḥkām al-Qur'ān*, "The Compendium of the Rulings of the Qur'ān," indicates by its title that a major concern of this medieval Quranic exegete was to support the use of the Qur'ān as a source of law with Islam. However, al-Qurṭubī's work is not limited to that for it provides a vast source of opinion on the meaning of the Qur'ān, much of it presented with little indication of the author's preferred meaning of the text. Rather, the point of the work seems to be the demonstration of the potentiality of the text for conveying a multiplicity of meanings.

"The process of citing authorities and providing multiple readings is, in part, a declaration of loyalty: It defines the tradition within which one works. It is also a means to establish the individuality or the artistry of [the commentator]. The selection, presentation and organization of citations constitute always a process that is unique to one writer."[1] Although such compilations may strike us today as mere repetition of the ideas of others, it is a creative act that is the result of dedicated work of the author. Finally, the books themselves are, of course, one element in a theological message: the possibility of the community and the text containing a multiplicity of interpretation while remaining one community and one text is thereby asserted.

The desire to distil tradition into compact units suitable for study and for reflection may be seen in the work of Jalāl al-Dīn al-Maḥallī (d. 1459) which was completed by Jalāl al-Dīn al-Suyūṭī (d. 1505) known as *Tafsīr al-Jalālayn*, the "Commentary of the Two Jalāls." The work focuses upon grammatical issues which are presented succinctly in a manner appropriate to those who have a solid training in the subtleties of the Arabic language. Yet at the same time, al-Suyūṭī also complied another work of exegesis, *al-Durr al-Manthūr fī'l-Tafsīr bi'l-Ma'thūr*, "Scattered Pearls in the Interpretation [of the Qur'ān] by Tradition," which is a vast compendium of older sources brought together complete with abbreviated *isnād*s in order to provide an overview of opinion. This latter work is more in keeping, in fact, with the overall character of al-Suyūṭī's work. He was a polymath whose compilations on many subjects set the tone for a general understanding of this age of consolidation. His aim was clearly to compile, in card file fashion, a sum of useful knowledge as it had been transmitted from the past. Much of the same material finds itself repeated in multiple works all by al-Suyūṭī; the apparent vast number of his books is exaggerated by the tendency also to create separate works on individual subjects which are also found in his larger compendia. His classic work on the Quranic "sciences," *al-Itqān fī 'Ulūm al-Qur'ān*, "The Perfection Concerning the Sciences of the Qur'ān," brings together about eighty subjects, each related to the Qur'ān and its study: where pieces of it were revealed, how they were revealed, what difficult words there are in it, what foreign words there are in it, what metaphors there are, and so on. This encyclopaedist tendency provides a categorization of knowledge that is functional rather than necessarily original, although the classification system itself may be innovative in some cases; al-Suyūṭī himself builds upon a tradition of such matters in this case, working on the model provided by al-Zarkashī (d. 1392) in his *al-Burhān fī 'Ulūm al-Qur'ān*, "The Disclosure of the Sciences of the Qur'ān".

Counter-tendencies in exegesis

However, this expansive, encyclopaedist tendency also came in for criticism in a manner which resulted in a contraction of available information. Two names stand out in medieval times for this tendency: Ibn Taymiyya and Ibn Kathīr. 'Imād al-Dīn Ismā'īl ibn 'Umar ibn Kathīr was born in Basra in 1300 and moved to Damascus when he was six, where he studied with some of the most famous scholars of his time including the Ḥanbalī theologian, jurist and reformer Taqī al-Dīn Aḥmad ibn Taymiyya (d. 1328). Ibn Kathīr became known as a scholar of law and a teacher of *ḥadīth* as well as being praised as one of the most respected preachers and lecturers in Damascus. He died in 1373. His major work, a commentary on the Qur'ān entitled simply *Tafsīr al-Qur'ān*, provides a synopsis of earlier material in a readily accessible form, a factor which gave the work much popularity in subsequent generations. His reliance is totally upon *ḥadīth* material; the era of Ibn Kathīr, in fact, marks the final submersion of rationalism under the powers of traditionalism. No longer did even the measure of personal opinion displayed in the work of al-Ṭabarī or al-Zamakhsharī have any substantial place in the understanding of the Qur'ān. Ibn Kathīr frequently structures his commentary around extracts from the classical books of *ḥadīth*, citing those reports relevant to the passage in question. In doing so, the tradition of *tafsīr* is being contracted severely; no longer are the intellectual disciplines of grammar, law and theology being brought into dialogue and debate with the text.[2]

It was Ibn Taymiyya who provided the theoretical basis to Ibn Kathīr's approach, through his emphasis in his *Muqaddima fī Uṣūl al-Tafsīr*, "An Introduction to the Principles of *Tafsīr*," on the steps which one must take in explaining the Qur'ān.

> If someone says, "What is the best method of *tafsīr*?" the answer is [as follows]. The most sound method is that the Qur'ān be interpreted by the Qur'ān. What is summarized in one place may well be explained in another, and what is abbreviated in one place may well be expanded in another.

If that [approach] thwarts your efforts, then your should [inter-
pret the Qur'ān] by the *sunna*, for it is a commentary (*sharḥ*)
and an elucidator of the Qur'ān. ... About this the Messenger
of God said, "Is it not that I was given the Qur'ān and the like
of it with it?", that is, the *sunna*. The *sunna* was also revealed
to him by revelation (*waḥy*), just as the Qur'ān was revealed. It
is just that it is not recited as the Qur'ān is recited. ... The
objective of this [approach to understanding the Qur'ān] is that
you search for the interpretation of the Qur'ān within itself and
if you do not find it [there], then from within the *sunna*. ...
Whenever you do not find an explanation in the Qur'ān nor in
the *sunna*, you should look concerning that matter at the statements of the companions of Muḥammad (*ṣaḥāba*). They are the
most knowledgeable in that regard because of what they
witnessed [of the revelation] of the Qur'ān and the circumstances
by which they were distinguished and because they have
complete understanding and sound knowledge. This is especially
so of their scholars and elders who include the four rightly-
guided Caliphs and the rightly guided *imāms*. ...When you are
unable to find the interpretation in either the Qur'ān or the
sunna and you cannot find it on the authority of the Companions,
in that situation most learned people go to the statements of the
Successors. This includes people such as Mujāhid ibn Jabr, for
he is a mark by which *tafsīr* is known. This is as Muḥammad ibn
Isḥāq said, saying that Abān ibn Ṣāliḥ told him on the authority
of Mujāhid ibn Jabr that he said, "I went through the Qur'ān
with Ibn 'Abbās three times from beginning to end, stopping at
each of its verses and asking him about them."[3]

The goal of both Ibn Taymiyya and Ibn Kathīr was to render the
Qur'ān accessible and intelligible through an assertion of authority
of the *'ulamā'*. Elements of classical exegesis that were deemed
unnecessary and impractical were excluded and condemned as lies
or even the material of the enemies of Islam. The emphasis
on Muḥammad, the person, and his revelatory *sunna*, along with
his closest followers as the focus of authority in Islam, rather than
the intellectual tradition, is covered in the term *salaf*, the "pious
ancestors."

Clearly, such tendencies in all these exegetical works and their
conflicting aims can be explained to some extent by the differing
audiences which the authors contemplated for their works. However,
it is important to recognize the ideological stance which is conveyed

within these books, especially in its attitude towards the past. The "acquisitive" nature of the works of al-Qurṭubī or al-Suyūṭī, their gathering together of material from the past in a celebration of the significance of the living Islamic tradition is opposed to the more monovalent attitude of Ibn Kathīr. Of course, these expansive and contractive tendencies show the power of religion to renew itself through a constant movement of reinterpretation.

Developments in Sufism

A survey of works in the field of history, theology or law would reveal the same variety of tendencies and liveliness in intellectual activities among Muslims of the post-thirteenth century. Some special attention is needed to Sufism in this period because it, too, went through a period of development, significantly consolidating institutionally in the post-sixteenth century, and starting to follow new lines in ritual.[4] The setting of the stage for the developments of the nineteenth and twentieth centuries is clearly to be seen both in terms of the developments within Sufism and in the reactions against it during this period.

Most of the Ṣūfī *ṭarīqa*s were rather loosely organized for much of their history, with individual branches within a given order existing independently. It would not necessarily have been possible for a Ṣūfī to recognize a follower of his own order from a different area; no common mode of dress or practice was implemented. The commonality of such Ṣūfīs was located only in their respect for the founder of the order. Even the person of the *shaykh* was nominated by the local centres with no centralized control. The Ṣūfī orders were, therefore, of no particular significance in terms of general social movements in the earlier period; their influence was regional and not political.

This started to change, first within the context of the sixteenth-century Ottoman empire, where the Mawlawiyya (the Mevlevi order) and Bektāshiyya were prominent and had significant influence with the people and were, to some extent, controlled by the government as a result. Such organizational movements became more widespread in the eighteenth century, with, for example, Shaykh Khālid (d. 1826) of the Naqshbandiyya order creating a network of more than one hundred subsidiary *khalīfa*s or "deputies", each with his own geographical region of control.[5] At the same time, the notion of dynastic succession (rather than spiritual selection) in the designation of the *shaykh* became more common.

Furthermore, a tendency emerged towards requiring allegiance to a single Ṣūfī order. In earlier times, the spiritual benefit of Sufism was thought to be such that more such benefit could be gathered by belonging to more than one order. It is common to read of people being initiated into multiple orders. Furthermore, many Ṣūfī orders displayed (and continue to display) a syncretic nature in terms of matters of authority and ritual. Ṣūfī saints, who are apparently key figures in one order, will be appealed to by members of another order. Rituals commonly associated with one order, such as the whirling dance of the Mawlawiyya order, will be employed by another order which is normally associated with other rituals, such as the deep breathing Rifāʿiyya.⁶ However, the Khalwatiyya in eighteenth-century Egypt emphasized the need to belong to this one order and to leave all others behind. Such an attitude created a similar effect in other orders, notably the Tijāniyya of Aḥmad al-Tijānī (d. 1815) and its rival, the Qādiriyya in North Africa.

These changes tended to elevate the status of individual *shaykhs* in a manner which became reflected in ritual activities also. The centralized leadership of Shaykh Khālid of the Naqshbandiyya, for example, became the focus of devotional activities rather than the local leader (who, as the "spiritual guide," had formerly been the centre of attention). Other changes reflect more on the desire to popularize and spread Sufism rather than simple organizational manoeuvres. An interesting shift in the practice of the *dhikr* has been noted within disparate and different Ṣūfī orders, including the Naqshbandiyya in China and the Khalwatiyya in Egypt in the eighteenth century. The *dhikr* can be performed either silently by individuals or out loud by a group. The former procedure tended to be considered more orthodox, and those who wished to maintain a respectable image for Sufism were concerned to see that the tradition was maintained, especially since the vocal *dhikr* was often accompanied by music and dance which was frequently condemned by more conservative religious leaders. In moving to a vocal *dhikr*, it has been suggested that a larger number of common people were attracted to the performances, making the message of the orders that much more widespread but also indicating the greater influence upon society which these groups has despite their reaction which some of their practices provoked.⁷

It is apparent from the perspective of later history that all of these elements of change are significant within the development of Sufism and its impact upon Muslim society in general in the nineteenth and twentieth centuries. A strong organization coupled with a good deal of popular appeal made the Ṣūfī orders a force to be reckoned with. However, the changes in Sufism were not limited to the *ṭarīqa*s, but may also be noted in the emergence of several significant figures who added to the body of the imagery and theory of Sufism in particular ways. Ṣadr al-Dīn al-Shirāzī, known as Mullā Ṣadra (d. 1641) is perhaps the most significant. Working within the developed tradition of Sufism in the wake of Ibn 'Arabī in the context of Shī'ī thought, Mullā Ṣadra's works reflect an integration of those two elements with Greek philosophy.

Purification movements

A certain backlash against Sufism can also be seen within the medieval period. Ibn Taymiyya argued strenuously for purging Islam of various practices prevalent at his time, especially popular Ṣūfī practices such as excessive asceticism, tomb visitations and saint worship along with beliefs such as miracle working. Although Ibn Taymiyya himself appears to have aligned himself personally with Ṣūfī orders and was thus not opposed to Ṣūfīsm as such, he argued against these specific activities by appealing to the Qur'ān and the practice (*sunna*) of Muhammad; anything within Sufism which could not be justified on this basis was to be rejected. Thus, music and song were to be considered non-Islamic, for example. The entire Ṣūfī proposal of the ecstatic experience of God was not a valid criterion by which to judge what is right and wrong (which is one of the arguments which al-Ghazālī had used a few centuries earlier to legitimate Ṣūfī practices). Similar thoughts arose in the eighteenth century as well, primarily in the Arabian movement which became known as the Wahhābiyya, once again a movement against Sufism and the Shī'a. Led by Ibn 'Abd al-Wahhāb (1703–1787), the movement argued that the attitude of reverence towards saints had led to a blind acceptance of their authority and this was to be rejected and replaced by the sole authority of Islam, the Qur'ān and the *sunna*. Shāh Walī Allāh (1702–62), a mystic-theologian, represents a similar tendency in the Indian context, but he placed greater emphasis on gradual reform rather than the strident confrontations of Ibn 'Abd al-Wahhāb.

The movements connected to Ibn 'Abd al-Wahhāb and Shāh Walī Allāh may be termed "pre-modern", in the sense that they developed before the impact of the industrialized West had been felt. They may best be termed "purification" movements[8] and they certainly sowed the seeds for later social and legal change in the

Islamic world. They seem to have been caused by a dissatisfaction with the more rigid formulations of medieval Islam, especially in the legal schools. The movement also picks up on a well-established tradition in Islam regarding the *mujaddid*, or renewer of the faith, believed to be an essential part of each age.[9] Fazlur Rahman has characterized these pre-modernist groups as having the following characteristics:

> (i) a deep and transforming concern with the socio-moral degeneration of Muslim society; (ii) a call to "go back" to original Islam and shed the superstitions inculcated by popular forms of Sufism, to get rid of the idea of the fixity and finality of the traditional schools of law, and to attempt to perform *ijtihād*, that is, to rethink for oneself the meaning of the original message; (iii) a call to remove the crushing burden of a predeterministic outlook produced by popular religion but also materially contributed to by the almost ubiquitous influence of Ash'arī theology; and (iv) a call to carry out this revivalist reform through armed force (*jihād*) if necessary.[10]

The birthday of Muḥammad

Such stances towards Sufism also reflect some of the developing attitudes within ritual and law. An example may be seen in the festivities connected to the celebration of the birthday of Muḥammad. Known generally as *mawlid al-nabī*, "the birth of the prophet," the celebration of this day does not have an official status in Islam. The commemoration of the day is not recorded in the classical texts of Islamic law and it has no connection to the *sunna*. When jurists did contemplate it in later centuries, they often termed it a *bid'a ḥasana*, a "commendable innovation." Historically, the present festival is thought to stem from the twelfth century; this is when the historians of the period start to record various practices related to the twelfth day of the month of Rabī' I which was designated as Muḥammad's birthday.[11] The activities within the celebration are characteristic of general Muslim approach toward honouring local saints. *Mawlid*s were, and still are, held for the most popular holy men and women of Islamic history as a part of mystical devotion. A holy day is stimulated by a connection with a holy person, a day on which celebrations and devotions may be expected to bring great merits and benefits. The central events of such days are processions (frequently lit with candles or the like), chanting, singing and telling stories. A fair is often organized for children. The celebrations culminate in religious devotions to the holy person, producing "exaltation, fervor, rapture and in many a tranquil contentment."[12] Today, in most parts of the Muslim world, the birthday of Muḥammad is celebrated in a similar manner. Each area has its own particular form of celebration and in many countries it has become an official state holiday. This official character is reinforced by the presence of the head of state who will frequently attend the festivities held at the main mosque in the capital city.[13]

Characteristic of the celebration is the recitation of poetry in praise of Muḥammad, often known as *mawladiyya*. Much of the material found in the poems recited even today is derived from classical sources[14] which emphasizes the continued role of and devotion to the learning of the past, and the significant role that Muḥammad's miracles and his human qualities have played in the practiced faith of Islam. As well, the characteristics of the poetry reveal a definite mystical element which has permeated Muslim belief. One example of the Ṣūfī influence may be seen in the theory espoused in much of the poetry regarding the pre-existent "Muhammadan light," an element of the miraculous but also the salvific nature of the conception of Muḥammad through which this world is connected to the divine domain. A typical poem contains the following lines:

> The lights of Muḥammad streamed upon us,
> The full moons have hurried away; we have never seen such
>   beauty.
> Only you are the face of happiness.
> You are a sun; you are a full moon.
> You are light upon light.
> You are an elixir, very precious
> You light up [our] hearts, my Beloved Muḥammad.
> You are the bride of both East and West
> You are firmly backed [by God] and honored,
> You are the Imām of the two *qibla*s.
> Whoever gazed upon your face felt elated.
> You are from distinguished parentage and your background
>   is peerless.[15]

Together with the recitation of poetry in honour of Muḥammad on these occasions, a more definitive element of Ṣūfī practice is included. The poetry is often followed by litany of a *dhikr*. This will not always be the case on the actual day of the celebration of Muḥammad's birthday, but it frequently occurs on other occasions in which the person of Muḥammad is invoked for blessing, such as in marriages. The performance of the *mawlid* poetry becomes the task of entertainers hired for the purpose. The poetry is not limited to praise of Muḥammad, but that theme always "'brackets the proceedings."[16]

Reactions against the mawlid

The entire celebration of the *mawlid*, whether connected to Muḥammad or to specific Ṣūfī saints (the latter celebration often referred to by a variety of names), frequently raised the ire of those Muslims who wished to purify Islam of all elements that could not be explicitly supported by the regulations of the Qur'ān or the practice of Muḥammad.

However, the power of Sufism, both in its institutionalized form and in the way that its general influence has been felt in Islam as a whole, was such that that Ṣūfī brotherhoods and their associated practices remained a vital part of the religious environment and have done so down until today.[17] The desire for an emotional aspect to religious life, in combination with the appeal of images which glorify Muḥammad and, indeed, the divine, has a substantial place in Islam and this is frequently provided by the Ṣūfī tradition. Grouped around a spiritual leader and following certain practices designed to stimulate the experience of God, Ṣūfī brotherhoods flourished throughout the Muslim world, even if they were not always condoned by governments or establishment religious forces.

Part V

Modern visions
of Islam

Significant dates

632	death of MUHAMMAD
1798	NAPOLEON lands in Egypt
1897	death of reformer AL-AFGHĀNĪ
1898	death of reformer SAYYID AHMAD KHĀN
1905	death of modernist MUHAMMAD 'ABDUH
1935	death of modernist RASHĪD RIDĀ
1938	death of modernist MUHAMMAD IQBĀL
	death of the founder of Republican Turkey, ATATÜRK
1956	death of the writer MUHAMMAD HUSAYN HAYKAL
1966	death of Islamist SAYYID QUTB
1979	death of Islamist MAWDŪDĪ
1985	death of modernist GHULĀM AHMAD PARVĒZ
1988	death of scholar FAZLUR RAHMAN

12 Describing modernity

In 1798 Napoleon landed in Egypt, ostensibly to protect French merchants there from local misrule, but more especially as a base of operations against the British in India. The Egyptian Mamluk troops were helpless against him having maintained even less, than other Ottoman troops, an awareness of modern military developments. The population generally was likewise relatively parochial in outlook. The French set up as much as they could of the apparatus of the Enlightenment on Egyptian soil: modern hospitals, impersonal administration, scientific laboratories (they set about, among other things, recording in scientific detail the still prevailing non-technologically based ways, which were presumed about to vanish before modern French civilization); they invited the astonished local savants to inspect the show and acknowledge the moral superiority of the Revolution – claimed to be true Islam.[1]

With the French occupation of Egypt, the Middle East (and other parts of the world, of course) was confronted directly by a technologically advanced and expansionist Europe. The impact on Muslims has been both substantial and significant, especially as they debate whether or not Islam itself can or should change, and how it should change if it should, to meet the current challenges and remain relevant to the lives of individuals.

Studying modern Islam

It is hazardous to make generalized judgements about an entity as manifold as modern Islam from Indonesia to Morocco, in a time so turbulent as this century; whatever is said must be suitably modest and tentative.[2] It is especially dangerous, although many observers often seem to miss the point, to view the entire world as revolving around developments in Europe, as if the rest of the world had no significant existence prior to and independent of Europeans or has been irrelevant to the creation of what modern Europe is now. It is an important corrective to keep in mind that the transformation of European society over the last five centuries is not the culmination of a straight line from ancient Greece and Rome to modern France and Germany, but the result of the interplay of general human history.

Certainly, a transformation of European society did take place between the late 1500s and the late 1700s. It is highlighted by two significant changes: the industrial revolution ushering in the techno- logical age, and the French revolution, which altered basic social values. This transformation not only affected Europe where it initially took place, but the rest of the world as well, especially through the rise of European colonial expansion. However, one should not think that everything which has happened in the Muslim world and else- where during this period is simply a response to those changes on the "outside"; the Muslim world continues on its own path of organic growth and change which interacts with the rest of the world. Change is very much a two-way street.

One area which proves a great stumbling block in the study of modern Islam is the implicit (and even on occasion explicit) moral valuation of progress as it has manifested itself in the West through the transformations of the technological age. Countries which have benefited most from progress are seen to be "more advanced" or "better" than those which have not. However, while various useful changes in human life have come about, not all of them may be championed as necessarily good. Certainly some of them may well be thought of in this mode – modern medical advances and the erad- ication of smallpox, for example – but a facile judgment of the state of modern progress in one society versus another does not satisfy the demands of careful scholarship nor the understanding of human societies in their multiplicity.

The terms "traditional" and "modern" are a part of this value- laden system in common parlance, where traditional stands for the irrational, non-scientific world view, and modern for everything which opposes that. But it is possible to use these terms meaningfully, if carefully done. Traditional refers to taking the attitude that one is doing things in the way in which they have always been done, that is, looking to the past for authority on a given matter. Modern then becomes identified with the technological age, not necessarily more rational than the traditional way, but with a different view of the past, the authority of which has been displaced. The trouble is that the division is not as clear as such a definitional stance wishes to pretend. There is a tendency to assume a process of evolution from traditional to modern, but, in fact, the situation is far more of a flux. The traditional world deals with change by rejecting or subtly altering its inherited conceptions (and thus the traditional world most assuredly does change), while the modern world never frees itself totally from the authority of the past. The modern aspects of a society are generally seen as following along hand-in-hand with its traditional ones. In sum, one might say that the terms are, at best, generalizations and that they do not reflect the realities of life as it is lived but are intellectual abstractions which can, if used reflectively, aid understanding. "Modern" refers to the embracing of the technological aspects of contemporary society, that being understood in the broadest manner; "traditional" does not mean the rejection of the modern but the continuation in certain aspects of life in a mode authorized by the past, notably in areas of life where other people have changed to a modern view.

The methodological dilemma is somewhat further confused by the fact that many nineteenth- and twentieth-century Muslim spokesmen (and there have been, until more recent times, very few spokeswomen) adopted the chauvinistic European mode of understanding the world: that the highlight of world existence is, in fact, in the West, that the rest of the world had to evolve and progress to that level, and that the Islamic world had been unchanging since the rise of the Mongols in the twelfth century. Time and again in reading Muslim sources this kind of apologetic, which accepts the European perspective on the question, is encountered. So, methodologically, we become even further tangled. We wish to understand contemporary Muslim world views and to do so we must recognize the cultural biases with which we approach the subject. Yet those biases are precisely what much of the material is interacting with, responding to and even adopting. And that is, in fact, what we are interested in: how modern Muslims have constructed their world views.

The phenomenon of modernity

The real challenge that the Muslim society has had to face and is still facing is at the level of social institutions and social ethic as such. And the real nature of this crisis is not the fact that the Muslim social institutions in the past have been wrong or irrational but the fact that there has been a social system at all which now needs to be modified and adjusted. This social system has, in fact, been perfectly rational in the past, i.e. it has been working perfectly well, as perfectly well as any other social system. The disadvantage of the Muslim society at the present juncture is that whereas in the early centuries of development of social institutions in Islam, Islam started from a clean slate, as it were, and had to carve out *ab initio* a social fabric – an activity of which the product was the medieval social system – now, when Muslims have to face a situation of fundamental rethinking and reconstruction, their acute problem is precisely to determine how far to render the slate clean again and on what principles and by what methods, in order to create a new set of institutions.[3]

While Fazlur Rahman, the author of the above passage, is enunciating a particular position within the modernist Muslim debate, he strikes a central point common to all who try to contemplate the relevance of Islam today by speaking of a modern situation of "fundamental rethinking and reconstruction" in which Islam now finds itself. But, before tackling the proposed answers to that question, something more basic must first be approached: why and how has this situation of "fundamental rethinking and reconstruction" arisen? What are the characteristics of the modern age which have created this situation? Why has Islam had to face them? And why does facing them seem to be such a problem?

The characteristics of the "modern era"

There are many ways of analyzing the idea called "modernity." At its simplest level, it might be said that modernity is that which renders the past problematic. Notably (and this is what makes this definition so significant), once tradition – the past – has been questioned and examined, there is no going back. The ideas of the past (for example, in terms of historical facts) can never have the same weight again, even if the challenge of modernity is ultimately rejected.[4]

Modernity is that which has created fundamental changes in behaviour and belief about economics, politics, social organization and intellectual discourse. Once again, it is important to keep in mind that changes have happened throughout the world; this is not just a matter of western influences on the rest of the world. Modernity must be seen as a world phenomenon.

In the economic sphere, change is seen in terms of industrialization and consequent economic growth, the formation of large capital sums, the growth of science and the emergence of new classes of people and social mobility. In the political arena, it is the growth of political parties (and the belief in the moral evolution resulting from that growth), unions and youth groups. In the social dimension, the change in relations between the sexes (with its economic implications), mass communications, urbanization, travel and generally increased mobility are especially marked. In the intellectual realm, the prominence of the idea of progress, the emergence of secular-rational norms and the rise of historical studies[5] all make the phenomenon of change so apparent. All of this has brought with it or brought about as a consequence, a change in the historical reality in which we live.

The five pillars of modernity

Many attempts have been made to try to define more closely the characteristics of the modern period in order to say just how it is different from past eras. Peter Berger's "Toward a Critique of Modernity"[6] has become a classic statement of such a definition. He speaks of five "dilemmas of modernity":

1   Abstraction (in the way life confronts bureaucracy and technology especially).
2   Futurity (the future as the primary orientation for activity and the imagination, and life governed by the clock).
3   Individuation (the separation of the individual from any sense of a collective entity, thus producing alienation).
4   Liberation (life viewed as dominated by choice and not fate; "things could be other than what they have been").
5   Secularization (the massive threat to the plausibility of religious belief).

Harvey Cox[7] has modified these into a slightly more positive form and speaks of the aptly-named (for this context) "five pillars of modernity." The modern period is said to be characterized by the following aspects:

1   The emergence of sovereign national states as legally defined entities in a global political system, most of which have emerged in their present form at most 200 years ago.

2   Science-based technology as a principal source of images for life
     and its possibilities.
3   Bureaucratic rationalism as a way of organizing and adminis-
     tering human thought and activity, where institutions take on
     their own intellectual life producing people who feel alienated,
     powerless and apathetic ("I only work here").
4   The quest for profit maximization as a means to motivate work
     and distribute goods and services (thus both within capitalism
     and socialism) as manifested in, for example, the capitalist mode
     of production and marketing.
5   Secularization and trivialization of religion and the use of the
     spiritual for profane purposes manifested in the removal of reli-
     gion's concern with politics and economics.

Secularization needs further comment, given the context of our investigation. This concept may be defined[8] as the process of emancipation
of certain areas of social, cultural and political life from the domi-
nance or control of traditional religious ideas; it has been both a
contributing factor in modernization and a result of it. The terms
used to describe the modern era – enlightened, secular, rational,
disenchanted (i.e. the loss of magic), scientific, post-traditional – all
indicate the tendency of secularization.

In fact, the attitudes towards religion are central elements of what
many people identify as modern, at least in popular parlance. For
example, the demolition of the truth of the Bible, the rejection of
the divinity of Jesus, and the doubts expressed about the value of
much that has been taught for generations are all the most obvious
elements within Christianity.[9] But these are negative elements,
matters which have created fear and terror along with an almost
perverse attraction to this modern age. Speaking positively of the
modern age as coinciding with the emergence of the philosophical
principle of the self as the judge on matters of truth and validity,
Descartes' "I think therefore I am" remains the only basic certain
truth as opposed to traditional religious values and their claims to
eternal validity.

Some observers have noted that this tendency towards secularization especially, but the other aspects of modernity also, happened
in Europe initially but have become of crucial significance for the
rest of the world. Therefore, European religion (Christianity) has
had to respond to this situation from the beginning of the age of
industrialization and the ways in which it has done so have become
paradigmatic (at least to some extent) for other religions. To a degree,

this would appear to be intrinsically true, but it is also a position urged by some writers: that Muslims should learn from the Christian experience and be prepared to relinquish certain aspects of their traditional faith while maintaining others. This kind of writing about Islam especially has received a great deal of criticism recently[10] but continues nevertheless.[11]

Other people, perhaps with a greater political (rather than religious) orientation towards life, have isolated another series of adjectives which characterize the modern period: colonial, imperialist, missionary, western invasion. There can be no doubt that isolating such elements is important in understanding the perceptions of the modern period in the Muslim world. However, this view, tends to see the modern world in terms of confrontation between the West and the Islamic world; other people may wish to subsume these elements under broader categories, however, such as the world-wide emergence of national states. Still, the reality of this perception cannot be underplayed.

Characteristics of the modern era in the Muslim world

How has modernity made its impact on the Muslim world? The sense of the tension created in the modern context is one of the first things which strikes many travelers and may be seen in many films and other media portrayals: the absurd and distressing confrontation between modern and ancient ways of life. Donkeys are still vying for a place on the road as decrepit cars and trucks, amid the Mercedes, go whizzing by; the importation of the McDonald's–Coca-Cola consumer culture exists in the face of vast wealth and abject poverty without a period of time to allow for build-up to consumerism (a period of time which North American and European society certainly had). Consumer society "is at odds with the pre-take off stage of the Middle Eastern economy, creating new needs and raising expectations that the economy cannot deliver."[12] This becomes a powerful conservative argument against the West, for appealing to western values and aspirations is seen to be the cause of contemporary frustrations. Yet the Muslim world has, in certain ways, adapted to the modern world through the use of its ancient resources; these have proven a source of strength as well as a source of tension. The utilization and re-utilization of modern materials – the implicit rejection of the throw-away society and the planned obsolescence of the West – are frequently startling and encouraging to the observer accustomed to North American-style consumerism.

The impact of modernity on the Islamic world has been felt in a vast number of ways. Some can easily be isolated: the cycle of ascendancy and decline through which the Islamic world feels itself to have been historically, the impact of the nationalist and socialist challenge, the impact of Zionism, and the impact of oil revenues.

Ascendancy and decline

A recognition of the impotence of the Islamic world in the face of the newly emerged power of Europe along with a shared memory of a powerful past has produced a great deal of soul searching and analysis. What are the reasons for this decline into subjugation and exploitation? The answers have frequently been religious, a response fostered and encouraged by negative post-Enlightenment attitudes towards religion in general and towards Islam in particular.

Haunting all of the discussions within the Muslim world is the notion of the failure of Islam. Has Islam somehow fallen by the wayside, become unable to cope with the emerging world and the contemporary human situation? This, of course, is a shattering thought for any religion, but it is especially so for Islam because the idea of success in the world has been central to Islamic ideology from the very early period of Islam. Acting as a paradigm for later Islamic thinking, Muḥammad is pictured as moving from Mecca to Medina (the *hijra*) in the midst of his preaching career in order to be successful. Islam would not have been revealed to the world, as God's last statement, if it were not divinely pre-ordained to succeed. God's word cannot be frustrated by human obstinacy. Islamic history and the golden age of Islam, in the same time period as the dark ages of Europe, only reinforce the notion of the success of the religion in further, very tangible terms. The rise of Europe as a colonialist power, therefore, shattered a deeply held Muslim idea – even, it might be said, one of the basic presuppositions of Islamic existence. A crisis of identity faced those who did not get carried away on the western bandwagon and who wished to investigate the roots of the problem. The modern situation was perceived to be one of fundamental challenge to Islam, therefore; the failure to be able to respond would be the failure of Islam as a religion. What then is the status of Islam when it is not in political ascendancy in the world?

The answers to this problem have been varied: the extent to which Islam itself might be seen as the cause of the gradual decline of its civilization is, in part, the subject at debate. Is it Islam itself which needs modification in the modern world or is it Muslims who have not lived up to the demands of Islam and consequently the civilization has declined? This question arises most frequently in discussions over science and technology. The failure to embrace modern science (which, it is often championed, stems from Muslim medieval advances) along with the scientific mentality as embodied in the western educational system is the cause of Islam's decline according to some. Others, however, would say that it is faith in God which is more crucial than the technology itself and thus they reject this entire argument.

Nationalism and socialism

Modern political ideologies have been seen by some as a way out of the present dilemma of decline but also as an attractive modern option in and by themselves. Socialism especially has attracted attention both as an alternative to Islam and as a way to construct an entirely new society. But it has also been seen as the true embodiment of Islamic principles especially in aspects of equality and social justice and as anti-western capitalism. In this view, Muḥammad established socialist principles in his state, which means that such a structure of society should take precedence over capitalism. After the period of occupation by European nations, democracy as a system of government, in the argument of many people, has lost its glamour and its moral claim to supremacy. Yet the civic virtues of Europe still held their appeal for many. The impact of more recent developments – the collapse of the colonial empires – has resulted in further confusion in the overall picture. The emergence of new political states, areas which formerly had little unified identity in many cases, has fostered the new phenomenon of nationalism in ethnic and/or cultural terms which often does not include Islam, at least not as that religion has been classically portrayed. Events in 1991 in Iraq, the ongoing Kurdish rebellions in Turkey, the situation in Bosnia, and the emergence of Muslim states out of the now divided Soviet Union are evidence of the strength of such issues. This indicates that there have been significant changes in traditional, pre-modern loyalty patterns brought about by nationalism.[13]

Zionism

Zionism has led to a strengthening of Islamic identity according to many observers, although most would also comment that even so, no united front has appeared among the Islamic nations, especially the Arabs. The sense that the existence of Israel represents the absolute trough of the decline of Muslim civilization is felt by many. Whether Israel is perceived as a punishment for Muslim errors in the past or as a part of a continued western presence in the Middle East, the insult that the nation represents to the Muslim world cannot be underestimated. Some people have argued that Israel's success as a nation – economically, politically – is evidence of the need to adopt western ways. But, for the most part, many feel that Israel represents further evidence of the sinful ways of Muslims and the need for a purification of Islam. The 1967 war between Israel and the Arab world deeply affected the collective psyche of the Muslim people in the wake of the defeat of the Arab troops.[14] The rise of fundamentalist movements, a renewed interest in the symbolic role of Jerusalem and a host of other factors are frequently attributed to this war.

Oil

Oil revenues have produced an ambivalence similar to that caused by the existence of Israel: they are either a curse or a blessing, according to the perspective taken. The impact of the vast revenues has been to take Muslims away from Islam, to the point that Saudi Arabia is frequently pictured as the most corrupt and un-Islamic nation in the world, a land of wine drinking multi-millionaires who repress the less fortunate citizens of their own country and do nothing to enhance Islam. The Iraqi invasion of Kuwait and the various justifications which emerged for it, especially as revealed in statements from Muslims outside the Arab countries, echo this sentiment to a great extent. The opposite argument, that oil revenues now put the population of the Muslim world in a position of affecting the world, giving them the possibility to stand up for their own rights and permitting the propagation of Islam within the context of the modern world, is also frequently made: oil revenues are a gift from God to allow the Muslim world to function in the modern context.[15] The impact of oil is, of course, only a part of the whole discussion of the modern industrial-technological civilization and its impact upon the economic and social life of individuals in society.

Other factors

In presenting the situation of the modern Islamic world, Emmanuel Sivan[16] speaks of television as the most obvious and blatant symbol of the contemporary invasion and the most effective tool in modernity's propagation. Loose morality, instant gratification, life as centred in love and pleasure while oblivious to religious beliefs are all a part of the Hollywood image which is bringing the Islamic world into the global village.[17] Other points may be raised. Education makes no attempt to relate the modern scientific world to Islam, the modern family is reinforced over the traditional structure, and nationalism is more firmly established than the concept of the Islamic community. Of course, this analysis of society and its ills is by no means unique to Islam.[18] With their own cultural forms and their own sociocultural assumptions, these same sentiments are echoed by certain segments of the population throughout the world. Clifford Geertz has said,

> [In face of the modern world, people] lose their sensibility. Or they channel it into ideological fervor. Or they adopt an imported creed. Or they turn worriedly in upon themselves. Or they cling even more intensely to the faltering traditions. Or they try to rework those traditions into more effective forms. Or they split themselves in half, living spiritually in the past and physically in the present. Or they try to express their religiousness in secular activities. And a few simply fail to notice their world is moving or, noticing, just collapse.[19]

The role of Islam in the modern world

A basic point needs to be made in understanding the various discussions which relate to the role Islam should or could (or should not and could not) play in the modern world. Religion, and Islam specifically, is classically thought of as the element which provides the grounding for an individual's life, the interpretative core through which life's experiences may be understood. But the past-oriented nature of religion as it acts to preserve that grounding has meant that its role in the contemporary period has been problematic. The issue then revolves around the form Islam should present to the world in order to take its place in modern society.

As has already been suggested, much of the character of the modern period could be termed the impact of secularism upon a traditional religious system; in that way, the threat to Islam is the same as that posed to Judaism and Christianity. Whether Islam is viable in the modern world is the question, especially since Islam has classically been conceived (if not always manifested in history this way) as a politicized religion. The reality of the matter is that, in the modern context, politicization is even further distant than it was in medieval times. In those ancient times, at least the presence of the caliph as a religio-political authority figure was maintained, even if that person was, during many periods, powerless in front of the military rulers and the independent scholarly élite. The office of the caliphate was officially eliminated with the rise of Republican Turkey in 1924. The perception of some Muslims in the modern period is that secularization is thus attacking the heart of Islam at its theoretical basis.

Islam is the civilizational basis of the Muslim world in politics, in society and in life. In modern terminology, it provides the linguistic basis by which life is experienced, delimits how things are to be perceived and sets the limits to discourse.[20] Can Islam continue with this role in the modern world? Should it even try to? These are the fundamental questions which some Muslims have chosen to face, and continue to face. It is the nature of religion in and by itself which has rendered the questions so difficult.

Some would say that it is the traditional nature of religion as it is manifested in its attitude to authority, based upon a notion of sacredness, and which sees authority as stemming from the past in a continuous flow up to the present, that jars so much with the modern ethos. A value is placed on the past because it supports the authority which exists today. But modernity involves rapid and multi-faceted change. Religions have always had to face changing circumstances and they have developed a number of mechanisms by which this is handled. New ideas, whether emergent, borrowed or acquired, are legitimated in a number of paradigmatic ways: change is seen as a legitimate unfolding of the past; new ideas are proven to have been present always; new ideas are proven to have legitimacy by saying that they should have been present, but the faithful have ignored/suppressed them so that a more legitimate continuity with tradition is discovered through change; or new ideas are accepted through a cultural revolution, the most radical of all strategies.

Under the impact of the rapid change which the modern world has inflicted, many Muslims have experienced a severe weakening of the traditional conception of the eternal, unchanging Muslim legal code, the *sharī'a*. At the same time, it is within the *sharī'a* that various strategies have been employed in order to try to face the challenge of change. The Muslim law had been firmly established by the great jurists of the past. Within the traditional framework, there is room for interpretation and modification, but there cannot be a questioning of the nature and the basis of the authority and the relevance of the law. How to assess the law today, then, in light of those characteristics of modernity as suggested above, has proven to be a challenge, to say the least. This is especially a problem because of the range of topics covered by the *shari'a*: while matters such as politics and taxation remained only theoretically under the guidance of the religious code in medieval Islam, areas of personal law – marriage, divorce, inheritance – remained the stronghold of religion.[21] It is, however, precisely in many of those areas that the contemporary world has effected a great deal of change and where the pressures, especially of nineteenth-century European values, have been felt the most. Equally problematic has been the fact that during the nineteenth century (if not earlier) most Islamic states either adopted or had imposed upon them European law codes which simply displaced the traditional *shari'a*. This process provided a means by which to introduce reforms, for example in areas of women's and family rights, but the result has been that those who wished to see religion continue to play a significant role in their societies either had to demonstrate that their religion, in fact, supported the reforms (and this became the position of those commonly termed the Modernists) or demand that the secular law codes be repealed and simply replaced by Islamic ones (a stance characteristic of more conservative elements).

The response of modern Muslims to this situation has indeed been of every conceivable type. For some, the solution to the question of the role of Islam today is found in Islamic "totalism": that Islam should govern every part of life, from politics to personal conduct to scientific investigation. At the other end of the spectrum, some have argued that the former Muslim ideal of a religio-political mix is the main stumbling block to the modernization of Islam, itself a desirable aim; religion should be a personal, interior matter, an issue between the believer and God and only in that way will Islam remain a vital force in today's world. In between these two responses remains a variety of compromise solutions and non-solutions which do not foster an integrated way of being for the individual.

The post-modern phenomenon

For those on the outside, however, some of the Muslim discussions of this confrontation with the modern period often seem rather quaint. The arguments still seem to revolve around the relevance or danger of Darwin, Marx and Freud, as if those figures represent the state of western thinking. There is little evidence in the Muslim world of what is called in some circles post-modernism. Certainly, radical Marxism is present and that may be viewed as a reaction within the post-modern framework; it is one, however, that calls for a total rejection of Islam and thus it can hardly be termed an Islamic post-modern ideology.[22] The post-modern questioning of the basic presuppositions of religion within a religious framework – the structures of authority, its orientation to the past, its fixation on success – is extremely limited.

Furthermore, to some people, the descriptions given above of what characterizes the modern world are woefully inadequate. The world has already entered a new period of challenge. Mass communications have made the existence of independent states anachronistic; a world community is emerging, but its character is extremely unclear.[23] Recognition has come about of the limits to progress in science and the impact that faith in science has had on the world; the perception of an ecological crisis is a large part of this. The recognition of the threat of technology has raised questions of whether just because something can be done, it should be done. Despite earlier optimism, technology has not managed to solve the basic problems of the world such as starvation. Faith in the moral evolution of humanity (especially the trust in democracy) has been destroyed in the furnaces of Auschwitz; the reality of continuing racism and of the potential for evil that lurks in humanity is felt. The impact of the industrialization of the world in terms of unemployment, pollution, maldistribution of goods and the merging of cultures has been recognized. Feminism and the assertiveness of less-developed countries (with a view to directing their own future through their own value systems) have both accompanied and perhaps been precipitated by post-modernism. These issues are manifested in general terms by the post-modern realization of the powerlessness of the individual to effect change on what have become living institutions.[24] To paraphrase the words of Harvey Cox, if the problem of modernism is termed "we cannot pray," the problem of post-modernism is "we cannot (and others cannot) eat." Post-modernism entails confrontation with the social issues of the day, here conceived within a religious framework: feminism, peace and war, minority expressions of theology, political stances, economics and so forth.

Whether the post-modern situation is taken seriously is one of the differentiating factors in trends in modern thought in general. Fundamentalism tends not to confront the reality of the situation; it proposes in its crasser forms, for example, that homeless people are those who simply choose to live that way. The emergence of critical theology in Christian and Jewish circles is marked by a willingness to confront the post-modern condition with compassion and thoughtfulness.

To the extent that Muslim post-modernism does exist, its greatest manifestation is to be found outside the cultural sphere of the Muslim countries themselves. The future may offer a different situation, in some people's estimation, with the rise of the women's movement and the potential inversion of power structures which could result within the Muslim world. It is worthy of note now, however, that even here, the positions enunciated seem limited: we do not see many women enunciating a new *sharīʿa* that displaces the male prerogative nor many who work on a theology based upon a female (or all inclusive, gender-neutral) language, for example.

Classification of Muslim approaches to modernity

The main issues for Islam in the contemporary situation relate to the place of religion in public life – social, economic, legal, political, intellectual. It is precisely those dimensions which are crucial to a definition of modernity and which thus create the problems to be faced. The dimensions of the phenomenon of modernity focus on the changes which have taken place in all these aspects of public life. That the focus of the conflict is found in this sphere is confirmed by the complementary principle that, to an almost complete extent, there has been no calling into question of Islam itself as a private need or mode of personal devotion, nor have there been many major attempts at a theological reformulation of the faith in light of the modern world. Therefore, studying the reactions of Muslims to modernity is primarily a matter of addressing the question of what specific place the religion is to have in modern life rather than questioning the existence of the religion as such. Can answers to the dilemmas and problems of modern life be found in the religion? If so, how? Can religion at least provide a way to cope?

A tri-part division of religious ways of interacting with the modern age is suggested by many analyses: Traditionalist (sometimes termed Normative or Orthodox); Islamist (sometimes termed Fundamentalist, Neo-Normativist or Revivalist); and Modernist (sometimes termed Acculturating or Modernizing).[25] A simple, although controversial example can serve to illustrate how this sort of division works in the case of Islam: polygamy.

The Traditionalist group may be characterized by their acceptance of multiple-wife marriages, suggesting that to think otherwise is to accept western standards; Islamic tradition has allowed polygamy and that is the way things should be. The Modernist group would suggest a position based on the premise that men and women are equal and monogamy is morally good because it aims towards a concept of social welfare, while polygamy has potentially negative effects on family life; it is often argued that the Qur'ān supports this position.[26] The Islamist group will start from the Qur'ān and say that the Qur'ān was aiming for monogamy all along but made allowances for ancient habits which no longer have any relevance.

It must be remembered that these three divisions are theoretical categories only; people, in the realities of their life situations, can rarely, if ever, be fitted neatly into one position or the other. The categories are heuristic, helpful to indicate tendencies but rarely sufficient to support a full analysis. Furthermore, such categorizations do not allow for historical change within the categories themselves, as will become clear. Modernists, for example, have a substantially different face today than they did at the start of the twentieth century. While the characterizations of these groups, along with refinements to be added later, will be employed in subsequent parts of this book, they are too schematic and reductive to provide structure for a full analysis. The value of these characterizations lies in their ability to reflect the overall dimensions of discussions in modern Islam and thereby provide some tools for more critical analysis.

The Traditionalist group

Each of the above three main categories may be said to display a different attitude towards the authority of the past. The Traditionalist group holds to the full authority of the past and that change should not and does not affect the traditions of the past. Change is to be rejected. Such an expression of the essence of the Traditionalist group is misleading, however: to some extent it falls captive to the group's own rhetoric. Islam, as a cultural entity, has, after all, always been able to cope with change and has built into its structures ways of dealing with change. New situations were ably managed by the institutionalized juridical system. Certainly it is true that the basic sources of Islam – the Qur'ān and the *sunna* – are viewed as unchanging for they are, in some manner, representations in the world of the unchanging God. But this conception, contrary to some suggestions,[27] did not curtail all reaction to changing circumstances. Rather, the issue for the Traditionalists in the contemporary period has been one of substantial challenge to well-established patterns of life and methods of legitimizing change. The Traditionalist group contains within it many of the learned scholars (*'ulamā'*) who might be thought to have a vested interest in maintaining the status quo, many of the mystically oriented Ṣūfī groups, and the vast majority of those who have not been exposed to modern education and thus to a great extent have not experienced the challenge of modernity to such a degree as to consider it a personal problem.

One trend within Traditionalism can be termed "Neo-traditionalism." This is a tendency which has been seen as a transitional position from traditionalism to any of the other groups. It may be, however, that as a position it has its own inherent permanent protagonists; such a position (displayed in S. H. Nasr's writings and, perhaps, in the Iranian revolution) urges a gradual change, seeing the advantage in certain elements of modern technology, for example, but wanting to withstand the rush of the acceptance of it all. In the short term, urgent change may be required but, in the long run, Islam will reign supreme.

Islamism and revivalism

The Islamist group, in contrast to the Traditionalist, is characterized by its desire to accept change in a controlled fashion; it therefore uses the authoritative sources of the past to legitimize changes in the present day. This group has a long intellectual history in Islam, or, at least, that is the perception of its adherents. Picking up on the line of thought from Ibn Taymiyya through Ibn 'Abd al-Wahhāb, these revivalist tendencies emphasize the absolute character of the sources authority of Islam – the Qur'ān and the *sunna*. This reliance on text results in what is frequently termed literalism or fundamentalism but, at the same time, it opens up the possibilities of independent reasoning through the rejection of authority by that very process of the return to the text and the ignoring of traditional interpretation of those texts. Such thinking also tends toward an anti-intellectualism, especially anti-philosophy. This is perhaps one of the key points for differentiating Modernists and Islamists.[28]

These trends in thought are crucial to the writings of people associated with contemporary expressions of Islam revivalism led by the Islamists. Abū'l A'lā' Mawdūdī (1903–1979) is a prime example. His call was for a return to the Qur'ān and a purified *sunna* so that Islam might be revitalized; this could only truly happen if Islam became the constitution of the state and this was the political goal towards which he worked in Pakistan. Sayyid Quṭb (1906–66) of Egypt provides another example. He became the intellectual spokesman for the Muslim Brotherhood. He championed a return to "pure Islam" and a move away from the materialism of the West which he perceived as contaminating Islam. Allegiance should be to Islam alone, for that provides the perfect social system for all humanity, one which will cure all the ills of the modern world. Once a truly Islamic state is established, all aspects of life will fall into their proper place. Both of these thinkers will be dealt with in later chapters of this book.

Revolutionary radical Islamism – that fringe element which dominates the media picture of Islamic fundamentalism – is somewhat distinct in the emphasis it places on the corruption to Islam from within the community. True Islam is the cure and must be applied through armed uprising. Also notable is the tendency to view things as opposing spheres: for example, the Government of God versus the Great Satan in Iranian propaganda. Thus, for someone such as Sayyid Quṭb, everything is *jāhilī*, from the "age of barbarism," except Islam.

The Islamist movement is sometimes called "fundamentalism" although that latter term involves the use of a designation borrowed from early twentieth-century Christianity which some people see as inappropriate.[29] In its application to religious groupings, the word "fundamentalism" arose in the United States and was used by a coalition of theologically conservative Protestants who came together in 1920 to struggle against modernism and liberalism; it was coined because these people were said to be holding to the great fundamentals of their faith.[30] For Protestant Fundamentalists, the key fundamental is the inerrancy of the Bible, which is a defence of basic religious ideals – the seriousness of sin, the need for redemption and the idea that Jesus has granted that redemption. There is a great stress placed on individual salvation and personal morality. Fundamentalists are prepared to do battle for their fundamentals. The best examples are seen in court cases against the teaching of evolution in the 1920s and in the more contemporary Moral Majority movement.

In the Islamic world the term "fundamentalism" has been applied (mainly by Westerners) to those who call for a strict implementation of the *sharīʿa*, including the call for an Islamic state. Opposition to western ways and to the perceived corruption of Muslim society is important, and even, according to some,[31] the most important elements uniting fundamentalists of all religious persuasions. The issue of scripture marks a difference between Muslim and Christian fundamentalists. Virtually all Muslims are "fundamentalist" in their attitude to scripture. Protestant doctrines, on the other hand, which are seen as intimately linked to inerrancy (for example, the resurrection of Jesus) are rejected by all Muslims. Likewise, while Muslim fundamentalists stress political goals and implementation of religion in all areas of life, Christian fundamentalists can go either way and some become secularists by Muslim standards.

The oppositional stance of both Christian fundamentalists and Muslim Islamist groups is significant; they both "do battle" with western modernism. (Muslims also frequently attack elements within their own societies and desire a total restructuring.) That element of militancy (taken in either a figurative or literal sense) on behalf of God's way in the world unites both groups. The claim to be the authentic expression of the tradition is also prominent; somewhat ironically then, both groups – Christians and Muslims – emphasize the distinctive elements of their own faith. Both groups wish to take scripture very seriously (if not always literally, although in theory they may be more inclined that way than more Modernist groups). Absolutism in ethics follows from this and both groups emphasize the supernatural, seeing God's will at work in the world in very direct ways.

Islamic modernism and its history

The Modernist group has seen that greater advantage is to be found within the modern circumstance by embracing change and making religion itself subject to change. The Modernist position is frequently based upon a principle of differentiating basic moral precepts from specific legal prescriptions. This movement too has had a substantial history. It developed in the nineteenth century with people such as Jamāl al-Dīn al-Afghānī (1839–1897), Muḥammad 'Abduh (1849–1905) and Rashīd Riḍā (1865–1935) in Egypt and Sayyid Aḥmad Khān (1817–1898) and Muhammad Iqbāl (1876–1938) in India. Al-Afghānī is famous for his idea of Pan-Islamism which he saw as a way of reviving and uniting Islam against Europe; this idea was to be combined with an embracing of philosophy and science which, he argued, transcend particular communities. He greatly influenced 'Abduh, and through him, Riḍā, who worked further to synthesize those features of the West which seemed desirable (especially its scientific rationality) with the essential truths of Islam. The situation in India was very similar. Aḥmad Khān argued that modern knowledge and the use of reason were what was required in order to bring vitality back to Islam. Essentially this involved a separation between Islam as a religion of ritual and law, and reason or science which was not seen to be under the control of religious law although it was in keeping with the true principles of the faith itself. Deep down, the argument went, there was no conflict between Islam and modernity, for they both functioned on different planes. Islamic law is not fixed but must change in each situation, especially in the social realm. Iqbal's message, frequently couched in mystically inspired poetry, urged the same return to the essentials of Islam, to be found in its true sources.

Reconstruction, *iṣlāḥ*, became the catchword for this trend.[32] As a movement it may also be seen to have had a substantial influence on the Islamists as well, with its call of "back to the sources." But its emphasis on elements of the West as having some value for Islamic culture (as opposed to the self-sufficiency of Islam), and its tendency towards a definition of religion centered on the individual in his/her relationship with God along with its flexible attitude towards the social aspect of the faith, mark the Modernists as distinct. A number of factors may be isolated as contributing to the rise of the Modernists, which illustrates once again that speaking simply of modernism as a reaction to Europe does not represent an accurate summary of the issues involved. According to the analysis of Ali Merad, the pressures of pre-Modernist fundamentalism, the development of the printed word as a result of the introduction of the printing press in Arab countries around 1822, the influence of western culture, the liberal evolution of the Ottoman regime (for example, the introduction of a code of civil liberties in 1839) and the structural renovation of the Eastern Christian churches showing an example of "zeal in the service of a faith," all contributed substantially to stimulating a "renaissance," *nahḍa*, within the Arab countries especially which has become identified with the Modernist trend.[33]

Islamic modernism wants Islam to be the basis for political life as well as the religious, but it perceives a need to reinterpret those structures in light of contemporary needs, frequently with a clear and unapologetic adoption of western notions. This generally reflects an idea of the flexibility of Islam such that modern ideologies may be seen as fitting in with Islamic ones. Generally, Modernists (such as Fazlur Rahman and Ghulām Aḥmad Parvēz, to be discussed in a later chapter) argue that the juridical basis of Islam must be put aside for the modern use of independent judgement based on the

Qur'ān and (perhaps) the *sunna*. This is a way of limiting the binding nature of the past, thus allowing some flexibility, but note that it does not deny its authority. Rather, it allows for a radical reinterpretation of the past, enabling principles of the past to be seen in light of modern ideals, such as democracy, freedom, equality, tolerance and social justice. In fact, these and other ideals become general principles which Islam is seen as standing for, and through which Islam must be implemented in today's world. Other examples are to be seen in the value of work and the redistribution of excess wealth. Matters which do not fit within these ideals are deemed superstitions and must be done away with, for they are not in keeping with Islam. Notable too, is the frequent Modernist appeal to the Islamic basis of many western ideas: democracy being found in the early Islamic community; *dhimmī* – non-Muslim subjects living under Muslim rule – being the foundation of religious pluralism and so forth. This sort of tendency can lead to apologetics where the superiority of Islam over all things Western is argued, a tendency also to be seen perhaps less frequently in Islamism. Modernism, then, differs from secularism by the efforts it makes to find support in the Qur'ān and the *sunna*; from the critic's point of view, this method is only "a cover for what secularists do more openly."[34]

In looking at these three main divisions, Traditionalism, Islamism, and Modernism, one factor differentiates or becomes crucial in the definition: the attitude toward what is termed "Islamic totalism." To what extent is Islam seen as encompassing all of life in its social, political and economic spheres? To what extent is Islam seen as a guide to social action and public legislation? The extent of this can range from Islam governing the full social structure to Islam being a "religion" in a Protestant sense, that is, as a matter for the individual and his/her conscience alone. Here too, for Islamists, as we shall see, it is possible to separate modernization from Westernization. That is, Islam can modernize without being Western: Islam can be pictured as providing the basis for all of life without having anything to do with western ideas, and, at the same time, change may be embraced as fully as is desired in order to allow for that modernization.

There are other possibilities for a solution to the dilemmas which Islam faces which come from a rejection of Islam *per se*. For example, the arguments for agnosticism and atheism present themselves. The former, perhaps also to be seen as a simple embracing of secularism, is as rampant in many Muslim countries as it is elsewhere. Some may well argue that it is not really a solution as such; rather, it is a platform displaying a failure of nerve, the inability either to commit oneself to religion or to leave it totally. It is for many, however, a pragmatic solution where issues of religion are simply not as important in life as are matters of finding a job and maintaining a family. Our concern here, however, is primarily with those who are active in trying to find a religiously-based answer to the questions of today.

13 Muḥammad and modernity

It is crucial to any understanding of religion in the modern world that an assessment of the attitude towards the past be undertaken: how is the authority of the past dealt with in the modern situation? In the Islamic case, the many specific issues which arise stem from one major question: what is the status of Muḥammad and the Qur'ān in the view of modern Muslims?

In dealing with Muḥammad, there are a number of approaches that may be contemplated in order to embrace the totality of the subject. Muḥammad's role as a source of authority through the status of what he actually did during his lifetime, summed up in the word *sunna*, is crucial. There are other, more subtle ways in which Muḥammad is discussed in the modern context, however, each of which reflects the impact of modernity and differing conceptions of Islam. They are frequently implicit positions, versus the explicit ones found in the discussions of the *sunna* and its authority. They are frequently more popular and significant in terms of their influence.

The role of biography

All Muslim groups in the modern world join in their veneration of Muḥammad. In fact, within the context of the modern world, that must be taken as one of the defining elements of what Islam actually is. The writing of biographies of Muḥammad is, therefore, a singularly appropriate enterprise for all concerned, and it provides, thereby, a glimpse into the adjustments Muslims have as a response to modern context. Biography is a powerful mirror for the reflection of ideals, as well as standards, of the age in which they are written and thus may be seen to reflect the contemporary situation of their authors in the very construction of the facts which the works intend to record.

Because of Muḥammad's role in Islamic society as "teacher and exemplar"[1] – ideals embodied in the concept of the *sunna* – his life story has been used constantly as an inspirational source, manifesting itself in the writing of biographies. With the impact of change in the modern world, it has become necessary for a biographer to create a biography which may be read as having some relevance to the modern world: a relevance which will reflect the ideals and aspirations of the writer's perception of the needs of the Muslim community. For example, encouraging the use of reason, the pursuit of education, and the fostering of science have frequently been pictured as cures for the ills of the Muslim world. Providing women with a more active role in society has become another common goal. The support that the actual details of the life of Muḥammad can provide for these ideas is crucial to the process of legitimizing the change which is deemed necessary. The sense of legitimization is important for most reformers; if Islam is to remain relevant to human life, then the changes deemed desirable must be incorporated within it. There is also a pragmatic reason for the appeal to legitimization by Muḥammad: literature, especially of the biographical type, is a powerful tool of propaganda.

Furthermore, for reformers, biographies can become the vehicle for reform by being a message couched in traditional terms and thus not so subject to attack from the more conservative elements in society. The example of widely criticized reformers from the nineteenth century made a number of twentieth-century reformers feel the need to veil their ideas in a form acceptable (or less easy to reject out-of-hand) to the religious powers.

The character of biography

A number of motifs are found repeatedly in modern biographies of Muḥammad which are worthy of attention. Among these are the following:

1   The treatment of the process of revelation versus the role of reason – can the traditional view of revelation as a supernatural event be maintained in light of reason?
2   The issue of Muḥammad's sinlessness – does it really make sense that Muḥammad never committed an error during his life as has been traditionally held?
3   The nature of Muḥammad's heavenly journey, undertaken early in his prophetic career, according to traditional accounts, when

he traveled on the back of a winged horse to Jerusalem and ascended to heaven in order to meet the former prophets and receive a vision of God – was it in the body (as was classically emphasized) or by the soul only (perhaps as a vision)?[2]

4 The general status of miracles in Muhammad's life – can they be accounted for by rational scientific explanations?

5 Muhammad's personality as a husband and as a statesman, with *jihād*, "holy war," a major part of the issue – can these sorts of activities be accepted in a modern context?

These topics reflect two concerns, both prominently displayed in the biographies. One is the impact of modern scientific thought and ways of understanding phenomena such as prophecy and miraculous occurrences. The other is the impact of Orientalism and general Christian attacks on Islam, especially in charges of Muhammad's "immorality" (as reflected, for example, in concerns over the number of his marriages) and "war-mongering" (as reflected in the assessment of the many battles which he led against the various tribes in Arabia). This last point is somewhat more complex. Orientalists, especially those who worked within the framework of colonialist regimes, frequently spoke of Islam as being counter to modern ideals and progress – that concept being glossed to include morality and ethics. That is, the morality encouraged by Islam was not in keeping with the modern ethos and would only hold Muslims back from being able to embrace science and progress. An example would be the horror expressed by some writers at the idea of Muslim men being able to have four wives; no man could possibly be an active member of an industrialized work force and cope with four wives! Therefore, these two topics – modern scientific thought and the moral character of Islam – are frequently intertwined. Thus the Muslim pro-science argument will frequently be anti-Orientalist at the same time.

With regard to the Orientalist attention to Muhammad, while Muslim devotion to their prophet was obvious enough, Christian desires to discover the "historical Jesus" were undoubtedly being reflected in some of the attention being given to Muhammad. The temptation towards implicit or explicit comparisons between Jesus and Muhammad – always being conducted from the viewpoint of the superiority of Christianity, to be sure – was undoubtedly too hard to resist for many Orientalist writers.

The question of the historical reliability of sources and the rise of historical criticism has also affected the Muslim biographical enterprise to a great extent. In embracing ideals of modern scientific thought and in rejecting Orientalist aspersions cast upon Islam, a method of historical–critical writing arose. This rise of the study of history is one of the characteristics of the modern period, as was suggested above. There was, therefore, on the part of some modern Muslim writers, an effort to foster a historical–critical approach in their writings about Muḥammad. No longer, it was said, could events simply be narrated as they were in the past, but the sources must be subjected to analysis for bias and implausibility. For those reformers bent on introducing the scientific method into the Muslim world, what more appropriate (but potentially dangerous!) vehicle could there be than the biography of Muḥammad? Many writers, therefore, certainly raise these sorts of issues in their work, but, in many instances, the actual implementation of the historical method has been quite minimal. That fact, however, should not detract from the attention given to the influence the idea itself has had.

Biographies and history

The emphasis in many (but certainly not all) of the modern biographies is not on Muḥammad's actions as such – that is, not in the historical narratives found in the classical books written by people like Ibn Isḥāq – but on his spiritual attitude, his general outlook and his morals. In this sense, Muḥammad is portrayed as the truly modern man and, once that idea is fully understood, then Islam may not only be seen to be compatible with the modern era, but may also be seen to embody it fully.

As with the classical biographies of Muḥammad which provide a mythic portrayal of a pristine society at the time of the foundation of Islam, a picture of the Islamic ideal, so too the modern ones. Each wishes to portray the ideals of the community, but the fact is that those ideals have changed over time. For the classical biographer Ibn Isḥāq, valiant battles led by the divinely appointed leader of the community served as an example for all to follow. Muḥammad's special relationship to God was displayed by the permission granted to him to marry many wives. These were aspects of the argument for Islam at the time of Ibn Isḥāq. But for modern writers, the ideals and aspirations are different and narrating the factual realities of Muḥammad's life (as recorded in these classical sources) does not necessarily accomplish the desired goal of contemporary relevance. In fact, Muḥammad as a real, live person tends to fade in many of the modern biographies, slipping into the light of unreal absolute perfection in his heroic role, while at the same time there is a downplaying of the "irrational" prophetic elements in his life. Muḥammad's greatest miracle for many modern writers, unlike the ancient writers such as Ibn Isḥāq, is not the splitting of the moon, or the sighing palm trunk as he walked by, or talking sheep, but the moral and spiritual transformation which he accomplished in society.

Another aspect appears in some biographies which needs attention. The biographies frequently reflect the socio-political environment of the writer to the extent that support for specific political parties becomes manifest. The past becomes a source of inspiration, especially for nationalists, and nationalism was rife in Egypt in the 1930s, for example, reflecting internal developments but also trends in European political thought; Islam and Muḥammad became ideal channels through which nationalism could be expressed. There was a wave of biographical writing in Egypt during this period; as a result, treatments of Muḥammad became popular elsewhere in the Arab world, the biographical form being adopted as a vehicle for reform. Looking at some of these biographies briefly will indicate some of their scope. Most of the attention falls on Muḥammad Ḥusayn Haykal, the most significant and the most studied of all contemporary biographers.[3]

Muḥammad Ḥusayn Haykal

Muḥammad Haykal was born in 1888 and died in 1956. He studied law in Cairo and then pursued further education at the Sorbonne in Paris. He received his Doctorate in 1912 for studies in economics and law. He worked as a lawyer and educator as well as a member of the government, as a novelist and, most significantly, as a journalist. His first work, *Zaynab*, was written while he was in Paris and was published in 1914; it is generally cited as the first Arabic novel. He also founded a newspaper with a weekly literary supplement in the 1920s and much of his later work appeared in it.

Haykal was most concerned with establishing the rationality of Islam and rejecting every Orientalist objection to, and criticism of, the religion itself. Islam is, for Haykal, fully in keeping with modern life and reason. Modern rational standards may, in fact, be identified as inherently and originally Muslim, Greek and Egyptian. Writes Haykal,

> Long before the times of Moses and Jesus, the science of ancient Egypt as well as its philosophy and law had passed to Greece

and Rome, which had then spread their dominion. It was Egypt
that contributed to Greek philosophy and literature their noblest
ideas. The new rationalist awakening thus produced, warned and
convinced people that miracles constitute no argument at all
... it was God's pattern that reason shall constitute the apogee
of human life, as long as it is not composed of empty logic, not
devoid of feeling and spirit, and as long as it martials [sic: read
"marshals"] all these faculties in a synthesized effort to discover
the secrets of the universe and achieve intimate knowledge of
the cosmic pattern. Thus, it was decreed by God that soon the
Prophet of Islām would rise to call men to the truth through
reason, complemented by feeling and spirit, and that the one
miracle of such a gnoseological synthesis should be the Holy
Book revealed to His Prophet Muḥammad.[4]

Much of this paragraph is a reaction against Christian missionary
and Orientalist prejudice and is spoken of as a scientific inquiry into
Muḥammad, away from the biases of the Europeans. Haykal does
use European studies of Muḥammad as the basis of his work,
however, for he considered the traditional Arabic sources to be full
of superstition and impossible stories. To some extent, Haykal
suggests, the Orientalists are not to blame for their distortions of
Islam, for irrational elements are clearly to be found in the classical
sources. It should not be thought, however, that Haykal's method
employs the historical–critical method as expounded in the West;
rather his biography of Muḥammad is guided by the ideals and spirit
of Islam and by the sources moulded by the methodological principle that things "must have been" a certain way. It is generally not
a critical analysis entailing a comparison of various traditions, but
simply a choosing of the appropriate historical report through the
elimination of any elements deemed superstitious or in error
according to the modern sensibility.

Notably, Haykal also sees his approach as a rejection of Muslim
conservative elements. What is holding Muslims back is not Islam
but the tradition which is so fervently maintained by the religious
élite. Furthermore, the attitudes displayed by the conservative religious authorities only give the Orientalists and the Christian
missionaries more ammunition. The sources used by these unfriendly
writers are those dominated by the conservative elements, and the
conclusions which those critics come to are not the result of the
methodology which they employ – a methodology which Haykal
argues should be followed – but of the sources themselves.

The only absolutely reliable source for talking about Islam is the Qur'ān. Interpreting the other sources in light of the spirit of the Qur'ān would correct all misunderstandings. For Haykal, the message of the Qur'ān is clearly one of rationality and the search for scientific wisdom, and that is a message which the religious classes have perverted over the ages. Further, the Qur'ān supports ideas of social order and individual freedom, keys to a truly modern Islamic society and in agreement with Haykal's own political position.[5]

Haykal's Muḥammad

Haykal's work, *The Life of Muḥammad*, published as a book in 1935, has been extensively read, translated and studied, both in a popular way as well as in scholarly analyses. Its aim is to provide a fully modern biography, one written in accord with modern scientific reason. At the same time, it is not a critical biography: for the most part it is a reiteration of facts from the classical sources with no critical stance. Haykal started the work in 1932 and published pieces of it periodically over the following two years. The work has been through at least ten editions, gaining a few extra sections in the process.

Haykal argues that all biographers reflect the standards of their own day. That Ibn Isḥāq, for example, should speak of certain events as miraculous simply reflects his understanding of the workings of the world at his time. Likewise, the early biographers display a materialistic slant towards an issue such as Muḥammad's multiple marriages (emphasizing elements like tribal alliances and so forth) and fail to see the spiritual element implied by the prophet's activities.

Several points prove crucial in Haykal's biography, as they do in most modern biographies, for they reflect the central issues which have been emphasized in western attacks upon Muḥammad and Islam. This apologetic response of the biographers is frequently their most notable element. Haykal discusses the trustworthiness of Muḥammad to counter some of the charges laid against him. Involved here is the notion of Muḥammad's sinlessness. One special aspect of this is in regard to the Satanic verses, concerning which it is declared inconceivable that Muḥammad could have been deceived by Satan into uttering certain verses supposedly to be in the Qur'ān (but later withdrawn) which compromised the monotheism of Islam by allowing minor goddesses to be viewed as intercessors with Allāh (a story told in many classical sources). Muḥammad's marriages are dealt with in detail, especially those to Zaynab and Māriya where images of lust and seduction were often conjured up. The treatment of Muḥammad's use of violence, minimized as much as possible by Haykal, is especially noticeable in comparison with older texts in which Muḥammad's fighting is often seen as a part of his successful strategy and nothing to be played down: fighting took place under God's will and command. All these areas are focused upon by Orientalists, and Haykal clearly rejects the Orientalist conclusions and argues against the Orientalist methods. Finally, Haykal speaks from a certain time period in Egypt when democracy was being promoted; his biography clearly reflects those ideals as stemming from, and therefore legitimized by, the time of Muḥammad.

> While the non-Muslim inhabitants began to fear Muslim power – knowing well that it stemmed from the depth of hearts which had tasted sacrifice and persecution for the sake of faith, the Muslims collected the fruits of their patience and enjoyed their religious freedom. Their peace and freedom were now made constitutional by the Islamic principles that no man has any authority over any other, that religion belongs to God alone, that service is to Him alone, that before Him all men are absolutely equal, and that nothing differentiates them except their works and intentions. ... The theater was ready and the stage was set for Muḥammad to constitute by his conduct the ideal exemplification and embodiment of these teachings and principles, and for his laying down the foundation stone of Islamic civilization.[6]

Because of Haykal's sense of rationality, he sees fewer miracles playing a role in Muḥammad's life but puts an emphasis on natural processes to explain some of them. The heavenly journey is taken as psychological, for example. As well, the picture of Muḥammad is framed in terms of modern ideals – loving, forgiving, perfect.

ʿAbd al-Raḥmān al-Sharqāwī

Al-Sharqāwī (1920–87) was an Egyptian novelist and critic who, in 1962, published *Muḥammad, the Messenger of Freedom*. His previous writings were famous for their poetic spirit as well as their political commitment. His treatment of Muḥammad was not designed as a biography to replace the classical ones in their recounting of history; "everything has been said" on that topic, according to the author.

Rather, he was attempting to portray an image of Muḥammad as a man whose aim was to produce a unified humanity based on notions of love and mercy and whose ultimate goal was to produce a better future for his people. Inherent in Muḥammad's message was progress and liberation through a veritable revolution.[7]

Al-Sharqāwī hoped to provide a positive picture for non-Muslim readers, a potentially large and fruitful audience given the large population of Christian Copts in Egypt. His work also, and perhaps more successfully, reflects the political climate of Nasserite Socialism in Egypt, a revolt against capitalism (and thus against Europe). This is conveyed by picturing Muḥammad as a worker, rising up on behalf of others against the rich Quraysh tribe and the Jews; the latter are pictured throughout the work as the rich enemies whom Muḥammad constantly tried to befriend. Downplayed are the prophetic and miraculous elements in Muḥammad's life; his experiences are seen as dreams of the perfect state of human existence, free from the type of oppression which was prevalent in pre-Islamic Mecca where everything was done for the benefit of the rich. Al-Sharqāwī's biography then is apologetic while pursuing the clear political end of a modern vision of society legitimized through Muḥammad's life. As such, it aroused some opposition within Egyptian clerical circles for its failure to treat the traditional religious values of Muḥammad's career and Islam as a whole.

ʿAbd al-Raḥmān ʿAzzām

ʿAzzām (1893–1976) was an Egyptian diplomat and served as Secretary-General of the Arab League from 1945 to 1952. In 1938 he wrote an Arabic work entitled *The Hero of Heroes or the most Prominent Attribute of the Prophet Muḥammad*. A revised English version was published in 1965 as *The Eternal Message of Muḥammad*. The format of the book is worthy of attention. The life of Muḥammad itself is briefly sketched in a short twenty pages. Following that are sections dealing with the basic message of Islam, social reform, the state, international relations, dissemination of the message, the causes of world disturbances, and the search for "a spiritual bulwark for civilization." The point is clear: Muḥammad, through his person and his actions, has something to say about each of these aspects of modern (political) existence. Bravery, love, the ability to forgive, and eloquence are all attributes of Muḥammad that are emphasized, leading to the conclusion that the diplomatic nature of Muḥammad's life is one that provides an example for today in the resolution of conflicts. "The Message of Muḥammad recognizes neither nationalism nor racism in their modern contexts; the fatherland of the Muslim admits of no geographical delimitations – it coexists with the faith. ... Racism, or a fanatic attachment to tribe, nation, color, language, or culture, is rejected by the Message as a product of pre-Islamic idolatry."[8] Political manoeuvres and military insights are also championed.

> Recognizing the inherent and manifest evils of war, the Message of Muḥammad circumscribed warfare with common rules of right conduct (*adab*), defining its aims and limiting it to the repulsion of aggression, the protection of the freedom of belief, and the termination of battle with just and durable agreements. ... Certain states nowadays prefer surprise attacks on their enemies without any previous warning. Preliminary precautions prior to attack are such that the aggression-bent state can surprise its enemies completely by pretending all along to favor peace; often the true motives and pretenses for waging war may not be revealed prior to combat. ... There is nothing more distasteful to Islam than this, and the tenets of Muslim law reject it in spirit and in practice.[9]

Najīb Maḥfūẓ

Awarded the Nobel Prize for Literature in 1988, Najīb Maḥfūẓ (in English usually written Naguib Mahfouz) is probably the best known of all contemporary Arab writers. Born in 1911, he published his first novel in 1939 at a time when the Arabic novel as a form was in its infancy. His major works include *The Cairene Trilogy*, written 1956–57, which traces the story of three generations of a Cairo family, putting into novel form the changes in the daily life of middle-class people in the first half of the twentieth century. His works were cited by the Nobel Prize committee as being "rich in nuance, now clear-sightedly realistic, now evocatively ambiguous."

Maḥfūẓ, in at least some of his writings, critiques the stance and values of traditional religion, Islam included. Religion has not accomplished what it set out to do. The divine has become irrelevant to modern life because of the way in which He has been made absent from human existence. The prophets, sent by God, have had little effect on human existence, "unable after their demise to ensure any abiding salvation for mankind from the burden of being human."[10]

Maḥfūẓ's Muḥammad

Published first as a serial in the newspaper *al-Ahrām* in 1959, *Children of Gabalawi* is an allegory of God, His messengers through history, and their interaction with the world. Its treatment of Muḥammad is not therefore traditional biography by any means, although elements of his life as depicted in early works are clearly discernible in the character of Qāsim and his environs of the streets of Cairo. The names are changed "to protect the innocent," but the story remains the same. The book is even divided into 114 sections, echoing the 114 *sūra*s of the Qur'ān.

Maḥfūẓ's Muḥammad is a deeply committed man who challenges the established secular and religious powers. He leads a band of vigilantes whose aim is no less than setting the stage for a world where human rights are respected and the law of God is enacted; this they set out to accomplish by force, in a manner pictured as being midway between Moses' war mongering and Jesus' pacifism. Muḥammad's character embodies all the values that should be emulated, and this includes his ability to love women; no modern apologetic is needed to excuse Muḥammad's multiple marriages.[11]

Maḥfūẓ's main interest, however, is in the frustration of the goal of Muḥammad by later followers, and this is what the work goes on to explore in its final section. Science has become the prophet. The leaders of the past have been made into legends. The story finally leads to the death of Gabalawi (i.e. God). Muḥammad, in this way, is no different than the earlier prophets talked of in the book (Adam, Moses, Jesus) whose mission should have been sufficient to set the world aright but, in fact, matters did not work out that way. Muslims are now without God, even while they claim to be surrounded by Him; this is the result of the failure to pose the necessary and penetrating questions concerning the nature of God and existence.

This is a biography for the modern world, one in which the message is deeply veiled by the curtain of the medium and the form. One cannot help thinking of Salman Rushdie's attempt at the same feat, and this parallel has been pursued by some observers.[12] Maḥfūẓ's work created an outcry at the time of its publication and it did not appear in book form until it was published in 1967 in Beirut (the venue for many dissident Egyptian works). Kenneth Cragg's assessment of the work is fitting:

> Its haunting, wistful scepticism presents a searching challenge to ordinary believers. Served by eminent narrative skill and literary

art, it invites them to look into a void, to think themselves stripped of their familiar securities, to divest themselves of assumptions about God and His messengers which have always been instinctive to their minds and culture. It confronts them with the unthinkable, with the implication that everything on which they had relied might need, for its own sake, to be called in question.[13]

Fatima Mernissi

A sociologist and university teacher in Morocco, Fatima Mernissi (b. 1940) recently published *Women and Islam: An Historical and Theological Enquiry*, which is as close as one might conceive to a feminist biography of Muḥammad. The root problem of Muslim society today, according to Mernissi, one which the intrusion of the West has forced Muslims to confront, is that women have not been treated as full members of the community.

Mernissi does not see Islamic gender segregation as an isolated social phenomenon of a religious nature, but as a political expression of a specific distribution of power and authority and an economic reflection of a specific division of labor, both forming a total and coherent social order. When this Islamic segregation is shaken, the coherence of the traditional social order as a whole is put into question, especially if social reform is not able to set up an acceptable new system of values governing male–female relations.[14]

Women may have gained the right to vote in a country such as Morocco, from where Mernissi writes, but they have not gained the right to be elected, she says. Men continue to consider power the privilege of the male and cannot conceive of the need to have women participating in decisions regarding the future. Furthermore, in order to support their position, the appeal is made to the foundations of the faith of Islam. This accounts for the current surge in Islamist membership, where men find comfort against the inroads of female demands.

To counter these sorts of appeals to religion, Mernissi returns to the sources to extract a picture of Muḥammad as the supporter of women's rights, though her picture is a mixed one. On one level, she seems to say that Islam is inherently male oriented and there is a need to move "beyond": "One wonders if a desegregated society, where formerly secluded women have equal rights not only economically but sexually, would be an authentic Muslim society."[15] But, at the same time, she looks back to Muḥammad for inspiration and legitimization. This is an attempt perhaps to battle Islamist elements (glossed consistently as anti-women) on their own grounds – inter-Muslim apologetics. Muḥammad is the champion of women whose opinion is even overruled by God on occasion (the implications for the status of the Qur'ān in Mernissi's books will be a topic for consideration in the next chapter) who seems to have been more influenced by the pragmatics of male-oriented power structures than His prophet. The tendency towards reinforcing male power has been further aggravated by male interpreters of the sacred texts who saw only their own prerogatives at stake and who thought nothing of ignoring Muḥammad's intentions of improving the lot of women.

For Mernissi, Muḥammad's character reflects precisely what is lacking in contemporary male–female relations: "Muhammad was a chief of state who publicly acknowledged the importance of affection and sex in life. And, during expeditions, his wives were not just background figures, but shared with him his strategic concerns. He listened to their advice, which was sometimes the deciding factor in thorny negotiations."[16]

The institution of the *ḥijāb*, "veiling" – here to be taken to mean the entire social system which separates men and women in Muslim countries, as will be explored further in Chapter 15 below – became a part of Islam only because of male concerns for their own privileges and was put in place against the general principles which Muḥammad had initiated. Attacks were made on Muḥammad because of his private life in which his wives enjoyed a great deal of freedom and authority, contrary to the established practices of society at the time. "Hurt and weakened, [Muhammad] lost his ability to stand up to 'Umar [pictured here as the spokesman for the male prerogative], and he agreed to the confinement of women. He gave his consent to the *hijab*. He gave his consent to the reestablishment of male supremacy."[17]

Muḥammad, for Mernissi, aspired to the ideal society, but the pressures of the situation – a situation into which he had introduced radical change – would not allow these platforms to be maintained. But the equality of men and women and the freedom of women to control their own lives and to be a valuable part of society are what Muḥammad stood for, and it is the true core of Islam. The pragmatic value of providing safety for his wives had overcome his principles. Those principles are reflected in the very basis of the religion of Islam, except, it would seem, when it comes to dealing with women. Islam, for Mernissi, stands for the use of the intellect as the means by which good is to be separated from evil. The veiling of women imposed the language of violence and power, whereas individual responsibility was the essence of the society which God wished to be instituted. But the ignorant forces of male power could not accept that responsibility.

> Muhammad put great emphasis on politeness. He himself was very shy. Several verses [of the Qur'ān] attest to this aspect of his character, which . . . in the absence of tactfulness on the part of some men of his entourage forced him to adopt the *hijab*. He did not consider that having a house open to the world had to mean that people would invade his privacy. The *hijab* represented the exact opposite of what he had wanted to bring about. It was the incarnation of the absence of internal control; it was the veiling of the sovereign will, which is the source of good judgment and order in a society.[18]

Mernissi's biography is not a traditional one, then. While it covers a great deal of the life of Muḥammad, its focus is on the women around him and his attitude towards them. This is no different, albeit substantially more explicit, than Haykal arguing for the rationality of Muḥammad. That is, the point of the biography is made more explicit to the reader; it could well be that, with the rise in general literacy levels, works like that of Mernissi have become more appropriate and more convincing. No longer is it necessary to embed one's ideas so deeply in stories.

'Alī Dashtī

Biographies of Muḥammad are, of course, not limited to being written by Arabs. 'Alī Dashtī was an Iranian journalist, novelist and politician with a classical religious training; he served in the Senate of Iran from 1954 to 1979. His book, *Twenty-three Years: A Study of the Prophetic Career of Mohammad*, was published anonymously in 1974. He died shortly after the Iranian revolution at the age of about 85 under vague circumstances.

Dashtī's biography presents a full rationalization of prophethood and is a fairly extreme example at that. Muḥammad's experience of prophethood was his own conscience or inner mind speaking to him. Nothing supernatural occurred in Muḥammad's life; everything can be accounted for by modern psychology and sociology. Muḥammad's infallibility is rejected, and thus the "Satanic verses" are accepted. The Qur'ān – Muḥammad's book rather than God's – is spoken of as being full of grammatical errors, as should be expected from an illiterate man such as Muḥammad, and was taken from a variety of sources. The miracle of the Qur'ān lies in its results, not its literary formulation – it is as untranslatable as a poem by the famous Persian poet Ḥāfiẓ. This comparison is noteworthy because of its Iranian emphasis; Dashtī, in fact, accuses the Arabs of being responsible for most of the problems of Islam especially as it is manifested in today's Arab Islamism. With the rise of Islam, "the Arabs did not suddenly lose their materialistic outlook, their inability to think in abstract terms, their unconcern with spiritual matters, and their unruliness and obstinacy."[19] After only a few centuries of Islam did the Iranians place "no value on their nationhood and [imagine] the Hejaz to be the sole source of God's blessings to mankind."[20]

The lack of rationality in matters of belief has caused the spread of superstition and illusion, according to Dashtī. Religion in general is seen to blunt human reason, although there is no reason why this should be so. If people would just accept that Muḥammad was fully human, then they would understand that everything he did in his life may be seen to fit with general psychological reactions and human emotions. Muḥammad's actions must be assessed in the context of the social environment and in terms of their benefit to the community. No standard of firm ethics can be expected from Muḥammad. Apparently inhumane principles were used by Muḥammad based on expediency and not on consistency with any spiritual or moral principle. Laws from the time of Muḥammad are, in today's context, frequently useless and meaningless, as are even some ritual practices, for example, the pilgrimage. Concerning Muḥammad's wives and various references to them in scripture, Dashtī says, "Every reader of the Qor'an must be amazed to encounter these private matters in a scripture and moral code valid for all mankind and for all time."[21] In the context of a radical biography such as this, all traditional understandings both of the person of Muḥammad and his authority, along with the authority of the Qur'ān are brought into question.

Biography and reform

The examples and the geographical distribution of these biographies of Muḥammad from the modern period – both at the beginning and at the end of the twentieth century – could be multiplied substantially. Earlier publications from outside the Arab world – for example, Aḥmad Khān and Ameer Ali in India and Umar Cokroaminoto in Indonesia – indicate that the phenomenon is much larger than what has been sketched above. In fact, one could also point to a similar use of the biography and ethos of the Shīʿī Imām Ḥusayn ibn ʿAlī by Ayatollah Khomeini in the Iranian revolution of 1978–9. Khomeini's appeal to the life story of the leader of the nascent Shīʿī community who was killed by the Umayyad ruler, Yazīd, in the year 680 was both vivid and effective. This story is one which speaks to every member of the Shīʿa about the need to rebel against an unjust ruler and to be prepared to sacrifice one's own life on behalf of the good of the community. Such actions are seen as redemptive for the individual believer. By alluding to this story and suggesting implicitly that he himself could be viewed as Imam Ḥusayn, Khomeini was able to rally support for political and social reform in Iran despite the overwhelming odds which the clerics faced when confronted by the Shah's power.[22] This paradigmatic use of Ḥusayn achieved literary manifestation in the book by Shaykh Muḥammad Mahdī Shams al-Dīn called *The Rising of al-Ḥusayn*. Originally written in Arabic by this Lebanese Shīʿī leader, the English translation (published in the wake of the Iranian revolution, in 1985) has a foreword which summarizes well the continuing relevance of religious biography in Islam:

> Imam al-Ḥusayn, peace be with him, created a momentous Islamic revolution, which has continued to live as history has gone by and still provides writers with vitality and inspiring material. Despite the passing of time, it is a revolutionary torch whose light guides revolutionaries and those who struggle to proclaim and support the truth and to resist and oppose the symbols of falsehood. For more than thirteen centuries, writers of different groups, inclinations and ideas have continued to write books and studies about this revolution. Yet neither has its spring been exhausted nor have the streams which flow from it run dry. It is the same as it was at the blessed time it took place in terms of its great significance.[23]

The use of the English word "revolution" (in Arabic, *thawra*) is significant here and its usage continues throughout the translation. Furthermore, the author alludes to its contemporary relevance:

> From the time of Muʿāwiya ibn Abī Sufyān, the Shīʿite Muslim has endured different kinds of persecution, harassment and terrorisation. He has been pursued by the authorities and has seldom felt secure. . . .

The tragic situation for the Shīʿite has continued for long periods. Out of this situation, under which generations and generations have lived and died, a man has emerged who carries, in the depths of his being, a feeling of sorrow and a spirit of revolution. This situation has made him keep close to his historical symbols, in the vanguard of which is the revolution of Imam al-Ḥusayn, in particular, and the history of the Imams, in general.[24]

The outpouring of biographical material related to Muḥammad and other religious heroes seems endless. There appears to be good reason for this, too. The appeal to authority is a necessity, it would seem, and the life of Muḥammad is an obvious focal point with which to deal with the issue of reform. The life stories of Muḥammad have no authoritative status themselves; they are not the actual source of the *sunna* although they certainly have relevance in understanding the context of both Muḥammad's actions and the Qurʾān. Therefore, the subtle rewriting of his biography (as displayed in the examples above) or even the maintenance of the traditional picture (and there are many examples of that in the contemporary world also)[25] does not raise substantial doubts over the basis of Islamic faith, at least on the surface. It is notable, however, that embedded in a number of the biographies, especially the more recent ones, are some far more radical views of both the value of the *sunna* and of the Qurʾān as well.

Issues of authority

Lying behind and presumed within all biographical treatments of Muḥammad is the belief that Muḥammad has something to say to modern Muslims. Clearly, all Muslims would agree that the story of Muḥammad has didactic value; that is, there are lessons and wisdom which can be learned from the life story itself. Furthermore, there is fundamental religious inspiration to be gained from reading the story of the founder of the religion, his trials and tribulations, his victories and defeats. But a question still remains that underlies all of these treatments: to what extent is Muḥammad's life, in the sense of all those things which he did in his life, actually binding upon Muslims? Are there simply general principles to be learned from Muḥammad's life or are the very details themselves elements which should or must be emulated?

One Muslim scholar has expressed his views about this in the following way. "There is a difference between obedience to the

Prophet in his quality of prophet and obedience to him in his quality of *amir* [i.e., leader of the community]. In his quality of prophet he is to be obeyed until the Resurrection, since the Koran is for all times. But in his quality of *amir* he was only obeyed during his lifetime. . . . Instructions resulting from his *amir*-ship, will always remain temporary, because circumstances change."[26] The response to this, representing another point of view, is to say that the two roles cannot be distinguished: Muḥammad's example, his *sunna,* covers both aspects and only by following that *sunna* can salvation be assured.

Religion is, as has been mentioned several times before, traditional. It orients itself from the past with a view to the present; it sees authority as vested in and stemming from the past. Adherence to *ḥadīth* material, the source of the *sunna,* has generally been pictured as maintaining this cultural continuity within Islam. But at the same time, it has been argued that the material gathered in the *ḥadīth* reports often hampers attempts to adapt Islam. Thus, questions have arisen: are the *ḥadīth* reports an essential part of Islam? Is it that they are essential but that they must be subjected to a total reassessment? Are they fully applicable? Or are they totally irrelevant and illegitimate as a source? It is noteworthy that the authority of the Qur'ān remains virtually unquestioned, although, as will be seen in the next chapter, different ways of interpreting it have been urged and do, to some extent, bring its status into question also.

The *sunna* today

The overall question to be raised here, then, is what is the authority of the *sunna* today? Is it felt to give legitimacy to patterns of life, social and ethical codes? Two opposing paths may be used as examples and both will recall the discussion of biographies. On the one hand, Muḥammad is the "perfect man," a perfect embodiment of the message of the Qur'ān. His example, therefore, must be authoritative, although in modern discussions it is not as common to see this conceived to be actual revelation as it was in classical times. On the other hand, Muḥammad is merely human, therefore capable of error and conditioned by his time and circumstances. His example is, as a consequence, not overly relevant or at least not compelling for the modern person. From the Modernist position, this removal of the constraints of Muḥammad's example provides an opening for evolution or progress in Islam.

It should be asked, however, why it is that the *sunna* specifically has become the focus of these sorts of discussions, rather than the

Qur'ān? What is the point of these discussions? For those who enunciate a position which involves extensive questioning of the *sunna*, the aim is to distill Islam down to its essentials and thereby more easily facilitate the incorporation of modern ideals. Those who speak from this position certainly desire the survival of the relevance of Islam; this is true despite the rhetoric of their opponents who picture them as attempting to destroy the religion. Furthermore, one could also say that all parties desire an intensification of Islam. All parties agree with the concept of Islamic law, that is, that religion should have something to say about legal issues, but they disagree on matters of jurisprudence, that is, the extent to which the decisions of the past are binding on the present. As well, the character of that Islamic law – whose Islam? which Islam? – continues to fragment the various groups.

The Modernist vision is one of an Islam which will more readily incorporate change and, thus, the *sunna* has become the target for criticism and an avenue for aspirations. Part of the reason for targeting the *sunna* is because the custodians of the sacred law were those who were perceived by many reformers as doing the most to prevent the modernization of the Islamic world. Many of the critics came from a lay background; they were not fully trained in the traditional legal sciences of Islam and did not have great admiration for such educational methods. Added to this is the use of Orientalist notions regarding the *ḥadīth* by some reformers. The reports of what Muḥammad had done and said during his life were subjected to critical historical analysis by Europeans, especially by Ignaz Goldziher at the end of the nineteenth century, who emphasized the weakness of traditional Muslim evaluations of the material and, even more, the tendentious nature of many of the reports themselves. Some Muslims picked up on this and used these sorts of doubts about the veracity of the material to attack the authority of the *sunna*. This was primarily an Egyptian phenomenon; the criticism of the *sunna* as a whole, however, has much earlier roots, especially in India, where the problem was attacked in more of a theological manner than a historical one.

Discussions in India

The fact that many of the discussions concerning the status of the *sunna* took place in India, and continue to take place in areas distant from the Arab countries, may be significant. The way in which the *sunna* embodies, in a very literal way, Arabian customs may be the jarring point such that, while the Arabs may feel secure in their identity as reflected in the *sunna*, the same may not hold true for those in other parts of the globe. Some have suggested that the more direct contact of Europeans with the Indian population could have been a factor in this movement, at least to the extent that the pressures to adopt European ways was felt more strongly by some people. Also, the Indian heritage of discussions about the *sunna* is long: Shāh Walī Allāh, in the eighteenth century, is famous for his encouragement of a critical attitude towards *ḥadīth*, for example.

Arguments between two contemporary Indo-Pakistani figures display precisely the dimensions of the issues conceived to be at stake in the authority of the past for Muslims. Ghulām Aḥmad Parvēz represents what is clearly a minority position today in arguing for the illegitimacy of the constraints of the example of Muḥammad, the *sunna*. Abū 'l-ʿAlāʾ Mawdūdī is a far more significant figure in terms of Pakistani politics but also the general Islamic resurgence worldwide. His position, which urges a reassessment of the *ḥadīth* reports which underlie the *sunna* but still acknowledges the authority of the concept itself, is far more widespread than that of Parvēz. The discussions between the two indicate the tensions between the different reform positions within modern Islam.

These arguments did not start in India with Parvēz and Mawdūdī; in fact, the basic issues have been discussed ever since Indian Muslims have tried to grapple with European rule and the relative status of Islam. Sayyid Aḥmad Khān represents an example of nineteenth-century Modernist thought, and, on this point, is clearly a precursor to the twentieth-century discussions.

All three of these writers – Aḥmad Khān, Parvēz and Mawdūdī – challenge the traditional religious classes, the *ʿulamāʾ*; none of them emerged from the context of the religious scholarly élite. There was, therefore, no way for their views to be declared heretical since the people promulgating the ideas were not subject to expulsion from the religious circles of authority. However, at the same time, "none of them [is] advocating a situation in which every Muslim can believe as he likes";[27] the communal sense of Islam remains, just as do the limits of the authority of the past.

Aḥmad Khān

Sir Sayyid Aḥmad Khān was born in 1817 to a noble family of Delhi. He died in 1898. He joined the East India Company in 1839 and was loyal to the British during the uprising of 1857–8. He urged that all that Muslims needed in India was the freedom to perform public religious rituals; the British should be supported, therefore, as long as they protected the Muslims rather than suppressed them. Ultimately, he saw the separation of the Muslims from the Hindu majority as the only way that an independent India could allow for Muslim survival. Until that goal was achieved, rule by benevolent foreigners was a better solution. He was knighted in 1888.

Aḥmad Khān may be characterized as a rationalist: he considered the proposition "religion in conformity with human nature" as absolute. All elements of supernaturalism must be declared false; this would include miracles and the like. Ethics and practices, therefore, should be based in nature; the law of Islam gives further guidance only. Education about the natural world is essential. His major life involvement was in Muslim education, devoting his retirement from 1876 on to the establishment and development of the Anglo-Muhammadan Oriental College at Aligarh. Education was the only way in which Muslims were going to be able to recapture their proper status. The school in Aligarh was traditional in the sense that it was a Muslim theological college, but it accepted students from all denominations – Sunnī, Shīʿī and Hindu – and "aimed at the liberalization of ideas, broad humanism, a scientific world view, and a pragmatic approach to politics."[28] Its goal was to have its graduates enter government service and thus eventually pave the way for Muslim separatism within India under this new leadership.

Aḥmad Khān and the authority of the past

Deeply influenced by European ideas of history and change, Aḥmad Khan embraced the notion that Indian and Islamic history should be studied within the perspective of western methodologies. He wrote a work on the life of Muḥammad (1870), using manuscript sources found in London. This opening of the past to re-examination also led to the possibility of questioning the basis of its authority. His approach was also supported by his theological attitude which saw the need to reopen the discussions concerning very fundamental ideas of Islam; all of this was marked by a severe anti-traditionalism and a strident nineteenth-century modernism. The past interpretations of Islam had become too embroiled in minor details and had lost the essence of the faith. In fact, Muslims had built themselves a structure of law based not upon an infallible source but upon the ideas and attitudes of Muslims from the first centuries of Islam; this was embodied in the *ḥadīth* material.

While the authority of the *ḥadīth* had been established in the past, Aḥmad Khan felt that the issue needed to be reopened so as to provide a basis for re-evaluating the *sharīʿa* as a whole; individual reasoning, *ijtihād*, must be used. This argues, as Sheila McDonough suggests,[29] that nineteenth-century people are as much in touch with determining the norms of Islamic society as the earlier ninth-century community which set the standards still followed in Islamic societies. Thus authority itself is not being questioned, only the formulation of it. The only valid *ḥadīth* reports are those which are in agreement with the statements of the Qurʾān, those which explain Quranic injunctions, and those which deal with basic issues not alluded to in scripture.[30]

Aḥmad Khan critiques the institution which has maintained the *sharīʿa* and the idea of that institution itself. Foreign influences are seen as one of the problems in the corruption of the *sharīʿa*. His aim was the liberalization of Islamic law in light of modern demands and the rationalization of other elements deemed to be essential.

Underlying Aḥmad Khan's ideas is the principle that true religion does not change but worldly affairs do and the two must be separated. "In his view," says McDonough,

> true religion should always be carefully distinguished from worldly affairs. True religion, he said, is unchanging, but worldly affairs are always changing. Originally, the great *ulema* used their personal opinions to give judgments on worldly affairs. This was in itself, he says, a valid thing for them to have done. Later, however, these opinions on temporary issues became identified with unchanging truth. This meant, he says, that the *ulema* were considered law-givers in the same sense as the Qurʾan; their human opinions became identified with the will of God.[31]

It is important to notice that in this conception the status of the Qurʾān as non-contingent in terms of worldly affairs is not challenged: only the legal structure of Islam needs to contend with change.

Parvēz

Ghulām Aḥmad Parvēz (in English sometimes Parwez) was born in 1903 in East Punjab, India, and died in 1985. He was raised in a religious home and was deeply influenced, according to his own account of his life story, by Muḥammad Iqbāl who pointed out for him the idea of a pure Islam without the centuries of foreign influence. He worked as a civil servant in India which is often seen as a career that set the pattern for him to see the need for definite planning and instruction for the future of Islam. His first book, a political tract against the Soviet Union, was published in 1926 or 1927 and it appeared anonymously because his government job allowed no political involvement. He also wrote articles for Abū'l A'lā' Mawdūdī's *Tarjumān al-Qur'ān* and other magazines. In 1938 he started publishing the magazine *Ṭulū'-i Islām* ("The Dawn of Islam") which has remained the main vehicle for his ideas since then and is now published in Karachi. He moved to Pakistan in 1948 and worked there as a government official until his retirement. He was a fervent opponent of Pakistan's religious classes whom he saw as the protectors of élite interests, not of true Islam and true rationality. His audience appears to have been mainly well educated young people, those who have presumably been deeply influenced by the West but are also searching for meaning within their own heritage.[32]

Parvēz saw that *ḥadīth* had been treated as a revelatory source by the religious classes of the past. This was not legitimate for him. The *sharī'a*, the "path" of life which Muslims follow, was, as a result of the status given to the *sunna* as a source of revealed knowledge, fundamentally wrong. All of the Muslim past, with the exception of the time of Muḥammad and the first four "righteous caliphs," must be rejected and considered a corruption of true Islam, because foreign influences, especially Byzantine and Persian, had become fully embedded in the *sharī'a*. For Parvēz, the Qur'ān alone can function in taking people from their complacent, destructive ways toward becoming full persons; reason is a base human instinct (but one which demands cultivating certainly) and needs revelation to complete it. At the time of Muḥammad there was the ideal political situation, everything being before God, with absolute authority vested in the leader. To restructure society into its pure Quranic foundations was Parvēz's goal. In this way, the decline of Muslim civilization – in terms of its power and conditions – would be halted.[33]

Parvēz on *ḥadīth*

Parvēz's argument has a number of aspects. The Qur'ān explains everything that an individual needs and no further source is needed. The Qur'ān contains no ruling saying that *ḥadīth* must be followed. Traditionalists claim that the word *ḥikma* in Qur'ān 2/129, "teach them the book and the *ḥikma*," refers to the *sunna* of Muḥammad, but Parvēz contends that this word is meant in the general sense of "wisdom." Likewise, *sūra* 59, verse 7, "Whatever the messenger gives you, take; whatever he forbids you, give over," relates only to distribution of spoils after battle for Parvēz, not to general things which Muḥammad proclaimed.[34] Muḥammad himself, on the basis of *ḥadīth* itself, argued against the continuing relevance of his person: "Do not write down anything from me except the Qur'ān."[35] The historical background to this *ḥadīth*, it should be noted, is undoubtedly to be found among those people who in the early centuries of Islam also took Parvēz's position on *ḥadīth*, seeing the Qur'ān as the only legitimate source.[36] *Ḥadith* and its authority were the result of a compromise, according to Parvēz, reached between the rulers and those who wished to uphold the Qur'ān alone.

Ḥadith reports occasionally contradict the Qur'ān; for example, the punishment for adultery is 100 lashes in the Qur'ān but stoning in the *ḥadīth*. Thus, for Parvēz, *ḥadīth* cannot be considered reliable. The unreliability of *ḥadīth* transmission also undermines its validity; any source will be garbled over time (except the Qur'ān which was widely transmitted in uniform style). Subjective judgements were made in the past regarding the transmitters of *ḥadīth*. According to Parvēz, even the companions of Muḥammad may have erred in their transmissions; this is a position which opposes all traditional theological statements which hold the companions of Muḥammad to have transmitted the material perfectly, limited only by their own perspective on the event being reported.

Furthermore, Muḥammad was an ordinary man according to Qur'ān 18/110 and he could have erred. The *ḥadīth* reports frequently include repugnant material, mixing ethical and doctrinal matters. The *ḥadīth* reports have fixed numerous elements of society in a static way in areas not governed by the Qur'ān; for example, in the Qur'ān it is commanded to give *zakāt*, "charity," which is seen to legislate the principle of "giving," whereas in *ḥadīth* it is stipulated that such and such an amount should be given. Says Parvēz, "If it had been the will of God that [the rate of *zakāt*] had to be 2½ percent [as the *sharīʿa* stipulates] until the Day of Resurrection, He would have stated it in the [Qur'ān]."[37]

Significance

Parvēz's position, in a manner similar to that of other Modernists, tends to separate existence into two parts. For Parvēz, the distinction is between *madhhab*, the ethnic (principally Iranian) elements implemented in revenge for military defeat at the hands of the Arabs (and now to be identified with society), versus *dīn*, "religion," which is the Qur'ān. His overall platform of urging people to go straight to the Qur'ān is one which accommodates the greatest possibilities for change while staying within a traditional understanding of the authority of the scripture; the Qur'ān is, after all, far less precise and detailed than the *sunna* as elaborated in medieval Islam, and thus adaptation is far easier to legitimize.

It is interesting to note that much of the emphasis in Parvēz's arguments is methodological and theological. Historical questions of whether Muḥammad did or did not do such things – questions which have motivated many scholarly studies of *ḥadīth* – seem subsidiary; the concerns are internal Muslim ones, despite the likelihood that western influence accounts for some of the impetus of the discussions. The overall impact of these arguments, for Parvēz, is that the decisions of the past made on the basis of *ḥadīth* are all open to question. Fazlur Rahman points out, however, at least one danger in this position: "the historical validity of the Koran itself is vouchsafed only by the tradition."[38] Some may not agree that the Qur'ān depends upon tradition to that degree, preferring to see the status of the scripture vested in the results it has had in society, for example. The point does demonstrate, however, the potential need for those who enunciate such positions to elaborate a full theological vision of Islam.

Mawdūdī

Parvēz found his opponent in the figure of Mawlānā Abū'l A'lā' Mawdūdī (1903–79). Mawdūdī was raised in a professional and religious family and was educated within a private, family setting in Hyderabad, India. He received no formal religious training, but his education was based on traditional Islamic knowledge. He learned Arabic and Persian in addition to his mother tongue, Urdu; later, he taught himself English and read widely in modern thought and science. He became a journalist at an early age, and by 1921 was editor of the Delhi newspaper *Muslim*; from 1925 to 1928, he was editor of *al-Jam'iyyat*. Both these papers were sponsored by an organization of Muslim scholars known as the *Jam'iyyat 'ulamā'-i Hind*. He started his personal writing, translating, and involvement in political activities during this period. In 1933 in Hyderabad, he became editor of *Tarjumān al-Qur'ān*, a monthly magazine which became the major vehicle for the enunciation of his views. His early writings of this period concentrated on the conflict between Islam and the western world view, all being judged on the basis of the Qur'ān and the *sunna*.

By the middle of the 1930s, Mawdūdī became more involved in political issues. He argued strenuously against nationalism as being a foreign invention and anti-Islamic and felt that within India such nationalism would result in the destruction of Muslim identity. In 1941 he founded Jamā'at-i Islāmī, the "Islamic Society," and remained its head until 1972. The goal of this organization was to effect a change in the life of Indian society, to make it more properly Islamic. However, in 1947, events forced Mawdūdī to emigrate to the recently formed Pakistan, and there he vowed to help establish a truly Islamic state; if this state for Muslims was to exist, he argued, it should be an Islamic one. His methods for urging this formation were the involvement of the Jamā'at-i Islāmī in Pakistani politics, constant criticism and inciting to action of the political powers, and a stream of writings, all of which aimed to explain the Islamic way of life. This political agitation led to prison terms for Mawdūdī, even to the sentence of death for a "seditious" pamphlet in 1953 (a sentence which was eventually commuted to two years in jail). He remained active in Pakistani politics throughout the 1960s.[39]

Mawdūdī's vision of Islam

Many of Mawdūdī's works clearly illustrate his basic view of Islam and portray him as a Islamist. His largest work, *Tafhīm al-Qur'ān*, is a translation and explanation of the Qur'ān in Urdu. Its aim is to present the message of the Qur'ān in a clear style for people of today, using the commentary to display how that message is relevant to modern-day concerns.

The fundamental structures of Islam all revolve around God who is in complete command of the universe and to whom all allegiance is owed. The natural order demands that people "submit," become Muslim; in order to facilitate that, God has sent prophets who bring the guidance which is needed for all humans to govern every aspect of their lives; this guidance is based on the idea of total loyalty to God. Any allegiance to something other than God – nationalism, modernism and the like – is anti-Islamic. Anything other than God which demands allegiance from a person belongs to the *jāhiliyya*, the term used in the Qur'ān for the non-Islamic ethos.[40] Islamic guidance, the form of divine guidance which is the most complete and totally pure which directs full allegiance to God, is embodied in the

Qur'ān and in the *sunna* of Muḥammad. The understanding and interpretation of these sources are not vested with the religious learned classes but are available to all by use of personal judgement; those judgements will be made by the yardstick of "Is it Islamic?" rather than "Is it rational?" as is done by so many Modernists.

Mawdūdī and the authority of the past

Mawdūdī argues, on the basis of the Qur'ān, that Muḥammad is to be taken as a good example for all Muslims at all times. Muḥammad as a prophet is inseparable from his being a full example. The very purpose of revelation is to use a person to enact the message; otherwise, God would just send an angel with a book and be done with it. Mawdūdī suggests, however, that the idea of Muḥammad as an exemplar does not validate slavish adherence to everything Muḥammad did. Not everyone should marry an Arab woman, for example![41] It is worth mentioning at this point that, for a Modernist, the issue remains in Mawdūdī's position of how to distinguish what should be followed from what should not. Parvēz certainly perceived this problem. J. M. S. Baljon notes that Parvēz accuses Mawdūdī of "denying tradition" when convenient, as in the length of his beard not necessarily being the same length as that of Muḥammad, yet condemning others for doing the very same thing – denying tradition. The accusation is made that those who claim to be able to determine which elements of the *ḥadīth* reports are to be followed and which are to be ignored – as Parvēz would suggest Mawdūdī is doing – are really claiming for themselves the status of prophethood. This is a veiled reference to the problems in Pakistant with Mīrzā Ghulām Aḥmad of the Aḥmadiyya (discussed below in Chapter 17).[42] The ultimate answer to this direction of the debate must lie in the concept of *ijmāʿ*, the consensus of the Muslim community, embodied in a more general notion of tradition. The real question, then, is to what extent are twentieth-century Muslims going to maintain those basic elements of the past in their search for modern Muslim identity?

Mawdūdī, like Parvēz, wants to find an Islamic flexibility which would legitimize change and allow Islam to continue to be relevant to life in the contemporary context. He is concerned, however, that the position which Parvēz argued *vis-à-vis* the *ḥadīth* reports, especially where it raises issues concerning their historical value, would eventually be applied to the Qur'ān, and Islam would crumble as a result. On the question of whether Muḥammad's example should be emulated in all times, he asserts that the Quranic evidence argues that it must; the prophetic example is the guarantor of the meaning of revelation and is indispensable to accepting the Qur'ān as revelation. The *ḥadīth* reports are reliable as texts because memorization was a highly developed skill among the Arabs and Muḥammad was an important person whose words and actions people would have remembered. Certainly, fabrication of *ḥadīth* reports did occur, but this is no reason to dismiss the entire package. The scientific procedures of the past used to assess *ḥadīth* reports were good but subject to error and were only based upon probability. In an argument typical of Mawdūdī's rationalism, the point is made that all of life is based upon probability and we all must use our God-given judgment to decide what to trust. "Blind imitation," *taqlīd*, is no longer sufficient, even though from a traditional standpoint that imitation is the best anyone can attain. To put one's trust in the learned people of the past and follow their interpretations is, from the traditional viewpoint, the appropriate manner of behaviour rather than follow one's own insights, which will be sure to be influenced by personal desires and lack of knowledge. Mawdūdī rejects this, for him the learned classes have failed to preserve true Islam and are only acting to preserve their own self-interests. In Charles Adams' words:

> Mawdūdī puts particular emphasis on the argument from probability, saying once more that the fact of a piece of information being only probable does not make it necessarily either wrong or untrustworthy. The proper thing for a serious man is neither to reject all the *ẓannī ḥadīth* [probable reports] nor to accept them all but to investigate each one individually. The vast majority of *ḥadīth*, because they are *akhbār-i-āḥād* [reports transmitted via one *isnād* only] fall into the *ẓannī* category. One should accept those he is able to prove to be reliable, reject those which he cannot prove, and reserve his judgment about any that fall in the neutral ground between proof and its lack. This he holds to be a reasonable stand and one that is in accord with Islam since Islam is a reasonable religion.[43]

Mawdūdī's answer to modernity is rigorous discipline and self-sufficiency along with revolt against Muslim rulers who do not support Islam appropriately. His call is to a return to Medina, the perfect political time of Muḥammad when true Islam existed and true interpretations were available; the true collectivity of the Muslim community in this period is the final goal of the present time.

However, this will only be arrived at by an initial return to the Islamic revolution through quiet conversion as displayed in Mecca. Parvēz's call, on the other hand, is to Mecca alone: Islam is internal, and Mecca was the era of pure faith, before time and place constricted Islam in Medina.[44]

Authority

The controversy over the *sunna* – and it has taken place throughout the Muslim world, not only in India and Pakistan – points straight to the heart of the views about Islam in the modern period. What is the essential part of Islam that must be maintained and passed on to future generations and what may be discarded as trappings from the past? This is the universal problem for all religions today. All parties in these discussions agree that Islam needs to be revitalized so that its relevance to modern life can be perceived and so that it may be advantageous for individual believers. But what is the proper Islamic way of deciding the basic question of the authority of the past? Does the *sunna* in fact have any authority within an Islamic framework or was this, as Parvēz suggests, simply a construct created in the past for political expediency? Is the *sunna* a vital part of Islam which has simply become mired in the analyses of the past? These are very fundamental questions about the structural bases of Islam and the answers to them produce radically different views on what Islam might be in the future. Most answers, when they are in fact produced, seem to urge a gradual reassessment of the past, one which will not produce a severe fracture with practices which are already a part of Muslim society. For some, this is too slow a solution and for them a more radical approach is needed. Others may try to side-step the issue and instead turn to the Qur'ān, the agreed upon locus of Islamic identity, and attempt a positive formulation of Islam on that basis. Chapter 14 will pay attention to the implications of these discussions about the Qur'ān.

14 The Qur'ān and modernity

In a manner which would seem to be quite exceptional within contemporary world religions,[1] there is an impressive amount of activity occurring in writing works of Qur'ān interpretation throughout the Muslim world. The reasons for this must be examined. Clearly, the search for Islamic identity, for the Islamic answer to the problems of the modern world, has led many Islamic thinkers to make recourse to the original resources of Islam: it has led them back to the Qur'ān. This tendency is widespread and not overly surprising; Islam has always been a scripturalist faith and few have wanted to question that basic orientation to the revealed text. Be that as it may, the writing of commentaries on scripture still needs some explanation to account for its prominence and significance.

The field of *tafsīr*, the Arabic word for "commentary," is a traditional one. The act of writing a *tafsīr* is an expression of individual piety on the part of the writer, but it also acts to enunciate each writer's particular view of Islam and its relevance to his or her age. Therefore, each writer faces a basic difficulty anew (although each works from the basis of what had been said in previous generations): how to make the text communicate meaningfully within his or her own time and cultural framework. Clearly, explaining the text to Malaysians in the twentieth century requires a different approach than it would have in Arabia of the tenth century.

The mode of commentary writing has not changed substantially since the classical medieval, although the use of certain modern forms – magazines, newspapers – may be noted. Modern Qur'ān interpretation is marked, in many of its manifestations, by three interrelated principles:

1 The attempt is made to interpret the Qur'ān in light of scientific reason and methodology. "To interpret the Qur'ān by the

Qur'ān" is the phrase frequently used to express this, implying the rejection of all the extraneous material provided by tradition in the form of *ḥadīth* reports and earlier commentaries.

2 Following from the previous principle, the attempt is made, through the expediency of interpretation, to divest the Qur'ān of all legendary traits, primitive ideas, fantastic stories, magic, fables, and superstitions; symbolic interpretation is the primary means for such resolutions.

3 The attempt is made to support doctrine by finding it in, or justifying it by, the Qur'ān.

Overall, it is common to find in modern commentaries an emphasis on the spiritual content of the Qur'ān and its guidance. As well, some Modernist approaches are marked by an attitude of viewing the Qur'ān as the work of Muḥammad's mind, at least to the extent of speaking of the text not as descending from heaven in its actual wording (as was classically expressed and is still held in many circles), but as being the spirit of revelation filtered through Muḥammad's psyche and thus being expressed within the limits of his intellect and linguistic abilities. As has been remarked by Fazlur Rahman, however, this has not always led to "historical inquiry into the Koranic revelation on scientific lines, [but] has enhanced the emotional intensity for the Prophet's person."[2] The ramifications of that have been sketched in the previous chapter.

The beginnings

The earliest focal point of Modernist *tafsīr* activity was in India. Sayyid Aḥmad Khān (1817–98) wrote the first major explicitly Modernist commentary, entitled simply *Tafsīr al-Qur'ān*. His book was directed towards making all Muslims aware of the fact that western influences in the world required a new vision of Islam, for Islam as it was actually practised and believed in by most of its adherents would be seriously threatened by modern advances in thought and science. Where, therefore, was the true core of Islam to be found? How was its centre to be defined? For Aḥmad Khān, these questions were to be answered through reference to the Qur'ān, which, if it were properly understood through the use of the powers of reason, would provide the necessary answers. The basis of the required social and educational reforms, for example, were to be found in the Qur'ān. By returning to the source of Islam, the religion would be revitalized and the proper future would be secure.

Muḥammad ʿAbduh

Generally considered the most significant Modernist figure in the crucial nineteenth-century developments in Egypt, Muḥammad ʿAbduh lived from 1849 to 1905. He was born in lower Egypt and was educated at the home of Islamic orthodoxy in Cairo, al-Azhar. He studied philosophy with Jamāl al-Dīn al-Afghānī and started writing on social and political issues, reflecting many of Afghānī's views. In 1877 he started teaching at al-Azhar and, shortly after that, at Dār al-ʿUlūm in Cairo. When the British invaded Egypt in 1882 (after the Egyptian army had taken over governing the country from the ruler Ismāʿīl), ʿAbduh, who had emerged as a leader of the civilian wing of opposition to Ismāʿīl, was exiled for a time to France along with Afghānī. He taught for a period in Beirut, and his lectures there form his book *Risālat al-Tawḥīd*, "The Theology of Unity," one of the few explicit attempts made to write a modernist Islamic theology. In 1888 he returned to Egypt and spent the rest of his career as a judge (*muftī*) giving decisions (*fatwā*s) which embodied his Modernist stance. He became the chief *muftī* of Egypt in 1897.

For ʿAbduh, the central problem which had to be faced was the decay of Islamic society.[3] Changing circumstances, unforeseen by Muḥammad in forming the Muslim community, had resulted in the status of Islam deteriorating within the community. New codes of law were being imposed, ones which some felt were more compatible with modern economic and social realities. New schools and institutions were emerging throughout society. These changes created a basic issue which had to be confronted: what is it that actually makes Muslim society Muslim?

ʿAbduh saw change as inevitable and beneficial, but he also saw the danger of the increasing separation of Islamic spheres of influence and areas controlled by the modern sense of human reason. Bringing these two together became the central platform of his Modernism. The simple transplantation of European law, for example, would not provide a viable basis for an Islamic society. Traditional Islamic schools were stagnant and modern schools were devoid of a religious ethos, and this resulted in the further splitting of Egyptian society into traditional and European-influenced sectors.

ʿAbduh's answer to this dilemma was to link the principles of change to Islam; Islam would be the controller of change, providing the criteria for selecting what was good and necessary in modern life. His aim was not to convince the traditional learned classes of the need for change, but rather to demonstrate to the more secular-influenced group that it was possible to be devout in the modern age. He hoped thereby that a new learned class would emerge which would be able to articulate the new, revitalized, rational Islam. His book, *The Theology of Unity*, is a good example of the way in which he worked out this position. The book is structured in the form of a classical work of theology, starting with epistemology and moving through the topics of God, prophets, revelation and Islam. Throughout the work the emphasis is on logical argumentation such that the conclusion that Islam is the one, true religion must be accepted by all rational people. The logical argumentation, however, avoids the "excesses" connected to probing into matters declared to be "unprofitable" for speculation.[4]

Fundamental to this revitalized Islam was the identification of elements in traditional Islam which were consonant with modern thought. Islam was to be seen as a "civilization" and an activity in life. *Ijmāʿ*, the principle of consensus in law, was to be identified with public opinion. *Shūrā*, consultation of the elders, was, in this view, parliamentary democracy. *Maṣlaḥa*, a legal principle reflecting the ideal of the public interest, could be identified with utilitarianism, in which legal opinion always aims toward the position from which the greatest good will flow.

In order to accomplish his aims, ʿAbduh urged a "return to the sources" in order to reassess them in light of the modern predicament and with the assistance of human reason. This task is reflected in his Qur'ān commentary and has made him the reference point for many Modernist writers as well as Islamist groups who highlight his scripturalist emphasis.

ʿAbduh and the Qur'ān

Leading the way for a changed Quranic interpretation, ʿAbduh struggled against the traditional enterprise of *tafsīr*. He argued for the need to make Qur'ān commentary available to the people as a whole. The intellectual efforts of the past had made the text "illegible"; any sense of a distinction between what was important and what was not had been lost. As well, the efforts of the past did not respond to the needs and questions of his day. ʿAbduh thus embarked on a commentary that would be minus the theological speculations, the detailed grammatical discussions, and the obtuse scholarship which characterized the commentaries of the past. The similarities in impulse and direction to those of the Protestant Reformation of Europe may be noted – Luther's Bible translation taking the text out of the hands of the clergy alone and giving it to the common person – along with the impact of the printing press, which became a major factor in the development of Egypt, with the first press established there in the 1820s.

'Abduh's commentary, which was published under the title *Tafsīr al-Manār* and was based upon his class lectures and the texts of his legal decisions, is marked by a moderate rationalist spirit coupled with an emphasis on the moral directions for the modern world as provided by the spiritual and religious guidance of the Qur'ān.[5] The search for knowledge, the use of the intellect, the need for education and the prerequisite of political independence were all to be found in and justified by the Qur'ān. What is unknown should be left unknown, rather than embrace the traditional folk tales that attempt to explain them. Any ambiguity which exists in the Qur'ān as a result is there for a reason: in order to divert attention away from the material world toward the spiritual. "If more details were useful, God would have added them." This, it should be noted, leads to a marked attitude of rejecting interpretations which find modern science in the Qur'ān. This tendency is even more pronounced in the work of Rashīd Riḍā, 'Abduh's follower who completed 'Abduh's *tafsīr* after the latter's death. For 'Abduh himself, the Qur'ān certainly tolerates (even encourages) scientific investigation, but science is not seen to reveal the true meaning of the Qur'ān. References in the text of scripture to telephones and spaceships are functions of the imagination according to 'Abduh and are not based upon sound principles of interpretation, contrary to the opinion of some other prominent writers who will be discussed below.

That the moral point of the Qur'ān is the text's highest and ultimate aim in 'Abduh's view, may be nicely illustrated by his commentary on the Quranic passage dealing with marriage of multiple wives:

> God has made the condition that one keep far from injustice to be the basis for his giving of a law (concerning marriage). This confirms the fact that justice is enjoined as a condition and that duty consists in striving for it.
>
> . . . Polygamy is like one of those necessities which is permitted to the one to whom it is allowed (only) with the stipulation that he act fairly, with trustworthiness, and that he be immune from injustice. . . . In view of this restriction, when one now considers what corruption results from polygamy in modern times, then one will know for certain that a people . . . cannot be trained so

that their remedy lies in polygamy, since, in a family in which a single man has two wives, no beneficial situation and no order prevail.[6]

Abū'l-Kalām Āzād

Āzād, who lived from 1888 to 1958, was an Indian politician who was influenced in his modernism by Aḥmad Khān and thought highly of his educational ideas. Āzād is also said to have been in contact with Muḥammad 'Abduh's ideas when he travelled in the Middle East in the early 1900s. He started his career as a journalist and continued to work for his political causes through journalism throughout his life. He was president of the Congress Party in India in 1923 and 1940 and was Minister of Education from 1947 to 1958 in independent India. Journalism was his main activity but, in everything he wrote, he manifested his aims concerning the nation of India. He opposed the creation of a separate Muslim state in India and served, from 1937 on, as Gandhi's adviser on Muslim issues. He urged the necessity for Hindu–Muslim cooperation in India in the struggle for independence from the British.

True religion is universal for Āzād, echoing a stance of modern Indian pluralism and of opposition to the India–Pakistan split. To recognize this unity is to recognize the unity of humanity. Antagonism between religions has emerged only because people have come to think that they have a monopoly on truth within their own faith; in fact, all religions share in the truth. All religious people should return to the true form of their own religion; this is what the Qur'ān instructs. All should submit to God and lead a life of right action according to their own religion. This religious spirit of cooperation reflects Āzād's ideals concerning the Indian political situation. All Muslims should return to the Qur'ān and the *sunna* and purify their religious tradition from all foreign additions. Care must be taken not to over-emphasize the importance of ritual and law of any faith, for this is what has produced conflict between religions in the past.

Āzād wrote his *Tarjumān al-Qur'ān* in the late 1920s as an explanatory translation, but his treatment of *sūra* 1 is a full commentary which presents all the basic concepts of Islam. *Dīn* is what has been given to all prophets everywhere and this is Islam. *Sharī'a* or *minhaj*, used by Āzād to refer to the path of Islam, varies with time and conditions, although it is an absolutely necessary and desirable part of all religions.

The Qur'ān presents its message as one based on truth, justice and righteousness. Its method of presentation is equally important:

> The primary and the most important feature of the method of presentation followed by the Qur'an is the appeal to reason that it makes. It lays repeated emphasis on the search for truth, on the need of exercising one's reason and insight, of reflecting over the outward experience of life and drawing valid conclusion. In fact, there is no chapter in the Qur'an wherein it has not made an earnest appeal to man to reflect upon everything.[7]

Āzād's comments on *sūra* 1, verse 4, "[God is] the Lord of the Day of Judgement," illustrates how he finds the theme permeating the text:

> The current religious beliefs had invested God with the characteristics of an absolute and moody monarch who, when he was pleased, showered gifts all around him or, when he was displeased, inflicted dire punishment. Thus arose the custom of offering sacrifices to appease God's wrath and win His favour. The Quran's conception of God, however, is not that of an arbitrary ruler who governs according to his moods and whims. On the contrary, the law of divine reward and retribution is a natural law of cause and effect which has universal application. We see its operation in the physical world around us all the time and should therefore have no difficulty in understanding its operation in relation to our spiritual conduct.
>
> So, just as man needs the protection of God the Preserver and the grace and bounty of God the Merciful [as presented in the previous verse of the Qur'ān], he cannot do without the divine quality of justice, which makes for organised good life and eliminates, or at least minimises, the elements of harm and mischief.[8]

Sayyid Quṭb

Born in 1906 and executed in 1966 for his role in plotting against the rule of Egyptian President Abdul Nasser, Sayyid Quṭb was spokesman for the radical manifestation of the Islamist Egyptian Muslim Brotherhood, al-Ikhwān al-Muslimūn, and continues to be a powerful, martyred voice for the movement. He represents, therefore, not the Modernism of 'Abduh, but an activist Islamic totalism, one initiated by Ḥasan al-Bannā' in 1928 and a major force in Egypt in the 1940s and 1950s. The thrust behind the Brotherhood was the desire to purify Islam of the corruption of western morals and influence in general. This was to be done through revolutionary social action, bringing Islamic policies into action in Egypt.[9] Islam was argued to be a comprehensive ideology, one which held the only possible answer to the ills and despair of the day. Islam would and should regulate life totally and, with the full acceptance of the *sharī'a* in public life, social justice and political freedom would follow. Reason and public welfare are the operative principles in life, but these must work within the moral principles of Islam alone. Islamic order rests on three basic principles: justice of the ruler, obedience of the ruled and the notion of consultation (*shūrā*) by which the ruler is elected, controlled and, if need be, deposed. It is thus a political platform under which all political parties would be outlawed, the law reformed to the *sharī'a*, and administrative posts given to those with religious education. This type of Islamism has proven very popular in many places in the Muslim world especially among the better educated young who have rejected both the traditional approach to scripturalism (as manifested in the works of the scholarly élite) and western modernity. Mawdūdī, whose ideas have already been examined, and Quṭb represent the most successful manifestations of the enunciation of this Islamist tendency.

Quṭb himself embraced Westernization early in his life but became disenchanted with it, so it is reported, after Israel's formation and after experiencing first hand what he spoke of as the anti-Arab sentiment in the United States during a stay there in 1949–51. He did not think much of the entire western way of life:

> I do know how people live in America, the country of the great production, extreme wealth, and indulgent pleasure. ... I saw them there as nervous tension devoured their lives despite all the evidence of wealth, plenty, and gadgets that they have. Their enjoyment is nervous excitement, animal merriment. One gets the image that they are constantly running from ghosts that are pursuing them. They are as machines that move with madness, speed, and convulsion that does not cease. Many times I thought it was as though the people were in a grinding machine that does not stop day or night, morning or evening. It grinds them and they are devoured without a moment's rest. They have no faith in themselves or in life around them.[10]

These attitudes towards the West and its materialistic trappings are reflected in Quṭb's *tafsīr* called *Fī Ẓilāl al-Qur'ān*, "In the Shade of the Qur'ān." Islam is the "final, comprehensive, perfect and accomplished message" from God. This Islam is not merely the religious principles of the Modernists, but a full system of life, perfect in its integration of freedom, equality and social justice, one which is in perfect accord with the cosmic order.[11] This is expressed in the *tafsīr* in the following way:

> *Those who believe and do righteous deeds are the best of all creatures* [Qur'ān 98/7]. This is also an absolute verdict that makes for no dispute or argument. Its condition is also clear, free from any ambiguity or deception. The condition is faith, not merely being born in a land which claims to be Islamic, or in a family which claims to belong to Islam. Neither is it a few words which one repeats again and again. It is the acceptance of faith which establishes its effects on the actual life, *and do righteous deeds*. It is entirely different from the words which go no further than the lips. As for the *righteous deeds*, these are everything which Allāh has commanded to be done in matters of worship, behaviour, action and day-to-day dealings. The first and most important of these *righteous deeds* is the establishment of Allāh's law on this planet, and the government of people according to what Allāh has legislated.[12]

Everything outside Islam is, as for Mawdūdī, *jāhiliyya*, derived from the spirit of barbarism and contrary to everything Islam stands for. Unbridled individualism and depravity are the marks of the modern world, and these have culminated in moral and social decline. Islamic society has not simply degenerated; it has, in fact, left Islam and become non-Muslim by negating God's sovereignty and substituting materialism. Modernization and development are plots to colonialize, in material, moral and cultural ways, the entire Muslim world. The reassertion of Islam and the condemnation of *jāhiliyya* are the ways to combat this threat. A group such as the Muslim Brotherhood must exist in order to create an alternative counter-society which will produce a model generation of true Muslims.[13]

A study of Qutb's commentary reveals the careful way in which his vision of Islam and society is embedded in the text. A. H. Johns, for example, has looked at the way Qutb treats the story of Moses in the Qur'ān.[14] Moses is the "great figure of moral and social liberation" and provides Qutb with a fitting vehicle for his ideas. Pharaoh is the tyrant ruler of every age who wishes to destroy religion; Moses is the model for all who wish to proclaim the triumph of God's word.

Egypt – despite Quṭb's emphasis on the whole of the Islamic community, as Johns points out – is the "cradle" of the world, a green, fertile valley providing all the necessities of life. Threats of jail made by the tyrant to the devotee of God do not cause loss of self-control but only produce demonstrations of the truth of the message, guided by God's power. And this message will resound in the hearts of the people who have lost their faith because of the humiliation they have suffered at the hands of the tyrant. But the remnant of their faith which remains in their hearts will be rebuilt. All of this, of course, while acting to interpret in vivid fashion the story of Moses as told in the Qur'ān, is a reflection of Quṭb's life itself, his struggles on behalf of religion against the hypocritical powers of the world, a struggle which radical Islamists continue down to today.

Quṭb also based his position on an argument about the merits of the Qur'ān and his style of presentation in his commentary reflects this urge. The lack of artistic appreciation of the text on the part of Muslims has meant that the holistic emphasis of the message has been missed; this is especially the fault in traditional commentaries which took an atomistic approach to the text. The unity of the Qur'ān as a book, as reflected in its artistry, is a mirror of divine unity and an image of the cohesive unity of Islam, the religion and social order. The dramatic elements of the Qur'ān are a reflection of the drama of human life and the text must therefore be lived for it to be meaningful. Quṭb reveals here his own earlier avocation as a *belle lettriste*.[15]

Ṭanṭāwī Jawharī

As has already been mentioned, both Aḥmad Khān and Muḥammad 'Abduh were intent on encouraging their compatriots to welcome the scientific outlook of the West in order to share in the progress of the modern world. Often this effort involved little more than simply stating that the Qur'ān enjoins its readers to seek and use rational knowledge. However, at other times, it also involved the historical claim that Islam had developed science in the first place and had then passed it on to Europe, so that, in embracing the scientific outlook in the present situation, Muslims were only reclaiming what was truly Islamic. A more distinctive trend in *tafsīr* emerges also, for example in the writings of Ṭanṭāwī Jawharī (1862–1940), an Egyptian secondary school teacher who published, among many other educational, religious and spiritualist works, a twenty-six-volume work entitled *Al-Jawāhir fī Tafsīr al-Qur'ān* ("Jewels in the Interpretation of the Qur'ān") between 1923 and 1935.[16]

Jawharī's writings are permeated by two main themes, common to much Modernist writing from the turn of the century: first, Islam is in perfect accord with human nature and second, Islam, as found in the Qur'ān, contains within it an explanation of the scientific workings of the world. God would not have revealed the Qur'ān had He not included in it everything that people needed to know; science is obviously necessary in the modern world, so it should not be surprising to find all of science in the Qur'ān when that scripture is properly understood. Jawharī also makes reference to the classical notion of the miraculous character or inimitability of the Qur'ān (*i'jāz*), which he takes to refer primarily to the content of the text in terms of its knowledge concerning matters which are only now becoming clear to humanity. Since the scientific knowledge contained in the text is proof of its miraculous character, references are found in the Qur'ān for numerous modern inventions (electricity, for example) and scientific discoveries (the fact that the earth revolves around the sun). Jawharī always claimed that his exegesis was no more far-fetched than the traditional legal approach to the text. Scientific exegesis stems from a view of the Qur'ān and the *sunna* as providing all the knowledge that people would need. The Qur'ān therefore anticipates modern science. What is more, as a tendency in interpretation, this exegetical approach has an honorable pedigree with classical precedents, for example in al-Mursī (d. 1257) who found astronomy, medicine, weaving, spinning, agriculture and pearl-diving mentioned in the Qur'ān.

The tendency to scientific interpretation (although now markedly out-of-date in the actual scientific information provided in the instance of Jawharī himself) has become widespread, and it is often used as a popular means of trying to convince non-Muslims of the divine nature of the Qur'ān and Islam. A startling example which was in circulation in Turkey in an English language publication (and thus presumably designed for tourist/non-Muslim consumption) comments in the following manner on Qur'ān 66/6, "The fire whose fuel is men and stones":

> A vast amount of energy lies locked in the nuclei of matter. In accordance with Einstein's equation, $E = mc^2$, it is known that a single gram of matter, if converted into energy, would yield energy equivalent to that contained in 2,500 tons of coal. If the atoms of men and stones could be converted directly to energy, we would be faced with inexhaustible amounts of fuel.

The real aim of the sacred verse, then, is to direct our attention to this fact. In other words, it intends to teach us the truth hidden in the essence of matter.[17]

Apologetics is not the only accomplishment of scientific exegesis, however. Muslims have found their faith enhanced and renewed through exposure to these types of claims. Typical is the following testimony from an Egyptian Doctor of Pharmacy, published in a 1991 textbook of world religions:

> Some of the statements in the Qur'an had no meaning at that time, 1,400 years ago, but they have meaning now. For example, "We have created this universe and we have made it expanding." "We have made the earth look like an egg." Such statements cannot come from just an average person living 1,400 years ago. Among ancient Egyptians, ancient Syrians we cannot find this information. I started to believe that someone was giving the knowledge to Muhammad. I'm not a very good believer – don't ask me to believe just because there is a book. But this information cannot come from any source except One Source.[18]

The argument against this type of approach, as enunciated by some Muslims, is that it suggests that the language of the text was not that of Muhammad[19] and his times; that is a lexically unsound approach, according to these critics. The word *samawāt* (literally "heavens") translated as "universe" in the previous quotation, for example, would have conveyed a certain meaning to Muhammad and his followers which would have been quite different from what is conveyed by the word "universe" today. As well, of course, such interpretations are opposed to the common Modernist idea that the Qur'ān's value is in its spirit and general guidance and it is not a source book of facts.[20] The ever-changing scientific ideas of the nineteenth and twentieth centuries should not be identified with the unchanging value of the Qur'ān, say many opponents. Shabbir Akhtar points out that these "arguments, if indeed that is the appropriate term for them, carry conviction only with devotees." Rarely, Akhtar notes, is the criterion of scientific consistency applied throughout the text:

> If the koranic claims tally with scientific views, it is cause for celebration in the religious camp; if not, it is declared either that the beliefs currently prevalent in the scientific community are,

conveniently enough for Muslims, erroneous or else that secular scientific truths are irrelevant to judgements about the truth of revealed claims. ... For to accept a consistent application of the criterion is, as the religionists themselves vaguely sense in some moods, in effect to impose a very exacting demand upon revelation. Is the Koran's authority, then, dependent upon its being able to achieve conformity with current scientific scholarship?[21]

Tafsīr in other parts of the Islamic world

The writing of commentaries goes on throughout the Muslim world, not just in India and Egypt. Ibn Bādis (1889–1940) was a famous Algerian Modernist reformer who turned to *tafsīr* to provide a vehicle for his ideas about contemporary political questions.[22] In Iran, Sayyid Muḥammad Ḥusayn al-Ṭabāṭabā'ī (1903–82) published an Arabic work entitled *al-Mīzān* ("The Balance"), some of which is available in English translation, which presents a totalist vision of Islam with a Neo-traditionalist flavour.[23] In Indonesia, people such as Ahmad Soorkatie presented the Modernist ideas of Muḥammad 'Abduh in the form of Quranic commentary embedded in lectures given in Arabic.[24]

As should be apparent from the above discussions, books of Quranic interpretation have become a vehicle for the spread of diverse ideas in the Islamic world. Support for various conceptions of Islam are found in the scriptural text, along with many passages which are deemed to have the answer to the dilemmas faced by Muslims and their faith in the modern world. All such works urge the relevance of Islam to the modern day, but it must be an Islam that is properly understood; and that is where the differences between the approaches begin to appear. Each approach argues for its own definition of what is essential in Islam. It is notable that the discussions and presentations thus far illustrated have not raised fundamental questions about the nature of the Qur'ān and how that is to be understood in the modern world.

Types of critical approach

Practical examples of looking at texts from the Qur'ān provide the best illustration of the issues which are at stake in talking about types of Muslim critical approach to the Qur'ān, the problems which they raise, and the limits which the interpretations will reach. Here is a good exercise for the reader: read the following three sections of the Qur'ān[25] and consider their problematic aspects within the modern context. Assume the stance of a Modernist Muslim: what do you perceive as problematic? Assume the stance of an Islamist: what is your response to a western perception of difficulties with these texts? Assume the stance of a Traditonalist: how would the passage be interpreted?

The first example

Sūra 56, verses 11 to 24:

> These will be
> Those Nearest to God:
> In Gardens of Bliss:
> A number of people
> From those of old,
> And a few from those
> Of later times.
> (They will be) on Thrones
> Encrusted (with gold
> And precious stones),
> Reclining on them,
> Facing each other.
> Round about them will (serve)
> Youths of perpetual (freshness),
> With goblets, (shining) beakers,
> And cups (filled) out of
> Clear-flowing fountains:
> No after-ache will they
> Receive therefrom, nor will they
> Suffer intoxication:
> And with fruits,
> Any that they may select;
> And the flesh of fowls,
> Any that they may desire.
> And (there will be) Companions
> With beautiful, big,
> And lustrous eyes, –
> Like unto Pearls
> Well-guarded.
> A Reward for the Deeds
> Of their past (Life).

This sensual picture of the rewards of heaven can evoke a variety of responses. For the Modernist, such portraits are potentially objectionable for what they imply about the relations between the sexes and for their material imagery in dealing with the rewards in the hereafter. Furthermore, Modernists will react to the Orientalist-missionary suggestion that this afterlife picture is somehow unspiritual (with the insinuation that Christianity has a more elevated view). Such a position may wish to propose that the picture is to be understood as mythic; this is not a description of reality as such, but is a figure which is expressed in a language which would appeal to those at the time of Muḥammad and would motivate them to convert and "submit" to the will of God. Such a resolution of the perceived problem suggests a certain relativization of the Quranic message in history such that parts of it may only be directly relevant to a certain age.

Muslims of the Islamist persuasion will insist that the passage reflects a reality, but that the reality is spoken of in metaphors and similar figures of speech. The "Companions," often translated less euphemistically as "fair maidens" (in Arabic: *hūr*) are not maidens at all, but priests who will minister to all, for example. The accuracy of the text, therefore, is not to be relativized but to be reinterpreted in a fashion amenable to the modern spirit – but the reality is still there in the text. Traditionalists have no difficulty with such a passage. There is no reason to suggest that the hereafter will be the least bit different than its literal description as provided by God in the Qur'ān. The only evidence which we have for the nature of the afterlife is provided in scripture and God will have described it accurately and will have designed it in a manner pleasing to Him and to humanity.

The second example

Sūra 23, verses 12 to 18:

> Man We did create
> From a quintessence (of clay);
> Then We placed him
> As (a drop of) sperm
> In a place of rest,
> Firmly fixed;
> Then We made the sperm
> Into a clot of congealed blood;
> Then of that clot We made

A (foetus) lump; then We
Made out of that lump
Bones and clothed the bones
With flesh; then We developed
Out of it another creature.
So blessed be God,
The Best to create!
After that, at length
Ye will die.
Again, on the Day
Of Judgment, will ye be
Raised up.
And We have made, above you,
Seven tracts; and We
Are never unmindful
Of (Our) Creation.
And We send down water
From the sky according to
(Due) measure, and We cause it
To soak in the soil;
And We certainly are able
To drain it off (with ease).

The previous passage suggested a situation about which humans have no evidence other than scripture. Here we are dealing with issues which relate to our knowledge of the natural world: birth, the notion of heavens ("tracts"), and rain. From some perspectives this information must be either right or wrong. For the Islamist, all this information must correspond to scientific knowledge, when both are properly understood. The very translation of the words relating to birth, for example, already reflects the assumption that the words were understood at the time of revelation in a semi-scientific fashion which agrees with current investigations into the stages of development of a foetus. More problematic, perhaps, is "seven tracts" or "heavens," but, even there, various layers in the earth's atmosphere can be identified with these seven. It is significant to note the implication here that the proper interpretation of these passages would only have become clear to Muslims in the latter part of the twentieth century, according to this view.

Scripture, for the Islamist, cannot be relativized to the point of saying that the text reflects the state of knowledge of the world at the time of Muḥammad, as would be the position of some (more radical) Modernists. These passages, Modernists might suggest, do not attempt to tell us of the facts of the world. Rather they reflect basic ideas that all suggest the glory and power of God; the importance of the text lies not directly in what it says but in what it points to.

For more traditional thinkers, any apparent conflict between such passages and modern science only illustrates the changing nature of scientific knowledge. The reality of the world is in the accurate description given by God. When observation of the world is done properly (and investigation is generally to be encouraged), the truth of the Qur'ān will be borne out.

The third example

Sūra 4, verse 34:

> Men are the protectors
> And maintainers of women
> Because God has given
> The one more (strength)
> Than the other, and because
> They support them
> From their means.
> Therefore the righteous women
> Are devoutly obedient, and guard
> In (the husband's) absence
> What God would have them guard.
> As to those women
> On whose part ye fear
> Disloyalty and ill-conduct,
> Admonish them (first),
> (Next), refuse to share their beds,
> (And last) beat them (lightly);
> But if they return to obedience,
> Seek not against them
> Means (of annoyance):
> For God is Most High,
> Great (above you all).

It is unlikely that any other passage in the Qur'ān has created more furore in the contemporary period than this. Pivotal is the word *wa-ḍribūhunna*, translated as "(and last) beat them (lightly)"; other translators soften the tone further with "chastise them"[26] or other similar sentiments. The Arabic word is commonly used to mean "beat," and there is no doubt that traditional Islam has taken the word in that physical sense. For the Islamist, there are two options, depending on the view of society and family values. First, the passage can be taken literally but with an emphasis placed on the legal requirements which are associated with the passage. For example, the necessity to "fear" disobedience would have to be taken very seriously. The strict application of the passage could then be argued to be "for the woman's own good," to protect her from herself. Implicit here (and, in fact, frequently made explicit) is the rejection of what is considered to be a western norm of family and male–female relations that would suggest that using physical force to ensure obedience is necessarily wrong. Some would claim that the ethical code promulgated by this passage under this interpretation is, in fact, the way things should be; the failure to embrace a proper (that is, Islamic) family structure is what has led to the degeneracy of the West – the "spare the rod, spoil the child/woman" syndrome.

However, another Islamist position on this passage would be to reinterpret the word "beat them." Phrases such as "chastise them" leave the text of scripture intact, and suggest that Islam has its own standards which are, in fact, better than those encouraged in the West but are fully respectful of the responsibilities of both men and women. It is Modernists who encounter the greatest problem in dealing with this passage. To declare the law appropriate for an earlier time, appropriate for a stage when people were still evolving morally, is to suggest that even the legal content of the Qur'ān is contingent upon history; only the basic religious impulse of the Qur'ān – the existence of God, His omnipotence and majesty – remains as the everlasting message of scripture.

This position of the contingency of the law is not accepted by many among the vocal promulgators of Islam in the contemporary period, for the absolute nature of the law of the Qur'ān is generally considered one of the central tags for the identification of Islam. Many Muslims fear – especially those of the Islamist persuasion, but the feeling is more widespread than that – that relativizing the Qur'ān to the standards of today (as in equality between men and women) will lead to "immorality" and similar sins, and will eventually lead down the "slippery slope" to the abandonment of Islam.

The issues at stake

There are two main questions which arise in modern discussions of the Qur'ān which illustrate, in a more abstract fashion, the limits to which these critical approaches may go in dealing with the contingency of the text. The first begins from the question of the miraculousness of the Qur'ān and moves into the general question of the rationality of the Qur'ān and the second raises the question of the difference between legal and moral regulations. Both of these are interconnected, one leading to the next, at least in the thought of some people.

The miraculousness of the Qur'ān

Classically, the doctrine of the *i'jāz* ("miraculousness," "inimitability") of the Qur'ān has been seen to assert the totally non-contingent nature of the text: it is fully divine and the language is that of God. The Qur'ān is the word of God *per se*. It has no relationship in its form to the passage of historical time. It literally descended from heaven, having been written on the pre-existent divine tablet. Any conflicts created by this attitude to the ultimate authority of the Qur'ān have always been solved by pointing to the limits of human knowledge – we simply do not fully understand. Some Muslims have urged a somewhat modified understanding of the miraculousness of the Qur'ān. In general, this conviction may be viewed as an aspect of the anti-supernaturalism and the support of rationalism which has already been noted, especially in discussions of Muḥammad's biography. But the question remains, to what extent can anti-supernaturalism be taken regarding the Qur'ān without destroying Islam, while remembering that underlying that question is always a second one, what is Islam?

A frequent response, as in the case of 'Alī Dashtī, is that the miracle of the Qur'ān lies not in its form, which is the most important aspect of the classical statements on the matter, but in the divine guidance which the book provides and the success which it has had. Thus the elevated, divine status of the Qur'ān (and, therefore, in one sense, its miraculousness) is maintained, but the traditional interpretation of each doctrine is done away with. This, then, allows two further thoughts for some people: a removal of all other supernatural elements within the Qur'ān and a questioning of the precise understanding of the non-contingency of the text.[27]

Another common tendency is to conceive the Qur'ān not as revealed literally but as installed in Muḥammad's heart and then spoken through the human faculties of the prophet. The language, therefore, is Muḥammad's, although it is still possible to hold that this is ultimately God's word also.[28] The impetus behind these discussions rests with the basic drive of the Modernist movements: the need to modernize, reform, and rejuvenate Islam. The means to do this is found in removing what is envisioned to be the stumbling block: anti-rationalistic ideas along with norms which are perceived as not being in keeping with modern society.

In addition, there has been the methodological influence of the historical–critical method as developed in Europe. Basic to this method are a number of assumptions – all revolving around the scientific rational impulse – that history moves by causality and that those causes may be determined and studied. History must be studied according to the laws of reason for that is the way the world works. Religion is nothing special in this regard: it is like any philosophy or literature and like nature itself. It must be coherent, logical, and capable of being incorporated into an understanding of human history. Biblical scholarship of the eighteenth century enunciated this stance quite plainly, for example in the case of Johann Salamo Semler who published a study of the Bible between 1771 and 1775 which "called for a purely historical-philological interpretation of the Bible, in the light of the circumstances surrounding the origin of the various books, without any concern for edification."[29] Detached from theological and philosophical restraints in the nineteenth century under the impact of Schleiermacher, Biblical studies in the early twentieth century "made impartial and objective research the ideal."[30] The end result of this is summarized in the following: "The only scientifically responsible interpretation of the Bible is that investigation of the biblical texts that, with a methodologically consistent use of historical understanding in the present state of its art, seeks via reconstruction to recognize and describe the meaning these texts have had in the context of the tradition history of early Christianity."[31]

For the most part, the impact of the historical–critical method has been slow to be felt in the Muslim world, at least within the study of the Qur'ān. The reasons for this lie within the traditional discussions concerning the nature of the Qur'ān which have just been mentioned. It must be remembered how much Muslims perceive to be at stake here. The existence of Islam classically depends upon the miracle of the Qur'ān. Thus, for those who have determined that this is the reform route to follow, caution is a continuous feature. Assessing the basic character and nature of the Qur'ān must be accomplished first, and that means raising questions of the rationality of the text and of its relationship to historical fact. The issue still lingers, as the following examples will show, of just how far Muslims can go in pursuing these questions while still remaining Islamic.

Muḥammad Khalaf Allāh and historical specificity

Rationality or anti-supernaturalism is one area where the limits of interpretation are confronted; the desire to see scripture as fully in keeping with reason can only be taken so far before those who maintain a more traditional view of Islam raise their objections. Another area where these limits are confronted is seen in the relationship between the text and historical reality, often spoken of in terms of the conflict between "truth" and "reality." Muḥammad Aḥmad Khalaf Allāh (b. 1916, d. 1997), in a thesis submitted to Cairo University in 1947, brought this issue to prominence in the Islamic world. While the issue had been broached by others before him, especially his teacher Amīn al-Khūlī (1895–1966),[32] in Khalaf Allāh's instance public reaction was fairly rapid. He wrote that the prophetic stories in the Qur'ān were not historical as such but kerygmatic: that they were being repeated for their moral/religious aims, and were reiterated in different forms according to Muḥammad's needs in a given situation. They were therefore contingent upon history even in their aims. This is the distinction between what may be termed "truth" (in a spiritual sense) and "reality" (as reflected in historical fact).

Khalaf Allāh was accused of "atheism and gross ignorance" and had to rewrite his thesis several times before it was accepted; it was published in 1950–1 but he was subsequently forced out of his university teaching post. Traditionally, all the stories of the Qur'ān have been seen to be of equal value and to be of a historical nature. This position raised a number of questions in the modern world, however. What of stories which did not seem to be in agreement with other, earlier sources? For example, in the Qur'ān Hamān is presented as Pharaoh's minister while in the Bible he is a minister to the Persian king of a much later period. What is a modern Muslim to believe? Are the facts of the Qur'ān all necessarily true historically and all other sources false? How will this attitude work in conjunction with the historical-critical method which clearly values older sources over newer ones? One of Khalaf Allāh's concerns was apologetic: how to save the Qur'ān from the attacks of the Orientalists who continued to cite all these problems within the text.

Khalaf Allāh's resolution of the problem was to say that the concern of the Qur'ān is to employ striking literary expressions through which psychological and religious truths are expressed. Its concern is not necessarily with historical or material truth (that is, "reality"). Literary genres, specifically historical-literary, parable and allegory, have been employed within the Qur'ān to embody these spiritual truths. The aim of the Qur'ān was to "admonish and exhort," not to instruct in history. Hence, information about time and place is generally missing in the Quranic narratives.[33]

Such controversies continue to replay down until today. Another scholar in the tradition of al-Khūlī, Naṣr Abū Zayd, was charged with apostasy in 1995 before the Egyptian Family Court. The Court found him guilty on the following grounds:

1   he had allegedly denied the existence of angels and devils referred to in the Qur'ān;
2   he had described certain images in the Qur'ān used of heaven and hell as mythical;
3   he had described the text of the Qur'ān as a human production (it is a "historically determined and culturally constructed" text);
4   he had advocated the use of the intellect to replace concepts derived literally from the text of the Qur'ān especially in regards to matters related to inheritance, women, Christians and Jews, and female slaves.

For these writings, Naṣr Abū Zayd was held to be an apostate and his marriage was annulled.[34] He and his wife fled the country as a result. Abū Zayd's response is simply to note that such ideas have a long heritage in Islam. They were the key notions held by the Mu'tazila during the formative centuries of Islam. Such ideas cannot simply be readopted within Islam, however; there is a need for a new modern theology of Islam which will "accommodate the literary study of the Qur'ān."[35]

The examples of Khalaf Allāh and Abū Zayd raise issues about the limits to which Muslims are prepared to take reinterpretation of the Qur'ān. Rationalism, the underlying principle of the historical–critical method, is fully applied in these cases in order to resolve the problems perceived within a general Modernist tendency. Neither writer actually doubts the authenticity of the text of scripture, only whether the words themselves are to be taken as intending to convey precisely what it has been traditionally thought that they say.

A contemporary response

Much of the response to Khalaf Allāh's work at the time of its publication dealt with it by saying that the author was using history as a criterion of truth higher than the Qur'ān, something which no Muslim could accept. The ultimate truth of the text of scripture exists, in these responses, *a priori*. A more subtle argument is made by Shabbir Akhtar who does not raise the example of Khalaf Allāh specifically but certainly deals with the principle in his book, *A Faith for All Seasons*. He approaches the problem as though it had only affected the Christian study of their scripture; he may well not be aware of the extent to which Muslims have already broached these questions. Regardless, the case of the "sophisticated Christians" (as an example he cites Richard Swinburne), provides a cautionary tale for Muslims, according to Akhtar, who wish to maintain their faith in light of philosophical approaches to scripture. Akhtar points out that it was Darwin who made it so necessary for Christians to distinguish between "the false non-religious husk and the concomitant true religious kernel."[36] This has gone to the extent now that Christians are willing to talk about false cultural trappings in which scripture has expressed truths for ignorant people of the past. Some statements of the Bible, or the Qur'ān, in this view, may be taken as "unempirical or false." For Akhtar, the problem with this is: how can one be sure that the underlying religious claims, which have been embodied in these false statements, are necessarily true? There is no way, he contends, to "distinguish in any unquestion-begging way . . . , between the religious message presumed to be true and the culturally specific incarnation presumed to be false."[37] After entertaining several possible ways around this problem – that God incorporated errors in scripture to keep us on our toes, or that apparent errors are matters which are simply beyond human reason – he concludes by saying that any concession to the idea of false claims in scripture must be resisted. If this is not so, then while "today we disown what we take to be factually erroneous, perhaps tomorrow we will reject apparent moral anachronisms – such as scriptural claims about the relatively low status of women or the impropriety of deviant sexual behaviour, not to speak of the occasional questionable doctrine about the nature or activity of the Deity."[38] Revelation, for Akhtar, is an all or nothing affair; that is the only way to construct a philosophically defensible Islam. Watering down the doctrine of the non-contingent nature of the text too far will lead to no defence against claims that the entire basis of the religion may be false.

The contingent nature of Qur'ānic law

Khalaf Allāh did not confront the question of the nature of the law; in fact, he studiously avoided raising the issue. Neither did he question the divine nature of the Qur'ān. It should be noticed that, from his perspective, it is not necessary to question the Qur'ān's status as the actual word of God; God may reveal speech which does not have the intent of providing historical facts, but it may still be conceived of as God's word. But when this kind of approach confronts the legal parts of the Qur'ān, further issues arise. Are the laws contingent, that is, applicable only to the time of Muḥammad? Are they embedded in the history of the early Muslim community or are they expressions of the eternal will of God?

Fazlur Rahman

Fazlur Rahman (1919–88) was Director of the Islamic Research Institute in Pakistan from 1962 to 1968 but, after pressure from conservative elements in that country, was forced to leave; he became Professor of Islamic Thought at the University of Chicago in the United States and achieved a reputation of being one of the great scholars in the field.[39]

Rahman was a fervent Modernist. In approaching the text of the Qur'ān, he wished to differentiate legal regulations from moral regulations, the former being contingent, the latter non-contingent. Legal rulings must be considered binding in a moral sense, even if not in their literal wording.[40] Much of the law of classical Islam has been wrongly formulated because the jurists ignored the moral ideal behind the text and the words were read as literal legal enactments, according to this view. The Quranic acceptance of slavery, a form of ownership of people which has fallen into disrepute under the impact of modernity, is treated in the following way by Rahman:

> As an immediate solution, the Qur'ān accepts the institution of slavery on the legal plane. No alternative was possible since slavery was ingrained in the structure of society, and its overnight wholesale liquidation would have created problems which it

would have been absolutely impossible to solve, and only a dreamer could have issued such a visionary statement. But at the same time every legal and moral effort was made to free the slaves and to create a milieu where slavery ought to disappear. ... Here again we are confronted by a situation where the clear logic of the Qur'ānic attitude was not worked out in actual history by Muslims. ... These examples [also including women and wine], therefore, make it abundantly clear that whereas the spirit of the Qur'ānic legislation exhibits an obvious direction towards the progressive embodiment of the fundamental human values of freedom and responsibility in fresh legislation, nevertheless the actual legislation of the Qur'ān had partly to accept the then existing society as a term of reference. This clearly means that the actual legislation of the Qur'ān cannot have been meant to be literally eternal by the Qur'ān itself.[41]

It is not only on legal topics that Rahman has approached the Qur'ān in this manner, although it is in that area where the extent of his demythologization becomes most clear. The psychological intention of the text as opposed to the descriptive meaning is frequently employed as a principle in his work, *Major Themes of the Qur'ān*. God's power, humans being predestined, intercession in the afterlife, divine punishment of humans, and the existence of the *jinn* are all interpreted not for their literal sense but for what they were driving at in terms of motivating humans toward the proper attitude regarding God, life and creation.

This position fits into an overall neo-modernist stance, according to Rahman himself, one which recognizes the complexities of life as opposed to the Islamist idea of everything (especially Islam) being "simple." Once again, it is the history of Islam which has taken Muslims away from the proper understanding of the Qur'ān; the text of scripture itself is still a perfect reflection of standards as they should be, as long as it is properly understood. Rahman blames the educational institutions developed in the early Muslim centuries for the failure to appreciate the true import of the Qur'ān. The educational system created what it called the Quranic sciences along with the legal structures of society. It separated these religious sciences from the rational or secular sciences (Rahman traces this division back to al-Ghazālī) and, with the growing disrepute of the latter studies, Islamic civilization fell into stagnation. The worst consequence of this was the rejection of Islamic philosophy, which could have kept open ways of enquiring into the foundations of Islam, but was unable to. No longer was the Qur'ān treated as a "vibrant and revolutionary document"; rather, it became "buried under the debris of grammar and rhetoric," a trend reaching its apex with the notion that only super-commentaries could and should be written.[42] The way Islam can free itself from this burden of the past is by studying history critically, in order to comprehend how the impetus of the Qur'ān has been understood in the past and how Muslims have interacted with it. Thereby, the essentials of the faith may be differentiated from that which has simply attached itself unnecessarily.

Pushing the "limits"

Some Muslims would take this further or perhaps even question the very presuppositions of the historical–critical method and approach the issue in a totally different way. We have seen in the previous chapter, for example, how Fatima Mernissi perceives the Quranic attitudes toward women: that they reflect male ideas put in the mouth of a male God. The law of the Qur'ān – through language – is culturally conditioned from beginning to end.

The same sense emerges from the writings of Mohammed Arkoun.[43] In dealing with the Qur'ān specifically, Arkoun pays attention to the historical development of interpretation of the scripture, a process which serves to establish how the Qur'ān takes on meaning in the Islamic context. This then leads to the observation that, from within the modern context, Muslims are attempting to read the Qur'ān as if modern reason was in all ways identical to the linguistic shape of the Qur'ān and Muḥammad's epistemological environment. The logic of the Qur'ān, from Arkoun's perspective, however, is a poetic logic rather than a rational logic. Ironically perhaps, it is precisely because the Qur'ān is written with this poetic logic that it can be read as if modern rationality were reflected in it. For Arkoun, of course, the Qur'ān conveys a mythical discourse rather than a historical one, but by that very fact it allows a historical interpretation.

The necessity today is, for Arkoun, to approach the Qur'ān with today's categories which are composed of the totality of the human sciences. The selection of these forms a refrain – even a litany according to one of his reviewers: ethnology, anthropology, history of religions, psychoanalysis, semiotics, and with human consciousness to be viewed mythically, historically, socially, economically, politically, philosophically, morally, aesthetically, religiously and so forth. The aim of this is to discover the way in which all elements

of culture are bound ideologically with history. All of human existence is founded upon and created by history and only through the
realization of this can the past, present and future become clear.
This is demythologization at its extreme.

As an example of what this might mean in a practical sense, an
issue of law is useful. For Arkoun:

> The basic difference between the Quran and the Shari'a is that
> the first makes use of contingent data in order to emphasize the
> relationship between God and man and to fill men's minds with
> a consciousness that there is a world beyond this world of events,
> values, norms and possessions. All this is clothed in mythical
> language and structure which opens the way to problems rather
> than excluding them. The second, on the other hand, system-
> atizes, within the framework of a code of law, the pragmatic
> solutions that were adopted at an early period. It is under-
> standable, then, why it is wrong to call norms that have been
> included in this code and perpetuated by an inflexible teaching
> Islamic.[44]

The Qur'ān then does not provide answers but problems, ones which
must be struggled with in human life. It is the aim of Arkoun's method
to get "outside" the dualities of contemporary discussions which
still deal with the understanding of the world in historicist terms. The
historical–critical method is not the answer for the needs of the
Muslim consciousness in the latter part of the twentieth century.[45]

This approach does not even seem to entertain the idea of
Rahman's moral ideals within the Qur'ān. Could it be said that
Mernissi and Arkoun get to the point of challenging the authority
of the Qur'ān text itself? In traditional understandings of "text" and
"authority" they clearly do. Their understandings seem to call for a
re-expression of the Qur'ān – one that stands, however, completely
within the Muslim ethos. Mernissi wonders, for example, if an Islam
which gave women freedom could really be called Islam at all.[46] It
might be termed post-Islamic, I would suggest. One of the reasons
for the radicalness of these positions is that neither writer stands
within the now-traditional method of historical criticism, although
the reasons for this may well be different in the two cases. Mernissi's
use of the feminist interpretative framework brings her face-to-face
with the historical issues, and there is a tendency in her writing to
step back from what might seem to be the inevitable conclusion.
Arkoun, on the other hand, wishes to change the very terms of the

discussion and eliminate the duality of the discussion between contingent and non-contingent, for example, for those very terms imply that there can be human knowledge which is outside the framework of historicity and language. From this perspective, "limits" to critical approaches make little sense, for the limits are those imposed by linguistic structures; the deconstruction of those limitations is the entire purpose of the exercise.

15 Issues of identity

In the discussion of the emergence of Islam in the seventh through tenth centuries, three matters were isolated that provided the key elements of Islamic identity. Theology, law and ritual were crucial to those activities which would serve to identify Islam as a religion over against other faiths (primarily Judaism and Christianity). This motif has remained stable throughout Islamic history down to current times, although the background against which that identity must be read is now much more multifaceted than in previous centuries. It is still possible to isolate the same three elements as crucial, although theology perhaps has taken a substantial back seat to law which now manifests itself primarily within the arena of politics and the role of Islam within it. Ritual, on the other hand, remains a very important aspect, both from the perspective of self-identity and for identity from the outside.

Each era has its way of interacting with these symbols of identity. Subtly altered understandings of the basic ritual activities of Islam illustrate some aspects of the transformations which are taking place in modern Muslim faith. Once again, these changed understandings and interpretations flow from changes in attitude toward the fundamental sources of Islam, the Qur'ān and the *sunna*. In most instances, however, the abstract intellectual discussions regarding these sources are not brought to the forefront when Muslims conceptualize their basic religious practices within the modern context. What continues to be of interest for our purposes is the way in which the issues and approaches as employed in the considerations of the Qur'ān and the *sunna* are also manifested in the approaches to the various issues which surround the role and function of ritual practice in the contemporary context.

The pillars of Islam

The traditional definitional elements of Muslim faith – the summaries of belief and the ritual "five pillars" – remain virtually intact in the modern context. Any movement toward prayers being said in the vernacular rather than Arabic, for example, or being able to perform the fast of Ramaḍān during a more "convenient" month, has proven singularly unsuccessful. But this should not be taken to suggest that the modern world has not had its impact felt in Muslim practice at all. Attention to Islamic ritual activities and their practice provides a means of looking at ways Muslims have attempted to express their religiosity in general; within the modern context, several factors lead to these ritual aspects of Islam having a significant bearing on the question of the contemporary manifestation of Islam.

What might be termed the politicization of Muslims, a worldwide phenomenon in Islam but especially prevalent in diaspora populations in North America and Europe, has led to a heightened sense of identity being felt through the affirmation of distinctive Islamic practices. Another way of expressing this is as "the Islamization of the self," and the use of Islamic symbols to provide identity on a personal level.[1] This tendency is connected not only with the move of individuals from a rural to an urban society, but also, one might contend, from a "Muslim" society to a "non-Muslim" one. Village society has always been characterized by the idea that "the life of the village is the religion of the village;" that is, the rhythm of life reflects the Islamic way and is integral within each member's life. Modern society, especially that of a predominantly non-Muslim country, displays a separation between religious life and secular life which has led to a tendency toward affirming various aspects of Muslim existence – notably those associated with ritual activity and self-study of the Qur'ān – as central tenets of identity. Identity in these cases is a personal one, not a collectively-affirmed one as in the community-based village life. The idea of women's veiling, *hijāb*, being a personal, home-focused idea serves as a specific example of this reorientation. Such personalization of faith is frequently a core element of Islamism, it may be remarked.[2]

This tendency toward personalization of faith may be the result of the general globalization of Islam within the world community. While Islam certainly spread widely in previous centuries, the present-day mobility of world populations along with massive dislocations of various groups within many countries has had some significant consequences. The status of Muslim minorities around the world has become an issue for Muslims, not perhaps impinging upon their self-definition within Islam in the same way as the creation of a diaspora-centred Judaism did but significant nevertheless, and it may well have an even greater impact in the future.[3]

Islam has always defined itself ritually as being focused on the "five pillars." In connection with each ritual, the impact of the modern world may be noted, not so much in the practices themselves necessarily but in the interpretation which is put forth of the activities. It is, therefore, not a matter of continuing to legitimize the activities themselves in the modern context but a question of how to mould them to the modern age within an Islamic framework and how to conceptualize them in relation to ideas of self-definition. It is this principle which displays, in a very practical sense, the ramifications of the approaches toward reinterpretation of the Qur'ān and the *sunna*, as discussed earlier in the previous chapters.

Witness to faith (shahāda)

The *shahāda*, or "witness to faith," is the first of the classical five pillars of Islam, repeating in Arabic the two phrases, "There is no god but God" and "Muḥammad is the messenger of God". An example of the contextualization of the *shahāda* in contemporary American society is provided by the following statement within a wedding ceremony, addressed to the bride who intended to convert to Islam:

> "There is no priesthood in Islam. Anyone can perform the [wedding] ceremony, even you yourselves, or a trusted representative of the bride and groom. I do not like the term conversion. Sister, you are not converting, you are reforming. Islam is not only the religion of Muhammad, it is also the religion of Moses and Jesus. The term Christianity was not used by Jesus but only by later generations, who modified his teachings. Thus, when we say, There is only one religion and that is Islam, we mean that all the prophets carried the same message from the same God. Sister, you are not obliged to convert to Islam. You may keep your religion intact if you wish to do so." Sue indicates her need to "reform." Nasem says, "Then let it be so." He explains the three foundations of Islam: oneness of God, prophethood, and resurrection.
>
> Then come the two testimonies: "Sister, repeat after me, I witness there is no God but God, Muhammad is His servant

slave and His messenger." Then prayer: all present raise their hands and pray that she might be a good Muslim and have a happy, prosperous life. Then the marriage ceremony.[4]

Islamists have often attempted to define Islam in terms of the witness to faith alone, by emphasizing the concept of *tawḥīd*, the oneness and unity of God, as expressed in *shahāda*. This follows from a statement made by Muḥammad as reported within the *ḥadīth* material to the effect that he brought nothing more important than the *shahāda*. The idea of *tawḥīd*, then, for the Islamists, expresses everything which Islam stands for and is the basis of all Islamic thought; such a summary is a crucial part of the suggestion that Islam is a "simple" religion, in that once the truth of this affirmation of the oneness of God is perceived, then everything else in Islam flows from it.

So, when you recite these words [of the *shahāda*], you should be conscious what an important commitment you are making to your God, with the whole world as your witness, and what a great responsibility you are taking on as a result of your commitment. Once you have made the affirmation consciously, the Kalimah [literally "the word," meaning the words of the *shahāda*] must inform all your thoughts and reign supreme in your whole lives: no idea contrary to it should form part of your mental furniture. Whatever runs counter to the Kalimah you must always consider false and the Kalimah alone true.

If you recite the Kalimah in this manner, only then can you become true Muslims, only then is created that overwhelming difference between man and man.[5]

The statement of the *shahāda*, then, is the essence of the Islamist totalism in the vision of Islam.

Prayer (*ṣalāt*)

Five specific periods of prayer a day are a ritual requirement in Islam. The globalization of the Muslim population has created a number of incongruous situations illustrating the way in which Islam has been confronted with the realities of the modern context.[6] In Surinam, Indians, brought by the Dutch to that country in the period 1873–1916 (in 1982, there were 50,000 such people) are members of the Ḥanafiyya in their legal school alignment. They conduct their sermon (*khuṭba*) during the Friday noon prayer in Urdu, and they face the east (their *qibla*) during all the prayer. The Javanese present in Surinam, on the other hand, are members of the Shāfiʿiyya according to their legal school and have a *qibla* to the west. These people were indentured labourers brought by the Dutch in the period 1850–1931, and in 1982 there were 90,000 of them. "The qibla is towards the west simply because it is in this direction in Java, although Mecca is situated from Surinam in the easterly direction," according to Rolf Reichert who researched this issue.[6] This is, of course, not a "problem" for Islam in any sense; that any group of people would continue to follow their traditional direction of prayer in any given place does not impinge upon significant elements of Muslim self-definition. It does indicate, however, that as the process of globalization continues, such elements may continue to grow and may well provoke questioning on the part of Muslims themselves.

A similar, and likewise essentially trivial, element is presented by Muslims flying in outer space and locating the direction of prayer and the time of prayer; this latter point also applies to those in polar regions where timings as related to the sun's position provide the suitable intervals for prayer. In most such situation, people agree that the timings of prayer in Mecca should be followed. The point here is that the modern context provokes a situation in which the fundamental principles of ritual activity in Islam must be faced. The solutions are argued on a legal basis, employing well-established juristic principles, extrapolated for the required situation.

More substantial issues related to prayer most certainly do exist and they reflect the extent to which Muslims have been willing to adapt ritual to the social context in which they live. The implementation of Sunday as the day of congregational prayer (*jumʿa*) rather than Friday has been one such issue. In 1935, Turkish leader Atatürk made Sunday the weekly day of closing for offices, factories and so forth. Such a "day of rest" had not been instituted during the pre-industrial age of Islamic society and had never been seen as a religiously-based necessity (the Qurʾān suggests that the sabbath as a day of rest was a special legal provision for the Jews). Atatürk's action was justified by him in terms of practical concern for life in the modern age.[7] Such a step did not, however, transform Muslim worship with its focus on Friday noon for communal prayer. In other countries, however, especially those with Muslim groups living within a primarily Christian context, the move to Sunday become an entire transformation of the Muslim day of communal gathering. Like similar movements within Reform Judaism which tried sabbath worship on Sundays rather than Saturdays within the context of European (Christian) society, this was a relatively short-lived accommodation to the society around them. For Muslims, Friday was (re-)asserted to be the day which was attached to a very basic sense of Islamic identity. What still remains in more contemporary times is the use of Sunday as a "family day" with mosque-centred activities (for example "Sunday school" as religious training for children).

For the performance of the Friday communal prayer, a prayer leader, *imām*, is required; his function is to lead the community in prayer, keeping the actions in unison, and he will frequently (but not always) be called upon to deliver the *khuṭba* or sermon. This has raised another issue related to the wide dispersal of Muslims today in countries where Muslims are not the majority of the population. In many instances, an *imām* is recruited from outside the country. This is often done as a way of helping to maintain the identity of the minorities, but in some situations this only emphasizes the foreignness of a minority group. Furthermore, these imported *imām*s are often felt to be out of touch with the realities of life in the new countries in which they are living. Malise Ruthven has pointed this out as a factor in acerbating the "Rushdie affair" in England. The *imām*s, in this case brought in from Pakistan to Bradford, reinforced

> the ties with the homeland, creating an anchor with the certainties of the past. It also reinforces isolation: few of the *imam*s know English; fewer still are aware of the wider British society around them with its complexities and diversified spiritual resources. The leaders add spiritual authority to a vision of society already viewed, one might say distorted, through the prism of faith: the society that corresponds to the *jahiliyya* of the Prophet's time, a godless, materialistic society wholly dedicated to the pursuit of worldly wealth and sensual pleasure.[8]

Equally significant in this regard, however, is the extent to which these prayer leaders have been thrust into a situation of adopting a general ministerial role, something essentially foreign to the nature of the office in the past and also in predominantly Muslim countries today. A new institution has essentially arisen within the North American and European context for Muslims.[9]

Overall, the interpretation of prayer in modern Muslim discussions has often taken on a certain spiritualized interpretation which may be usefully compared to the general remarks about the character of ritual at the conclusion of Chapter 7 above. Rarely is prayer presented as simply a duty to be fulfilled because it has been decreed by God. Rather, prayer is described as the primary defence of the Muslim against the encroachment of worldly concerns, for "it prevents an individual from all sorts of abominations and vices by providing him chances of direct communion with God."[10] The spiritual leader of Iran, Ayatollah Ali Khamenei is reported to have suggested the following: "no other channel is a better means for communicating with the Almighty, and ... a 'Salat' said with full cognizance of its deeper meanings and with a full heart is the best safeguard for against a tendency to succumb to a feeling of absurdity and moral weakness."[11]

Fasting (*ṣiyām, ṣawm*)

Abstention from all food and drink, as well as avoidance of sexual intercourse during daylight hours, is the mark of the Muslim thirty-day period of fasting, done during the month of Ramaḍān. Ramaḍān has always been considered by most Muslims as the most important of the ritual duties. Even if a person does not comply with the requirement of five prayers a day, observance of the fast is still likely. Contemporary Muslim fast participants do, however, exhibit subtle changes in the interpretation of their actions. While in earlier times a sense of the penitent value of fasting was certainly present, this has been downplayed in interpretations of recent decades. For many Modernists and Islamists, the fast is performed because it has been commanded by God, not for any individual benefit which may accrue to the individual in terms of his or her fate in the hereafter. Moral benefit in the here and now, however, is emphasized. The fast is a means of social levelling and reinforcing notions of social responsibility. When even the rich are hungry, the fate of the poor will be evident, so the argument goes. Even more, there is an overall sense of Muslim unity celebrated during the fast, especially in the festive aspects of nightlife during the month.

Various attempts have been made, especially under government impetus to modify this area of Muslim practice. President Bourguiba of Tunisia, in February of 1960, for example, urged the avoidance of Ramaḍān observances for government employees.[12] Religion should serve to ameliorate life, not make it more difficult, his argument went; in the present state of Tunisia's attempts to thrive as an independent country, fasting would only worsen the economic condition and the suffering which would result from the month of fasting was a type of penitence foreign to Islam. Certain religious scholars supported this stance on the grounds that *jihād,* "holy war," was needed in order to build the country economically, and fasting for those fighting in times of *jihād* was not necessary according to Islamic law.[13] Similar suggestions were reported in Egypt in the mid-1950s.[14] These "reforms," based upon an impetus toward greater efficiency in (capitalist) society, did, however, prove extremely unpopular, even among those who did not partake in the fasting. Those who argued against changing the requirements of Ramaḍān said that the legislation imposed by God could not be changed by the opinion of a lowly human being. Fasting, according to the argument against change, is intimately tied to hardship; that is the essence of it in fact ("Where is the fasting person who does not suffer hardship in fasting?", it was asked). Just because economic hardship might result from fasting did not give a reason not to fast; if it did, then nobody would bother to fast, everyone claiming that it involved hardship.[15] In fact, the whole logic of fasting was to provide the experience of hardship for those who might otherwise never experience it. The argument for the rationality of Islamic ritual is notable. Overall, these types of arguments and the tide of public sentiment led governments to a compromise position of restricting working hours in government offices and factories during the month.

It has been pointed out by some observers that the concern which Muslims expressed over this issue of Ramaḍān observance was far more severe than that expressed regarding many other changes which were taking place in the Muslim world at that time. Polygamy, for example, was banned in several countries during this period. The issue, therefore, was not perceived to be one of changing the law, as such, but one of an attack on Muslim identity:

> Ramadan had become in modern times the great manifestation of the unity of Islam, the month when Muslims believing or unbelieving become conscious of their past and affirmed their links with their ancestors, and the criticism [of the practice of Ramaḍān] was perhaps resented not because it ran counter to the Shari'a but rather because it threatened the solidarity of the Muslim community.[16]

The role of Ramaḍān as a social rather than religious requirement has also become apparent in recent times, with some young people declaring that fasting during Ramaḍān "is the thing to do" even, apparently, if one is not Muslim.[17] The extent to which fasting is a significant element of Muslim identity today is emphasized within the context of the often-noted assertiveness of Muslim minority groups in minority situations. One interesting instance of this contemporary politicization of Muslims may be illustrated through an incident at my own university. During the spring of 1991 and the winter of 1999, the final examination period for students fell during Ramaḍān. This, of course, is not the first time such would have happened, with Ramaḍān moving some eleven days earlier each solar calendar year. However, in recent years, the university administration has experienced an apparently new phenomenon: requests for "deferred final examinations" from Muslims on the grounds of the religious requirement of fasting during daylight hours which would, reasonably enough it was argued, make undertaking an examination difficult. It is the focus on Ramaḍān that is significant. North American society, after all, ignores all aspects of the Muslim ritual calendar. Students have not demanded that classes not take place during prayer times (not even Fridays) nor that those wishing to go on pilgrimage to Mecca be excused from any academic responsibilities. (Christmas and Easter remain central to the academic schedule, however.) Ramaḍān is an individual religious action which is particularly amenable to the general North American religious ethos; the assertion of its prominence in the ritual calendar, therefore, is a part of the contextualization of the Muslim community in the modern world.

Determining when Ramaḍān should start and the precise hours of fasting on any given day is increasingly accommodated to modern technology and order. Traditionally, the religious calendar has been established each month through the sighting of the moon.[18] For some people, this raises a question about the role of science within Islam. Science can now tell us with great accuracy when the month of Ramaḍān starts and ends. Back in Muḥammad's time, the only practical means of determining the month was by observation of the moon. It only makes sense (and God urges such in the Qur'ān), so the argument goes, that today Muslims should embrace the scientific accuracy which is available.

The traditional practice of the recitation of the Qur'ān during the nights of Ramaḍān continues, celebrating the revelation of the Qur'ān to Muḥammad during that month. Modern media participate in the event with radio stations playing Qur'ān recitation. Even in officially secular Turkey, the publication of the appropriate one-thirtieth section of the Qur'ān in Turkish translation each day in the newspaper is an ongoing practice.

Charity (*zakāt, ṣadaqa*)

The giving of alms (*zakāt*) has been, within the juridical system of classical Islam, a fully regulated system. Modern terminology and principles have been applied to *zakāt*, especially in countries outside the Muslim heartlands where the economic systems presuppose, if not demand, certain forms of financial participation. Thus we see "*zakāt* returns" just like "Income Tax returns," where statements of net worth are subject to calculation of the tax owing. Such "returns" often present an uneasy compromise between the realities of modern Euro-American life and the traditional categories of items on which *zakāt* is collectable; they may also feature certain aspects which might not be seen as being fully in keeping with a system of "Islamic economics" as that is proposed, and partially enacted, by some Islamists (such as taking into account interest paid on mortgages and loans).

Similar problems with the payment of *zakāt* must be faced in the more central Islamic lands also. Is *zakāt* to be paid on types of property unknown in classical Islamic times? Just what do stock certificates represent? Should the tax be paid in stock certificates or in cash? In what percentage? Likewise an issue over who should receive the *zakāt* arises, with the traditional list of the poor, new converts, travellers, missionaries, those who collect the tax, slaves (for buying their freedom) and those who have debts due to public service, frequently being extended to include modern charitable institutions.[19] Such issues are generally solved through the processes of Islamic law such as reasoning by analogy, but the significant fact, of course, is that the issue does have to be faced.[20]

Zakāt and politics have mixed extensively in Pakistan where charity and income tax have often been equated; it has been argued that only the modern state apparatus can actually handle the equitable distribution of these funds, given the complexities of modern life.[21] Likewise, *zakāt* and the idea of egalitarianism as fitting in with the socialist platforms were especially prominent under Abdul Nasser in Egypt of the 1960s.[22] Islamic charity is equated to a system of responsibility fundamental to Islamic social structures and social assumptions. The sharing of wealth legitimizes one's own possession of material goods and emphasizes the communal aspects of ownership in Islam. "To pay Zakat is a cleansing process for the wealth and its owner. Allah not only promises reward in the hereafter but also to bless an enterprise so that it becomes more profitable."[23]

Finally, another way of solving the entire problem of how *zakāt* is to be understood in the modern world has arisen. There has been a tendency to remove *zakāt* altogether from its juridical context and simply make it freewill offerings. This is one more aspect of the emergence of a personalized and individualized Islam, common among the Islamist group. But this exists in tension with ideas of Islamic economics in which the only legitimated system of taxation (and taxation would seem essential to the modern nation-state, Islamic or otherwise) is that of *zakāt*. It is also argued that *zakāt* must be given in the proportions which have been established in the *sunna*, regardless of whether they are needed or not; the basis of a secular taxation system, however, is that the amount "given" varies with the needs of the government. Fundamentally, this is an issue of whether or not charity is to be viewed as a purificatory rite for the devout: if so, then demands of a government to extract it subvert that sense of offering which seems essential to a purificatory view. Could Muslims ever view a compulsory tax which is assessed and deducted from one's pay cheque as a religious offering?[24] At the same time, the sense of the communal nature of Islam and the legitimizing of the political aspects of the religion through the model of Muḥammad leads more frequently to an assertion of the state's responsibility for collection of the tax. This would appear to be the motivation behind a 1991 suggestion in Malaysia that the government should legislate the giving of *zakāt* with penalties of up to three years in jail, an 1800 dollar fine and six strokes of the cane for non-payment. Even the threat of such legislation would seem to be having an effect, according to authorities who saw a 75 per cent rise in contributions to the Islamic Treasury in 1991 compared to 1990.[25] Other approaches are also suggested for Muslims is the diaspora:

> The imposition of an organized Zakat collection system should be the objective of every Islamic state, both for the benefit of social peace and religious fulfilment. This might create a problem where Muslims live side by side with non-Muslims. It would not be just to charge the Muslim with both civil and religious taxes while the non-Muslim neighbour pays only one tax. In the past, non-Muslims used to pay Jizya which was the counterpart of Zakat. This, however, is no longer the practice. The solution, therefore, should be to deduct Zakat from the secular tax. As Zakat is ear-marked for social benefits, it is of service to all citizens.[26]

Pilgrimage (*hajj*)

Lasting up to seven days, the pilgrimage focuses upon Mecca and its environs.[27] The pilgrimage presents ritual, legal, social, administrative, symbolic and ethical aspects, all of which have a particular and distinctive flavour in the modern period. There is a tendency in apologetic works towards rationalism in aspects of pilgrimage ritual. Regarding the black stone lodged in the side of the Ka'ba which pilgrims attempt to touch while circumambulating the shrine, for example, a symbolic status alone is often attributed to it; any connection of the stone to pre-Islamic times and to stone worship, as was classically affirmed by Muslim writers, will be ignored. The stone is just a natural stone from Mecca, according to the religious scholar Maḥmūd Shaltūt of Egypt. Such interpretations exist in tension, however, with those which emphasize the power of the stone and thus affirm its pre-Islamic significance.[28] Such issues have arisen primarily because of the confrontation of modern historical questioning and traditional religious conceptions. Some aspects relate to "irrational" matters: is the black stone really a rock descended from heaven as was held in the past? How could that possibly be?

More generally, according to one study of contemporary popular religious literature, there is a marked reluctance on the part of many writers to acknowledge any continuation of pre-Islamic practices within Islamic rituals such as the pilgrimage. The "Islamization" of pagan rituals is ignored, for it is felt, apparently, that such historical research may well be destructive to Islam, even though observations about these connections were widespread in classical Islam. The preferred view today is to see all elements of Islam as having been revealed by God, sometimes even to the point of ignoring the idea that there had been a pre-Islamic pilgrimage. Interestingly, Sayyid Quṭb provides a contrary view: "in these verses [of the Qur'ān] we see how Islam turned the [*hajj*] into an Islamic commandment, removed its pagan roots and made it into one of the supporting pillars of Islam, adorned it with Islamic notions and cleansed it from its blemishes and dregs . . . , indeed, this is the way of Islam with every custom and ceremony which it deemed right to maintain."[29]

The most popular way of understanding all the pilgrimage rituals is to emphasize their symbolic and spiritual value. For example, throwing stones at the pillars represents not the external Satan but the internal Satan in the individual's heart. In general, the acts of the pilgrimage may appear "irrational" but their performance provides a way for the individual to show devotion to God;

interpretation or relating the elements to their historical symbolic referents is unnecessary, if not undesirable, therefore. The pilgrimage is portrayed as an event in which the power and grandeur of God may be experienced by all Muslims, regardless of their origin or social status.[30] In some of the more imaginative symbolic interpretations, such as that of the Iranian ʿAlī Shariʿātī, various aspects of the *hajj* become symbols of Islamic life: the *saʿy*, which in its historical interpretation is the running back and forth in search of water of Hagar, becomes "activism," the struggle of life in the world for what is needed in daily living and the struggle against economic and political oppression. *Tawāf*, the circumambulation of the Kaʿba, is symbolic of "endeavour," especially in the striving toward a correct, divinely-oriented life of devotion.[31]

Beyond the interpretation of the activities of the pilgrimage, there are substantial issues related to the level of participation. Somewhere between one and two million people have participated every year over recent decades. The Saudi Arabian government counted 1,718,186 people at the 1998 *hajj*, including 1,132,344 pilgrims who arrived from foreign countries and 585,842 from within Saudi Arabia, the majority of whom were non-Saudi residents. Of the participants arriving from outside the country, 56 per cent were male and 44 per cent female.

The total number of pilgrims in any year can vary because of political circumstances. For example, in 1989, the total number was 774,560.[32] This was a substantial drop from the 960,386 in 1987, and may be explained by the absence of pilgrims from Iran (who in 1987 numbered 157,395). Behind this, then, is another modern issue for Islam, one which vexes Muslims tremendously. The pilgrimage, a ritual required for all Muslims who are able to undertake it, takes place not solely on a personal level but also as a ritual which is performed in a modern nation-state, Saudi Arabia. It is, therefore, both under the control of that state and also that state's responsibility. Thus one can see the emergence of complex visa regulations allowing for entrance into the country limited to the period around the pilgrimage.[33] In 1987, over 400 pilgrims, mainly Iranians, were killed during violent demonstrations. As a result, the Saudi government cut ties with Iran and limited the number of Iranian pilgrims to 45,000. Iran retaliated by refusing to allow participation in the *hajj* at all. This situation lasted until 1991 when Iranians once again joined in. More recently, Iraqis wishing to come overland to do the *hajj* have faced a problem due to the closed border between Iraq and Saudi Arabia. In 1999, this led to a war of words between the two countries over who it was that was responsible for the problem. The Saudi Arabian government declared that it "will not under any circumstance use the *Hajj* occasion and the performance of religious duties, for any political purpose,"[34] underlining its consciousness of the Muslim perception of the issue. The idea that participation in a fundamental ritual of the religion should be controlled by a given political regime has created substantial difficulties for some Muslims; calls for the internationalization of Mecca are sometimes voiced as a result. The political aspects of the issue – the alliances between Saudi Arabia and the United States being a focal point of many allegations – result in the pilgrimage frequently becoming a symbolic element in the struggle between modern nations. Ayatollah Khomeini of Iran, for example, described the pilgrimage as the most important time for Muslims to demonstrate their unity and their rejection of imperialism:

> What is the solution, and what is the responsibility of the Muslims and oppressed for dispelling these illusions [of their powerlessness]? The primary solution, from which emerges all other solutions for cutting the roots of these problems and eradicating corruption, is the unity of Muslims, rather the unity of all oppressed and enslaved peoples in the world. This unity is gained through widespread *tabligh* [missionizing] and invitation. And the centre for this invitation and *tabligh* is the holy city of Makkah [Mecca] during the congregation of Muslims to perform the Hajj. This was started by Ibrahim, continued by Muhammad and will be followed by Hadrat Mahdi [who, the Shīʿa believe, will return at the end of time]. It was enjoined on Ibrahim to call people to Hajj to attend to their needs – that is, the political, social, economic and cultural issues of the society – and so that they, could witness how God's Prophet laid upon the altar the fruit of his life, for the sake of God.
>
> We renounce the infidels during the Hajj rituals. This is a political-religious renunciation that the Prophet Muhammad, upon whom be peace, enjoined.[35]

On top of the question of political control of access, other implications also arise as a result of modern conveniences allowing participation in the pilgrimage. Most pilgrims now fly directly to Jedda in Saudi Arabia before commencing on their way to Mecca. (In 1998, 982,654 foreign pilgrims arrived by air, 32,528 by sea and 117,162 by land.) The numbers of pilgrims handled in Saudi Arabia has increased tremendously (in 1869, some 110,000 foreigners participated; in 1907, 250,000[36]) but the implications of this are felt all over the Muslim world, especially in the social significance which results from participation in the pilgrimage. Richard Antoun reports that, in the Jordanian village which he studied, a general rise in annual income (resulting from working in the Saudi Arabian oil industry), modern, safe and rapid transportation methods, and government encouragement of local pilgrim guides had all resulted in a marked rise in the proportion of the inhabitants who had performed the pilgrimage between the years 1959 and 1986.[37] This was accompanied, however, by a change in the ethos related to pilgrimage performance. It used to be, according to Antoun, that performing the pilgrimage brought both status within the community and the requirement from the pilgrim of appropriately pious behaviour; it was, therefore, something which was reserved for the older men of the community who, it was felt, would be able to carry the burden of that responsibility. Today, a far greater proportion of younger men (under 40 and generally well-educated) undertake the pilgrimage as a means of asserting religious identity.

Flying to Jedda to commence the pilgrimage has some direct ritual implications. Traditionally, the state of sanctity represented by the clothing know as the *iḥrām* (along with other associated rituals) would be entered before passing into the region of the *mawāqit* or boundaries of the sacred area, within which Jedda sits. Pilgrims coming by airplane, therefore, as a rule put their pilgrimage costume on in their home country before boarding the plane, although it is considered possible to do it in Jedda.[38] Certain other aspects of the rituals are now likely to be spread over a number of days rather than have all the pilgrims accomplish them all at once. This fact was brought home once again when an accident at Minā in 1998 in which 118 pilgrims died when a stampede occurred as the participants headed towards the area for the ritual stoning of Satan. For the 1999 pilgrimage, much effort was put into the coordination of the twenty-one hospitals (with a capacity of 7,103 beds) to be able to deal with an emergency. But also,

> Undersecretary for Pilgrimage Affairs Hatem Qadi announced that in order to avoid overcrowding at the Jamrat area in Mina, arrangements have been made with the *Tawafa* organizations for the stoning ritual to be performed by their pilgrims in groups at specified times. He stated that the success of the group system to be implemented this year depends upon the cooperation of

all pilgrims and *Hajj* missions. Electronic instruction boards will be installed on the Jamrat bridge to inform pilgrims in various languages on the situation in the area, and pilgrims will be urged to wait for some time if the area is crowded, and not proceed with the stoning.[39]

The huge numbers of people attending have also required an extra storey to be built at the mosque of Mecca, something which is considered in legal terms an innovation, yet one which was necessary. Some people have urged that the pilgrimage be stretched over a longer period of time so that everyone may be accommodated. Substitutions for the animal slaughter which is an integral part of the activity have been suggested, such that a person need to give up (i.e. sacrifice) something "held dear," just as Abraham was willing to give up his son, the action which the sacrifice recalls.[40] As it stands, the sacrifices have become centralized. The Islamic Development Bank's Sacrificial Meat Utilization Project is in charge of coordinating the annual sacrifice ritual and subsequent distribution of the meat. A sheep (of which some 440,000 were imported in 1999, mainly from Australia; 8,000 camels and cows were also available) is then slaughtered on behalf of the pilgrim in four modern abattoirs (built at the cost of 128.3 million dollars, employing 20,000 people to administer and perform the program) according to prescribed Muslim ritual slaughtering methods. The meat is quick frozen and later distributed to refugee populations in twenty-seven countries around the Muslim world.[41] Modern issues of hygiene clearly dictate that 440,000 animals cannot be slaughtered in the outdoor environs of Mecca. Such hygienic and safety concerns are also raised in relationship to the housing and facilitating the massive influx of pilgrims themselves; much publicity was given in 1999 to the construction of the required tent cities out of fireproof material due to accidents in previous years.

Islamic identity and politics

Ritual is not, of course, the only aspect of Muslim identity that has been affected in the modern context. In contemporary Muslim life much attention is given to the attempt to implement Islamic ideals within society in general. This may be summarized generally as the impact of Islam upon politics, although its basis in Islam is in the field of law. Primarily associated with the Islamists' totalist vision, the idea that Islam "encompasses all of life" has become the central pivot for political aspirations. Religion also becomes a political tool in this framework, as in the frequent charge that Islam is used by many political leaders simply to justify change and to keep the masses quiet. Here it is a matter of the social use of Islamic symbols rather than the personal use of them.[42] It is here, then, that we realize that Islam as a faith in the modern world has two faces: the personal, ever-searching and flexible, and the institutional, firm and imperialistic.[43]

The background to this search for the public, political face of Islam may best be considered in light of the growth of secularism, especially as promulgated by governments in countries which identify themselves as constituted by a majority Muslim population. Secularism exists in many different forms in these countries, but it always manifests itself in those who argue for Islam in the modern world as a purely religious phenomenon without political force, an argument which allows for massive social reorganization without having to take the full Islamic factor into account. The extreme form of this is radical secularism as was found in mid-twentieth century Albania where the aim had been to replace all of Islam. This is, therefore, not an Islamic example as such, although the people involved were Muslims by heritage and they were seeking a way to live within the modern world. More common is the type of secularism found in Turkey where there is a total separation of religion from politics and public life as a whole. Mustafa Kemal Atatürk (1881–1938) was the Turkish nationalist leader responsible for much of the character of that country as it is today. After leading the drive to expel the Greeks from Turkey after World War I, he moved the country towards official secularism, best typified symbolically by the change in the way Turkish was written: the Arabic script which had been used for five centuries under the Ottomans was abandoned and replaced by the Latin alphabet, modified slightly to account for certain peculiarities of Turkish. The suppression of Islamic legal and educational institutions, and the outlawing of mystical Ṣūfī groups were other steps in the removal of religion from the apparatus of the state. While certain elements of these positions have been modified in recent years with the back-and-forth movement of the parties in power and the continuing significant role of the armed forces, Turkey remains firmly secularist.

Islam in officially secular countries is replaced, on an ideological level – that is, as the system of thought which orients and interprets an individual's life within society – by nationalism, capitalism or socialism. Other cited examples of secularism are seen in the multi-faith system found in Indonesia and Muslim secularism as in the

Egypt of the 1970s where religion (or Islam specifically) had a role and a standing politically but was not the full basis of the society. The evidence for this is in the way in which law codes were implemented and adopted. While the Muslim religious legal code, the *sharīʿa*, was replaced in secular countries by other law codes, in each instance the dividing line between religious and secular varies, especially when compared to western models of secularism as, for example, in the religious control of divorce and marriage. One other way in which secularism is characterized is by the state control of all religions. Secularism has been used to champion progress and also to enhance unity in countries, especially where there are significant non-Muslim minorities. This, it is said, has been the most important factor in pushing countries such as Egypt and Indonesia toward official secularism.

It is against this background that the emergence or resurgence of Islam as a political force manifest in the Islamist groups must be seen. Starting in the 1970s, Islam thrust itself into world headlines with the revolution in Iran, the assassination of Anwar Sadat, the killings in Algeria, the Taliban in Afghanistan. The heritage of this resurgence goes back much further, of course, but the modern movements have had a particular focus upon the presence of Islam as a political identity.

The continuing pressure of the Islamists has led to an uneasy balance in many countries. Governments are using Islam to a greater extent, while cracking down on the more radical aspects of the Islamist groups. In recent years, some have spoken of a "post-Islamist" mood emerging among many people,[44] because of the significant re-emergence of Islam as a factor in politics which has undermined the need for the more moderate (and generally accepted) aspects of the Islamist agenda. This has been accomplished through a governmental appeal to Islam as the social basis of legal statutes, while being accompanied by a careful limiting of the realms in which the Islamic *sharīʿa* is to be implemented.[45] To those in power, this often makes a good deal of pragmatic sense, since the difficulties in determining how the *sharīʿa* can give guidance on current issues such as gun control, import duties and industrial monopolies are well understood. Discussion of such issues by Islamists has produced a number of responses, for example that the *sharīʿa* is designed for a "minimal" government (as in the platform of Ḥasan al-Turābī in the Sudan) or that one may weigh the rulings of the *sharīʿa* against the greater interests of the country (as in the platform of Imam Khomeini in Iran).

The rise of an Islamic political consciousness and the resultant wish for participation within the political system among a good portion of the general Muslim populace have had their own ramifications. While such political movements may have started with numerically insignificant groups of people, the rise of mass higher education and the emergence of inexpensive means of mass communications have produced the desire and the opportunity for many more people to become involved.[46] This rise in participation has had the effect of producing a significantly fractured voice within the Islamist movement; the greater the number of people involved, the greater the number of opinions. Because of this, it has become difficult, if not impossible, to say that such a "movement" actually exists in any real sense. Consequently, governments have been able to use their authority to fill the resultant lack of Islamist unity. The situation at the end of the twentieth century seems as unstable as ever as far as the political face of Islam goes.

Identity in the modern context

The interpretation of Islamic ritual and political activities illustrates the tension which would seem to be present in some of the conceptualizations of Islam today. Bringing the personal and the institutional together in a rapidly moving world of conflicting interests seems beyond most discussions, and when they do occur, they often take on the air of unreality, as for example in the treatment of "Islamic economics" or "Islamic ways of knowing." Underlying them all are the basic motifs already noticed in discussions of the place of Muḥammad and the Qurʾān: anti-supernaturalism, an accommodation with science, a debate over legal provisions versus moral imperatives. The presentations of Islam often seem to be on the defensive: Muslim activities are seen as the final barrier of the individual against modernity. It is not surprising, then, that for many Muslims, ritual has assumed the keystone of their self-identity as Muslim. It should not be forgotten, however, that for many Muslims this resurgence or added emphasis on ritual is a feature only of those alienated from their Islamic roots anyway. The integration of Muslim life in the more rural parts of the Muslim world continues as it ever has and may well continue in that manner for many generations to come.

Part VI
Re-visioning Islam

16 Feminism's Islam

The main focus of the examination of the modern period thus far has been the intellectual discussions conducted in Muslim circles over the past two centuries which have attempted to enunciate an understanding of the basis of Islam in its contemporary context. Certainly not all Muslims have taken part in the actual discussion of these issues sketched earlier, but they all do, in fact, have a position on them, whether they enunciate it or not. How the Qur'ān is to be understood and how Muḥammad is to be conceived are the hermeneutical fundamentals upon which Islam is based, and even those who simply follow what has "always" been thought on these topics are taking a position within the debate. Furthermore, it is clear that some of the discussions taking place today have had a profound impact upon the face of Islam as a whole, not only in its intellectual and ideological formulations, but also in its practical ramifications, as may be seen in the modern discussions surrounding ritual activities and politics.

No doubt, Muslims as individuals are far more concerned with the implementation of their religion as a vital part of their lives than they are with the theoretical understanding of the underpinnings of their faith. Islam is a "simple" religion, says a popular phrase in Islamist circles, and it is not in need of these intellectual discussions. And yet the point remains that the basic principles which surround the intellectual conceptualization of the fundamental elements of Islam – the Qur'ān and Muḥammad – make their mark even in the basic aspects of modern Muslim daily life, despite these claims. One area in which this may be demonstrated revolves around the discussions dealing with women's place in modern Islam, especially as this reflects further issues concerning the entire structure of Muslim society. In fact, it is in tangling with this concern that many thinkers believe that the traditional face of Islam will encounter its greatest challenge and from where new visions of what Islam might be in the future will emerge.

Obviously enough, women comprise about 50 percent of all Muslims. While all Muslims, male and female, would agree that Islam stands for and aspires to a single religion regardless of the gender of the adherent, the sociological facts speak otherwise. Islamic society has both encouraged and allowed specifically female modes of religiosity within the overall framework of the religion. This is the result of a number of factors which could be termed both negative and positive. The exclusion of women from the power structures of institutionalized Islam, along with the specific religious requirements for women, have jointly brought about specific female-oriented ramifications. Islamic law, with its enunciated roots firmly in the Qur'ān, has instituted a social system based upon the presumption of an extended family grouping within a patriarchal system. This has existed, quite successfully, in creative tension with the notion of the Muslim *umma*, the community within which all are one under their relationship to God. Within that overall social system with its assigned roles for women, certain women-focused religious activities have emerged. Feminists would say that women have sought to build a world to replace the one from which they have been excluded.[1]

The modern age has had a severe impact upon the social system of Islam, as has already been noted several times. At the same time, the place of the family within that social system remains central to much of the sense of Muslim identity.[2] Not surprisingly, therefore, issues of women in the context of the family receive what might considered a disproportionate amount of attention in the discussions of Islam in the modern context. This focus on women is not necessarily an apologetic response to the pressures of the day, nor is it necessarily "anti-Islamic" to focus upon it as is sometimes suggested. Family roles have always been fundamental elements of Islamic identity, and thus women's issues are central. Furthermore, the question of women's roles in society is an enormous problem at the present time for a number of reasons. The traditional assumptions about the way in which family life is structured are being questioned daily, not simply by intellectuals and western-educated individuals, but by the urban masses as well. The transition from rural to urban society, resulting in overcrowded cities, mass transit, poverty, unemployment and all the other characteristics of modern life, has meant a severe disruption in the roles played within the family. Education has also exaggerated the problem, not just by creating a reflective group of people who recognize that knowledge is power (only to have that insight rendered meaningless frequently by their failure to achieve any significant social power despite their education), but by radically changing the social structure. Both men and women have tended in recent times to delay marriage while education was being undertaken. This has resulted in the emergence of a group of people not even contemplated in the traditional Islamic social system: unmarried adolescents. The prime focal points of a jurist's social system are the female child and the married woman.[3]

Therefore, the question emerges for Muslims of every persuasion: what is to be done to make Islam relevant and even helpful in this new situation? It is the discord felt between modernity and the traditional religious forms that is stimulating the need for change. It is not that accusations are necessarily being made that Islam is somehow "at fault," but rather that attempts are being made to draw on traditional religious resources to find the answers for today. Islam has functioned, through its divinely-authorized social system, to provide identity for its members by drawing the social boundaries of individual existence in relationship to other members. Under the pressures of today, the identity provided is no longer commensurate with the aspirations of some people, many of whom are women; or, at least, the straightforward answers of the past no longer prove sufficient in responding to modern questioning. The issue of women, then, is one which displays, in a very vital form, the implications of the intellectual debates which have been discussed earlier and suggests, in some of its ideas, an emerging new vision of what Islam as a social system and even as a "religion" might be in the future.

Traditional patterns of women's religion

In practice, women have been excluded from substantial areas of Islamic ritual. Menstruation, while not implying a ritual contagion in Islam (for "pollution" does not get transmitted from one person to another in Islamic thinking), serves as a barrier to ritual performance for the woman concerned. Thus, while men have nothing to fear from women being present at prayer, the ritual status of a woman would be on communal view if her attendance at public worship, for example, were to be required whenever she was able to attain a ritually pure state. Islam, therefore, instituted what might be termed a paternalism, generally excluding women from public performance of the daily prayer for the benefit of their privacy. Other reasons for this exclusion are frequently proffered, especially within apologetic presentations of Islam. Women prove a distraction to men at prayer, some claim, not allowing the believers to concentrate fully upon the divine; praying separately is therefore advantageous for both genders. In addition, women have other responsibilities within the family structure which preclude their participation in regularly scheduled events; this explanation for different ritual requirements according to the gender of the believer is also common in Jewish apologetics.

The result of this separation has not been the establishment of rival female institutions in which women may perform their rituals separately. Rather, in many places in the Muslim world, specific popular religious practices often associated with mysticism and saint worship (something which many Muslim reformers have targeted as "non-Islamic") have emerged, activities which exist outside the male-dominated institutionalized forms of Islam. Such cults are seen to have provided women with a sense of solidarity and independence from men. The magical aspects of this worship, manifested in trances, vows and oaths, are viewed as powerful tools in the relationship between men and women. Fear is often seen to be instilled in men because, through their wives' activities in these saint cults, power is believed to be held over a man's virility and fertility.[4]

Another popular Islamic institution, resulting from the legal institution of ritual cleansing and from the practicalities of society, is the public bath. Here, women gather within the intimacy of their own gender and participate in social circles beyond their own kin grouping. Observers have noted that women emerge with a significant form of power from this structure because they are able to move between family groupings in these contexts to a far greater extent than men are able in male-oriented situations. The "inside track" on social, political and economic movement is available to women, frequently then to be shared with their husbands within the confines of their own homes, a factor of some value in domestic power arrangements.

Seclusion

Seclusion of women has become the most firmly lodged image of Islamic society in the western popular imagination. That is an image which reflects a reality and a basic principle of the Islamic social system, although the precise form which it takes varies with geographical location (and implied cultural differences), social status and a variety of other factors. The honour of the family is what is traditionally seen to be at stake, although this is critiqued frequently by pointing out that it is the male sense of honour which is being protected on the assumption of a female tendency towards independence and uncontrolled sexuality which must be restrained. Behaviour of the female is therefore to be controlled to preserve the male honour.

The word used to refer to this seclusion varies: *ḥijāb* and *purdah* both refer to a principle which frequently becomes manifest in the clothing of women which is expressed more accurately in contemporary terms as *al-ziyy al-Islāmī*, Islamic modest dress, and denotes a covering of the hair and an obscuring of the shape of the body. Seclusion as a whole is an ideal aspired to but which cannot always be afforded. For women in total seclusion, servants are required in order to run errands; this was, and is, beyond the means of many families. As well, in the modern world, it is often easier for a woman to find a job to provide a source of income for her family than it is for an uneducated man to do so; this means that a woman will, of necessity, be thrust into society outside the home. In rural societies, the restrictions on the movement of women were always of little consequence; the family, within which a women has no restrictions, was seen to extend throughout the village and thus freedom of movement (required for women to participate in agricultural tasks and so forth) created no difficulty.

The concept of seclusion has produced a great deal of debate in Islam, with some people stating that seclusion is not a part of the religion, and others saying that it is. As is frequently the case, this is as much a matter of definition of words as anything else. The total veiling of women – taken as a way of implementing a "movable seclusion" – is not stated as a requirement in the Qur'ān and, on that basis, is often suggested to be simply a cultural trait and not a part of Islam. Such is true only, however, if attention is paid to the outer form of clothing alone. Veiling is, in fact, the logical (although, strictly speaking, perhaps not necessary) outgrowth of various Quranic statements taken to their limits. Full veiling institutes the Islamic attitude towards social interactions between men and women in its fullest degree, in a manner that ensures that violations are extremely difficult. Of course, why this specific issue – the seclusion of women – should be the one that Islamic jurists took to such an extreme formulation as compared to other aspects of Islamic law may well be questioned. Overall, however, one of the implications of the symbolism which seclusion suggests is that women are conceived to have power while needing (in the male view, it would seem) to being restrained at the same time.[5]

In terms of legal standing in the Islamic system, women's rank, logically enough, reflects the assumptions of the social structure. This is how it should be, after all; a social system is unlikely to function well if the confines of that system do not allow a group of people to assert the status which the system grants. Thus the Qur'ān establishes that the testimony of two women is required to equal that of one man (Qur'ān 2/282). The portion of a woman's inheritance is less than that of a man (Qur'ān 4/11). Divorce is allowable upon the woman's instigation only for a set number of reasons, whereas a man needs no specific pretext at all. A great deal of concern is displayed over establishing the lineage of children: while men are free to remarry after divorce, women must wait (while being supported by their ex-spouse) to see if they are pregnant. The male rules the house in all matters. The religion of the male is presumed to be the religion of the entire household; thus a Muslim male may marry a Jewish or Christian woman, but a Muslim female may marry only another Muslim (Qur'ān 5/6). A man may marry up to four wives at a time, but a woman may marry only one husband. Discipline (Qur'ān 4/34) and sex (Qur'ān 2/223) are the prerogatives of the male to which the female is subject.

There is a sense conveyed in the Quranic statements which suggests that women will not wish to cooperate in society and will need to be coerced. For example, that a woman must wait a certain period after divorce or after becoming a widow in case she should be pregnant so that paternity may be firmly established would seem necessary only on the assumption that a woman would wish to hide relevant information about her sexual liaisons. Additionally, Fatima Mernissi has argued that Islam is based not on the misogyny which characterizes western society, but on the fear of heterosexuality.[6] Mernissi's view is echoed by other writers, for example in the fiction of Alifa Rifaat.[7] The women of these short stories, poignantly illustrated by the unnamed woman of the title story *Distant View of a Minaret*, at first seem to crave for more love and life and yet they are constantly disappointed by their male companions. As a result they find their only solace in performing the worship of God within the context of female religious practices.

It might be possible to invert Mernissi's argument and say that this guarded attitude toward sex is precisely what is appropriate. The Islamic social system is set so that women will not distract men from worship and are themselves then forced to worship for their own comfort. But the objection would remain that this had been accomplished at the price of the full human-ness of both genders. If it is thought that the purpose of religion in general, and Islam specifically, is to allow the achievement of that human-ness, then the existence of a problem will be felt.

Modern demands

"Equality" has become a catchword world-wide when speaking of women's issues. The concept is slippery, however, and needs a clear definition in order to be able to anchor an analysis. In most cautious feminist discussions, equality does not mean "sameness", as some opponents might try to suggest in their attempts to trivialize the issues. Equality refers to potentiality of human-ness, a self-determination for "life options". These are issues of opportunities, not roles. The experience of gender is the most prominent aspect in the discussions of the issue. The social process of the internalization of gender is seen to determine the limits in achievement of humanness which, it is suggested, we are all entitled to. There is, in Judeo–Christian–Muslim society in general, a relationship between power and gender, and gender internalization is a means of control to the advantage of patriarchy; gender roles and the control involved thereby serve to the advantage of the already established prerogatives of the male in society. Mernissi summarizes this aspect of the problem of being a woman: "Why can't I stroll peacefully in the alleys of the Medina?"[8] That is, the very fact of being a woman in society limits the activities which she might wish to undertake, and these activities are ones which men take for granted in their lives.

Another term frequently used in discussions about women is "status," but that, too, is rather evasive conceptually. "Status" frequently seems to imply that there are some given categories into which social roles may be categorized and that these may be used to compare social functions. This, however, ignores the fact that different social systems reflect different assumptions; looking only at something called "status," therefore, views only the superficial manifestations of a social system and not its underlying structure which would seem to be far more of a key to understanding.

Notably, a great deal of the analysis of gender structure is not specific to Islam itself, but to patriarchy in general as a world-wide phenomenon. And Islam's assumptions certainly reflect a patriarchy within its society. Thus, from some points of view, Islam has not allowed the possibilities for women which it has for men; if the social system of Islam reflects the best possible solution for all, then why is it that a woman cannot stroll around the Medina, to repeat Mernissi's phrase? "Inferiority," a popular idea of what the complaint of women is all about when it comes to discussion of their status, really misses the point. Mernissi argues that the issue is really one of subjugation. That is, society does not reflect ideological positions regarding women which are necessary to its functioning as such, but rather reflects assumptions about power structures.

The idea of the complementarity of the genders is often used in talking about the Islamic understanding of the roles of men and women in society; the concept is especially popular in Islamist circles whose approach to the Qur'ān necessitates the continuation of legal differentiation between men and women. Women have their role to play in society as mothers and home-makers while men shoulder the responsibilities for maintenance of the family in financial ways. The question from this position is not one of "subjugation" or "inferiority," but rather "natural order" reflected in the concept "equal though different." The complementarity notion suggests that women want and need to be isolated in society and do not wish to play a more active role in the world at large; this, the theory suggests, is "natural."

> The function of the husband and wife are quite distinct, and each is entrusted with the functions which are best suited for his or her nature. The Qur'ān says that God has made man and woman to excel each other in certain respects. The man excels the woman in constitution and physique, which is capable of bearing greater hardships and facing greater dangers than the physique of woman. On the other hand, the woman excels the man in the qualities of love and affection. Nature, for her own purpose of helping in the growth of creation, has endowed the female among men, as well as the lower animals, with the quality of love to a much higher degree than the male. Hence there is a natural division as between man and woman of the main work which is to be carried on for the progress of humanity. Man is suited to face the hard struggles of life on account of his stronger physique; woman is suited to bring up the children because of the preponderance of the quality of love in her. The duty of the maintenance of the family has therefore been entrusted to the man, and the duty of bringing up the children to the woman. And each is vested with authority suited to the function with which he or she is entrusted. Hence it is that men are spoken

of as being the maintainers of women and women as "rulers over the household and the children."[9]

Furthermore, any of the so-called restrictions on women resulting from this assessment of the situation are argued to be for the benefit of women themselves, and are seen to be based upon the differences in nature between men and women, differences which are, after all, at the bottom of any assertion about complementary roles.

> Possessors of beauty are comparatively few in number, and the natural course of life changes the appearance of those and renders them homely. When women without the veil mingle with men, the favorable attention of the latter will be drawn only to beautiful women and charming young girls. Naturally unattractive women would be considered undesirable, and this would result in their being cut off from society and companionship. This would mean, on the one hand, a decrease in the population and, on the other hand, since men are not always able to procure beautiful wives, that their attention would be drawn to handsome children. Therefore if one looks at this question from the standpoint of reason and justice, he will see that the veil prevents corruption.[10]

Objectors to the theory of complementarity note that it is based upon an idea of men and women having antagonistic wills such that the two genders need to be separated into different spheres of competence, since, it would appear to be fundamentally assumed, they could never cooperate. These assumptions, however, are cultural constructs according to feminist critiques; they are ideas which are designed to preserve male power and to control female power, and, implicitly at least, have become embedded in the Qur'ān and the *sunna*. Interestingly, the Islamic view of society according to this vision of complementarity is based upon a strong notion of women's power which must be restrained.[11] It is, therefore, a part of the double notion that pervades gender construction in Islamic society (and perhaps generally): woman as powerful along with woman as needing to be dominated. There is a further irony and a contradiction involved in this. Women achieve a secure sense of gender identity through restrictive and oppressive controls over their being (and especially their sexuality); the very controls which are imposed have the result of identifying women strongly as women.[12]

Islamic answers

Most writings by Muslim women on Islam and the "problem" of women emphasize that the problem is, in fact, not a religious one; religion is the answer, not the problem or the source, according to these authors.[13] Religion, as found in the Qur'ān and the *sunna*, provides a definition of the "natural order" of things and the proper implementation of this will lead to the satisfaction of all people – men and women – in society.

One very popular expression of this, a traditional one in Christianity also, is to see the husband in relationship to his family as a mirror of the relationship between God and humanity.[14] This is a cosmic reflection, then, of the natural order of things, which is also echoed in the biological differences between men and women: woman as nurturer, man as aggressor. The basis for this is, of course, to be found in the divine affirmation that two genders have been created – not one, but two. If God had intended each human being to have been capable of all dimensions of life, he would have created only one gender. Furthermore, Muslim apologists point out, women are not burdened by the Biblical image of being the source of evil because, in the Qur'ān, the story of Adam and Eve does not reflect those ideas in its retelling. Likewise, the "gender" of God is not an issue. Arabic only has two grammatical genders and their separation is, to a large extent, arbitrary. The fact that the noun for God is grammatically masculine does not reflect, according to this view, any pre-eminence of the male. This kind of apologetic trend dominates the discussions and there seems to be little evidence of any attempt at a feminist theological vision of Islam. The questions may well be broached at some point in the future: what would it mean, for example, for all people, male and female, to be members of a community of *Muslimāt* (that is, the feminine plural of Muslim, itself the singular masculine form) rather than the *Muslimūn*, as it is now expressed in the masculine plural form? Writers such as Riffat Hassan[15] come the closest to raising such issues but this is generally done in academic circles and even then does not lack the apologetic tendency. It may well be, however, that women writers will emerge, writing in Arabic, Persian or Urdu, who do not feel the same needs to challenge "western misunderstanding" about Islam, and who will start to define a female theological vision.[16]

The use of the past

The most frequent observation made, rarely without patronizing overtones, is that the "status of women" given in the Qur'ān is a vast improvement over that of the pre-Islamic period. Before Muḥammad, female children were subject to infanticide, women were the possessions of men without any rights, and so forth. "In the days of Ignorance, it was common among women to freely mix [in] public. They exposed any part whatsoever of their [bodies] to the public gaze. It was not considered indecent or immoral."[17] The coming of Islam empowered women, to the point that their legal rights exceeded those of European women until very recently. This view, however, is opposed by other writings which speak of the power and prestige that women had in the pre-Islamic period which men, under the guise of a (mis-)interpreted Qur'ān, have gradually removed.[18] 'Ā'isha, the wife of Muḥammad who is a frequent source of authority in *ḥadīth* and famous as a leader of a revolt in early Islamic times, is the central role model of such perspectives.[19] Even more radical approaches to the material suggest that Islam itself was responsible for the movement away from women's power (a power sometimes even linked to a matriarchal system) toward the present position of subjugation.[20]

From the perspective of a historian, it may be pointed out that all these views are based upon selective citation of evidence. Women in pre-Islamic Arabia may be portrayed as powerful and active, or as tyrannized with no power, according to which facts are presented. What must be remarked, therefore, is that all of these approaches are attempts to remythologize society with a more productive vision. That vision will be one which embraces the ideals of the group concerned: for the Islamist, the "myth" of empowerment via Islam, for the feminist, the "myth" of women's potential gradually removed by men (either as embodied in Islam or as "misinterpretation" of Islam). The problem remains that these are myths which are easy to deconstruct.

Classical Islam itself provides a mythological picture of pre-Islamic society, as was pointed out in Chapter 1 above. By Islamic definition, *jāhiliyya*, the age of ignorance, is everything that Islam has come to remove. The picture found in classical texts, therefore, of a matriarchal society in which women played an active role is a part of the Islamic myth itself. That is how Muslim males of the ninth and tenth centuries pictured a society which was at its lowest point morally and socially: women in control! This myth stands in tension with the other aspect of the pre-Islamic mythic picture which sees Islam as providing moral growth from the pre-Islamic period – thus the picture of the improvement in women's rights – but the aspect of women in this mythic story provides only part of the story. Rather, this myth provides a general evaluation of the overall legal accomplishment of Islam. Each element of Quranic law has become embedded in narrative detail as evidence of this transformation accomplished by Islam. In a typical development of structural myths, both aspects exist side by side, acting to control society and justify present practice; each probably has its origin in a specific historical situation and reflects aspirations or frustrations of a certain period. Their continued existence together poses a problem only for modern historians who tend to isolate one element from the narrative structure in the desire to create coherence out of the historical records, and for those who wish to remythologize.

Ḥijāb in the modern context

The preservation of the home as an Islamic focal point of life has become a central defence of much of Muslim life in the modern world, especially in geographical areas which are not predominantly Islamic. With secular society encroaching from all sides, the home becomes the representation of an Islamic paradise, an oasis of divinely-structured society located in a context fully awash with everything Islam rejects. *Ḥijāb*, in this mode of behaviour, becomes a home-oriented activity. Once again, this personalization of religion may be suggested to be both the result and the cause of this particular interpretation and way of being Muslim. One's own religious behaviour becomes the most important aspect of the exercise of Islam, rather than in its communal manifestation, and seeing its implementation as limited to one's own home (at least in the religion's social implications) seems to act as a line of defence. The possibility exists of taking the personalization of Islam to its fullest extent and, in the specific case of the Islamic notion of the seclusion of women, speaking of the necessity of the *ḥijāb* of the heart as the only requirement. While such interpretations certainly have a heritage in Islamic mysticism, their role in legitimating personal behaviour in secularized society should not be underestimated.

Women in the Muslim *umma*

An oft-quoted statement of Egyptian feminist Nawāl al-Saʿdāwī is worth repeating; she is arguing against Islamist suggestions that the natural place for women is in the home and that corruption will occur if women are encouraged to seek employment outside the home:

> These men [who make this argument] ignore the fact that the majority of women in Egypt (80 per cent or more) are peasants and have never worn the veil. They leave their houses every morning to work with a hoe in the fields or to carry loads of dung or pails of water on their heads. Does this mean that these men think these millions of Egyptian women have abandoned their femininity which nature has given them, and are exposed to moral corruption or lack of protection for their religion and honor? If so, why have these men kept quiet? ... Why have they not demanded that the peasant women be protected inside the homes and not be made to go to work in the fields?
>
> Since we have not heard of any of them making such a demand, does that mean that they consider these millions of Egyptian women corrupt in their morals or lacking in femininity or having little honor and religion? Or do they believe that femininity and honor are qualities enjoyed only by a small minority of Egyptian women?[21]

Saʿdāwī's argument brings two points to the fore. One, powerful feminist voices do have a presence in the Islamic world, despite the media presentations. Two, and more salutary, Saʿdāwī reminds us that, in fact, for the vast proportion of Muslim women, the "crisis" of modernity has brought a negligible effect. Islamist arguments are, to a large extent, phenomena of the urban centres, where social and economic factors loom as the stimulus behind the rejection of feminist argumentation regarding the place of women in society. For women in rural areas, the Islamic social system remains intact and coherent, rendering men and women significant social actors within their own particular fields of control. Those fields of control, it is to be remembered, regulate not only relations within each gender but also between them: men and women establish power structures both over each other and among their own same gender groupings.

The reality of the situation in the urban context cannot be denied, however. The (re-)assertion of male authority over women, characteristic of Islamism, and in many cases the assertion of the state's power to control women's activities, are symptoms of economic and social pressures resulting from the radical restructuring of society taking place in so many areas of the Muslim world.[22] The economic roles of women in society have changed substantially and the declaration of Islamists that women belong in the home is a cry of sorrow to return to the safe values of the past as elaborated in the Qur'ān and the *sunna*, where men's economic and social roles were firmly established. That is a phenomenon not unique to the Muslim world, of course. Nor is it only a matter of male concern. When there are few, if any, roles for women to play in society outside the (traditionally) prescribed ones, the (re-)adoption of things such as Islamic dress or the rejection of feminist ideology may be taken as an expression of women's own frustration at social and economic conditions. It is out of this frustration and rethinking that may yet emerge a new vision of Islam.

17 Visions for Islam in the twenty-first century and beyond

With the move into the twentieth-first century, the question may well be asked, what of Islam (or, indeed, religion in general) in the new millennium? Few will doubt that Islam will continue to exist. Rather, it is the variety of forms in which it will be found that is of interest. Doubtless, the main trends which have already been sketched above will be the most significant. Islam, however, will face challenges on a variety of fronts which will likely both change it and strengthen its determination in the ongoing march of human history. Some of those challenges will come from within; others will come from without. Some of the modern thinkers within Islam, such as Mohammad Arkoun and Shabbir Akhtar, who may well stimulate these new lines of thought, have already been mentioned previously in the context of discussions of Muslim sources of authority. Others, such as Farid Esack who attempts to face human problems from his own sense of Muslim identity not constrained by traditional Islamic practices,[1] are just starting to make their impact. From the outside, it is not only the forces of creeping secularism but strident humanist voices who pose a new challenge, along with rival religious groups. Among the latter, it is especially groups whose origins are from within the Islamic milieu that are particularly significant, since their appeal is precisely to those familiar with Muslim claims and activities. Other religions, including Hinduism and especially Christianity, play a major role as a challenge to Islam as well, of course, but they fall outside the purview of this book, although their influence is to be noted in many places.

The move outside Islam

It is a common phenomenon in religion that, if the questioning of the authority of the past is taken far enough in the desire to be able to accommodate or compensate for the changes of the modern period, there is a need for a new source of authority. This may even account for the rise of each religion in its formative period also. Modernity, as such, may not be the root cause of the emergence of these movements, therefore, but they may stem from a very basic dislocation in human existence. Such an understanding can be used to characterize various offshoots of Islam in the modern period which clearly have a modernist stance and a renewed sense of authority.

The Aḥmadiyya is one such group, founded by Mīrzā Ghulām Aḥmad (1835–1908) and now comprised of some four million members.[2] Ghulām Aḥmad was educated with law or government service under the British in mind but in 1877 he started devoting himself to the cause of Islam. His earliest writings aim towards a revitalization of Islam within the modernizing platform. As early as 1882, he claimed to be the *mujaddid*, "renewer" of Islam and, by 1891, had put forth the proclamation that he was the promised Messiah of the Muslim community. Later, he suggested he was also an avatar of Krishna, Jesus returned to earth, and the manifestation of Muḥammad. He claimed to be a prophet in receipt of revelation, but one who was sent without a book of scripture or a new religion (and thus he always asserted that he was subordinate to Muḥammad). His function was to return Islam to its proper formulation, by means of a prophetic-revelatory authority within a messianic-eschatological context. Debate has followed Ghulām Aḥmad, dividing both his followers and the Muslim community as a whole, concerning both the extent of and the validity of his claims and the status of the finality of Muḥammad's prophethood and revelation, doctrines which are considered central to Islam, as it has been classically defined. For our purposes here, however, it is sufficient to note that the Aḥmadiyya vests authority in Ghulām Aḥmad beyond that normally associated even with a *mujaddid*. This was done in support of a Modernist stance, embracing modern science and many moral ideals associated with the Enlightenment, in combination with a return to the essence of Islam as it is revealed in the Qur'ān and through the guidance of the person of Mīrzā Ghulām Aḥmad. For the Aḥmadiyya, the correct interpretation of Islam has been vested with the authority of revelation.

The members of the Aḥmadiyya proclaim themselves to be Muslims, although in countries such as Pakistan they have been declared outside the Islamic community and, in many places, severe concern has been raised concerning their missionary activity, which remains a very strong emphasis of the movement reflecting an effort from the very beginning to counter Christian missionary activity in India, and is also associated with an active Qur'ān translation programme, something generally not encouraged within more traditional circles. The situation is quite different for the Bahá'ís who do not wish to consider themselves Islamic but rather proclaim themselves to be members of a new "World Faith" which supersedes Islam.

The Bahá'ís trace their origins to 'Alī Muḥammad Shīrāzī (1819–50) of Iran who referred to himself as the Bāb, the "Gate," and proclaimed himself to be the returned Hidden Imām, longed for by the Shī'a, and a prophet of God. His appearance is taken to imply the abrogation of Islam and the initiation of a new religious dispensation. After the Bāb's death, Mīrzā Ḥusayn 'Alī Nūrī (1817–92), who took the name Bahá'u'lláh, proclaimed himself the Messiah who had been promised by the Bāb in the words, "He whom God shall make manifest." Bahá'u'lláh's platform was strongly Modernist from the Muslim perspective within which it arose, and the Bahá'í faith remains that way. Legal reforms on matters such as women and family rights were implemented; disarmament, world government and inter-religious harmony became central proclamations, much in keeping with certain nineteenth-century European ideals (parallel to Christian and Jewish movements at the time). From the perspective of the history of religions, this was an attempt to reuniversalize Islam (even religion in general), by taking it out of its culturally-bound forms and into the modern context.[3]

As with the Aḥmadiyya, the Bahá'ís support a programme of modernization emerging from the context of Islam, but, in this case, not by a return to the sources and a renewal of the past; rather, this takes place by a replacement of the sources of authority (even though the Bahá'ís do revere the Qur'ān, as they do all other scriptures, as the "word of God"). This sort of radical rupture with the past is, of course, precisely what more conservative elements of society fear Modernists of all types are actually aiming towards.

The role of Muslim intellectualism

Many of the modernist voices that are being heard from within, rather than from outside, the Muslim context have at least one common element among them: they speak from an intellectual context. This is an often neglected source of Islamic thinking in surveys of (and categories) of modern Islamic trends. This neglect may come as something of a surprise to students of other religions, since it would not seem possible to study modern Christianity without taking into account Hans Küng, for example, nor could we consider modern Judaism without Emil Fackenheim. None of these people can claim to represent a very substantial portion of the believers within the religion as their followers, it might be argued, yet it would seem that a picture of those religions within the modern world would just be incomplete without them.

In fact, in the cases of Judaism and Christianity, I do not perceive that there is much difficulty in including such figures in a survey of modern thought; it is more likely, in fact, that the conservative sides of those two religions are going to be dismissed as having no significantly enunciated platform to be discussed. When we come to the study of the future of modern Islam, however, the case seems to be different. Attention to the intellectual side seems to be sadly lacking. Many reasons for this can be suggested. Often the excuse is made that the intellectual trend does not seem significant numerically within Islam (especially as compared to modern Judaism and Christianity). Where are we supposed to turn to find the impact of such people? But yet, it would seem overly paranoid to suggest, in this era of the ramifications of attacks on Orientalism by people such as Edward Said,[4] that the suspicion is that this ignoring of the intellectual trend is a part of the necessary degradation of Islam itself by Orientalists. To credit Islam with the possibility of such persons existing would seem to be counter to the basic Orientalist stance of picturing Islam as a constraining and reactionary force.[5]

Mohammed Arkoun, an Algerian living in Paris and writing primarily in French, is one of those intellectuals who is often ignored, not being considered representative of anything to do with modern Islam itself. The first impression some people receive of a figure such as Arkoun is one of a person who has "sold out" to the West, a person who has adopted so much of the European intellectual tradition that there is no Islamic root left in any meaningful way. Of course, it is a fact that, in general, many of the intellectuals found in modern religions do live and work in the university context and conduct themselves as academics with all that requires – learned papers, prolific production of books and articles – and this seems to give some credence to the stance that such people do not need to be considered part of the intellectual construct of the given religion as such. This may account for some of the reality behind the idea that there do not seem to be many people like Arkoun in Islam. Many perhaps are lurking within universities without ever identifying themselves in a particularly overt way.

Arkoun himself wants to use the term "the critical tendency in current Islamic thought" when speaking of the "intellectual and scientific directions" in modern Muslim thinking. Significantly, in terms of understanding how his position fits into the overall picture, he has clearly attempted to embrace what he would term a *contemporary* theoretical stance (as opposed to simply modern, that being equated to a historicist perspective) and this he sees as the basis of his work. Arkoun poses the question in an essay written as an introduction to a translation of the Qur'ān and then reprinted in his *Lectures du Coran*: "How should the Qur'ān be read?" with an emphasis on the the idea of "How should it be read today?"[6] This is not a question commonly posed in the Muslim framework and reveals immediately Arkoun's concerns. The point is not really one of simply how to read it, but how to understand the book in light of modern intellectual thought. The problem is, as the Christian postmodernist theologian Mark C. Taylor expresses it:

[T]he "texts" that have guided and grounded previous generations often appear illegible in the modern and postmodern worlds. Instead of expressing a single story or coherent plot, human lives tend to be inscribed in multiple and often contradictory texts. What makes sense and is meaningful in one situation frequently seems senseless and meaningless in another setting. The resulting conflict creates confusion that extends far beyond the pages of the book.[7]

How, then, is one to retrieve the Qur'ān both from the mountains of learned philological knowledge and from the literalist tendencies of many modern Islamic movements, and to discover something which speaks to the modern, intelligent individual? As Arkoun suggests, the task is one that is already underway in Judaism and Christianity but is still to be confronted in the Islamic context. It means coming to an understanding of the social and historical conditioning of all human existence, including language, leading to a liberation from the categories of thought imposed by past places and eras. This is not simply a study of history, because that discipline, in much of its Orientalist manifestation, is still deeply entrenched in the nineteenth-century notion of a search for absolutes and essentials. Rather, the historicity of knowledge will be discovered by the totality of the methods of the social sciences, according to Arkoun, asking questions not of "what really happened" (in the formulation of the discipline of history) but how it is that certain ideas came to be a part of the social imagination[8] and the role that those ideas play in construction of reality for society.

Mohammed Arkoun passionately believes that what he has to say is of relevance not only to the university academic tradition, but also to the Muslim faith. The claim is that what he says should have some bearing on the basic understanding of faith in the modern world and how that faith should be expressed and understood, not only in the academic framework but also from within the faith perspective. His position may represent a thread of Islamic Modernism in the intellectual, theological sense, but it is one which is very attuned to the close of the twentieth century. Other Modernists, from a lay background (as is apparently the case with Arkoun) have pursued scholarship but have frequently found theological liberalism too dangerous a course to follow. Whether that will change in the future we must wait and see.

In the posing of these questions Arkoun is marked as "post" the Modernists of Islam, as one who ventures into post-modernism, or even a "post-Islamic" position, if that be understood in the same manner that post-modernism is intimately linked with modernism. However, the adverse reaction which such positions evoke amongst other enunciators of modern visions of Islam cannot be over-estimated. The historicity of Islam is seen as being rejected in the attempt by Arkoun and others like him to escape from the dualisms of religion and society; as in similar suggestions in contemporary Christian thought, such views are often termed destructive of everything which people hold dear in their religion.

New voices in a Traditionalist framework

An example of theological reflection within Islam that presents a more conservative framework for discussion is to be seen in the works of Shabbir Akhtar who has been cited a number of times already.[9] Akhtar became famous during the uproar over Salman Rushdie's *The Satanic Verses*; he was an extremely eloquent spokesman for the Muslim community, especially in Bradford, England, where much of the controversy centred. Akhtar has a Doctorate in Philosophy of Religion and brings to the modern expression of Islam precisely that which is said to be missing: a theological re-evaluation of Islam, expressed in modern philosophical terms. Consider the following:

> The silence of God in this increasingly religionless age is certainly damaging to the faithful outlook. It does seem to open up the

possibility of supplying impressively plausible cases for the atheistic stance. Indeed it creates a serious doubt about God's alleged miraculous activities even in the past. Is it not an arguably superior assumption that the different human claims about the miraculous are better explicable in terms of a cultural shift in our thinking rather than in terms of God's decision to introduce in recent years a basic alteration in his ways? Given the credulity and gullibility of early man, his ignorance of the moods of Nature – an ignorance poorly compensated by the pagan appeal to magic and its illusory technique – the atheist's suggestion is surely not altogether implausible.

The current silence of Allah could spell a crisis for Muslim faith. Nature is as revealing as it is ambiguous, hence of course the need for a revelation in a sacred language in the first place. The God of Islam seems to have retreated from Nature and community, the two matrices in which, according to religious believers, he typically used to reveal himself.[10]

Akhtar's point is that the challenges of contemporary philosophy to the tenability of religious faith as a whole have been ignored by Muslims but they can only continue to be ignored at the peril of the survival of the faith itself. Christianity, for Akhtar, has virtually self-destructed through the efforts of (Protestant) theologians bending over backwards to assimilate the latest theories of secularism to their faith. This too will happen to Islam if the example of Christianity is not studied carefully and profit taken from the mistakes made in that arena.

Akhtar's theological position tends to support the moderate side of Islamism. Most significant in this is the all encompassing nature of Islam (Christianity's "render unto Caesar what is Caesar's" has, it would appear for Akhtar, been misused in recent centuries to support separation of church and state). But it is in the reformulation of philosophically supported arguments in favour of traditional Islamic doctrine – the inerrancy of the Qur'ān,[11] the eternal message of scripture, the concept of the one God – where Akhtar, as he says of himself, breaks new ground. Just what the future might hold for this development is certainly unclear. For many Muslims, it would seem that even the opening of such questions for debate is going too far. For Akhtar, however, the failure to treat such questions openly and honestly could spell the end to Islam as a viable religion in the modern, secular context. Akhtar's future inquiries could well move him out of the Islamist camp which he has defended "out of a desire to empathise with members of his own community, to avoid taking the road that enticed the intellectually gifted sons of Islam into the enemy camp, so to speak."[12] In other words, Akhtar has not yet created for himself (and those like him) a philosophically integrated and consistent stance within Islam; further work in the area and, as Malise Ruthven has pointed out, greater exposure to the classics of Muslim philosophy, theology and history may well yet produce that new vision. Indeed, as time goes by, Akhtar himself seems to be discouraged by the possibilities; in 1997, after three years of university lecturing on philosophy and comparative religion in Malaysia, he resigned his position. He found his fellow Muslim intellectuals totally lacking "a sense of history" and was appalled when told "Believers ... [have] nothing new to learn. Western style free inquiry is aimless. Besides what is the point of free inquiry if God has already revealed to us the whole truth?" He was totally dismayed at the lack of intellectual freedom: "Freedom is a precondition of profundity: no wonder philosophy has no place in the cultural life of Muslims."[13] Akhtar's line of thought is full of possibility for a "re-visioning" of Islam, but the likelihood of it being taken up by a new generation of Muslim intellectuals is uncertain.

Challenges to Akhtar's position exist also, precisely in the way in which he, himself, sees them as coming. Ibn Warraq is one of those writers who sees the failure of freedom of thought in Islam, along with what he describes as a dismal track record of concern with basic human rights, as reason enough to abandon Islam (and all religion). For Ibn Warraq, "Muslims cannot hide forever from the philosophical insights of Nietzsche, Freud, Marx, Feuerbach, Hennell, Strauss, Bauer, Wrede, Wells, and Renan."[14] For him, however, religion becomes impossible when viewed in light of modern thought, and he willingly declares himself an apostate and a "secular humanist." Islam cannot be redeemed in any way because it is fundamentally flawed. "Perhaps the worst legacy of Muhammad was his insistence that the Koran was the literal word of God, and true once and for all, thereby closing the possibility of new intellectual ideas and freedom of thought that are the only way the Islamic world is going to progress into the twenty-first century."[15] On the evidence of the people discussed in this book, by no means do all Muslims find Ibn Warraq's conclusions compelling. Some certainly recognize more than others the need for carefully considered contemplation of the future role and structure of Islam. But the value of Islam as a source of identity, as a grounding in life, as a way to understand existence, and as a way to relate to God is far too strong for the challenges of today not to be faced up to.

Putting matters in perspective

The challenges to Islam and the future directions it could take are apparent. Underlying all such discussions are the topics related to the status and interpretation of the fundamental religious sources of authority. It is important, however, to reflect just briefly upon what all this might mean in terms of Muslim religiosity, although that is a question which is not easy to approach. Richard Antoun puts it well:

> How are we to determine, for instance, whether the building of new mosques, the establishment of government-sponsored religious publishing houses, the setting aside of special places in parliament for prayer, the establishment of religious political parties, or the establishment of bureaus to safeguard the Holy Quran are indications of religious mindedness, indications of a shift in the attitudes of elites only, or simply an increase in political action in the name of Islam? Is an increasing use of Arabic, an increase in veiling, an increase in attendance at the Friday congregational prayer, or an increase in pilgrimage to be taken as an increase in piety, religious-mindedness, or hypocrisy?[16]

The fact is that the range of contemporary Muslim religiosity varies tremendously. One of the reasons for this is that people understand and "use" religion in a variety of ways; that is true whether we are dealing with Islam or Christianity or any other religion. The following summary within a recent anthropological study provides an interesting perception of the ways in which Islam manifests itself:

> In this village, Islam can take the form of a bland legalism or a consuming devotion to the good of others; an ideology legitimizing established status and power or a critical theology challenging this very status and power; a devotive quietism or fervent zealotism; a dynamic political activism or self-absorbed mysticism; a virtuoso religiosity or humble trust in God's compassion; a rigid fundamentalism or reformist modernism; a ritualism steeped in folklore and magic or a scriptural purism.[17]

The basis for these variations appears to depend on a wide variety of factors: childhood experiences, individual personality, education, general social context and so forth. All the variations, however, emphasize the independence of thought which is possible even within a society frequently characterized by its apparent uniformity. Plainly, Islam is a multi-faceted phenomenon which is able to encompass within its fold many different views of the world and of religion in general.

This list of variations in religious practice is useful for stimulating further thought; it may serve to place the discussions into which we have delved in their proper perspective. While such issues deserve extensive treatment in their own right, for our purposes here it is sufficient to remember that devotion to the learning of the past continues to live in conjunction with interaction with the pressures of the contemporary world. By no means are all aspects of Muslim religiosity mired in debate.

Muslim faith is a complex phenomenon, just as is any other religion. It may be tempting to suggest that there are two different faces to Muslim religiosity: the intellectual debate over principles of the faith confronting the personal practice of individual Muslims. The danger here is that we may exaggerate a dichotomy which, while it may have a certain analytical convenience, may lead to a distortion of the presentation of Muslim faith. Better would be a conception which sees faith on a continuum, attempting self-conscious definition at times and reaching into the experiential dimension of religion in order to refresh those definitions at other times. This would seem to be the genius of religion, and of Islam especially.

Notes

Transliteration and other technical considerations

1 Unfortunately, the various editions of the *Encyclopaedia of Islam* are not consistent in their transliteration. The older edition, for example, uses "ai" for the diphthong "ay." The transliteration used in this book is that of the New Edition, with the exceptions noted.

Introduction

1 Hans Mol, *Identity and the Sacred: A Sketch for a New Social-scientific Theory of Religion*, New York, The Free Press, 1976, p. 55.

1 Prehistory

1 A brief and useful summary of the history of this period with excellent attention to the religious factors involved is to be found in F. E. Peters, *Allah's Commonwealth: A History of Islam in the Near East 600–1100 A.D.*, New York, Simon and Schuster, 1973, introduction. For an illustration of a variety of scholarly views on the pre-Islamic period, see the collection of articles assembled in F. E. Peters (ed.), *Arabs and Arabia on the Eve of Islam*, Aldershot, Ashgate/Variorum, 1999.

2 See J. Spencer Trimingham, *Christianity among the Arabs in Pre-Islamic Times*, London, Longman, 1979, chapter 5.

3 On the matter of the role of trade in south Arabia and its bearing on the rise of Islam, see Patricia Crone, *Meccan Trade and the Rise of Islam*, Princeton, Princeton University Press, 1987, pp. 12ff, 27.

4 On this aspect of south Arabian religion, see Ulf Oldenburg, "Above the Stars of El. El in Ancient South Arabian Religion," *Zeitschrift für die alttestamentliche Wissenschaft*, 82 (1970), 187–208.

5 See G. Ryckmans, "Heaven and earth in the South Arabian inscriptions," *Journal of Semitic Studies*, 3 (1958), 225–36.

6 See Andrew Rippin, "RHMNN and the Ḥanīfs," in Wael B. Hallaq and Donald P. Little (eds), *Islamic Studies Presented to Charles J. Adams*, Leiden, E. J. Brill, 1991, 153–68.

7 See P. Crone, *Meccan Trade*, esp. pp. 149–67 for details on the likely extent of the trade.

8 See Joseph Henninger, "Pre-islamic Bedouin Religion," in Merlin L. Swartz (trans. and ed.), *Studies on Islam*, New York, Oxford University Press, 1981, pp. 3–22, although much of the detail in this article is open to grave doubt.

9 See G. R. Hawting, "The Origins of the Muslim Sanctuary at Mecca," in G. H. A. Juynboll (ed.), *Studies in the First Century of Islamic Society*, Carbondale, Southern Illinois University Press, 1982, pp. 23–47.

10 See Edward Shils, "Tradition," *Comparative Studies in Society and History*, 13 (1971), 122–59.

11 See, e.g. al-Wāḥidī, *Kitāb Asbāb al-Nuzūlg*, Aḥmad Ṣaqr (ed.), Cairo, Dār al-Kitāb al-Jadīd, 1969, pp. 43–4. On the interpretation of this type of anecdote, see A. Rippin, "The Exegetical Function of *Asbāb al-Nuzūl* Material," *Bulletin of the School of Oriental and African Studies*, 51 (1988), 1–20.

12 Compare Qur'ān 5/103.

13 See, for example, Michael Cook, *Muḥammad*, Oxford, Oxford University Press, 1983, Chapter 7.

14 Al-Wāḥidī, *Asbāb*, p. 42.

15 Al-Qurṭubī, *al-Jāmiʿ li-Aḥkām al-Qur'ān*, Beirut, Dār Iḥyāʾ al-Turāth al-ʿArabī, 1967, vol. 2, p. 178. On this passage and its interpretation, see Mahmoud M. Ayoub, *The Qur'ān and its Interpreters*, volume 1, Albany, State University of New York Press, 1984, pp. 176–9.

16 See Michael Cook, "Early Islamic Dietary Law," *Jerusalem Studies in Arabic and Islam*, 7 (1986), 217–77, especially pp. 270–1.

17 See G. R. Hawting, "The Literary Context of the Traditional Accounts of Pre-Islamic Arab Idolatry," *Jerusalem Studies in Arabic and Islam*, 21 (1997), 21–41.

18 Ibn al-Kalbī, *Kitāb al-Aṣnām*, R. Klinke-Rosenberger (ed.), Leipzig, Otto Harrassowitz, 1941, pp. 3–4; a full English translation of this work is available, Nabih Amin Faris, *The Book of Idols, being a Translation from the Arabic of the* Kitāb al-Aṣnām *by Hishām ibn al-Kalbi*, Princeton, Princeton University Press, 1952. See below, Chapter 7, for an explanation of the details of the Muslim *ḥajj*.

19 See Reuven Firestone, "Abraham's Association with the Meccan Sanctuary and the Pilgrimage in the Pre-Islamic and Early Islamic Periods," *Le Muséon*, 104 (1991), 359–87.

2 The Qur'ān

1 For an illustration of a variety of scholarly approaches to the analysis of the Qur'ān, see the collection of articles assembled in Andrew Rippin (ed.), *The Qur'ān: Style and Content*, Aldershot, Ashgate/Variorum, 2000.

2 See *Encyclopaedia of Islam, New Edition*, "*Malā'ika*" (by D. B. MacDonald).

3 See Norman Calder, "From Midrash to Scripture: the Sacrifice of Abraham in the Early Islamic Tradition," *Le Muséon*, 101 (1988), 375–402.

4 See Geoffrey Parrinder, *Jesus in the Qur'ān*, London, Faber and Faber, 1965, esp. pp. 22–9.

5 See Arthur Jeffery, "The Qur'ān as Scripture," *The Muslim World*, 40 (1950), especially pp. 202–6.

6 Such observations have provoked a great deal of academic work (some of it markedly polemical); see the collection of scholarly articles on this topic in Ibn Warraq (ed.), *The Origins of the Koran*, Amherst, NY, Prometheus Press, 1998.

7 This is not the only possible way of dividing up the *sūra*, of course; for another view, see Neal Robinson, *Discovering the Qur'ān*, London, SCM Press, 1996, pp. 201–23.

8 See John Burton, *The Collection of the Qur'ān*, Cambridge, Cambridge University Press, 1977, for a treatment of these various accounts and their potential significance.

9 The most readily available source of information about these manuscripts and some of the controversy about them is to be found in Toby Lester, "What is the Koran?" *The Atlantic Monthly*, 283, i (January 1999), 43–56. The text of the article is available on the Web in *The Atlantic Monthly* archives (www.theatlantic.com).

10 Gerd-R. Puin, "Neue Wege der Koranforschung: II. Über die Bedeutung der ältesten Koranfragmente aus Sanaa (Jemen) für die Orthographie-geschichte des Korans," *Universität des Saarlandes Magazin Forschung*, 1 (1999), 37–40, esp. p. 40.

11 See John Wansbrough, *Quranic Studies: Sources and Methods of Scriptural Interpretation*, Oxford, Oxford University Press, 1977, part 4, on which see Andrew Rippin, "*Quranic Studies*, part IV: some methodological notes," *Method and Theory in the Study of Religion*, 9 (1997), 39–46.

12 William Muir, *The Apology of al-Kindy, Written at the Court of al-Māmūn (A. H. 215; A. D. 830) in Defence of Christianity against Islam*, London, Smith, Elder and Co., 1882, pp. 18–19 and 28, passages slightly modified.

13 Al-Rummānī, *al-Nukat fī I'jāz al-Qur'ān*, in Muḥammad Zaghlūl Sallām, Khalaf Allāh Aḥmad (eds), *Thalāth Rasā'il fī I'jāz al-Qur'ān*, Cairo, Dār al-Ma'ārif, 1956, esp. pp. 76–80; a partial English translation of the text is available in Andrew Rippin and Jan Knappert, *Textual Sources for the Study of Islam*, Manchester, Manchester University Press, 1986, section 2.3.

14 One volume of this work is available in English translation: J. Cooper, *The Commentary on the Qur'ān by Abū Ja'far Muḥammad b. Jarīr al-Ṭabarī*, Oxford, Oxford University Press, 1987. For further bibliography of Quranic interpretation see Andrew Rippin, "The Present Status of Tafsīr Studies," *The Muslim World*, 72 (1982), 224–38; for an introduction to *tafsīr* and its early form and structure, see the collection of scholarly articles assembled in Andrew Rippin (ed.), *The Qur'an: Formative Interpretation*, Aldershot, Ashgate/Variorum, 1999.

15 Al-Ṭabarī, *Jāmi' al-Bayān 'an Ta'wīl Āy al-Qur'ān*, Aḥmad and Maḥmūd Shākir (eds), Cairo, Dār al-Ma'ārif, 1971, vol. 6, pp. 170–1.

16 See Muslim ibn al-Ḥajjāj, *Ṣaḥīḥ Muslim, Kitāb al-Ṣalāt*, Muḥammad Fu'ād 'Abd al-Bāqī (ed.), Cairo, Dār Iḥyā' al-Kutub al-'Arabiyya, 1955–6, vol. 1, pp. 295–8, traditions 34–46, translated in Rippin and Knappert, *Textual Sources*, section 3.2.3.2. A full English translation of Muslim ibn al-Ḥajjāj's work is available: Abdul Hameed Siddique, *Sahih Muslim*, Lahore, M. Ashraf, 1971.

17 See al-Bukhārī, *al-Ṣaḥīḥ, Kitāb Faḍā'il al-Qur'ān*, Muḥammad Muḥsin Khān (ed. and trans.), New Delhi, Kitab Bhavan, 1984, 5th edition, vol. 6, pp. 489–96. For a somewhat later treatment of the same subject see A. E. Christensen, *Xavāṣṣ-i-Āyāt. Notices et extraits d'un manuscrit persan traitant la magie des versets du Coran*, Copenhagen, A. F. Høst and Son, 1920.

18 For interesting examples of this see Bess Allen Donaldson, *The Wild Rue: A Study of Muḥammadan Magic and Folklore in Iran*, London, Luzac, 1938, chapter 16.

3 Muḥammad

1 On the overall historical problem of Muḥammad, see F. E. Peters, "The Quest for the Historical Muhammad," *International Journal of Middle East Studies*, 23 (1991), 291–315. For an illustration of a variety of scholarly approaches to the study of Muḥammad, see the collection of articles assembled in Uri Rubin (ed.), *The Life of Muḥammad*, Aldershot, Ashgate/Variorum, 1998.

2 See the use made of this material made Patricia Crone and Michael Cook, *Hagarism: The Making of the Islamic World*, Cambridge, Cambridge University Press, 1977; Michael Cook, *Muḥammad*, Oxford, Oxford University Press, 1983. All of the original source material is gathered together in Robert G. Hoyland, *Seeing Islam as Others Saw It: A Survey and Evaluation of Christian, Jewish and Zoroastrian Writings on Early Islam*, Princeton, Darwin Press, 1997. A useful supplement to this is Robert G. Hoyland, "The Content and Context of Early Arabic Inscriptions," *Jerusalem Studies in Arabic and Islam*, 21 (1997), 77–102.

3 For an attempt to use the Qur'ān as a historical source for the life of Muḥammad see A. T. Welch, "Muḥammad's Understanding of Himself: the Koranic Data," in R. G. Hovannisian and S. Vryonis Jr. (eds), *Islam's Understanding of Itself*, Malibu, CA, Undena Publications, 1983, pp. 15–52. It must be remembered, however, that the only way the author is able to draw the conclusions which he does is by assuming, *a priori*, the basic framework provided by the *Sīra* material. On the overall question, see Andrew Rippin, "Muḥammad in the Qur'ān: Reading Scripture in the 21st Century," in Harald Motzki (ed.), *The Biography of Muḥammad: The Issue of the Sources*, Leiden, E. J. Brill, 2000, pp. 298–309.

4 For details of the understanding of this see Andrew Rippin, "Al-Zarkashī and al-Suyūṭī on the Function of the 'Occasion of Revelation' Material," *Islamic Culture*, 59 (1985), 243–58.

5 See Lawrence I. Conrad, "Abraha and Muḥammad: some Observations apropos of Chronology and Literary *topoi* in the Early Arabic Historical Tradition," *Bulletin of the School of Oriental and African Studies*, 50 (1987), 225–40; on a similar tendency in historical texts also see his "Seven and the *Tasbī*': On the Implications of Numerical Symbolism for the Study of Medieval Islamic History," *Journal of the Economic and Social History of the Orient*, 31 (1988), 42–73.

6 See Crone and Cook, *Hagarism*, p. 157, n. 39 and p. 160, n. 56; also see Patricia Crone, "The First-century Concept of *Hiğra*," *Arabica*, 41 (1994), 352–87, for ideas related to the underlying meaning of *hijra*.

7 Ibn Hisham, *al-Sīra al-Nabawiyya*, Muṣṭafā al-Saqā, *et al.* (eds), Cairo, Ḥalabī, 1955, vol. 1, pp. 504; A. Guillaume, *The Life of Muḥammad: A Translation of* [*Ibn*] *Isḥāq's Sirāt Rasūl Allāh*, Oxford, Oxford University Press, 1955, p. 233.

8 Compare this standard presentation with Patricia Crone, *Meccan Trade and the Rise of Islam*, Princeton, Princeton University Press, 1987, for some insights into the historical problems of Muḥammad's biography.

9 See John Wansbrough, *The Sectarian Milieu: Content and Composition of Islamic Salvation History*, Oxford, Oxford University Press, 1978, p. 32.

10 Wansbrough, *Sectarian Milieu*, p. 56.

11 al-Bukhārī, *al-Ṣaḥīḥ*, *Kitāb Faḍā'il al-Qur'ān*, Muḥammad Muḥsin Khān (ed. and trans.), New Delhi, Kitab Bhavan, 1984, 5th edition, vol. 6, pp. 517–18, tradition number 574.

12 Muslim ibn al-Ḥajjāj, *Ṣaḥīḥ Muslim, Muqaddima*, Muḥammad Fu'ād 'Abd al-Bāqī (ed.), Cairo, Dār Iḥyā' al-Kutub al-'Arabiyya, 1955–6, vol. 1, p. 9, tradition number 1.

13 Al-Tirmidhī, *al-Jāmi' al-Ṣaḥīḥ*, *Kitāb al-Qadar*, Aḥmad Shākir (ed.), Beirut, Dār al-Kutub al-'Ilmiyya, 1987, vol. 4, pp. 387–8, tradition number 2135; also cited in Kenneth Cragg and Marston Speight (eds), *Islam from Within: Anthology of a Religion*, Belmont, CA, Wadsworth Publishing, 1980, p. 82.

14 Classic scholarly statements of this understanding of the growth of *ḥadīth* are to be found in Ignaz Goldziher, *Muslim Studies*, London, George Allen and Unwin, 1971 (original German edition, 1890), vol. 2, pp. 17–251, and Joseph Schacht, *The Origins of Muhammadan Jurisprudence*, Oxford, Clarendon Press, 1950.

15 See the works of M. J. Kister, *Studies in Jāhiliyya and Early Islam*, London, Variorum, 1980; also Harris Birkeland, *The Lord Guideth: Studies on Primitive Islam*, Oslo, H. Aschehoug, 1950.

16 Al-Ghazālī, *Iḥyā' 'Ulūm al-Dīn*, Cairo, al-Maktaba al-Tijāra al-Kubrā, 1965, vol. 2, p. 381, quoted in Kees Wagtendonk, "Images in Islam, Discussion of a Paradox," in Dirk van der Plas (ed.), *Effigies Dei: Essays on the History of Religion*, Leiden, E. J. Brill, 1987, p. 123. The entire Book 20 of al-Ghazālī's *Iḥyā'* is devoted to the character of Muḥammad as the "perfect Muslim".

17 See Marie Rose Seguy, *The Miraculous Journey of Mahomet: Miraj Nameh*, New York, George Braziller, 1977. Jamel Eddine Bencheikh, *Le voyage nocturne de Mahomet*, Paris, Imprimerie Nationale, 1988, combines an excellent collection of illustrations with some useful analysis.

18 *Sūra* 53 is also sometimes connected to the night journey; see Josef van Ess, "Vision and Ascension: *Sūrat al-Najm* and its Relationship with Muḥammad's *mi'rāj*," *Journal of Qur'anic Studies*, 1 (1999), 47–62.

19 For the significance of this motif, see Ilai Alon, "Interpretation as Compromise: the Case of the Five Daily Islamic Prayers," in Shlomo Biderman and Ben-Ami Scharfstein (eds), *Interpretation of Religion*, Leiden, E. J. Brill, 1992, pp. 207–27.

20 Ibn Hishām, *Sīra*, vol. 1, pp. 402–3; A. Guillaume, *Life of Muhammad*, p. 184.

21 See, for example, Najm al-Dīn al-Ghaytī (d. 1573), *Qiṣṣa miʿrāj al-nabī*, found in a Swahili version by al-Amīn ibn ʿAlī in J. Knappert, *Swahili Islamic Poetry*, Leiden, E. J. Brill, 1971, vol. 3, 227–75.

22 See Harris Birkeland, *The Legend of the Opening of Muḥammad's Breast*, Oslo, Jacob Dybwad, 1955.

23 Jane Idleman Smith (ed.), *The Precious Pearl: A Translation from the Arabic*, Missoula, MT: Scholars Press, 1979, pp. 59, 60.

4 Political action and theory

1 See Patricia Crone and Michael Cook, *Hagarism: The Making of the Islamic World*, Cambridge, Cambridge University Press, 1977, but cf. the many adverse reviews of the book.

2 See the works of Yehuda D. Nevo, whose insights are based primarily on archaeological findings in the Negev desert: "Towards a Prehistory of Islam," *Jerusalem Studies in Arabic and Islam*, 17 (1994), 108–41; Yehuda D. Nevo and Judith Koren, "The Origins of the Muslim Descriptions of the Jāhilī Meccan Sanctuary," *Journal of Near Eastern Studies*, 49 (1990), 23–44.

3 See G. R. Hawting, "The Significance of the Slogan *lā hukmᵃ illā lillāh* and References to the *Ḥudūd* in the Traditions about the Fitna and the Murder of ʿUthmān," *Bulletin of the School of Oriental and African Studies*, 41 (1978), 453–63, and his *The First Dynasty of Islam: The Umayyad Caliphate AD 661–750*, London, Croom Helm, 1986.

4 For the full text of these inscriptions see Christel Kessler, "ʿAbd al-Malik's Inscription in the Dome of the Rock: a Reconsideration," *Journal of the Royal Asiatic Society*, 1970, 2–14. On the Dome in general see Oleg Grabar, "The Umayyad Dome of the Rock in Jerusalem," *Ars Orientalis*, 3 (1959), 33–62, reprinted in his *Studies in Medieval Islamic Art*, London, Variorum, 1976, chapter 2, and his article in *Encyclopaedia of Islam, New Edition*, "al-Ḳuds" [i.e. Jerusalem], part B, "monuments."

5 See Oleg Grabar *et al.*, *The Shape of the Holy: Early Islamic Jerusalem*, Princeton, Princeton University Press, 1996, pp. 60–1, on these inscriptions.

6 On all of these points see Grabar, "Umayyad Dome"; Grabar, *Shape of the Holy*, chapter 2; F. E. Peters, *Jerusalem and Mecca: The Typology of the Holy City in the Near East*, New York, New York University Press, 1986; Guy le Strange, *Palestine Under the Moslems*, London, Palestine Exploration Fund, 1890.

7 See Peters, *Jerusalem and Mecca*, chapter 4. Also see Myriam Rosen-Ayalon, *The Early Islamic Monuments of al-Ḥaram al-Sharīf: An Iconographical Study*, Jerusalem, Institute of Archaeology, Hebrew University, 1989, who emphasizes the decorative aspects of the mosaics as a picture of paradise, linking the building to the common Jewish/Christian belief in Jerusalem's role on the Day of Judgement.

8 See K. A. C. Creswell, *Early Muslim Architecture*, second edition, Oxford, Clarendon Press, 1969, vol. 1, part 1, pp. 101–9.

9 See Howard Crosby Butler, *Early Churches in Syria, Fourth to Seventh Centuries*, Amsterdam, Adolf M. Hakkert, 1969.

10 Patricia Crone and Martin Hinds, *God's Caliph: Religious Authority in the First Centuries of Islam*, Cambridge, Cambridge University Press, 1986, but cf. the review by Norman Calder in *Journal of Semitic Studies*, 32 (1987), 375–8; also Ira M. Lapidus, "The Separation of State and Religion in the Development of Early Islamic Society," *International Journal of Middle East Studies*, 6 (1975), 363–85.

11 On the interpretation of the *miḥna*, see John A. Nawas, "A Reexamination of Three Current Explanations for al-Ma'mun's Introduction of the *Miḥna*," *International Journal of Middle East Studies*, 26 (1994), 615–29.

12 See Lapidus, "Separation of State and Religion". For the role of the *'ulamā'* in a somewhat later period (although still displaying precisely the same tensions as in earlier times) see Emmanuel Sivan, *"'Ulamā'* and Power," in his *Interpretations of Islam*, Princeton, Darwin Press, 1985, pp. 107–32.

13 Hamilton A. R. Gibb, "Some Considerations on the Sunni Theory of the Caliphate," in his *Studies on the Civilization of Islam*, Boston, Beacon Press, 1962, p. 148.

5 Theological exposition

1 See G. R. Hawting, "The Significance of the Slogan *lā ḥukm*^{a} *illā lillāh* and References to the *Ḥudūd* in the Traditions about the Fitna and the Murder of 'Uthmān," *Bulletin of the School of Oriental and African Studies*, 41 (1978), 453–63.

2 See W. Madelung, "Early Sunnī Doctrine concerning Faith as Reflected in the Kitāb al-Īmān of Abū 'Ubayd al-Qāsim b. Sallām (d. 224/839)," *Studia Islamica*, 32 (1970), 248–9, reprinted in his *Religious Schools and Sects in Medieval Islam*, London, Variorum, 1985. Also see J. Meric Pessagno, "The Murji'a, Īmān and Abū 'Ubayd," *Journal of the American Oriental Society*, 95 (1975), 382–94.

3 John Alden Williams (ed.), *Islam*, New York, Washington Square Press, 1963, p. 164, from the "Epistle to 'Uthmān al-Battī," slightly modified.

4 See Wilferd Madelung, "The Spread of Māturīdism and the Turks," in *Actas do IV Congresso de Estudos Arabes e Islamicos, Coimbra-Lisboa 1968*, Leiden, E. J. Brill, 1971, pp. 109–68, reprinted in Madelung, *Religious Schools and Sects*.

5 See A. J. Wensinck, *Muslim Creed, its Genesis and Historical Development*, Cambridge, Cambridge University Press, 1932, Chapter 6.

6 See Williams, *Islam*, pp. 162–5, although note that the full text has not been translated. Among other important texts attributed to Abū Ḥanīfa but, in fact, written by his pupils, are Abū Muqātil al-Samarqandī (d. 823), *Kitāb al-ʾĀlim waʾl-Mutaʿallim* (see Joseph Schacht, "An Early Murciʾite Treatise: the Kitāb al-ʿAlim wal-Mutaʿallim," *Oriens*, 17 [1964], 96–117) and Abū Muṭīʿ al-Balkhī (d. 799), *al-Fiqh al-Absaṭ* (see Wensinck, *Muslim Creed*, Chapter 6, esp. p. 123, and Hans Daiber, *The Islamic Concept of Belief in the 4th/10th Century*, Tokyo, Institute for the Study of Languages and Cultures of Asia and Africa, 1995).

7 Kenneth Cragg and Marston Speight, *Islam from Within: Anthology of a Religion*, Belmont, CA, Wadsworth Publishing, 1980, p. 119, quoting

from a creed ascribed to Ibn Ḥanbal found in Ibn Abī Yaʿlā, *Ṭabaqāt al-Ḥanābila*. For a translation of another work by Ibn Ḥanbal, his "Refutation of the Dualists and the Anthropomorphists," see Morris Seale, *Muslim Theology: A Study of Origins with Reference to the Church Fathers*, 2nd edition, London, Luzac, 1980.

8 John Burton, *Abū ʿUbaid al-Qāsim b. Sallām's K. al-Nāsikh wa-l-Mansūkh*, Edited with a Commentary, Cambridge, E. J. W. Gibb Memorial Trust, 1987, p. 46.

9 See Patricia Crone and Martin Hinds, *God's Caliph: Religious Authority in the First Centuries of Islam*, Cambridge, Cambridge University Press, 1986, esp. Chapter 3.

10 For some details on this debate see Michael Cook, *Early Muslim Dogma: A Source-critical Study*, Cambridge, Cambridge University Press, 1981, Chapter 12; for the text itself, see Julian Obermann, "Political Theology in Early Islam: Ḥasan al-Baṣrī's Treatise on Qadar," *Journal of the American Oriental Society*, 55 (1935), 138–62; Michael Schwarz, "The Letter of al-Ḥasan al-Baṣrī," *Oriens*, 20 (1967–9), 15–30; partial translation in Andrew Rippin and Jan Knappert, *Textual Sources for the Study of Islam*, Manchester, Manchester University Press, 1986, section 6.1.

11 See M. A. Cook, "The Origins of *Kalām*," *Bulletin of the School of Oriental and African Studies*, 43 (1980), 32–43.

12 A. N. Nader (ed. and trans.), *Kitāb al-intiṣār. Le livre du triomphe et de la refutation d'Ibn Rawandī l'hérétique par Abū al-Ḥusayn b. ʿOthmān al Khayyāṭ le Muʿtazil*, Beirut, Editions les lettres Orientales, 1957, French p. 110, Arabic p. 89.

13 See Harry Austryn Wolfson, *The Philosophy of the Kalam*, Cambridge, MA, Harvard University Press, 1976, Chapter 3, for a full discussion of the topic and its relationship to Jewish and Christian notions.

14 See Wolfson, *Philosophy*, pp. 251–5, for further discussion of the whole issue. Also see Wilferd Madelung, "The Origins of the Controversy Concerning the Creation of the Koran," in J. M. Barral (ed.), *Orientalia Hispanica sive studia F. M. Pareja octogenario dicata*, volume 1, part 1, Leiden, E. J. Brill, 1974, pp. 504–25, reprinted in Madelung, *Religious Schools and Sects*.

15 See Wolfson, *Philosophy*, Chapter 2, for a full treatment of this topic.

16 See George F. Hourani, *Islamic Rationalism: The Ethics of ʿAbd al-Jabbar*, Oxford, Clarendon Press, 1971, p. 131.

17 See George F. Hourani, "Divine Justice and Human Reason in Muʿtazilite Ethical Theology," in Richard G. Hovannisian (ed.), *Ethics in Islam*, Malibu, CA, Undena Publications, 1985, pp. 73–83, especially section VII.

18 See Wilferd Madelung, "Imamism and Muʿtazilite Theology," in T. Fahd (ed.), *Le Shiʿisme imamite*, Paris, Presses Universitaire de France, 1979, pp. 13–29, reprinted in Madelung, *Religious Schools and Sects*. Also see below, Chapter 8.

19 Walter C. Klein (trans.), *Abu ʾl-Ḥasan ʿAlī ibn Ismāʿīl al-Ašʿarī's al-Ibānah ʿan Uṣūl ad-Diyānah (The Elucidation of Islam's Foundation)*, New Haven, CT, American Oriental Society, 1940, p. 47.

20 Klein, *al-Ibānah*, p. 103.

21 See Richard J. McCarthy (trans.), *The Theology of al-Ashʿarī*, Beirut, Imprimerie Catholique, 1953, especially Chapters 1–3 of the translation of al-Ashʿarī's *Kitāb al-Lumaʿ*.

22 McCarthy, *Theology*, English p. 14, Arabic p. 11.

23 Fathalla Kholeif (ed.), *Kitāb al-Tawḥīd: Abū Manṣūr Muḥammad ibn Muḥammad ibn Maḥmūd al-Māturīdī al-Samarqandī*, Beirut, Dar el-Machreq Editeurs, 1970, with an English summary of the contents. See also the studies by J. Meric Pessagno, for example, *"Irāda, Ikhtiyār, Qudra, Kasb*: the View of Abū Manṣūr al-Māturīdī," *Journal of the American Oriental Society*, 104 (1984), 177–91.

24 The creed is translated in Arthur Jeffery (ed.), *A Reader on Islam: Passages from Standard Arabic Writings Illustrative of the Beliefs and Practices of Muslims*, 's-Gravenhage, Mouton, 1962, pp. 347–52; for a commentary on it from the perspective of the Ashʿarī school, see the work of al-Taftazānī (d. 1388) as found in Earl Edgar Elder (trans.), *A Commentary on the Creed of Islam*, New York, Columbia University Press, 1950.

6 Legal developments

1 See George Makdisi, "Ashʿarī and the Ashʿarites in Islamic Religious History," *Studia Islamica*, 17 (1962), 37–80, 18 (1963), 19–39.

2 On these terms see A. Kevin Reinhart, "Islamic Law as Islamic Ethics," *Journal of Religious Ethics*, 11 (1983), 186–203. For a good overall summary of the development of the *uṣūl al-fiqh*, see *Encyclopaedia of Islam, New Edition*, *"Fiḳh"* (by Joseph Schacht).

3 For one detailed example see Patricia Crone, *Roman, Provincial and Islamic Law: The Origins of the Islamic Patronate*, Cambridge, Cambridge University Press, 1987.

4 See Patricia Crone and Martin Hinds, *God's Caliph: Religious Authority in the First Centuries of Islam*, Cambridge, Cambridge University Press, 1986, pp. 48ff.

5 See Joseph Schacht, *An Introduction to Islamic Law*, Oxford, Oxford University Press, 1964, pp. 17–8, 29–30.

6 George Makdisi, "The Significance of the Sunni Schools of Law in Islamic Religious History," *International Journal of Middle East Studies*, 10 (1979), especially p. 1.

7 For a good summary of this development see Chapter 2 of Crone, *Roman, Provincial and Islamic Law*.

8 For an examination of these different tendencies as displayed in specific laws see Michael Cook, "Early Islamic Dietary Law," *Jerusalem Studies in Arabic and Islam*, 7 (1986), 217–77.

9 Wael B. Hallaq, "Was al-Shafiʿi the Master Architect of Islamic Jurisprudence?" *International Journal of Middle East Studies*, 25 (1993), 587–605, argues that the immediate impact of al-Shāfiʿī may not have been as great as previous scholars have tended to portray and that it may have taken several centuries before other jurists effected this reconciliation of rationalism and traditionalism.

10 Al-Shāfiʿī, *Kitāb al-Umm*, Cairo, Būlāq, 1903–7, vol. 7, p. 271, as quoted in Joseph Schacht, *The Origins of Muhammadan Jurisprudence*, Oxford, Oxford University Press, 1950, p. 16.

11 Al-Shāfiʿī, *al-Risāla fī Uṣūl al-Fiqh*, Muḥammad Sayyid Kilānī (ed.), Cairo, Ḥalabī, 1983, p. 204, para. 1312; also available in English translation, Majid Khadduri (trans.), *Islamic Jurisprudence: Shāfiʿī's Risāla*, Baltimore, Johns Hopkins University Press, 1961; reprint, Cambridge, Islamic Texts Society, 1987, p. 286.

12 On this book see Norman Calder, *Studies in Early Muslim Jurisprudence*, Oxford, Clarendon Press, 1993, chapter 2; for an opposing view on the composition of the text (with a good introduction to the text itself), see Yasin Dutton, *The Origins of Islamic Law: The Qurʾān, the* Muwaṭṭaʾ *and Madinan* ʿAmal, Richmond, Curzon Press, 1999, Chapter 2. A translation of the *Muwaṭṭaʾ* is available: Aisha Abdurrahman Bewley (trans.), *Al-Muwatta of Imam Malik ibn Anas: The First Formulation of Islamic Law*, London, Kegan Paul, 1989.

13 See Norman Calder, "Law" in Seyyed Hossein Nasr, Oliver Leaman (eds), *History of Islamic Philosophy*, London, Routledge, 1996, part II, 979–98.

14 See Wael B. Hallaq, "On the Authoritativeness of Sunni Consensus," *International Journal of Middle East Studies*, 18 (1986), esp. p. 448.

15 See N. J. Coulson, *A History of Islamic Law*, Edinburgh, Edinburgh University Press, 1964, p. 71.

16 See Wael B. Hallaq, "Was the Gate of Ijtihad Closed?" *International Journal of Middle East Studies*, 16 (1984), esp. p. 10.

17 Hallaq, "Ijtihad", p. 11.

18 A. J. Wensinck, *The Muslim Creed, its Genesis and Historical Development*, Cambridge, Cambridge University Press, 1932, pp. 112–13, article 7 from the Fiqh Akbar I.

19 ʿAbd al-Qāhir al-Baghdādī (d. 1037), *Kitāb al-Nāsikh waʾl-Mansūkh*, Ḥilmī Kamil Asʿad ʿAbd al-Hādī (ed.), Amman, Dār al-ʿAdawī, 1987, pp. 104–5 ; further material from this same section of al-Baghdādī's book is translated in Andrew Rippin and Jan Knappert, *Textual Sources for the Study of Islam*, Manchester, Manchester University Press, 1986, section 5.1.

20 Al-Marghinānī, *al-Hidāya: Sharḥ Bidāyat al-Mubtadiʾ*, Cairo, Ḥalabī, 1975, vol. 1, pp. 226–29; a larger portion of this text is translated in Rippin, Knappert, *Textual Sources*, section 5.4.

21 Daniel Brown, "Islamic Ethics in Comparative Perspective," *The Muslim World*, 89 (1999), 191.

22 See Bernard Lewis (ed. and trans.), *Islam from the Prophet Muhammad to the Capture of Constantinople*, volume 2: *Religion and Society*, New York, Harper and Row, 1974, pp. 40–2, from al-Māwardī (d. 1058).

23 As is displayed in the theological discussions over ʿUthmān and ʿAlī; see above Chapter 5.

24 Coulson, *History*, p. 126. Also see Norman Calder, "Friday Prayer and the Juristic Theory of Government: Sarakhsī, Shīrāzī, Māwardī," *Bulletin of the School of Oriental and African Studies*, 49 (1986), 35–47.

25 For more details of these offices and several others see Reuben Levy, *The Social Structure of Islam*, Cambridge, Cambridge University Press, 1957, Chapter 7.

26 A good basic overview of the legal status of the "protected communities" is available in Majid Khadduri, *War and Peace in the Law of Islam*, Baltimore, Johns Hopkins University Press, 1955, Chapter 17.

7 Ritual practice

1 See 'Abd al-Qāhir al-Baghdādī, *Kitāb Uṣūl al-Din*, Istanbul, Dār al-Funūn al-Tūrkiyya, 1928, pp. 186–93.
2 See al-Shāfi'ī, *al-Risāla fī Uṣūl al-Fiqh*, Muḥammad Sayyid Kaylānī (ed.), Cairo, Ḥalabī, 1983, p. 15, para. 56; Majid Khadduri (trans.), *Islamic Jurisprudence: Shāfi'ī's Risāla*, Baltimore, Johns Hopkins University Press, 1961, p. 68.
3 See Yehuda D. Nevo and Judith Koren, "The Origins of the Muslim Descriptions of the Jāhilī Meccan Sanctuary," *Journal of Near Eastern Studies* 49 (1990), 23–44.
4 Al-Baghdādī, *Uṣūl*, p. 186.
5 See Patricia Crone and Martin Hinds, *God's Caliph: Religious Authority in the First Centuries of Islam*, Cambridge, Cambridge University Press, 1986, p. 25, n. 8, and the more detailed study in John Walker, *A Catalogue of the Muhammadan Coins in the British Museum*, volumes 1 and 2, London, Trustees of the British Museum, 1941, 1956.
6 See Muslim ibn al-Ḥajjāj, *Ṣaḥīḥ Muslim*, *Kitāb al-Īmān*, Muḥammad Fu'ād 'Abd al-Bāqī (ed.), Cairo, Dār Iḥyā' al-Kutub al-'Arabiyya, 1951, vol. 1, p. 45, tradition no. 21; other traditions in this chapter of Muslim ibn al-Ḥajjāj display a diverse way of expressing the *shahāda* (e.g., tradition no. 20 which states that one witnesses that "you worship God and disbelieve in what is other than Him").
7 See Edward William Lane, *An Account of the Manners and Customs of the Modern Egyptians Written in Egypt During the Years 1833–35*, London, John Murray, 1836, pp. 69–96 for a full description (with diagrams) of the intricacies of the prayer ritual. Also see Alford T. Welch, "Islam," in John R. Hinnells (ed.), *A New Handbook of Living Religion*, London, Penguin, 1997, pp. 181–91.
8 See S. D. Goitein, "Prayer in Islam," in his *Studies in Islamic History and Institutions*, Leiden, E. J. Brill, 1966, pp. 73–89 on the prayer in general, and pp. 84–5 on this specific point.
9 For an attempt at reconstructing the history of the Friday prayer see S. D. Goitein, "The Origin and Development of the Muslim Friday Worship," in his *Studies*, pp. 111–25.
10 Al-Baghdādī, *Uṣūl*, p. 190.
11 For more on issues related to this topic and its inverse – the changing of mosques into churches – see Timothy Insoll, *The Archaeology of Islam*, Oxford, Blackwell, 1999, 35–40, 54–8.
12 See Oleg Grabar, *The Formation of Islamic Art*, New Haven, CT, Yale University Press, 1973, pp. 121–3; the whole chapter, "Islamic Religious Art: the Mosque," is of central importance.
13 See Ulrich Haarmann, "Islamic Duties in History," *The Muslim World*, 68 (1978), 12–13.
14 For a full treatment of the Quranic details on fasting see K. Wagtendonk, *Fasting in the Koran*, Leiden, E. J. Brill, 1968.
15 For full details of the pilgrimage including the text of the prayers see Ahmad Kamal, *The Sacred Journey, being Pilgrimage to Mekkah*, London, George Allen and Unwin, 1961. Also valuable for its pictures is Ezzedine Guellouz, *Mecca, the Muslim Pilgrimage*, London, Paddington Press, 1979.

16 See William Graham, "Islam in the Mirror of Ritual," in Richard G. Hovannisian and Speros Vryonis Jr. (eds), *Islam's Understanding of Itself*, Malibu, CA, Undena Publications, 1983, p. 69.

8 The Shīʿa

1 See John Wansbrough, *The Sectarian Milieu: Content and Composition of Islamic Salvation History*, Oxford, Oxford University Press, 1978, p. 120.

2 Al-Tirmidhī, *al-Jāmiʿ al-Ṣaḥīḥ: Kitāb al-Manāqib*, Aḥmad Shākir *et al.* (eds), Beirut, Dār al-Kutub al-ʿIlmiyya, 1987, vol. 5, p. 596, tradition number 3724, translation from Moojan Momen, *An Introduction to Shiʿi Islam*, New Haven, CT, Yale University Press, 1985, p. 15.

3 See B. Todd Lawson, "Note for the Study of a 'Shīʿī Qurʾān'," *Journal of Semitic Studies*, 36 (1991), 279–95, with a full bibliography of earlier scholarship on the issue; also Hossein Modarresi, "Early Debates on the Integrity of the Qurʾān," *Studia Islamica*, 77 (1993), 5–39; M. M. Bar-Asher, "Variant Readings and Additions of the Imāmī-Šiʿa to the Quran," *Israel Oriental Studies*, 13 (1993), 39–74.

4 See E. Kohlberg, "Shīʿī Ḥadīth," in A. F. L. Beeston, T. M. Johnstone, R. B. Serjeant and G. R. Smith (eds), *Arabic Literature to the End of the Umayyad Period*, Cambridge, Cambridge University Press, 1983, pp. 299–307.

5 E. Kohlberg, "From Imāmiyya to Ithnā-ʿashariyya," *Bulletin of the School of Oriental and African Studies*, 39 (1976), 521–34.

6 See Abdulaziz Abdulhussein Sachedina, *Islamic Messianism: The Idea of the Mahdi in Twelver Shiʿism*, Albany, State University of New York Press, 1981.

7 See E. P. Sanders, *Jesus and Judaism*, London, SCM Press, 1985, pp. 95–106.

8 See H. A. R. Gibb, "Government and Islam under the Early ʿAbbasids. The Political Collapse of Islam," in *L'élaboration de l'Islam*, Paris, Presses Universitaires de France, 1961, p. 118.

9 A. A. A. Fyzee, *A Shīʿī Creed: A Translation of Risālatuʾl-Iʿqadāt [of Ibn Babawayh]*, Oxford, Oxford University Press, 1942, pp. 31–2.

10 Fyzee [Ibn Babawayh], *Shīʿī Creed*, p. 43 (translation slightly modified).

11 For the theology of al-Shaykh al-Mufīd in comparison with that of the Muʿtazila, Ibn Babawayh (Ibn Babūyā) and al-Sharīf al-Murtaḍā, see Martin J. McDermott, *The Theology of al-Shaykh al-Mufīd (d. 413/1022)*, Beirut, Dar el-Machreq, 1978. Also see Wilferd Madelung, "Imāmism and Muʿtazilite Theology," in T. Fahd (ed.), *Le Shîʿisme Imâmite*, Paris, Presses Universitaires de France, 1979, pp. 13–29, reprinted in his *Religious Schools and Sects in Medieval Islam*, London, Variorum, 1985.

12 Al-Sharīf al-Murtaḍā, *al-Uṣūl al-Iʿtiqādiyya*, in Āl Yāsīn (ed.), *Nafāʾis makhṭūṭāt*, Baghdad, al-Maʿārif, 1954, vol. 2, p. 81 as quoted in McDermott, *Theology*, p. 385.

13 See Momen, *Shīʿī Islam*, p. 189.

14 See Norman Calder, "Judicial Authority in Imāmī Shīʿī Jurisprudence," *British Society for Middle Eastern Studies Bulletin*, 6 (1979), 104–8. Also see Wilferd Madelung, "Authority in Twelver Shiism in the Absence of

the Imam," in *La notion d'authorité au Moyen Age: Islam, Byzance, Occident. Colloques internationaux de la Napoule 1978*, Paris, Presses Universitaires de France, 1982, pp. 163–73, reprinted in Madelung, *Religious Schools and Sects.*

15 For details more on juridical development among the Shīʿa see Norman Calder, "*Zakāt* in Imāmī Shīʿī Jurisprudence, from the Tenth to the Sixteenth Century A.D.," *Bulletin of the School of Oriental and African Studies*, 44 (1981), 468–80, and his "Khums in Imāmī Shīʿī Jurisprudence, from the Tenth to the Sixteenth Century A.D.," *Bulletin of the School of Oriental and African Studies*, 45 (1982), 39–47.

16 See Arthur Gribetz, *Strange Bedfellows:* Mutʿat al-Nisāʾ *and* Mutʿat al-Ḥajj. *A Study Based on Sunnī and Shīʿī Sources of* Tafsīr, Ḥadīth *and* Fiqh, Berlin, Klaus Schwartz Verlag, 1994.

17 See Joseph Eliash, "On the Genesis and Development of the Twelver-Shīʿī Three-tenet Shahādah," *Der Islam*, 47 (1971), 265–72.

18 See Fyzee [Ibn Babawayh], *Shīʿī Creed*, p. 61.

19 See Mahmoud Ayoub, *Redemptive Suffering in Islam: A Study of the Devotional Aspects of ʿAshura' in Twelver Shiʿism*, The Hague, Mouton, 1978.

20 See Bess Allen Donaldson, *The Wild Rue: A Study of Muhammadan Magic and Folklore in Iran*, London, Luzac, 1938, for information on a number of Shīʿī practices in the modern era.

9 Ṣūfī devotion

1 Ibn Ḥanbal, *Kitāb al-Zuhd*, Beirut, Dār al-Kutub al-ʿIlmiyya, 1976, p. 3.

2 See M. A. Amir Moezzi, *Le voyage iniatique en terre d'Islam. Ascensions célestes et itineraries spirituals*, Louvain, Peeters, 1996.

3 See Ignaz Goldziher, *Muslim Studies*, London, George Allen and Unwin, 1971, vol. 2, pp. 356–60.

4 See Norman Calder, "Ḥinth, Birr, Tabarrur, Taḥannuth: an Inquiry into the Arabic Vocabulary of Vows," *Bulletin of the School of Oriental and African Studies*, 51 (1988), 214–39.

5 See Margaret Smith, *An Early Mystic of Baghdad*, London, Sheldon Press, 1935; also Ignaz Goldziher, *Introduction to Islamic Theology and Law*, Princeton, Princeton University Press, 1981, p. 130, citing a study by D. S. Margoliouth.

6 For a treatment of a developed formulation of the *dhikr*, see Hamid Algar, "Silent and Vocal Dhikr in the Naqshbandī Order," in Albert Dietrich (ed.), *Akten der VII. Kongresses für Arabistik und Islamwissenschaft*, Göttingen, Vandenhoeck and Ruprecht, 1976, pp. 39–46.

7 Ali Hassan Abdel-Kader, *The Life, Personality and Writings of al-Junayd*, London, Luzac, 1976, p. 89, quoting from al-Junayd, *al-Risāla*.

8 For further on this type of Sufism see Carl W. Ernst, *Words of Ecstasy in Sufism*, Albany, State University of New York Press, 1985.

9 Margaret Smith (ed. and trans.), *Readings from the Mystics of Islam*, London, Luzac, 1950, p. 43.

10 See Seyyed Hossein Nasr, "The Spiritual States in Sufism," in his *Sufi Essays*, New York, Schocken Books, 1977, pp. 68–83, and A. J. Arberry,

Sufism, an Account of the Mystics of Islam, London, George Allen and Unwin, 1950, Chapter 7.

11 Al-Ghazālī, *Bidāyat al-Hidāya*, Cairo, Ḥalabī, 1934, p. 4, translated in W. Montgomery Watt, *The Faith and Practice of al-Ghazali*, Lahore, Sh. Muḥammad Ashraf, 1963, p. 90.

12 See J. Spencer Trimingham, *The Sufi Orders in Islam*, Oxford, Oxford University Press, 1971, p. 14 and passim for further information.

13 This text is found in Muhammad ibn Yaḥyā al-Tādhifī al-Ḥanbalī, *Qalā'id al-Jawāhir fī Manāqib al-Shaykh ʿAbd al-Qādir*. The translation is based on that found at the web site http://www.islam.co.za/abdalqadirjilani/necklaces_8.htm. The full printed translation by Muhtar Holland is forthcoming from al-Baz Publishing, Hollywood, FL, under the title *Necklaces of Gems*.

14 See Canon Sell, *The Religious Orders of Islam*, Madras, London, SPCK, 1908, p. 40. For more information on general Ṣūfī practices, see Jean-Louis Michon, "The Spiritual Practices of Sufism," in Seyyed Hossein Nasr (ed.), *Islamic Spirituality: Foundations*, New York, Crossroads, 1987, pp. 265–93.

15 See the many works of Henry Corbin, for example, his *Creative Imagination in the Sufism of Ibn ʿArabi*, Princeton, Princeton University Press, 1969.

10 Intellectual culture

1 Edgar V. McKnight, *Post-modern Use of the Bible: The Emergence of Reader-oriented Criticism*, Nashville, Abingdon Press, 1988, p. 108.

2 See Lawrence I. Conrad, "The Arab-Islamic Medical Tradition," in L. I. Conrad et al., *The Western Medical Tradition, 800 BC to AD 1800*, Cambridge, Cambridge University Press, 1995, pp. 93–138.

3 Conrad, "Medical Tradition", p. 103.

4 See G. R. Hawting, "The Development of the Biography of al-Ḥārith ibn Kalada and the Relationship Between Medicine and Islam," in C. E. Bosworth, et al. (eds), *The Islamic World From Classical to Modern Times: Essays in Honor of Bernard Lewis*, Princeton, Darwin Press, 1989, pp. 127–40.

5 See Michael W. Dols, *The Black Death in the Middle East*, Princeton, Princeton University Press, 1977.

6 Ibn Khaldūn, *al-Muqaddima*, as quoted in Dols, *Black Death*, p. 90.

7 Dols, *Black Death*, p. 109.

8 Franz Rosenthal, "The Defense of Medicine in the Medieval Muslim World," *Bulletin of the History of Medicine*, 43 (1969), 523, reprinted in his *Science and Medicine in Islam: A Collection of Essays*, Aldershot, Variorum, 1990, chapter 8.

9 For further details on this issue see David A. King, "Science in the Service of Religion: the Case of Islam," *Impact of Science on Society*, 159 (1990), 245–62, reprinted in his *Astronomy in the Service of Islam*, Aldershot, Variorum/Ashgate, 1993, chapter 1.

10 Translation based on the material found at the web site http://users.erols.com/gmqm/euromed3.html. The full text is available in translation: William Alexander Greenhill, *A Treatise on the Small-pox and Measles*

Notes 305

by *Abú Becr Mohammed ibn Zacaríyá al-Rází*, London, Sydenham Society, 1848.

11 G. Anawati, "Science," in P. M. Holt, A. K. S. Lambton and B. Lewis (eds), *The Cambridge History of Islam*, Cambridge, Cambridge University Press, 1970, vol. 2, pp. 743–4.

12 Majid Fakhry, *A Short Introduction to Islamic Philosophy, Theology and Mysticism*, Oxford, Oneworld, 1997, p. 48.

13 Ibn Qutayba, *'Uyūn al-Akhbār*, Cairo, Dār al-Kutub Press, 1925–30, as quoted in Dimitri Gutas, *Greek Thought, Arabic Culture: The Graeco-Arabic Translation Movement in Baghdad and Early 'Abbāsid Society (2nd–4th/8th–10th Centuries)*, London, Routledge, 1998, p. 159.

11 Medieval visions of Islam

1 Norman Calder, "Tafsīr from Ṭabarī to Ibn Kathīr. Problems in the Description of a Genre Illustrated with Reference to the Story of Abraham," in G. R. Hawting and A.-K. A. Shareef, *Approaches to the Qur'ān*, London, Routledge, 1993, pp. 103–4.

2 See Calder, "Tafsīr," pp. 130–1.

3 Ibn Taymiyya, *Muqaddima fī Uṣūl al-Tafsīr*, in his *Daqā'iq a-Tafsīr*, Muḥammad Jalaynad (ed.), Cairo, Dār al-Anṣār, 1978, vol. 1, pp. 76–81 (portions only).

4 Nehemia Levtzion, "Eighteenth Century Sufi Brotherhoods: Structural, Organizational and Ritual Changes," in Peter G. Riddell and Tony Street (eds), *Islam: Essays on Scripture, Thought and Society: A Festschrift in Honour of Anthony H. Johns*, Leiden, E. J. Brill, 1997, pp. 147–60.

5 Levtzion, "Eighteenth Century," pp. 150–1.

6 Both of these matters are vividly displayed in the documentary film "Souhait d'extase: *dhikr* de la Rifa'iyya de Damas (Syrie)", a CNRS film directed by Jean-Claude Penrad (Paris, 1997) in which the *silsila* of the group incorporates 'Abd al-Qādir al-Jilānī and al-Rifā'ī. Mortification of the flesh, perhaps more commonly noted among the Qādiriyya, is also displayed. The appeal to Ḥusayn, son of 'Alī, which occurs at one point in the film, may not be so much a matter of classical syncretism as a result of the contemporary environment of Syria.

7 Levtzion "Eighteenth Century," p. 152; Hamid Algar, "Silent and Vocal *Dhikr* in the Naqshbandī Order," in Albert Dietrich (ed.), *Akten des VII. Kongresses für Arabistik und Islamwissenschaft*, Göttingen, Vandenhoeck und Ruprecht, 1976, pp. 39–46.

8 Fazlur Rahman, "Internal Religious Developments in the Present Century Islam," *Cahiers d'histoire mondiale/Journal of World History*, 2 (1955), 863–4.

9 For this point in its overall context see Yvonne Haddad, "Muslim Revivalist Thought in the Arab World," *The Muslim World*, 76 (1986), 143–67; for more details see also John O. Voll, "Renewal and Reform in Islamic History: Tajdid and Islah," in John L. Esposito (ed.), *Voices of Resurgent Islam*, New York, Oxford University Press, 1983, pp. 32–47.

10 Fazlur Rahman, "Islam: Challenges and Opportunities," in Alford T. Welch and Pierre Cachia (eds), *Islam: Past Influences and Future Challenges*, Edinburgh, Edinburgh University Press, 1979, p. 317.

11 See P. Shinar, "Traditional and Reformist Mawlid Celebrations in the Maghrib," in Myriam Rosen-Ayalon (ed.), *Studies in Memory of Gaston Wiet*, Jerusalem, Institute of Asian and African Studies, Hebrew University, 1977, pp. 371–413; N. J. G. Kaptein, *Muḥammad's Birthday Festival: Early History in the Central Muslim Lands and Development in the Muslim West until the 10th/16th century*, Leiden, E. J. Brill, 1993.

12 Morroe Berger, *Islam in Egypt Today: Social and Political Aspects of Popular Religion*, Cambridge, Cambridge University Press, 1970, p. 83 (see pp. 81–4 on the *mawlid*s in general); see also J. W. McPherson, *The Moulids of Egypt (Egyptian Saint-days)*, Cairo, N. M. Press, 1941, who lists 126 *mawlid*s among both Muslims and Christians.

13 The way in which this aspect functions in Moroccan society – the monarchy as legitimized through its association with Muḥammad – is the emphasis of M. E. Combs-Schilling, *Sacred Performances: Islam, Sexuality, and Sacrifice*, New York, Columbia University Press, 1989, esp. pp. 160–74 on the *mawlid*.

14 See, for example, the poem by al-Barzanjī (d. 1766) an extract of which (on the birth of Muḥammad) is quoted in Andrew Rippin and Jan Knappert, *Textual Sources for the Study of Islam*, Manchester, Manchester University Press, 1986, section 3.2.1.

15 Earle H. Waugh, *The Munshidīn of Egypt: Their World and their Song*, Columbia, University of South Carolina Press, 1989, p. 189, quoted and translated from a book entitled *Al-Qāmūs al-Jadīd fī'l-Qaṣā'id wa'l-Anāshīd*, Cairo, n.d., which Waugh describes as a collection of panegyric poems used by professional religious singers in contemporary Egypt.

16 Waugh, *Munshidīn*, p. 100.

17 An excellent summary of the position of Sufism in the eighteenth through twentieth centuries, with relevant bibliography, is found in Chapter 4 of Julian Baldick, *Mystical Islam: An Introduction to Sufism*, London, I. B. Taurus, 1989.

12 Describing modernity

1 M. G. S. Hodgson, *The Venture of Islam: Conscience and History in a World Civilization*, vol. 3: *The Gunpowder Empires and Modern Times*, Chicago, University of Chicago Press, 1974, p. 216.

2 Kenneth Cragg, "Religious Developments in Islam in the 20th Century," *Cahiers d'histoire mondiale/Journal of World History*, 3 (1956), 505.

3 Fazlur Rahman, *Islam*, 2nd edition, Chicago, University of Chicago Press, 1979, p. 214.

4 Harvey Cox, *Religion in the Secular City: Toward a Postmodern Theology*, New York, Simon and Schuster, 1984, p. 182.

5 See David Lowenthal, *The Past is a Foreign Country*, Cambridge, Cambridge University Press, 1985, for illustrations of a variety of aspects of this.

6 In his *Facing Up to Modernity: Excursions in Society, Politics, and Religion*, New York, Basic Books, 1977, pp. 70–80.

7 See Cox, *Religion in the Secular City*, p. 183.

8 See R. J. Zwi Werblowsky, *Beyond Tradition and Modernity: Changing Religions in a Changing World*, London, The Athlone Press, 1976, p. 11.

9 See Werblowsky, *Beyond Tradition*, pp. 23–6.
10 See Edward Said, *Orientalism,* New York, Pantheon Books, 1978.
11 See, for example, W. M. Watt, *Islamic Fundamentalism and Modernity,* London, Routledge, 1988, and my review of that book in *Journal of Semitic Studies,* 36 (1991), 367–9.
12 Cited from an unnamed source in Emmanuel Sivan, *Radical Islam: Medieval Theology and Modern Politics,* New Haven, CT, Yale University Press, 1985, p. 11.
13 See John J. Donohue, "Islam and the Search for Identity in the Arab World', in John L. Esposito (ed.), *Voices of Resurgent Islam,* New York, Oxford University Press, 1983, pp. 48–61.
14 See Fouad Ajami, *The Arab Predicament: Arab Political Thought and Practice since 1967,* Cambridge, Cambridge University Press, 1981, for some views (many quite controversial) on the impact of the 1967 Arab-Israeli war and the 1973 oil boycott.
15 See Bruce B. Lawrence, *Defenders of God: The Fundamentalist Revolt against the Modern Age,* San Francisco, Harper and Row, 1989, p. 195, who refers to this with the nice formulation, "the mythologization of oil."
16 Sivan, *Radical Islam,* p. 11.
17 Film has proven an ideal medium for conveying these issues, both in stimulating the problem and in critiquing it. See, for example, the biting social critique of modern Arab life presented in the 1989 Algerian/French film "De Hollywood à Tamanrasset" directed by Mahmoud Zemmouri. In a more subtle way, the Iranian films of Abbas Kiarostami provide a similar vision.
18 Allan Bloom, *The Closing of the American Mind,* New York, Simon and Schuster, 1987, pp. 69, 73, 74. The American public's self-flagellation in creating a best-seller of this work must be understood as a part of the general ambivalence felt by many toward the modern period.
19 Clifford Geertz, *Islam Observed: Religious Development in Morocco and Indonesia,* New Haven, CT, Yale University Press, 1968, p. 3.
20 See, for example, the discussion of these concepts in Mohammed Arkoun, *Rethinking Islam Today,* Washington, DC, Center for Contemporary Arab Studies, Georgetown University, 1987, pp. 13–14.
21 Seyyid Hossein Nasr, "The Shari'ah and Changing Historical Conditions," in his *Islamic Life and Thought,* Albany, State University of New York Press, 1981, pp. 27–30.
22 Werblowsky, *Beyond Tradition,* p. 19.
23 See Cox, *Religion in the Secular City,* p. 186.
24 Cox, *Religion in the Secular City,* pp. 186–7.
25 The terms "normative," "neo-normative," and "acculturating" are used in Yvonne Y. Haddad, *Contemporary Islam and the Challenge of History,* Albany, State University of New York Press, 1982, pp. 7–12. See also William E. Shepard, "Islam and Ideology: Towards a Typology," *International Journal of Middle East Studies,* 19 (1987), 307–36, esp. pp. 327–8, note 2, for a full review of other terms and categories used in various analyses. It may also be observed that this kind of separation makes some sense in comparative religion terms if the categories are seen in terms of both authority of the past and attitude to change: Judaism's

division between Orthodox, Conservative and Reform and even Christianity's Catholic, Evangelical and Protestant may all be analysed in
these terms. The history of the development of these groups makes the
situation of each religion quite different, however.

26 See John Esposito, "Tradition and Modernization in Islam," in Charles
Wei-hsun Fu and Gerhard E. Spiegler (eds), *Movements and Issues in
World Religions. A Sourcebook and Analysis of Developments since 1945:
Religion, Ideology, and Politics*, New York, Greenwood Press, 1987, p.
96.

27 Watt, *Islamic Fundamentalism*, Chapter 1, argues that this position is
inherent in Islam because of its view of religion as unchanging, linked
to the notion of the eternal word of God, etc. He also sees this as a
reflection of ancient bedouin notions of the world which are fully
engrained in the Islamic ethos. This all seems highly doubtful.

28 See Fazlur Rahman, "Islam: Challenges and Opportunities," in Alford
T. Welch and Pierre Cachia (eds), *Islam: Past Influence and Present
Challenge*, Edinburgh, Edinburgh University Press, 1979, pp. 317–18.

29 See William Shepard, "'Fundamentalism' Christian and Islamic,"
Religion, 17 (1987), 355–78; see also his "What is 'Islamic fundamentalism'?" *Studies in Religion*, 17 (1988), 5–26.

30 See Shepard, "'Fundamentalism',," and the critiques of it by Bruce
Lawrence and Azim Nanji, *Religion*, 19 (1989), 275–84.

31 Lawrence, *Defenders of God*, passim, e.g., p. 201.

32 See *Encyclopaedia of Islam, New Edition*, "*Iṣlāḥ*" (by Ali Merad).

33 See Ali Merad, "Reformism in Modern Islam," *Cultures*, 4 (1977), 108–27.

34 Shepard, "Islam and Ideology," p. 313.

13 Muḥammad and modernity

1 See James E. Royster, "Muḥammad as Teacher and Exemplar," *The
Muslim World*, 68 (1978), 235–56, although note that not all of his sources
are from the contemporary period.

2 For a summary of various modern views on this aspect of Muḥammad's
biography see Jamel Eddine Bencheikh, *Le voyage nocturne de Mahomet*,
Paris, Imprimerie Nationale, 1988, pp. 251–7.

3 For an overview of the topic see Annemarie Schimmel, *And Muḥammad
is His Messenger: The Veneration of the Prophet in Islamic Piety*, Chapel
Hill, University of North Carolina Press, 1985, especially the last two
chapters; the work also has an excellent bibliography.

4 Muḥammad Ḥusayn Haykal, *The Life of Muḥammad*, Isma'il Ragi A.
al Faruqi (trans.), Indianapolis, IN, North American Trust Publications,
1976, pp. 579–80.

5 See Charles D. Smith, *Islam and the Search for Social Order in Modern
Egypt: A Biography of Muḥammad Ḥusayn Haykal*, Albany, NY, State
University of New York Press, 1983, pp. 113–25.

6 Haykal, *Muḥammad*, pp. 184–5.

7 Jacques Jomier, "Une vie de Mohammad, apôtre de la liberté," *Mélanges
d'institut dominicain d'études orientales du Caire*, 8 (1964–6), 395–400;
also Antoine Wessels, *A Modern Arabic Biography of Muḥammad:
A Critical Study of Muḥammad Ḥusayn Haykal's Ḥayāt Muḥammad*,

Leiden, E. J. Brill, 1972, pp. 19–24; M. M. Badawi, "Islam in Modern Egyptian Literature," in his *Modern Arabic Literature and the West*, London, Ithaca Press, 1985, pp. 61–3.

8 Abd al-Rahman Azzam, *The Eternal Message of Muḥammad*, New York, Devin-Adair, 1964; Mentor Books, 1965, pp. 204–5.

9 Azzam, *Eternal Message*, pp. 141–2.

10 Kenneth Cragg, *The Pen and the Faith: Eight Modern Muslim Writers and the Qur'ān*, London, George Allen and Unwin, 1985, p. 159. It should be noted that some have argued against this sort of interpretation of Maḥfūẓ's work, but such tendencies seem to aim more toward saving Maḥfūẓ from charges of blasphemy than appreciation of the literary merits of the work; as an example, see Jareer Abu-Haidar, "Awlād Ḥāratinā by Najīb Maḥfūẓ: an Event in the Arab World," *Journal of Arabic Literature*, 16 (1985), 119–31.

11 Wessels, *Modern Arabic Biography*, pp. 24–9.

12 See Malise Ruthven in *The (London) Times Literary Supplement*, November 25–December 1, 1988, p. 1312.

13 Cragg, *Pen and the Faith*, pp. 157–8.

14 Issa J. Boullata, *Trends and Issues in Contemporary Arab Thought*, Albany, State University of New York Press, 1990, p. 132.

15 Fatima Mernissi, *Beyond the Veil: Male–Female Dynamics in Modern Muslim Society*, revised edition, Bloomington, Indiana University Press, 1987, p. 9.

16 Fatima Mernissi, *Women and Islam: An Historical and Theological Enquiry*, Oxford, Basil Blackwell, 1991, p. 104. This is the translation of Mernissi's French work *Le harem politique: le prophète et les femmes*, Paris, A. Michel, 1987, which has been published in the United States under the title *The Veil and the Male Elite: A Feminist Interpretation of Women's Rights in Islam*, Reading, MA, Addison-Wesley, 1991.

17 Mernissi, *Women and Islam*, pp. 163–4.

18 Mernissi, *Women and Islam*, p. 185.

19 Ali Dashti, *Twenty-Three Years: A Study of the Prophetic Career of Mohammad*, F. R. C. Bagley (trans.), London, George Allen and Unwin, 1985, p. 158; also see my review of this book in *Bulletin of the School of Oriental and African Studies*, 50 (1987), 547–8.

20 Dashti, *Twenty-Three Years*, p. 208.

21 Dashti, *Twenty-Three Years*, p. 137.

22 On Khomeini's use of Shī'ī symbols in general see Mangol Bayat, "The Iranian Revolution of 1978–79: Fundamentalist or Modern," *Middle East Journal*, 7 (1983), 30–42.

23 Shaykh Muḥammad Mahdī Shams al-Dīn, *The Rising of al-Ḥusayn: Its Impact on the Consciousness of Muslim Society*, I. K. A. Howard (trans.), London, Muhammadi Trust, 1985, p. xiii. The foreword, from which this quote comes, is signed "The Muhammadi Trust." The book was one in a series planned to consist of four titles written in the 1970s by Muḥammad Mahdī Shams al-Dīn on Ḥusayn.

24 Shams al-Din, *Rising*, p. 23.

25 An example of this in English would be Martin Lings, *Muḥammad: His Life Based on the Earliest Sources*, London, George Allen and Unwin, 1983.

26 Aslam Jayrājpūrī, teacher of Ghulām Aḥmad Parvēz, as cited in J. M. S. Baljon, "Pakistani Views of Ḥadīth," *Die Welt des Islams*, NS 5 (1958), 225. Also see Daniel W. Brown, *Rethinking Tradition in Modern Islamic Thought*, Cambridge, Cambridge University Press, 1996, pp. 68–80.

27 Sheila McDonough, *The Authority of the Past: A Study of Three Muslim Modernists*, Chambersburg, PA, American Academy of Religion, p. 3.

28 Aziz Ahmad, *Islamic Modernism in India and Pakistan 1857–1964*, London, Oxford University Press, 1967, p. 37.

29 McDonough, *Authority*, p. 12.

30 Ahmad, *Islamic Modernism*, p. 50.

31 McDonough, *Authority*, p. 14.

32 See R. A. Butler, "Ghulam Ahmad Parvez: Ideological Revolution Through the Qur'an," *Al-Mushir*, 17 (1975), 1–37.

33 G. A. Parwez, *Islam: A Challenge to Religion*, Lahore, Idara-e-Tulu-e-Islam, 1968, provides a good introduction to his general thought as connected to the Qur'ān.

34 J. M. S. Baljon, *Modern Muslim Koran Interpretation (1880–1960)*, Leiden, E. J. Brill, 1961, pp. 17–19; also Baljon, "Pakistani Views of Ḥadīth," pp. 219–27.

35 Muslim ibn al-Ḥajjāj, *Ṣaḥīḥ Muslim, Kitāb al-Zuhd wa'l-Raqā'iq*, Muḥammad Fu'ād ʿAbd al-Bāqī (ed.), Cairo, Dār Iḥyā' al-Kutub al-ʿArabiyya, 1951, vol. 4, pp. 2298–9, tradition no. 72. See the treatment of the discussion of this point in Egypt in G. H. A. Juynboll, *The Authenticity of the Tradition Literature: Discussions in Modern Egypt*, Leiden, E. J. Brill, 1969, chapter 5, esp. pp. 49–50.

36 The motivation in the past appears to have been conservatism – the "fear of innovation" – as compared to today's "rejection of innovation in the past" as pointed out by Baljon, "Pakistani Views of Ḥadith," p. 227, but this may really only indicate the relativeness of all such terms.

37 Quoted in Baljon, "Pakistani Views of Ḥadīth," p. 224, from Parvez's *Maqām-i Ḥadith*.

38 Fazlur Rahman, "Internal Religious Developments in the Present Century Islam," *Cahiers d'histoire mondiale/Journal of World History*, 2 (1955), 873.

39 Charles J. Adams, "The Ideology of Mawlana Mawdudi," in Donald Eugene Smith (ed.), *South Asian Politics and Religion*, Princeton, Princeton University Press, 1966, pp. 371–97; idem., "Mawdudi and the Islamic State," in John L. Esposito (ed.), *Voices of Resurgent Islam*, New York, Oxford University Press, 1983, pp. 99–133; Kurshid Ahmad and Zafar Ishaq Ansari, "Mawlānā Sayyid Abul Aʿlā Mawdūdī: An Introduction to his Vision of Islam and Islamic Revival," in their edited volume, *Islamic Perspectives: Studies in Honour of Mawlānā Sayyid Abul Aʿlā Mawdūdī*, Jedda, Saudi Publishing House; Leicester, The Islamic Foundation, 1979, pp. 359–83.

40 See Elizabeth Sirriyeh, "Modern Muslim Interpretations of Shirk," *Religion*, 20 (1990), 139–59 (esp. 149–51).

41 Baljon, "Pakistani Views of Ḥadith," p. 225.

42 Baljon, "Pakistani Views of Ḥadith," pp. 225–6. For the polemic in the other direction – Mawdūdī against Parvēz – see Maryam Jameelah, "Islam Minus *Sunnah*: a Critical Review of the Work of Ghulam Ahmad

Parvez," in her *Islam and Modernism*, Lahore, Mohammad Yusuf Khan, 1975, pp. 97–104.

43 Charles J. Adams, "The Authority of the Prophetic *Ḥadith* in the Eyes of Some Modern Muslims," in Donald P. Little (ed.), *Essays on Islamic Civilization presented to Niyazi Berkes*, Leiden, E. J. Brill, 1976, p. 35.

44 The Mecca/Medina split has become a motif in some Muslim Islamist movments; see, for example, the use made of it by Maḥmūd Muḥammad Ṭāhā (d. 1985) of the Sudan in his *The Second Message of Islam*, Syracuse, Syracuse University Press, 1987.

14 The Qur'ān and modernity

1 Cf. John B. Henderson, *Scripture, Canon and Commentary: A Comparison of Confucian and Western Exegesis*, Princeton, Princeton University Press, 1991, p. 221: "The abandonment or supersession of commentarial forms in the intellectual culture of early-modern times has often gone unremarked. Yet this development is probably of greater significance in the intellectual transition between the medieval and modern worlds than most of the great ideas of leading philosophers and scientists of this same age. For the form of the commentary influenced modes of thought, and did not just provide the format for their expression."

2 Fazlur Rahman, "Internal Religious Developments in the Present Century Islam," *Cahiers d'histoire mondiale/Journal of World History,* 2 (1955), 872.

3 On 'Abduh, see Charles C. Adams, *Islam and Modernism in Egypt: A Study of the Modern Reform Movement inaugurated by Muḥammad 'Abduh*, London, Oxford University Press, 1933; also H. A. R. Gibb, *Modern Trends in Islam*, Chicago, University of Chicago Press, 1947, Chapters 2 and 3.

4 See Muḥammad 'Abduh, *The Theology of Unity*, Ishaq Musa'ad and Kenneth Cragg (trans.), London, George Allen and Unwin, 1966.

5 See Jacques Jomier, *Le commentaire coranique du Manar. Tendances modernes de l'exégèse coranique en Egypte*, Paris: Maisonneuve, 1954. In more recent times, Maḥmūd Shaltūt, head of al-Azhar University in Cairo from 1958–63, has continued with this type of moderate modernism in the context of Quranic interpretation; see Kate Zebiri, *Maḥmūd Shaltūt and Islamic Modernism*, Oxford, Clarendon Press, 1993, which also provides an excellent overview of Qur'ān interpretation in the modern context.

6 Helmut Gatje, *The Qur'ān and its Exegesis: Selected Texts with Classical and Modern Muslim interpretations*, Berkeley, University of California Press, 1976, p. 249.

7 Āzād as cited in I. H. Azad Faruqi, *The Tarjuman al-Qur'an: A Critical Analysis of Mawlana Abu'l-Kalam Azad's Approach to the Understanding of the Qur'an*, New Delhi, Vikas Publishing, 1982, p. 73.

8 Ashfaque Husain, *The Quintessence of Islam: A Summary of the Commentary of Maulana Abul Kalam Azad on al-Fateha, the First Chapter of the Quran*, Bombay, Asia Publishing House, 1960, pp. 68, 69 (originally published in 1958 under the title *The Spirit of Islam*).

9 An excellent presentation of the core ideas of the Brotherhood is found

312   *Notes*

in Yvonne Yazbeck Haddad, "The Qur'anic Justification for an Islamic Revolution: the View of Sayyid Qutb," *The Middle East Journal*, 37 (1983), 14–29; also see her "Sayyid Qutb, Ideologue of the Islamic Revival," in John Esposito (ed.), *Voices of Resurgent Islam*, New York, Oxford University Press, 1983, pp. 67–98.

10 Sayyid Qutb, *Fī'l-Ta'rīkh: Fikra wa-Minhaj*, as quoted in Yvonne Y. Haddad, *Contemporary Islam and the Challenge of History*, Albany, State University of New York Press, 1982, p. 90.

11 These are, of course, the ideals claimed for the western liberal, democratic tradition but Qutb emphasizes the absolute sovereignty of God within a truly Islamic society; see Leonard Binder, *Islamic Liberalism: A Critique of Development Ideologies*, Chicago, University of Chicago Press, 1988, Chapter 5.

12 Sayyid Qutb, *Fī Ẓilāl al-Qur'ān*, Beirut, Dār al-Shurūq, 1973–4, translated as *In the Shade of the Qur'ān*, M. Adil Saladi and Ashur A. Shamis (trans.), London, MWH London Publishers, 1979, vol. 30, p. 249. On the commentary as a whole, see Ronald Nettler, "A Modern Islamic Confession of Faith and Conception of Religion: Sayyid Qutb's Introduction to the *Tafsīr, Fī Ẓilāl al-Qur'ān*," *British Journal of Middle East Studies*, 21 (1994), 102–14.

13 See Emmanuel Sivan, *Radical Islam: Medieval Theology and Modern Politics*, New Haven, CT, Yale University Press, 1985, Chapter 2.

14 A. H. Johns, "Let my People Go! Sayyid Qutb and the Vocation of Moses," *Islam and Christian-Muslim Relations*, 1 (1990), 143–70.

15 See Binder, *Islamic Liberalism*, pp. 190ff in reference to Sayyid Qutb's work *al-Taṣwīr al-Fannī fī'l-Qur'ān*; also see Johns, "Let My People Go!" p. 148 and Issa J. Boullata "The Rhetorical Interpretation of the Qur'ān: I'jāz and Related Topics," in Andrew Rippin (ed.), *Approaches to the History of the Interpretation of the Qur'ān*, Oxford, Oxford University Press, 1988, pp. 150–1.

16 See J. Jomier, "Le Cheikh Tantawi Jawhari (1862–1940) et son commentaire du Coran," *Mélanges de l'institut dominicain d'études orientales du Caire*, 5 (1958), 115–74; F. de Jong, "The Works of Ṭanṭāwī Jawharī (1862–1940): Some Bibliographical and Biographical Notes," *Bibliotheca Orientalis*, 34 (1977), 153–61.

17 Haluk Nurbaki, *Verses from the Glorious Koran and the Facts of Science* (V), Metin Beynam (trans.), Ankara, Turkish Foundation for Religious Publications, 1986, p. 44. There are many other examples of such books in English; see, for example, Ghulam Sarwar, *Philosophy of the Quran*, Lahore, Muhammad Ashraf, 1938.

18 This statement comes from an interview with Khaled aly Khaled in a side-bar called "Living Islam" in Mary Pat Fisher and Robert Luyster, *Living Religions*, Englewood Cliffs, NJ, Prentice-Hall, 1991, p. 277.

19 See Issa J. Boullata, "Modern Qur'ān Exegesis: a Study of Bint al-Shāti'"s Method," *The Muslim World*, 64 (1974), 103–13.

20 See also J. Jomier, "L'éxègese scientifique du Coran d'après le Cheikh Amin al-Khouli," *Mélanges de l'institut dominicain d'études orientales du Caire*, 4 (1957), 269–80.

21 Shabbir Akhtar, *A Faith for All Seasons: Islam and Western Modernity*, London, Bellew, 1990, p. 54.

22 See Ali Merad, *Ibn Badis, commentateur du Coran*, Paris, Librairie Orientaliste Paul Geuthner, 1971.

23 See his *The Quran in Islam: Its Impact and Influence on the Life of Muslims*, Assadullah ad-Dhaakir Yate (trans.), London, Zahra Publications, 1987; also S. H. Nasr, H. Dabashi, S. Vali Reza Nasr (eds), *Shi'ism: Doctrines, Thought and Spirituality*, Albany, State University of New York Press, 1988, Chapter 3, on Ṭabāṭabā'ī and another contemporary Iranian thinker, Ayatollah Murtaḍā Muṭahharī.

24 See A. H. Johns, "Quranic Exegesis in the Malay World: In Search of a Profile," in Rippin (ed.), *Approaches*, pp. 275–8. For contemporary, printed *tafsīr*s, see Howard M. Federspiel, "An Introduction to Qur'anic Commentaries in Contemporary Southeast Asia," *The Muslim World*, 81 (1991), 149–65, and idem, *Popular Indonesian Literature of the Qur'ān*, Ithaca, NY, Modern Indonesia Project, 1992.

25 Rather than provide my own translation of these three Quranic passages, I have used the translation of Abdullah Yusuf Ali, *The Holy Qur-an*, Beirut, Dar al-Arabia, 1968, but many prints exist; this translation is accompanied by an extensive commentary in the footnotes which exhibit Modernist tendencies (especially in the desire to "spiritualize"' various aspects) which are also reflected in the translation itself.

26 As for example in the Aḥmadī translation by Maulawi Sher Ali.

27 Akhtar, *Faith*, chapter 3, also argues against the traditional assessment of the Qur'ān in terms of its form – an argument which has no persuasive value among opponents, he says – and prefers the argument from results. He does not use this as a basis for questioning the non-contingent nature of the text (which he maintains) but simply as a more effective argument.

28 See, for example, Fazlur Rahman, *Major Themes of the Qur'ān*, Minneapolis, MN, Bibliotheca Islamica, 1982, p. 98.

29 Edgar Krentz, *The Historical Critical Method*, Philadelphia, Fortress Press, 1975, p. 19.

30 Krentz, *Historical Critical Method*, p. 24.

31 Krentz, *Historical Critical Method*, p. 33, quoting and translating Ulrich Wilckens, "Über die Bedeutung historischer Kritik in der modernen Bibelexegese," in *Was heisst Auslegung der Heiligen Schrift?*, Regensburg, Friedrich Pustet, 1966, p. 133.

32 See Jacques Jomier, "Quelques positions actuelles de l'éxègese coranique en Egypte révélées par une polemique recente (1947–1951)," *Mélanges d'institut dominicain d'études orientales du Caire*, 1 (1954), 39–72, in connection with the Arabic translation of the *Encyclopaedia of Islam* article on *tafsīr* by al-Khūlī.

33 See Haddad, *Contemporary Islam*, pp. 46–53; see also Haddad's article, "Islamic 'Awakening' in Egypt," *Arab Studies Quarterly*, 9 (1987), 241, for observations on Khalaf Allāh's present political role in presenting the religious plank of a leftist-leaning party in Egypt. Donald Malcolm Reid, "Cairo University and the Orientalists," *International Journal of Middle East Studies*, 19 (1987), 51–76, usefully views Khalaf Allāh in the light of the broader social context of the time.

34 The judicial aspects of the case are reviewed in Kilian Bälz, "Submitting Faith to Judicial Scrutiny through the Family Trial: The 'Abû Zayd' Case," *Die Welt des Islams*, 37 (1997), 133–55

35 Nasr Abu Zayd, "The Dilemma of the Literary Approach to the Qur'ān: A Study of Amīn al-Khūlī's Thought," in N. Abu Zayd and D. van der Meij (eds), *Qur'anic Studies on the Eve of the 21st Century,* forthcoming (typescript p. 21). The main work of Abū Zayd which develops his ideas regarding the Qur'ān is *Mafhūm al-Naṣṣ: Dirāsa fī 'Ulūm al-Qur'ān* ("The Concept of the Text: A Study in the Sciences of the Qur'ān"), Cairo, Marzak al-Thaqāfī 'l-'Arabī, 1990.

36 Akhtar, *Faith,* p. 69.

37 Akhtar, *Faith,* pp. 70–1.

38 Akhtar, *Faith,* p. 74.

39 For a brief, but well expressed appreciation, see W. A. Bijlefeld, "In Memoriam: Dr. Fazlur Rahman," *The Muslim World,* 79 (1989), 80–1.

40 Rahman, *Major Themes,* p. 48, deals with moral ideals versus the legal plane on the issue of polygamy as an example of this.

41 Fazlur Rahman, *Islam,* second edition, Chicago, University of Chicago Press, 1979, pp. 38–9.

42 See Fazlur Rahman, *Islam and Modernity: Transformation of an Intellectual Tradition,* Chicago, University of Chicago Press, 1982, Chapter 1.

43 A lucid introduction to his work may be found in Issa J. Boullata, *Trends and Issues in Contemporary Arab Thought,* Albany, State University of New York Press, 1990, pp. 79–85.

44 Mohammed Arkoun, "The Death Penalty and Torture in Islamic Thought," *Concilium,* 120 (1979), 78.

45 See Boullata, *Trends and Issues,* pp. 80–1.

46 Fatima Mernissi, *Beyond the Veil: Male–Female Dynamics in Modern Muslim Society,* revised edition, Bloomington, Indiana University Press, 1987, p. 9.

15 Issues of identity

1 See the observations in Charles J. Adams, "Islamic Resurgence: Religion and Politics in the Muslim World," in Nigel Biggar, Jamie S. Scott and William Schweiker (eds), *Cities of Gods: Faith, Politics and Pluralism in Judaism, Christianity and Islam,* New York, Greenwood Press, 1986, pp. 167–91, esp. p. 169.

2 See Malise Ruthven, *A Satanic Affair: Salman Rushdie and the Rage of Islam,* London, Chatto and Windus, 1990, pp. 132–3, for further reflections along this line.

3 Note, for example, the study by M. Ali Kettani, *Muslim Minorities in the World Today,* London, Mansell, 1986, and the focus of interest revealed in the *Journal: Institute of Muslim Minority Affairs.*

4 Michael M. J. Fischer, Mehdi Abedi, *Debating Muslims: Cultural Dialogues in Postmodernity and Tradition,* Madison, University of Wisconsin Press, 1990, p. 303. This book is a valuable treatment from an anthropological perspective of diaspora Muslim adjustment (as well as covering many other topics of interest).

5 Sayyid Abul A'la Mawdudi, *Let Us be Muslims,* Khurram Murad (ed. and trans.), Leicester, The Islamic Foundation, 1985, p. 71 (first published in Urdu in 1940; also translated under the title *The Fundamentals of Islam*).

6 Rolf Reichert, "Muslims in the Guyanas: A Socio-economic Overview," *Journal: Institute of Muslim Minority Affairs,* 3/ii (1981), 123; also cited in Kettani, *Muslim Minorities*, pp. 203–5. The problem is said by Reichert (pp. 123–4) to stem from the "ignorance" of the *sharīʿa* on the part of the Javanese but that hardly seems sufficient as an explanation of the issue.

7 S. D. Goitein, "The Origin and Nature of the Muslim Friday Worship," in his *Studies in Islamic History and Institutions*, Leiden, E. J. Brill, 1966, p. 125.

8 Ruthven, *Satanic Affair*, p. 72, also p. 158.

9 For some reflections on this issue, see Earle H. Waugh, "The Imam in the New World. Models and Modifications," in Frank E. Reynolds and Theodore M. Ludwig (eds), *Transitions and Transformations in the History of Religions: Essays in Honor of Joseph M. Kitagawa*, Leiden, E. J. Brill, 1980, pp. 124–49.

10 This statement is found in the pamphlet, "Concepts of Worship in Islam," distributed by the World Assembly of Muslim Youth from Riyadh, Saudi Arabia.

11 "The True Religious Value of Daily Prayers," *Hong Kong Muslim Herald*, vol. 14, no. 5 (Rabi-Thani 1412 AH [October 1991]), p. 2–2 [sic].

12 Habib Bourguiba, "For Ramadan Reform," in Benjamin Rivlin, Joseph S. Szyliowicz (eds), *The Contemporary Middle East: Tradition and Innovation*, New York, Random House, 1965, pp. 169–73 (reprinted from an address by President Bourguiba on February 6, 1961, according to this source, translated and published by the Tunisian Secretariat of State for Information); Francis Hours, "A propos du jeûne du mois de Ramadan en Tunisie," *Orient*, 13 (1960), 43–52; S. D. Goitein, "Ramadan, the Muslim Month of Fasting," in his *Studies*, pp. 106–8.

13 Hava Lazarus-Yafeh, "Contemporary Religious Thought among the 'Ulama of al-Azhar," in her *Some Religious Aspects of Islam: A Collection of Articles*, Leiden, E. J. Brill, 1981, p. 98.

14 J. Jomier and J. Corbon, "Le Ramadan, au Caire, en 1956," *Mélanges d'institut dominicain d'études orientales du Caire,* 3 (1956), 1–74, esp. pp. 46–8.

15 Kamil al-Shinnawi, "Against Ramadan Reform," reprinted in Rivlin and Szyliowicz (eds), *Contemporary Middle East*, pp. 174–8.

16 Albert Hourani, *Arabic Thought in the Liberal Age 1798–1939*, 2nd edition, Cambridge, Cambridge University Press, 1983, p. 350.

17 "Ramadan 'Hip' on the Club Scene: Tradition now Fashionable among Young Urbanites in Ramallah," *The (Toronto) Globe and Mail*, January 7, 2000, page A8.

18 See Cyril Glassé, *The Concise Encyclopedia of Islam*, New York, HarperCollins, 1989, pp. 81–4, s.v. "Calendar"; see also the discussion in Jomier and Corbon, "Le Ramadan," pp. 8–12.

19 See Lazarus-Yafeh, "Contemporary Religious Thought," p. 96.

20 See M.A. Mannan, *Islamic Economics: Theory and Practice*, new and revised edition, London, Hodder and Stoughton, 1986, esp. Chapter 13, "Some Aspects of Public Finance in Islam." Mannan grapples with some of the difficulties with the modern implementation of *zakāt* as a tax system, for example regarding the impact of inflation.

21 See the discussion in Ann Elizabeth Mayer, "Islamization and Taxation in Pakistan," in Anita M. Weiss (ed.), *Islamic Reassertion in Pakistan: The Application of Islamic Laws in a Modern State*, Syracuse, NY, Syracuse University Press, 1986, pp. 59–77, which also points out the difficulties involved in the differences between Sunnī and Shīʿī taxation systems and the implications of the government imposition of the Sunnī version.

22 Lazarus-Yafeh, "Contemporary Religious Thought," pp. 101–2.

23 Zaki Badawi, "Zakat: A New Source of Development Finance?" *Q News: A Muslim Magazine*, 310 (August 1999), p. 32.

24 Kenneth Craig, *The Dome and the Rock: Jerusalem Studies in Islam*, London, SPCK, 1964, p. 52, an argument attributed to Maḥmūd Shaltūt.

25 "The Way of *Zakāt*," *Asia Week*, Sept. 13, 1991, p. 63.

26 Badawi, "Zakat," p. 33.

27 For an overview, see J. Jomier, "Le pèlerinage musulman vu du Caire vers 1960," *Mélanges d'institut dominicain d'études orientales du Caire*, 9 (1967), 1–72.

28 Hava Lazarus-Yafeh, "Modern Muslim Attitudes towards the Kaʿba and the Ḥadjdj: the Rise of Neo-fundamentalism in Contemporary Islam," in her *Some Religious Aspects of Islam*, pp. 106–29.

29 Quoted in Lazarus-Yafeh, "Modern Muslim Attitudes," p. 111.

30 See J. Michot, "'La signification du pèlerinage (Hajj) dans trois brochures populaires égyptiennes'", *Mélanges d'institut dominicain d'études orientales du Caire*, 18 (1988), 211–42.

31 See Richard Antoun's analysis of ʿAlī Sharīʿātī's book *Hajj* in his *Muslim Preacher in the Modern World: A Jordanian Case Study in Comparative Perspective*, Princeton, NJ, Princeton University Press, 1989, pp. 176–82. Also see Fischer, Abedi, *Debating Muslims*, chapter 3.

32 These figures come from Fouad al-Farsy, *Modernity and Tradition: The Saudi Equation*, London, Kegan Paul International, 1990, pp. 28–33, derived from information provided by the Deputy Ministry of the Interior for Passport and Civil Status. This book was distributed in 1991 by the Ministry of Information, Kingdom of Saudi Arabia; it also provides a breakdown by country for pilgrimage participation in 1987, giving, according to the author, "some indication of the religious devotion of Muslims of the different countries." More current figures are available in the press releases at the Web site of the Embassy of Saudi Arabia in the United States (www.saudiembassy.net).

33 See the Web site www.iad.org/books/HU-visa.html and /POI.html (pages of the "Islamic Affairs Department" at the Embassy of Saudi Arabia in the United States).

34 Embassy of Saudi Arabia press release, March 20, 1999, found at www.saudiembassy.net/press_release/99_spa/hajj99.html#Nayef

35 "Hajj and the Ummah's Modern International Relations," in Kalim Siddiqui (ed.), *Issues in the Islamic Movement 1983–4*, London, Open Press, 1985, pp. 98–9.

36 David Long, *The Hajj Today: A Survey of the Contemporary Makkan Pilgrimage*, Albany, State University of New York Press, 1979, p. 127; this work is an excellent presentation of the many issues related to the pilgrimage raised in the modern context.

37 Antoun, *Muslim Preacher*, p. 168. This mode of analysis of the *hajj* is also found in Juan Eduardo Campo, "The Mecca Pilgrimage in the Formation of Islam in Modern Egypt," in Jamie Scott and Paul Simpson-Housley (eds), *Sacred Places and Profane Spaces: Essays in the Geographies of Judaism, Christianity and Islam*, Westport, CT, Greenwood Press, 1991, pp. 145–61; Campo's emphasis falls on the impact of *hajj* participation within three levels of religious discourse: governmental, oppositional and popular.

38 Lazarus-Yafeh, "Contemporary Religious Thought," p. 96. See Glassé, *Concise Encyclopedia*, p. 444, for a map of the *mawāqit* and pp. 180–2 for his article on the *iḥrām*.

39 Embassy of Saudi Arabia press release February 14, 1999, at the Web site www.saudiembassy.net/press_release/99_spa/hajj99.html#prep

40 See Richard C. Martin, "Pilgrimage; Muslim Pilgrimage," *Encyclopedia of Religion*, New York, Macmillan, 1987, vol. 11, p. 345. Other specific legal aspects which have been modified in most understandings of the *hajj* ritual are detailed in Jomier, "Le pèlerinage," pp. 68–71, most of which reflect the impact of the large number of people involved and the precise scheduling of events.

41 On the overall economic impact of the *hajj* see the articles in *The Middle East* for August 1987 (pp. 25–6) and August 1988 (p. 31); also see Fischer, Abedi, *Debating Muslims*, pp. 168–70; King, *Hajj Today*, pp. 95–104.

42 C. J. Adams, "Islamic Resurgence," p. 169.

43 Fischer, Abedi, *Debating Muslims*, p. 153.

44 See the volume devoted to "Le post-islamisme," *Revue du monde musulman et de la Méditerranée*, 85–86 (1999).

45 See Nathan J. Brown, "Shariʿa and State in the Modern Muslim Middle East," *International Journal of Middle East Studies*, 29 (1997), 359–76.

46 See Dale F. Eickelman and Jon W. Anderson, "Print, Islam, and the Prospects for Civic Pluralism: New Religious Writings and their Audiences," *Journal of Islamic Studies*, 8 (1997), 43–62.

16 Feminism's Islam

1 For the reaction of men to these pressures see Yvonne Y. Haddad, *Contemporary Islam and the Challenge of History*, Albany, State University of New York Press, 1982, pp. 54–70; our focus here is more on women's discussions than male polemic-apologetic.

2 See the reflections of Susan E. Marshall, "Paradoxes of Change: Culture Crisis, Islamic Revival, and the Reactivation of Patriarchy," *Journal of Asian and African Studies*, 19 (1984), 1–17.

3 Fatima Mernissi, *Beyond the Veil: Male–Female Dynamics in Modern Muslim Society*, revised edition, Bloomington, Indiana University Press, 1987, pp. xxii–xxix. The status of older women may comprise a third category in between these two, but it is far less problematic a group for the jurists in the way in which they have understood the legal requirements. Other groups – unmarried older women, for example – are primarily conceived of as a danger to the social system and, in that sense, are not taken into account except when they violate the status of the other two categories.

4 Lois Beck, "The Religious Lives of Muslim Women," in Jane I. Smith (ed.), *Women in Contemporary Muslim Societies*, Lewisburg, PA, Bucknell University Press, 1980, pp. 27–60. See also Fatima Mernissi, "Women, Saints, and Sanctuaries," *Signs: Journal of Women in Culture and Society*, 3 (1977), 101–12; Robert A. Fernea and Elizabeth W. Fernea, "Variation in Religious Observance among Islamic Women," in Nikki R. Keddie (ed.), *Scholars, Saints, and Sufis: Muslim Religious Institutions in the Middle East since 1500*, Berkeley, University of California Press, 1972, pp. 385–401; among the many anthropological studies which examine the roles women play in Muslim societies, see the exemplary book of Janice Boddy, *Wombs and Alien Spirits: Women, Men and the Zar Cult in Northern Sudan*, Madison, University of Wisconsin Press, 1989.

5 Mohammad Fadel, "Two Women, One Man: Knowledge, Power, and Gender in Medieval Sunni Legal Thought," *International Journal of Middle East Studies*, 29 (1997), 185–204, points out that according to the jurist al-Qarāfī (d. 1285), the discrimination against women in Islamic law, where it is applicable, is there to discourage the role of women in legal situations where it would unnecessarily remove them from their seclusion (see p. 193).

6 Mernissi, *Beyond the Veil*, p. 82.

7 Alifa Rifaat, *Distant View of a Minaret and Other Stories*, Denys Johnston-Davies (trans.), London, Heinemann, 1985.

8 Mernissi, *Beyond the Veil*, p. xv.

9 Maulānā Muhammad 'Alī, *The Religion of Islām: A Comprehensive Discussion of the Sources, Principles and Practices of Islām*, Columbus, OH, Ahmadiyya Anjuman Ishā'at Islām, 1990, revised sixth edition; first published 1936. While this quote comes from an Ahmadī writer (and thus from a "suspect" source in many parts of the Islamic world), most Muslims would have no difficulty in agreeing with the sentiment expressed in it at this point; the modernist stance of Muhammad Ali's writing indicates that the idea of the natural inclinations of men and women as dictating their roles in society is far more widespread than belonging just to Islamist circles (in which it is the standard motif of the discussions). Whether it is possible to deny these "natural" differences (or to what extent one may do so) continues to plague North American feminist thought; see Carol Tavris, *The Mismeasure of Woman*, New York, Simon and Schuster, 1992, who argues, for example, that studies show that men placed in the role of nurturer do just as well as women, and that women are as capable as men of acts of extreme violence.

10 Hajji Shaykh Yusuf (Charles R. Pittman, trans.), "In Defense of the Veil," *The Muslim World*, 33 (1943), 209, reprinted in Benjamin Rivlin, Joseph S. Szyliowicz (eds), *The Contemporary Middle East*, New York, Random House, 1965, p. 358.

11 An idea echoed in certain North American feminist analyses of their own society: see, for example, the feminist classic, Susan Brownmiller, *Against Our Will: Men, Women and Rape*, New York, Simon and Schuster, 1975.

12 See the discussion of this point in Deniz A. Kandiyoti, "Emancipated but Unliberated? Reflections on the Turkish Case," *Feminist Studies*, 13 (1987), 317–38. Some people of course may argue that a "secure sense of gender identity" is not necessarily a welcome end.

13 See the statement by Saddeka Arebi, "Gender Anthropology in the Middle East: the Politics of Muslim Women's Misrepresentation," *American Journal of Islamic Social Sciences*, 8 (1991), 99–108.

14 Jane I. Smith, "The Experience of Muslim Women," in Yvonne Y. Haddad, Byron Haines and Ellison Findly (eds), *The Islamic Impact*, Syracuse, Syracuse University Press, 1984, p. 112, n. 21, citing Mawdūdī.

15 Among her many writings, see Riffat Hassan, "Women in Islam and Christianity: A Comparison," in H. Küng and J. Moltmann (eds), *Islam: A Challenge for Christianity*, Concilium 1999/3, London, SCM Press, 1994, pp. 18–22; "An Islamic Perspective," in Jeanne Becher (ed.), *Women, Religion and Sexuality: Studies on the Impact of Religious Teachings on Women*, Philadelphia, PA, Trinity Press, 1991, pp. 93–128; idem, "Equal Before Allah? Woman-man Equality in the Islamic Tradition," *Harvard Divinity Bulletin*, 17, number 2 (January-May, 1987), 2–4; idem, "On Human Rights and the Qur'ānic Perspective," *Journal of Ecumenical Studies*, 19 (1982), 51–65.

16 Some sense of this may emerge in Nighat Said Khan, *Voices Within: Dialogues with Women on Islam*, Lahore, ASR Publications, 1992.

17 Miss Shaista Aziz Alam, "Purdah and the Qur'ān," *Hamdard Islamicus*, 13 (1990), 82.

18 See the discussion in Jane I. Smith, "Women in Islam: Equity, Equality, and the Search for the Natural Order," *Journal of the American Academy of Religion*, 47 (1979), 517–37.

19 See D. A. Spellberg, *Politics, Gender, and the Islamic Past: The Legacy of 'A'isha bint Abi Bakr*, New York, Columbia University Press, 1994.

20 See Leila Ahmed, "Women and the Advent of Islam," *Signs: Journal of Women in Culture and Society*, 11 (1986), 665–91, and her book, *Women and Gender in Islam: Historical Roots of a Modern Debate*, New Haven, CT, Yale University Press, 1992.

21 Nawāl al-Sa'dāwī, *Qāḍiyat al-Mar'a al-Miṣriyya al-Siyāsiyya wa'l-Jinsiyya*, Cairo, 1977, as translated and quoted in Valerie J. Hoffman-Ladd, "Polemics on the Modesty and Segregation of Women in Contemporary Egypt," *International Journal of Middle East Studies*, 19 (1987), 35. For further on Sa'dāwī, see Ramzi Saiti, "Paradise, Heaven, and Other Oppressive Spaces: A Critical Examination of the Life and Works of Nawal el-Saadawi," *Journal of Arabic Literature*, 25 (1994), 152–74.

22 See the comments in Yvonne Y. Haddad, "Islam, Women and Revolution in Twentieth-century Arab Thought," *The Muslim World*, 74 (1984), 137–60.

17 Visions for Islam in the twenty-first century and beyond

1 See his *Qur'ān, Liberation and Pluralism: An Islamic Perspective on Interreligious Solidarity Against Oppression*, Oxford, Oneworld, 1997,

and *On Being a Muslim: Finding a Religious Path in the World Today*, Oxford, Oneworld, 1999.

2 For more on the Aḥmadiyya see Antonio R. Gualtieri, *Conscience and Coercion: Ahmadi Muslims and Orthodoxy in Pakistan*, Montreal, Guernica, 1989; Yohannan Friedmann, *Prophecy Continuous: Aspects of Ahmadi Religious Thought and Its Medieval Background*, Berkeley, University of California Press, 1989.

3 On the Bahá'í's in the context of modern Islam, see Christopher Buck, "Bahá'u'lláh as 'World Reformer'," *The Journal of Bahá'í Studies*, 3, iv (1991), 23–70; Juan R. I. Cole, *Modernity and the Millennium: The Genesis of the Baha'i Faith in the Nineteenth-Century Middle East*, New York, Columbia University Press, 1998.

4 Edward Said, *Orientalism*, New York, Pantheon Books, 1978; also his *Covering Islam: How the Media and the Experts Determine How We See the Rest of the World*, New York, Pantheon Books, 1981. The impact of these books on contemporary western scholarship will form an interesting piece of research; see Emmanuel Sivan, *Interpretations of Islam, Past and Present*, Princeton, NJ, Darwin Press, 1985, Chapter 5, on the Arab reaction to Said's work, but see also my review of Sivan's book, *Bulletin of the School of Oriental and African Studies*, 51 (1988), 329–30.

5 See Mohammed Arkoun, *Rethinking Islam: Common Questions, Uncommon Answers*, Boulder, CO, Westview Press, 1994, esp. p. 2: "The great majority of Orientalists who specialize in the study of Islam remain indifferent to upheavals linked to the 'postmodern condition'."

6 Note that, given the context of the publication of this essay, its likely audience was conceived to be people without ability to read the Qur'ān in Arabic, i.e. non-Muslims and Muslims without formal religious training.

7 Mark C. Taylor, *Erring: A Postmodern A/theology*, Chicago, University of Chicago Press, 1984, p. 3

8 The concept of the *imaginaire*, not really captured by the English "imagination," is central to Arkoun's thought. See the discussion in Arkoun, *Rethinking Islam Today*, Washington, DC, Center for Contemporary Arab Studies, Georgetown University, 1987, esp. pp. 20–3.

9 Shabbir Akhtar, *A Faith for All Seasons: Islam and Western Modernity*, London, Bellew, 1990.

10 Akhtar, *Faith*, p. 84.

11 Malise Ruthven, *A Satanic Affair: Salman Rushdie and the Rage of Islam*, London, Chatto and Windus, 1990, p. 128, questions Akhtar regarding the status of women as indicated in the Qur'ān: that a woman's testimony is worth half that of a man's, Akhtar said, is "a scandal of faith. . . . God decrees what He pleases. We have to accept it, that's the scandal of faith. God's commands sometimes seem impossible: but we are duty-bound to obey."

12 Ruthven, *Satanic Affair*, p. 129. Ruthven did not have the benefit of reading Akhtar's book when writing this work; his remarks are extremely perceptive.

13 Shabbir Akhtar, "Ex-defender of the Faith", *The Times Higher Education Supplement*, August 22, 1997.

14 Ibn Warraq, *Why I am not a Muslim*, Amherst, NY, Prometheus Books, 1995, p. 33.
15 Ibn Warraq, *Why*, p. 350.
16 Richard T. Antoun, *Muslim Preacher in the Modern World: A Jordanian Case Study in Comparative Perspective*, Princeton, Princeton University Press, 1989, p. 248.
17 Reinhold Loeffler, *Islam in Practice: Religious Beliefs in a Persian Village*, Albany, State University of New York Press, 1988, p. 246.

Glossary

Abbasids   dynasty of caliphs ruling from 750, through the era of the flowering of Islam, and coming to a final end in 1258, although it had lost any meaningful power several centuries earlier with the rise of the Buwayhids.

adab   "morals" or "courtesy"; the habitual way of acting in accordance with social standards.

adhān   the call to prayer.

Allāh   Arabic for God.

amīr   commander or prince, frequently used in reference to the person who leads the community.

Ash'ariyya   the theological school named after al-Ash'arī (d. 935).

āya   verse of the Qur'ān; also used in a general meaning of "sign" from God.

baqā'   Ṣūfī term for the mystic's "continuance" of existence with God.

basmala   the statement at the beginning of each *sūra* of the Qur'an (except *sūra* 9), "In the name of God, the Merciful, the Compassionate", also used by Muslims as an invocation.

Burāq   the winged creature which carried Muḥammad on his "night journey" (*isrā'*) from Mecca to Jerusalem.

Buwayhids   dynasty of Shī'ī Persian military rulers who took over rule in 945 and lasted until the takeover by the Sunnī Seljuq rulers in 1055 (also spelled Būyids).

dhikr   "mentioning" or "remembrance"; term used for the chant in Ṣūfī meditations.

dhimmī   a member of a protected community, especially referring to the Jews and Christians who live under Muslim rule. The right to practise their own religion was guaranteed by their payment of a special poll tax, the *jizya*.

dīn   religion; the word is used in the Qur'ān to refer to the specific beliefs and practices of people.

du'ā'   "calling" upon God, used for informal prayer and supplication, as compared to *ṣalāt*.

fanā' Ṣūfī term for the "passing away" or absorption of the individual into God.

fātiḥa "opening", the first *sūra* of the Qur'ān, used especially in prayer.

fatwā a legal decision rendered by a *muftī*, who is a jurist qualified to make decisions of a general religious nature.

fiqh jurisprudence, the science of religious law, as described by the jurists known as the *fuqahā'* (of which the singular is *faqīh*).

ghayba "occultation" of the last Imām in the Shī'ī tradition.

ghusl major ablution, requiring a full washing.

ḥadd the restrictive ordinances of God as stated in the Qur'ān, all of which have a specific penalty involved for their violation.

ḥadīth a tradition or written report, being the source material for the *sunna* of Muḥammad, gathered together in the six books of authoritative traditions in Sunnī Islam.

ḥajj pilgrimage to Mecca performed in the month of Dhū'l-ḥijja, one of the "Five Pillars" of Islam; a requirement for all Muslims, if they are able, once in a lifetime.

Ḥanābila the Sunnī school of law (the "Ḥanbalī school") named after Aḥmad ibn Ḥanbal (d. 855).

Ḥanafiyya the Sunnī school of law named after Abū Ḥanīfa (d. 767), the "Ḥanafī school".

ḥanīf the attribute, especially ascribed to Abraham in the Qur'ān, of being a sincere believer in God.

ḥijāb the veil or partition which prevents men from gazing at the "charms of women". A variety of styles exist but most emphasize covering the hair and hiding the shape of the body.

Ḥijāz region in the west of central Arabia, the birthplace of Muḥammad.

hijra Muḥammad's emigration from Mecca to Medina in the year 622 CE, understood as the date for the beginning of the Muslim *hijrī* calendar.

iḥrām the state of consecration into which the pilgrim enters (thus becoming a *muḥrim*) in order to perform the *ḥajj* or the *'umra*.

i'jāz doctrine which states that the Qur'ān cannot be imitated; the "inimitability" of the Qur'ān.

ijmā' "consensus", one of the four sources of law in Sunnī Islam, the others being Qur'ān, *sunna*, and *qiyās*.

ijtihād the use of one's "personal effort" in order to make a decision on a point of law not explicitly covered by the Qur'ān or the *sunna*; the person with the authority to do this is called a *mujtahid*.

imām literally the "model", here generally referring to the prayer leader in the *ṣalāt* who stands in front of the rows of worshipers, keeping their actions in unison during the prayer. The word is also used in other contexts. It is a title of the revered early leaders of the Shī'a who are the source of authority in that community; these Imāms are 'Alī ibn abī Ṭālib and certain of his descendants who were designated as holding the position. The word is also commonly used as a title of the founders of the Sunnī schools of law – Abū Ḥanīfa, Mālik ibn Anas, al-Shāfiʿī and Ibn Ḥanbal – and similarly for other significant religious figures.

Imāmī generic name given to the largest group of the Shīʿa, the Ithnā ʿAshariyya.

īmān faith; one who has faith is a *muʾmin*.

iṣlāḥ "reformism", especially in the nineteenth-century Arab world as proposed by people such as Muḥammad ʿAbduh.

Islam the name of the religion preached by Muḥammad, so named in the Qurʾān, literally meaning "submission"; those who adhere to Islam are called Muslims.

Islamist a contemporary movement among Muslims which emphasizes a "return" to the Qurʾān and *sunna* as the basis of a revival of Islam, with an emphasis on Islam as the basis of society; often called "fundamentalist".

ʿiṣma a doctrine which states that the prophets, and especially Muḥammad, were protected from sin (*maʿṣūm*) during their lifetimes. It is also applied to the Shīʿī Imāms.

isnād the chain of authorities through whom a *ḥadīth* report has passed; the list of these people forms the first part of the *ḥadīth* report, the text which comes after it being called the *matn*.

isrāʾ Muḥammad's "night journey" to Jerusalem, connected to the heavenly ascension, *miʿrāj*.

jāhiliyya the "Age of Ignorance", historically seen to be before Muḥammad but in a general religious sense referring to ignoring, or ignorance of, Islam; especially used with moral overtones.

jihād "striving for the faith" or "holy war", sometimes seen as a "sixth pillar" of Islam.

jinn genies, another dimension of animate creation on earth.

jumʿa in reference to prayer, *ṣalāt*; it is the Friday noon gathering of the community which is enjoined in the Qurʾān and which takes place in the *jāmiʿ* or congregational mosque.

Kaʿba the sacred black cube building in the middle of the mosque in Mecca; Muslims face in the direction of the Kaʿba when they perform the ritual prayer (*ṣalāt*) and circumambulate it when they perform the pilgrimage (*ḥajj* or *ʿumra*).

kalām literally, "speech"; refers to a mode of theological discussion framed in terms of an argument and thence to speculative theology as a whole.

khalīfa Caliph, the leader of the Sunnī community, the "successor" to Muḥammad.

khaṭīb the person at the Friday noon prayer who delivers the address, the *khuṭba*.

Khawārij   group in early Islam who believed in absolute devotion as the mark of a true Muslim, all others being unbelievers (singular: Khārijī) *khuṭba*   the address given at the Friday noon prayer by the *khaṭīb*.

madhhab   a school of law formed around one of the four early figures significant in juristic discussions (Abū Ḥanīfa, Mālik ibn Anas, al-Shāfiʿī, Ibn Ḥanbal); plural: *madhāhib*.

Mālikiyya   followers of the legal school named after Mālik ibn Anas (d. 795).

maʿrifa   mystical knowledge.

maṣlaḥa   "general good" and "public interest", used as a basis for legal decisions.

matn   the text of a *ḥadīth* report, as compared to the *isnād*, the chain of transmission.

mawlid   birthday; specifically the celebration of the birthday of Muḥammad.

miḥna   the "inquisition", primarily under the Abbasid caliph al-Maʾmūn (ruled 813–33), which demanded that government officials and religious leaders adhere to the doctrine of the "created Qurʾān".

miḥrāb   the niche in the wall of a mosque marking the *qibla*, or direction of prayer towards Mecca.

Minbar   the "pulpit" on which the *khaṭīb* gives the address (*khuṭba*).

miʿrāj   the "heavenly ascension" of Muḥammad, reported to have taken place around the year 6 of the *hijra*, in which he met with the prophets of the past, was given visions of heaven and hell, gazed upon God and was given the command of five prayers a day for all Muslims.

Modernist   a contemporary movement among Muslims which emphasizes the need to reform Islam in keeping with modern times; and frequently emphasizes the personal and rational nature of religion as a way of accommodating change.

muftī   a jurist who is authorized to give a *fatwā* or legal decision on a religious matter.

mujaddid   a renewer or the faith, stated in a *ḥadīth* report to appear in the Muslim community every 100 years, in order to revive the true spirit of Islam through the process of *tajdīd*, "renewal".

mujtahid   a jurist who is qualified to exercise *ijtihād* or personal effort in making legal decisions on matters where there is no explicit text of the Qurʾān or the *sunna* to be followed.

Murjiʾa   group in early Islam who held the "status quo" position in the debates over faith, generally connected to Abū Ḥanīfa (d. 767)

Muslim   a person who follows the Islamic religion.

Muʿtazila   a theological school of thought which blossomed in the eigth and ninth centuries; it stressed human free will and the unity and justice of God, and embraced Greek rationalist modes of argumentation. In modern times, certain thinkers (e.g., Muḥammad ʿAbduh) are sometimes considered "neo-Muʿtazilī" because of their reintroduction of some of these ideas.

muwāqit   the locations at which the pilgrim's *iḥrām* clothing is put on for the performance of the pilgrimage (*ḥajj*).

nahḍa   the renaissance of the Muslim world in general that was pictured by reformers as resulting from the cultural renewal which would take place in modern times.

Orientalist   basically those who study the Orient, specifically meaning Europeans (and in more recent time North Americans) who have studied Islam. The connection of such people to Christian missionizing and to colonial ruling powers has led to the term have negative connotations, especially in the wake of the analysis of Edward Said, *Orientalism* (New York, Pantheon Books, 1978) which argued that the Orientalist's perception of Islam was structured by the fundamental power relationship between the Islamic world and the colonial rulers.

purdah   a term from India referring to seclusion and veiling of women; the same as *ḥijāb*.

qadar   preordination of events by God.
Qadariyya   group in early Islam who argued for free will in the theological debates, precursors of the Muʿtazila.
qāḍī   a judge who makes decisions on the basis of the religious law.
qibla   the direction in which one faces in prayer (Mecca), marked by the *miḥrāb* in the mosque.
qiyās   "analogy", one of the four sources of law in Sunnī Islam, the others being Qur'ān, *sunna*, and *ijmāʿ*.

rakʿa   cycle of postures through which a person goes in performing the *ṣalāt*: standing, bowing, prostrating, sitting.

salaf   the "pious ancestors," the first three generations of Muslims, who some modern Islamists hold up as embodying the ideal manifestation of Islam.
ṣalāt   the prescribed five prayers a day, one the "Five Pillars" required of all Muslims.
ṣawm   fasting performed in the month of Ramaḍān, one of the "Five Pillars" required of all Muslims (also called *ṣiyām*).
Shāfiʿiyya   followers of the school of law named after al-Shāfiʿī (d. 820).
shahāda   "witness to faith"; saying (in Arabic), "There is no god but God and Muḥammad is His messenger"; one of the "Five Pillars" required of all Muslims, indicating conversion to Islam but also a part of the ritual prayer (*ṣalāt*).
sharīʿa   the religious law derived from the four sources of law in Sunnī Islam (Qur'ān, *sunna*, *qiyās*, and *ijmāʿ*).

shaykh literally, "an old man" and used as a term of respect for a religious teacher; used especially of a Ṣūfī master.

Shīʿa the religio-political party championing the claims of ʿAlī ibn abī Ṭālib and his heirs to the rightful leadership of the community and to their status as Imāms; since the beginning of the sixteenth century, the Shīʿī position has been the official state religion of Iran and most of its followers live there. They comprise about 10 percent of the world population of Muslims.

shūrā "consultation", a concept to which Islamists frequently appeal when speaking of Islamic ways of structuring governments.

silsila the Ṣūfī "chain" of authority which traces spiritual lineage.

Sīra the biography of Muḥammad as found in written form.

Ṣūfī an adherent to the mystical way of Islam, Sufism, *taṣawwuf*.

sunna "custom"; the way Muḥammad acted which is then emulated by Muslims. The source material for the *sunna* is found in the *ḥadīth* reports. The *sunna* is one of the four sources of law for Sunnī Islam, along with Qurʾān, *qiyās*, and *ijmāʿ*.

Sunnīs the majority form of Islam, those who follow the *sunna* (thus being called the *ahl al-sunna*), who do not recognize the authority of the Shīʿī Imāms.

sūra a chapter of the Qurʾān.

tafsīr interpretation of the Qurʾān, especially as found in written form. Such books generally follow the order of the Quranic text and pay attention to the meaning of each word or sentence.

taqlīd the reliance upon decisions made in the past in matters of religious law; the word is set in opposition to *ijtihād*, "personal effort", and frequently has a negative sense in the modern context.

ṭarīqa "the way" of Sufism; a Ṣūfī order or brotherhood.

taṣawwuf Sufism, the mystical way in Islam.

ṭawāf the ritual of the circumambulation of the Kaʿba during the pilgrimage.

tawakkul "trust" in God, especially among the Ṣūfīs.

tawḥīd doctrine holding to the proclamation of the unity of God.

Traditionalists term used primarily for the followers of Ibn Ḥanbal (d. 855) who rejected the claims of rationalism especially in early theological discussions. The inheritors of that position in modern times may follow any legal school but maintain an attitude of adherence to the legal (and religious) decisions of the past.

ʿulamāʾ the learned class, especially those learned in religious matters (singular: *ʿālim*)

Umayyads the first dynasty of caliphs, ruling from 661 until the takeover of the Abbasids in 750.

umma the community; the body of Muslims.

ʿumra   the "visitation" of the holy places in Mecca, the lesser pilgrimage; it can be performed at any time of the year but is also joined with the *ḥajj*.

Wahhābiyya   the followers of Ibn ʿAbd al-Wahhāb (d. 1787); a revivalist-purificatory movement in Arabia which became (and continues to be) the official religious policy of Saudi Arabia.

wilāya   position of ʿAlī as the "friend" (*walī*) of God.

wuḍūʾ   minor ablution required prior to some ritual performances.

zakāt   alms tax, one of the "Five Pillars" required of all Muslims.

Further reading

The following reading list comprises some of the more significant and informative works, primarily in English, for the study of Islamic religious history and thought. Reference should be made to the notes of this book for further readings on specific issues.

Abrahamov, Binyamin, *Islamic Theology: Traditionalism and Rationalism*, Edinburgh, Edinburgh University Press, 1998.

Abu-Rabiʿ, Ibrahim M., *Intellectual Origins of Islamic Resurgence in the Modern Arab World*, Albany, State University of New York Press, 1996.

Adams, Charles C., *Islam and Modernism in Egypt: A Study of the Modern Reform Movement Inaugurated by Muhammad ʿAbduh*, London, Oxford University Press, 1933.

Ahmad, Aziz, *Islamic Modernism in India and Pakistan 1857–1964*, London, Oxford University Press, 1967.

—— and G. E. von Grunebaum, *Muslim Self-statement in India and Pakistan 1857–1968*, Wiesbaden, Otto Harrassowitz, 1970.

Arberry, A. J., *Sufism: An Account of the Mystics of Islam*, London, George Allen and Unwin, 1950.

Arkoun, Mohammed, *Lectures du Coran*, Paris, Editions G.-P. Maisonneuve et Larose, 1982; second edition, Tunis, Editions Alif, 1991.

Baljon, J. M. S., *Modern Muslim Koran Interpretation (1880–1960)*, Leiden, E. J. Brill, 1961.

Binder, Leonard, *Islamic Liberalism, a Critique of Development Ideologies*, Chicago, University of Chicago Press, 1988.

Boullata, Issa J., *Trends and Issues in Contemporary Arab Thought*, Albany, State University of New York Press, 1990.

Brown, Daniel W., *Rethinking Tradition in Modern Islamic Thought*, Cambridge, Cambridge University Press, 1996.

Calder, Norman, *Studies in Early Muslim Jurisprudence*, Oxford, Clarendon Press, 1993.

Carré, Olivier, *Mystique et politique. Lecture révolutionnaire du Coran par Sayyid Qutb, frère musulman radical*, Paris, Les éditions du Cerf/Presses de la fondation nationale des Sciences Politiques, 1984.

Cook, Michael, *Early Muslim Dogma: A Source-critical Study*, Cambridge, Cambridge University Press, 1981.

——, *Muhammad*, Oxford, Oxford University Press, 1983.

Cragg, Kenneth, *Counsels in Contemporary Islam*, Edinburgh, Edinburgh University Press, 1965.

——, *The Pen and the Faith: Eight Modern Muslim Writers and the Qur'an*, London, George Allen and Unwin, 1985.

Crone, Patricia, *Meccan Trade and the Rise of Islam*, Princeton, Princeton University Press, 1987.

——, and Michael Cook, *Hagarism: The Making of the Islamic World*, Cambridge, Cambridge University Press, 1977.

——, and Martin Hinds, *God's Caliph: Religious Authority in the First Centuries of Islam*, Cambridge, Cambridge University Press, 1986.

Donner, Fred, *Narratives of Islamic Origins: The Beginnings of Islamic Historical Writing*, Princeton, Darwin Press, 1998.

Ede, David, *et al.*, *Guide to Islam*, Boston, G. K. Hall, 1983. Bibliographical overview of standard sources mainly in English.

Eickelman, Dale F. and James Piscatori, *Muslim Politics*, Princeton, Princeton University Press, 1996.

Esposito, John L. (ed.), *Voices of Resurgent Islam*, New York, Oxford University Press, 1983.

——, *Islam and Politics*, Syracuse, Syracuse University Press, 1984, 2nd edition 1987.

—— (ed.), *Oxford Encyclopaedia of the Modern Islamic World*, New York, Oxford University Press, 1995. A valuable resource for all modern topics.

—— and John J. Donohue (eds), *Islam in Transition: Muslim Perspectives*, New York, Oxford University Press, 1982.

Ess, Josef van, "The Beginnings of Islamic Theology," in J. E. Murdoch, and E. D. Sylla (eds), *The Cultural Context of Medieval Learning*, Dordrecht, Holland, D. Reidel Publishing, 1975, pp. 87–111. All of van Ess' works are essential to the study of Islamic theology, but most are written in German; the two English articles provide a good introduction to his perspective.

——, "Early Development of *Kalām*," in G. H. A. Juynboll (ed.), *Studies on the First Century of Islamic Society*, Carbondale, Southern Illinois University Press, 1982, pp. 109–23.

——, *Theologie und Gesellschaft im 2. und 3. Jahrhundert Hidschra. Eine Geschichte des religiösen Denkens im frühen Islam*, Berlin, W. de Gruyter, 1991–7.

Fischer, Michael M. J. and Mehdi Abedi, *Debating Muslims: Cultural Dialogues in Postmodernity and Tradition*, Madison, University of Wisconsin Press, 1990.

Geertz, Clifford, *Islam Observed: Religious Developments in Morocco and Indonesia*, New Haven, Yale University Press, 1968.

Gibb, Hamilton A. R., *Modern Trends in Islam*, Chicago, University of Chicago Press, 1947.

Gilliot, Claude, *Exégèse, langue, et théologie en Islam. L'exégèse coranique de Tabari (m. 311/923)*, Paris, J. Vrin, 1990.

Gilsenan, Michael, *Recognizing Islam: Religion, and Society in the Modern Middle East*, London, Croom Helm, 1982.

Glassé, Cyril, *The Concise Encyclopedia of Islam*, New York, HarperCollins, 1989; paperback edition San Francisco, Harper, 1991. A reference work useful for many points of fact. Some of the entries in this book need to be handled with care, however, due to their universalistic mystical interpretations.

Goldziher, Ignaz, *Muslim Studies*, two volumes, London, George Allen and Unwin, 1966, 1971 (German original 1889–90).

——, *The Ẓāhirīs, Their Doctrine and Their History*, Leiden, E. J. Brill, 1971 (German original 1884).

——, *Introduction to Islamic Theology and Law*, Princeton, Princeton University Press, 1981 (German original 1910).

Grabar, Oleg, *The Formation of Islamic Art*, New Haven, Yale University Press, 1973.

Groom, Nigel, *Frankincense and Myrrh: A Study of the Arabian Incense Trade*, London, Longman, 1981.

Grunebaum, Gustave E. von, *Muhammadan Festivals*, New York, Henry Schuman, 1951.

——, *Modern Islam: The Search for Cultural Identity*, Berkeley, University of California Press, 1962.

——, *Classical Islam: A History 600 AD–1258 AD*, Chicago, Aldine Publishing, 1970.

Haddad, Yvonne Yazbeck. *Contemporary Islam and the Challenge of History*, Albany, State University of New York Press, 1982.

—— (ed.), *The Muslims of America*, New York, Oxford University Press, 1991.

—— and Adair T. Lummis, *Islamic Values in the United States: A Comparative Study*, New York, Oxford University Press, 1987.

——, John Obert Voll and John L. Esposito, *The Contemporary Islamic Revival: A Critical Survey and Bibliography*, New York, Greenwood Press, 1991.

Hawting, G. R., *The First Dynasty of Islam: The Umayyad Caliphate AD 661–750*, London, Croom Helm, 1986.

——, *The Idea of Idolatry and the Emergence of Islam: From Polemic to History*, Cambridge, Cambridge University Press, 1999.

Hourani, Albert, *Arabic Thought in the Liberal Age, 1798–1939*, London, Oxford University Press, 1962.

Jansen, J. J. G., *The Interpretation of the Koran in Modern Egypt*, Leiden, E. J. Brill, 1974.

Juynboll, G. H. A., *The Authenticity of the Tradition Literature: Discussions in Modern Egypt*, Leiden, E. J. Brill, 1969.

Kerr, Malcolm H., *Islamic Reform: The Political and Legal Theories of*

Muhammad 'Abduh and Rashid Rida, Berkeley, University of California Press, 1966.

Kuban, Dogan, *Muslim Religious Architecture*, two parts, Leiden, E. J. Brill, 1974, 1985.

Kurzman, Charles (ed.), *Liberal Islam: A Sourcebook*, New York, Oxford University Press, 1998.

Lawrence, Bruce B., *Defenders of God: The Fundamentalist Revolt against the Modern Age*, San Francisco, Harper and Row, 1989.

—— , *Shattering the Myth: Islam beyond Violence*, Princeton, Princeton University Press, 1998.

Lecker, Michael, *Muslims, Jews and Pagans: Studies on Early Islamic Medina*, Leiden, E. J. Brill, 1995.

Lee, Robert D., *Overcoming Tradition and Modernity: The Search for Islamic Authenticity*, Boulder, CO, Westview Press, 1997. An examination of the ideas of Iqbāl, Quṭb, Sharī'atī, and Arkoun.

Lewis, Bernard, *The Arabs in History*, 4th edition, London, Hutchinson, 1966.

McDonough, Sheila, *The Authority of the Past: A Study of Three Muslim Modernists*, Chambersburg, PA, American Academy of Religion, 1970.

Martin, Richard, *et al.*, *Defenders of Reason in Islam: Mu'tazilism from Medieval School to Modern Symbol*, Oxford, Oneworld, 1997.

Momen, Moojan, *An Introduction to Shi'i Islam*, New Haven, Yale University Press, 1985.

Mortimer, Edward, *Faith and Power: The Politics of Islam*, New York, Random House, 1982.

Munson, Henry, Jr., *Islam and Revolution in the Middle East*, New Haven, Yale University Press, 1988.

Nasr, Sayyid Vali Reza, *Mawdudi and the Making of Islamic Revivalism*, New York, Oxford University Press, 1996.

Nasr, Seyyed Hossein (ed.), *Islamic Spirituality: Foundations*, New York, Crossroads, 1987.

Nielson, Jorgen, *Muslims in Western Europe*, Edinburgh, Edinburgh University Press, 1992.

Padwick, Constance E., *Muslim Devotions: A Study of Prayer-manuals in Common Use*, Oxford, Oneworld, 1996 (originally published 1961).

Parrinder, Geoffrey, *Jesus in the Qur'an*, London, Faber and Faber, 1965.

Peters, F. E., *A Reader in Classical Islam*, Princeton, Princeton University Press, 1994.

Rahman, Fazlur, *Islam*, 2nd edition, Chicago, University of Chicago Press, 1979.

—— , *Major Themes of the Qur'an*, Minneapolis, Bibliotheca Islamica, 1980.

—— , *Islam and Modernity: Transformation of an Intellectual Tradition*, Chicago, University of Chicago Press, 1982.

These works by Rahman provide a good overview of the subject from a critical modernist Muslim standpoint.

Robinson, Francis, *Atlas of the Islamic World Since 1500*, New York, Facts on File, 1982. A nicely illustrated and useful reference which provides a basic historical orientation to the subject.

Rubin, Uri, *The Eye of the Beholder: The Life of Muḥammad as Viewed by the Early Muslims: A Textual Analysis*, Princeton, Darwin Press, 1995.

Sabanegh, E. S., *Muhammad b. Abdallah, 'Le prophète'. Portraits contemporains Egypte 1930–1950*, Paris, Librairie J. Vrin, n.d..

Schacht, Joseph, *The Origins of Muhammadan Jurisprudence*, Oxford, Clarendon Press, 1950.

——, *An Introduction to Islamic Law*, Oxford, Clarendon Press, 1964.

—— and C. E. Bosworth (eds), *The Legacy of Islam*, second edition, Oxford, Oxford University Press, 1979.

Schimmel, Annemarie, *And Muhammad is His Messenger: The Veneration of the Prophet in Islamic Piety*, Chapel Hill, University of North Carolina Press, 1985.

——, *Mystical Dimensions of Islam*, Chapel Hill, University of North Carolina Press, 1975.

Sells, Michael, *Early Islamic Mysticism: Sufi, Qur'an, Mi'raj, Poetic and Theological Writings*, New York, Paulist Press, 1996. An excellent collection of translated sources.

——, *Approaching the Qur'án: The Early Revelations*, Ashland, OR, White Cloud Press, 1999. An accessible study and translation of sections of the Qur'ān complete with a CD of recitations.

Shepard, William E., *Sayyid Qutb and Islamic Activism: A Translation and Critical Analysis of Social Justice in Islam*, Leiden, E. J. Brill, 1996.

Sirriyeh, Elizabeth, *Sufis and Anti-Sufis: The Defence, Rethinking and Rejection of Sufism in the Modern World*, Richmond, Curzon, 1999.

Sivan, Emmanuel, *Radical Islam: Medieval Theology and Modern Politics*, New Haven, Yale University Press, 1985.

Smith, Margaret, *Rābiʿa the Mystic and Her Fellow-saints in Islam*, Cambridge, Cambridge University Press, 1928, 1984.

Smith, Wilfred Cantwell, *Islam in Modern History*, Princeton, Princeton University Press, 1957.

Stanton, H. U. Weitbrecht, *The Teaching of the Qur'an, With an Account of its Growth and a Subject Index*, London, SPCK, 1919, 1969.

Swartz, Merlin (ed.), *Studies in Islam*, New York, Oxford University Press, 1981.

Trimingham, J. Spencer, *The Sufi Orders in Islam*, Oxford, Oxford University Press, 1971.

Wansbrough, John, *Quranic Studies: Sources and Methods of Scriptural Interpretation*, Oxford, Oxford University Press, 1977.

——, *The Sectarian Milieu: Content and Composition of Islamic Salvation History*, Oxford, Oxford University Press, 1978. Both books by Wansbrough are essential reading for advanced students.

Wasserstrom, Steven M., *Between Muslim and Jew: The Problem of Symbiosis Under Early Islam*, Princeton, Princeton University Press, 1995.

Watt, W. Montgomery, *The Formative Period of Islamic Thought*, Edinburgh, Edinburgh University Press, 1973.

Wensinck, A. J., *The Muslim Creed: Its Genesis and Historical Development*, Cambridge, Cambridge University Press, 1932.

Zaman, Muhammad Qasim, *Religion and Politics Under the Early 'Abbasids: The Emergence of the Proto-Sunnī Elite*, Leiden, E. J. Brill, 1997.

Resources on the Internet

In order to support and update this book, a Web site of resources is maintained via the link to this book at

http://www.rippin.org

The following list of resources in "clickable format" is found there. As well, reference should be made there for lists of additional resources, both in print and on the Internet, as well as updates to the following addresses.

The amount of information regarding Islam that is available on the Internet is enormous. Using well organized listings of sites is by far the best place in which to start one's search for relevant information. Prof. A. Godlas at the University of Georgia has established an exemplary site at

http://www.arches.uga.edu/~godlas/

Links are found there to online Qur'ān and *hadīth* texts as well as information on every topic treated in this book (and more). Other important collections of links on Islamic subjects are

http://www.academicinfo.net/Islam.html

and

http://www.islamworld.net/

A less specialized collection of links but one which tends to view Islam within the context of Religious Studies is found at

http://www.library.regentcollege.ubc.ca/Wabash/islam.htm.

A very thorough and scholarly collection of links is to be found at Columbia University Library

http://www.columbia.edu/cu/libraries/indiv/area/MiddleEast/index.html

The Muslim Students Association at the University of Buffalo provides an extensive list of linked material of more Muslim popular interest at

http://wings.buffalo.edu/student-life/sa/muslim/isl/isl.html

Another Muslim site which has both extensive links and thousands of pages of useful information is

http://www.ummah.org.uk/

An excellent collection of links which features a good deal of material on modern cultural, political and religious issues is found at the University of Texas

http://menic.utexas.edu/menic.html

Women's issues in Islam are the focus of attention of the links at the Muslim Women's Homepage at

http://www.jannah.org/sisters/index.html

A notable site full of relevant source material is

http://www.al-islam.com

which provides direct access to many of the central Islamic texts in both Arabic and English and also has a link to a "Dictionary of Islam" which is a useful reference.

The Fordham University Internet History project has a significant collection of original and secondary source material in their Medieval Sourcebook available at

http://www.fordham.edu/halsall/islam/islamsbook.html

An on-line tutorial on Islamic history up to 1600 is available from the University of Calgary at

http://www.ucalgary.ca/HIST/tutor/islam/

The Internet has become an arena for a good deal of Muslim–Christian polemic especially regarding the Qur'ān and Muḥammad. A lot of scholarly information is available, but frequently it is found within a context that makes it difficult to discern the objectivity of the material. A major Muslim site which declares its purpose to be "to educate Muslims about the questions and issues frequently raised by the Christian missionaries" is

http://www.islamic-awareness.org/

The main target of the site is the Christian
http://answering-islam.org/

The Web facilitates access to a large assortment of material culture
artefacts. For example, illustrations of Islamic calligraphy (including
early Qur'ān manuscripts) are to be seen at
http://muslim-answers.org/calligraphy.htm

Samples of the Sana'a Qur'ān manuscripts may be viewed at
http://www.unesco.org/webworld/mdm/visite/sanaa/en/
present1.html
which presents a short summary of a CD-ROM which UNESCO has
produced on the manuscripts. For more general views of Islamic art
see
http://www.islamicart.com/

Useful tools easily accessible include a web page for calendar conversion:
http://bert.cs.pitt.edu/~tawfig/convert/
and for printing out calendars, thus allowing determination the date
of the Muslim new year etc.; see
http://www.assirat.org/Hcal/

Encyclopaedic references on Islam include the *Encyclopaedia of the
Orient*
http://i-cias.com/e.o/index.htm
and the *Encyclopaedia Iranica*
http://www.iranica.com/articles/index.html
which is currently available only for the entries "*dastūr*" through
"education", but it is a very valuable source of material that is worth
checking.

USENEWS groups can vary tremendously in value. To get a sense
of what contemporary Muslims are discussing on the Internet and
to see polemic and apologetics at work, monitor
soc.religion.islam

General index

Note: "al-" is ignored in alphabetizing; all Arabic characters ordered by English representation.

Index of Qur'ān citations